Oxford School Spelling Dictionary

Editors: Robert Allen & Sheila Dignen

Consultant: Michele Chapman

OXFORD
UNIVERSITY PRESS

Great Clarendon Street, Oxford OX2 6DP

Oxford University Press is a department of the University of Oxford.
It furthers the University's objective of excellence in research, scholarship,
and education by publishing worldwide in

Oxford New York

Auckland Cape Town Dar es Salaam Hong Kong Karachi
Kuala Lumpur Madrid Melbourne Mexico City Nairobi
New Delhi Shanghai Taipei Toronto

with offices in

Argentina Austria Brazil Chile Czech Republic France Greece
Guatemala Hungary Italy Japan Poland Portugal Singapore
South Korea Switzerland Thailand Turkey Ukraine Vietnam

First published 2001
Second edition 2003
This edition 2008

British Library cataloguing in Publication Data

Data available

ISBN: 978-0-19-911636-2

11

Typeset in OUP Argo and OUP Swift

Printed in Malaysia by Vivar Printing Sdn Bhd

Paper used in the production of this book is a natural, recyclable product made from wood grown in sustainable forests. The manufacturing process conforms to the environmental regulations of the country of origin.

Contents

Introduction

This new edition of the *Oxford School Spelling Dictionary* is designed to help students find correct spellings quickly and easily, without the distractions found in a large dictionary. With explanatory footnotes throughout, the *Oxford School Spelling Dictionary* will give you more support than electronic spellcheckers. It has been updated drawing on the Oxford English Corpus, the largest language research programme in the world. This database provides an extensive picture of current English and enables the dictionary to present the most accurate picture of spelling today. This new edition delivers all the KS2 curriculum vocabulary, the most up-to-date words, and recent spelling and hyphenation patterns.

Generally speaking there are three main areas of spelling difficulty for users of English whatever their age.

- Some words are difficult because they have unusual or unpredictable features. Eighth, guard, and niece are often spelled wrongly because they have awkward letter sequences. Disappear and embarrass are confusing because some letters are doubled while others are not. Words such as desperate and separate seem inconsistent because one has an e in the middle where the other has an a for no apparent reason.
- Then there are words that are easily confused. Vain, vein, and vane sound the same but have very different meanings. Some words change their spelling according to how they are used. For example, dependant as a *noun* is spelled with an a, but as an *adjective*, dependent is spelled with an e.
- The third type of difficulty arises when suffixes and endings are added to words. It is not easy to remember to keep an e in changeable, to replace y with i in happily, and not to double the p in galloping.

With increased interest in spelling, reading, and writing in schools today we hope that the *Oxford School Spelling Dictionary* will provide a valuable tool offering useful strategies for dealing with spelling difficulties. We also hope that it will support teachers and parents whose task is to enable young writers to become confident, accurate spellers and to express themselves with a voice of their own.

How to use this book

Entries

Words are listed alphabetically in blue and the part of speech or word class (e.g. *noun*, *verb*, *adjective*) follows in black. If the word has endings (called inflections), these are also listed in black below the headword.

Decide on the first sound of the word you are looking for. Some first sounds can be confusing. If you cannot find the word you are looking for, use the Try also tips which will guide you to other possible spellings.

Footnotes

Some words are marked with a small symbol. These identify words that have a footnote attached to them. The footnotes give extra information to help you check that you are using the correct word. For example, at bite you will find a footnote to tell you that there is another word that sounds like it but is spelled a different way, !byte. Words that sound the same but are spelled differently are called homophones. Some footnotes also give extra information on usage and grammar.

Panels

There are about 250 panels which highlight particular problems. For example, you may want to know which words are spelled -able like bendable, and which ones are spelled -ible like accessible. Or you may want to know how you form plurals of nouns ending in -f such as calf or roof. Use these information panels to build your knowledge of spelling rules and practices.

It may be useful to keep a spelling jotter for new words. When using a new word, say it aloud several times before you write it down. When you go on to use it in your writing, try not to copy it but to write the word from memory.

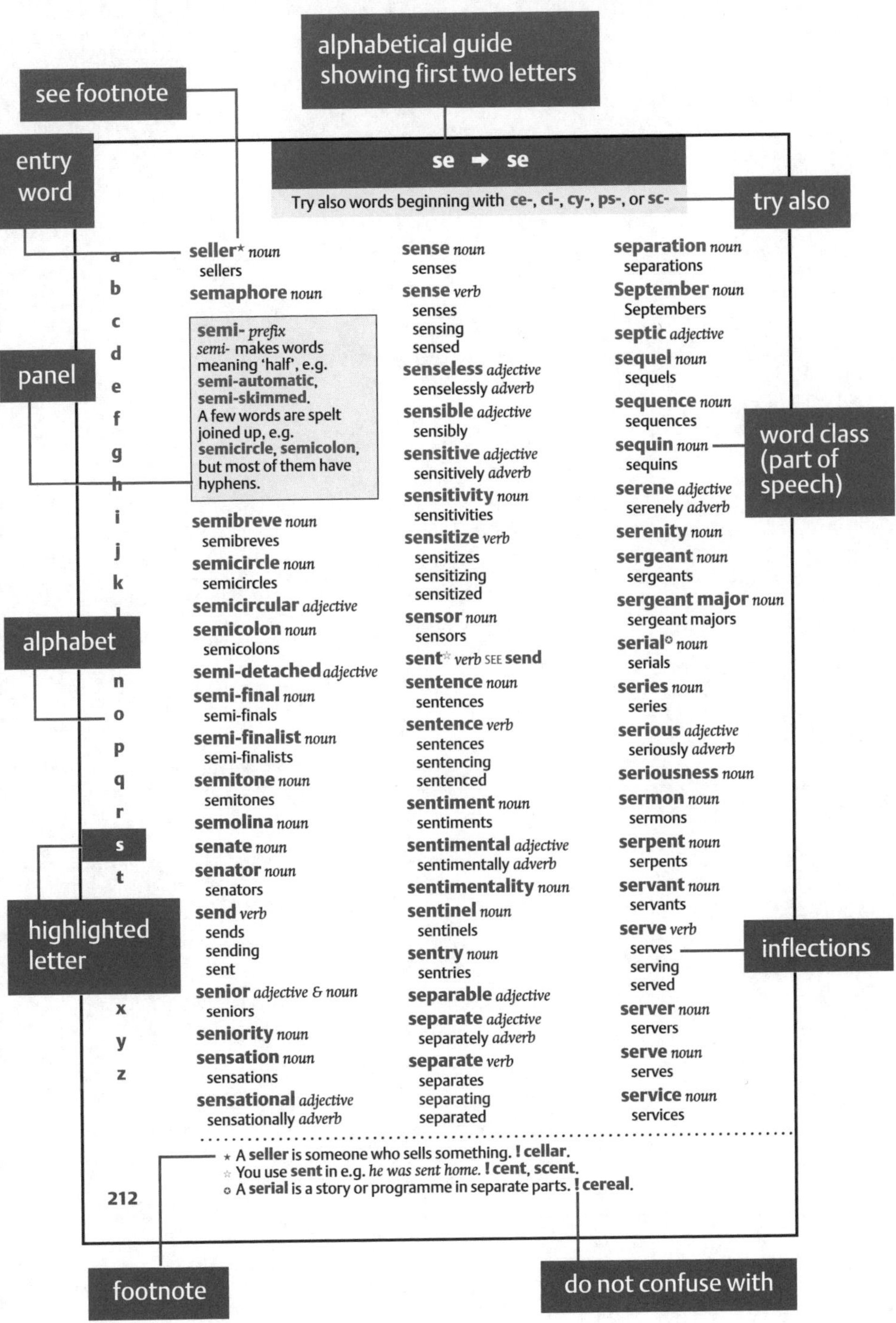
alphabetical guide showing first two letters
see footnote
entry word
se ➡ se
Try also words beginning with ce-, ci-, cy-, ps-, or sc-
try also
panel
word class (part of speech)
alphabet
highlighted letter
inflections
footnote
do not confuse with
a
b
c
d
e
f
g
h
i
j
k
n
o
p
q
r
s
t
x
y
z
seller* noun
sellers
semaphore noun
semi- prefix
semi- makes words meaning 'half', e.g. semi-automatic, semi-skimmed.
A few words are spelt joined up, e.g. semicircle, semicolon, but most of them have hyphens.
semibreve noun
semibreves
semicircle noun
semicircles
semicircular adjective
semicolon noun
semicolons
semi-detached adjective
semi-final noun
semi-finals
semi-finalist noun
semi-finalists
semitone noun
semitones
semolina noun
senate noun
senator noun
senators
send verb
sends
sending
sent
senior adjective & noun
seniors
seniority noun
sensation noun
sensations
sensational adjective
sensationally adverb
sense noun
senses
sense verb
senses
sensing
sensed
senseless adjective
senselessly adverb
sensible adjective
sensibly
sensitive adjective
sensitively adverb
sensitivity noun
sensitivities
sensitize verb
sensitizes
sensitizing
sensitized
sensor noun
sensors
sent☆ verb SEE send
sentence noun
sentences
sentence verb
sentences
sentencing
sentenced
sentiment noun
sentiments
sentimental adjective
sentimentally adverb
sentimentality noun
sentinel noun
sentinels
sentry noun
sentries
separable adjective
separate adjective
separately adverb
separate verb
separates
separating
separated
separation noun
separations
September noun
Septembers
septic adjective
sequel noun
sequels
sequence noun
sequences
sequin noun
sequins
serene adjective
serenely adverb
serenity noun
sergeant noun
sergeants
sergeant major noun
sergeant majors
serial° noun
serials
series noun
series
serious adjective
seriously adverb
seriousness noun
sermon noun
sermons
serpent noun
serpents
servant noun
servants
serve verb
serves
serving
served
server noun
servers
serve noun
serves
service noun
services
★ A seller is someone who sells something. ! cellar.
☆ You use sent in e.g. he was sent home. ! cent, scent.
○ A serial is a story or programme in separate parts. ! cereal.
212

Aa

-a *suffix*
Most nouns ending in *-a*, e.g. **amoeba**, **gala**, have plurals ending in *-as*, e.g. **amoebas**, **galas**. A few technical words have plurals ending in *-ae*, e.g. **antennae**.

aback *adverb*

abacus *noun*
abacuses

abandon *verb*
abandons
abandoning
abandoned

abbey *noun*
abbeys

abbot *noun*
abbots

abbreviate *verb*
abbreviates
abbreviating
abbreviated

abbreviation *noun*
abbreviations

abdomen *noun*
abdomens

abdominal *adjective*

abduct *verb*
abducts
abducting
abducted

abduction *noun*
abductions

abide *verb*
abides
abiding
abided

ability *noun*
abilities

ablaze *adjective*

able *adjective*
abler
ablest
ably *adverb*

-able and **-ible** *suffixes*
You add *-able* to a verb to make an adjective that means 'able to be done', e.g. **bendable** means 'able to be bent'. Some adjectives that have this meaning end in *-ible*, e.g. **accessible**, **convertible**, and **incredible**. You cannot use *-ible* to make new words as you can with *-able*.

abloom *adjective*

abnormal *adjective*
abnormally *adverb*

abnormality *noun*
abnormalities

aboard *adverb* & *preposition*

abode *noun*
abodes

abolish *verb*
abolishes
abolishing
abolished

abolition *noun*

abominable *adjective*
abominably *adverb*

aboriginal *adjective*

Aborigine *noun*
Aborigines

abort *verb*
aborts
aborting
aborted

abound *verb*
abounds
abounding
abounded

about *preposition*

above *adverb*

abrasive *adjective*

abreast *adverb*

abroad *adverb*

abrupt *adjective*
abruptly *adverb*

abscess *noun*
abscesses

abseil *verb*
abseils
abseiling
abseiled

absence *noun*
absences

absent *adjective*

absentee *noun*
absentees

absent-minded *adjective*
absent-mindedly *adverb*

absent-mindedness *noun*

absolute *adjective*
absolutely *adverb*

absorb *verb*
absorbs
absorbing
absorbed

absorbent *adjective*

absorption *noun*

abstract *adjective* & *noun*
abstracts

abstract *verb*
abstracts
abstracting
abstracted

absurd *adjective*
absurdly *adverb*

absurdity *noun*
absurdities

abundance *noun*

abundant *adjective*
abundantly *adverb*

abuse *verb*
abuses
abusing
abused

abuse *noun*
abuses

abusive *adjective*
abusively *adverb*

abysmal *adjective*
abysmally *adverb*

abyss *noun*
abysses

academic *adjective*

academy *noun*
academies

accelerate *verb*
accelerates
accelerating
accelerated

acceleration *noun*

accelerator *noun*
accelerators

accent *noun*
accents

accent *verb*
accents
accenting
accented

accept* *verb*
accepts
accepting
accepted

acceptable *adjective*
acceptably *adverb*

acceptance *noun*

access *noun*
accesses

access *verb*
accesses
accessing
accessed

accessibility *noun*

accessible *adjective*

accession *noun*
accessions

accessory *noun*
accessories

accident *noun*
accidents

accidental *adjective*
accidentally *adverb*

acclaim *verb*
acclaims
acclaiming
acclaimed

accommodate *verb*
accommodates
accommodating
accommodated

accommodation *noun*

accompaniment *noun*
accompaniments

accompanist *noun*
accompanists

accompany *verb*
accompanies
accompanying
accompanied

accomplish *verb*
accomplishes
accomplishing
accomplished

accomplished *adjective*

accomplishment *noun*
accomplishments

accord *noun*
accords

accordance *noun*

according *adverb*
accordingly

accordion *noun*
accordions

account *noun*
accounts

account *verb*
accounts
accounting
accounted

accountancy *noun*

accountant *noun*
accountants

accumulate *verb*
accumulates
accumulating
accumulated

accumulation *noun*

accuracy *noun*

accurate *adjective*
accurately *adverb*

accusation *noun*
accusations

accuse *verb*
accuses
accusing
accused

accustomed *verb*

ace *noun*
aces

ache *noun*
aches

ache *verb*
aches
aching
ached

achieve *verb*
achieves
achieving
achieved

achievement *noun*
achievements

acid *noun*
acids

acidic *adjective*

acidity *noun*

acknowledge *verb*
acknowledges
acknowledging
acknowledged

* To **accept** something is to take it. ! **except**.

acknowledgement *noun*
acknowledgements
acne *noun*
acorn *noun*
acorns
acoustic *adjective*
acoustics *plural noun*
acquaint *verb*
acquaints
acquainting
acquainted
acquaintance *noun*
acquaintances
acquire *verb*
acquires
acquiring
acquired
acquisition *noun*
acquisitions
acquit *verb*
acquits
acquitting
acquitted
acquittal *noun*
acquittals
acre *noun*
acres
acrobat *noun*
acrobats
acrobatic *adjective*
acrobatically *adverb*
acrobatics *noun*
acronym *noun*
acronyms
across *adverb & preposition*
act *noun*
acts
act *verb*
acts
acting
acted
action *noun*
actions
activate *verb*
activates
activating
activated

active *adjective*
actively *adverb*
activity *noun*
activities
actor *noun*
actors
actress *noun*
actresses
actual *adjective*
actually *adverb*
acupuncture *noun*
acute *adjective*
acutely *adverb*
Adam's apple *noun*
Adam's apples
adapt *verb*
adapts
adapting
adapted
adaptable *adjective*
adaptation *noun*
adaptor *noun*
adaptors
add *verb*
adds
adding
added
adder *noun*
adders
addict *noun*
addicts
addicted *adjective*
addiction *noun*
addictions
addictive *adjective*
addition *noun*
additions
additional *adjective*
additionally *adverb*
additive *noun*
additives
address *noun*
addresses
address *verb*
addresses
addressing
addressed

adenoids *plural noun*
adequate *adjective*
adequately *adverb*
adhere *verb*
adheres
adhering
adhered
adhesive *noun*
adhesives
adhesive *adjective*
Adi Granth *noun*
adjacent *adjective*
adjective *noun*
adjectives
adjourn *verb*
adjourns
adjourning
adjourned
adjournment *noun*
adjudicate *verb*
adjudicates
adjudicating
adjudicated
adjudication *noun*
adjudicator *noun*
adjudicators
adjust *verb*
adjusts
adjusting
adjusted
adjustment *noun*
adjustments
administer *verb*
administers
administering
administered
administration *noun*
administrations
administrative *adjective*
administrator *noun*
administrators
admirable *adjective*
admirably *adverb*
admiral *noun*
admirals
admiration *noun*

a b c d e f g h i j k l m n o p q r s t u v w x y z

admire *verb*
admires
admiring
admired

admirer *noun*
admirers

admission *noun*
admissions

admit *verb*
admits
admitting
admitted

admittance *noun*

admittedly *adverb*

ado *noun*

adolescence *noun*

adolescent *noun*
adolescents

adopt *verb*
adopts
adopting
adopted

adoption *noun*

adoptive *adjective*

adorable *adjective*
adorably *adverb*

adoration *noun*

adore *verb*
adores
adoring
adored

adorn *verb*
adorns
adorning
adorned

adornment *noun*

adrenalin *noun*

adrift *adjective & adverb*

adult *noun*
adults

advance *noun*
advances

advance *verb*
advances
advancing
advanced

advanced *verb*

advantage *noun*
advantages

advantageous *adjective*

advent* *noun*

Advent* *noun*

adventure *noun*
adventures

adventurous *adjective*
adventurously *adverb*

adverb *noun*
adverbs

adversary *noun*
adversaries

adverse *adjective*
adversely *adverb*

adversity *noun*
adversities

advertise *verb*
advertises
advertising
advertised

advertisement *noun*
advertisements

advice *noun*

advisable *adjective*

advise *verb*
advises
advising
advised

adviser *noun*
advisers

advisory *adjective*

advocate *noun*
advocates

advocate *verb*
advocates
advocating
advocated

aerial *adjective & noun*
aerials

> **aero-** *prefix*
> You use *aero-* to make words to do with the air or aircraft, e.g. **aerobatics**. If the word is a long one you spell it with a hyphen, e.g. **aero-engineering**.

aerobatic *adjective*

aerobatics *plural noun*

aerobics *plural noun*

aerodrome *noun*
aerodromes

aerodynamic *adjective*

aeronautical *adjective*

aeronautics *noun*

aeronaut *noun*
aeronauts

aeroplane *noun*
aeroplanes

aerosol *noun*
aerosols

aesthetic *adjective*
aesthetically *adverb*

affable *adjective*
affably *adverb*

affair *noun*
affairs

affect☆ *verb*
affects
affecting
affected

affection *noun*
affections

affectionate *adjective*
affectionately *adverb*

affirm *verb*
affirms
affirmed
affirming

* Use a capital A when you mean the period before Christmas.
☆ **Affect** means 'to make something change'. **! effect**.

affix *verb*
affixes
affixing
affixed
afflict *verb*
afflicts
afflicting
afflicted
affliction *noun*
afflictions
affluence *noun*
affluent *adjective*
afford *verb*
affords
affording
afforded
affordable *adjective*
afforestation *noun*
afield *adverb*
afloat *adjective & adverb*
afraid *adjective*
afresh *adverb*
African *adjective & noun*
Africans
after *preposition*
aftermath *noun*
afternoon *noun*
afternoons
afterwards *adverb*
again *adverb*
against *preposition*
age *noun*
ages
age *verb*
ages
ageing
aged
aged *adjective*
agency *noun*
agencies
agenda *noun*
agendas
agent *noun*
agents

aggravate *verb*
aggravates
aggravating
aggravated
aggravation *noun*
aggression *noun*
aggressive *adjective*
aggressively *adverb*
aggressor *noun*
aggressors
agile *adjective*
agility *noun*
agitate *verb*
agitates
agitating
agitated
agitation *noun*
aglitter *adjective*
agnostic *noun*
agnostics
ago *adverb*
agonizing *adjective*
agony *noun*
agonies
agoraphobia *noun*
agree *verb*
agrees
agreeing
agreed
agreeable *adjective*
agreeably *adverb*
agreement *noun*
agreements
agriculture *noun*
agricultural *adjective*
aground *adverb & adjective*
ahead *adverb*
ahoy *interjection*
aid *noun*
aids
aid *verb*
aids
aiding
aided

Aids *noun*
ailing *adjective*
ailment *noun*
ailments
aim *verb*
aims
aiming
aimed
aim *noun*
aims
aimless *adjective*
aimlessly *adverb*
air* *noun*
airs
air *verb*
airs
airing
aired
airborne *adjective*
air conditioned *adjective*
air conditioning *noun*
aircraft *noun*
aircraft
airfield *noun*
airfields
air force *noun*
air forces
airgun *noun*
airguns
airline *noun*
airlines
airlock *noun*
airlocks
airmail *noun*
airman *noun*
airmen
airport *noun*
airports
airship *noun*
airships
airstream *noun*
airstreams
airtight *adjective*

* You can use a plural in the phrase *to put on airs*.

airy *adjective*
airier
airiest
airily *adverb*
aisle★ *noun*
aisles
ajar *adverb & adjective*
alarm *verb*
alarms
alarming
alarmed
alarm *noun*
alarms
alas *interjection*
albatross *noun*
albatrosses
album *noun*
albums
alcohol *noun*
alcoholic *adjective & noun*
alcoholics
alcoholism *noun*
alcove *noun*
alcoves
alert *verb*
alerts
alerting
alerted
alert *adjective & noun*
alerts
algebra *noun*
algebraic *adjective*
alias *noun*
aliases
alibi *noun*
alibis
alien *adjective & noun*
aliens
alienate *verb*
alienates
alienating
alienated
alienation *noun*
alight *verb*
align *verb*
aligns
aligning
aligned
alike *adjective & adverb*
alive *adjective*
alkali *noun*
alkalis
alkaline *adjective*
alkalinity *noun*
all *adjective & pronoun*
Allah *noun*
allegation *noun*
allegations
allege *verb*
alleges
alleging
alleged
allegedly *adverb*
allegiance *noun*
allegiances
allegorical *adjective*
allegory *noun*
allegories
allergic *adjective*
allergy *noun*
allergies
alley *noun*
alleys
alliance *noun*
alliances
allied *adjective*
alligator *noun*
alligators
alliteration *noun*
allocate *verb*
allocates
allocating
allocated
allot *verb*
allots
allotting
allotted
allotment *noun*
allotments
allow☆ *verb*
allows
allowing
allowed
allowance *noun*
allowances
alloy *noun*
alloys
all right *adjective & adverb*
all-round *adjective*
all-rounder *noun*
ally *noun*
allies
ally *verb*
allies
allying
allied
almighty *adjective*
almond *noun*
almonds
almost *adverb*
aloft *adverb*
alone *adjective & adverb*
along *preposition*
alongside *preposition & adverb*
aloud✪ *adverb*
alphabet *noun*
alphabets
alphabetical *adjective*
alphabetically *adverb*
alpine *adjective*
already *adverb*
also *adverb*
altar✣ *noun*
altars

★ An **aisle** is a passage in a church or cinema. **! isle.**
☆ **Allowed** means to be permitted to do something. **! aloud.**
✪ **Aloud** means 'in a voice that can be heard'. **! allowed.**
✣ An **altar** is a raised surface in religious ceremonies. **! alter.**

alter★ *verb*
alters
altering
altered
alteration *noun*
alterations
alternate *adjective*
alternately *adverb*
alternate *verb*
alternates
alternating
alternated
alternating current *noun*
alternative *noun*
alternatives
alternative *adjective*
alternatively *adverb*
alternator *noun*
alternators
although *conjunction*
altitude *noun*
altitudes
altogether *adverb*
aluminium *noun*
always *adverb*
amalgamate *verb*
amalgamates
amalgamating
amalgamated
amalgamation *noun*
amateur *adjective* & *noun*
amateurs
amateurish *adjective*
amaze *verb*
amazes
amazing
amazed
amazement *noun*
ambassador *noun*
ambassadors
amber *noun*

ambiguity *noun*
ambiguities
ambiguous *adjective*
ambiguously *adverb*
ambition *noun*
ambitions
ambitious *adjective*
ambitiously *adverb*
amble *verb*
ambles
ambling
ambled
ambulance *noun*
ambulances
ambush *noun*
ambushes
ambush *verb*
ambushes
ambushing
ambushed
amen *interjection*
amend *verb*
amends
amending
amended
amendment *noun*
amendments
amenity *noun*
amenities
American *adjective* & *noun*
Americans
amiable *adjective*
amiably *adverb*
amicable *adjective*
amicably *adverb*
amid☆ *preposition*
amino acid *noun*
amino acids
ammonia *noun*
ammunition *noun*

amnesty *noun*
amnesties
amoeba *noun*
amoebas
among✪ *preposition*
amount *noun*
amounts
amount *verb*
amounts
amounting
amounted
amphibian *adjective* & *noun*
amphibians
amphibious *adjective*
ample *adjective*
ampler
amplest
amply *adverb*
amplification *noun*
amplifier *noun*
amplifiers
amplify *verb*
amplifies
amplifying
amplified
amputate *verb*
amputates
amputating
amputated
amputation *noun*
amuse *verb*
amuses
amusing
amused
amusement *noun*
amusements
amusing *adjective*
amusingly *adverb*
an✣ *adjective*
anaconda *noun*
anacondas

★ **Alter** means to change something. **! altar**.
☆ You can also spell this word *amidst*.
✪ You can also spell this word *amongst*.
✣ You use *an* instead of *a* before a word beginning with a vowel, e.g. *an apple*, or before an abbreviation that sounds as though it begins with a vowel, e.g. *an MP*.

a b c d e f g h i j k l m n o p q r s t u v w x y z

anaemia *noun*
anaemic *adjective*
anaesthetic *noun*
anaesthetics
anaesthetist *noun*
anaesthetists
anaesthetize *verb*
anaesthetizes
anaesthetizing
anaesthetized
anagram *noun*
anagrams
analogous *adjective*
analogue★ *adjective*
analogy *noun*
analogies
analyse *verb*
analyses
analysing
analysed
analysis *noun*
analyses
analytical *adjective*
anarchism *noun*
anarchist *noun*
anarchists
anarchy *noun*
anatomical *adjective*
anatomy *noun*

> **-ance** and **-ence**
> *suffixes*
> Most nouns ending in *-ance* come from verbs, e.g. **disturbance**, **endurance**. Some nouns end in *-ence*, e.g. **dependence**, **obedience**, and you need to be careful not to misspell these.

ancestor *noun*
ancestors
ancestral *adjective*
ancestry *noun*
ancestries
anchor *noun*
anchors
anchorage *noun*
anchorages
ancient *adjective*
anemone *noun*
anemones
angel *noun*
angels
angelic *adjective*
anger *noun*
anger *verb*
angers
angering
angered
angle *noun*
angles
angle *verb*
angles
angling
angled
angler *noun*
anglers
Anglican *adjective & noun*
Anglicans
Anglo-Saxon *adjective & noun*
Anglo-Saxons
angry *adjective*
angrier
angriest
angrily *adverb*
anguish *noun*
angular *adjective*
animal *noun*
animals
animated *adjective*
animation *noun*
animosity *noun*
animosities
ankle *noun*
ankles
annex *verb*
annexes
annexing
annexed
annexation *noun*
annexe *noun*
annexes
annihilate *verb*
annihilates
annihilating
annihilated
annihilation *noun*
anniversary *noun*
anniversaries
announce *verb*
announces
announcing
announced
announcer *noun*
announcers
announcement *noun*
announcements
annoy *verb*
annoys
annoying
annoyed
annoyance *noun*
annoyances
annual *adjective*
annually *adverb*
annual *noun*
annuals
anonymity☆ *noun*
anonymous *adjective*
anonymously *adverb*
anorak *noun*
anoraks
anorexia *noun*
anorexic *adjective*
another *adjective & pronoun*
answer *noun*
answers

★ You will sometimes see the spelling *analog*, especially when it is about computers.
☆ The noun from **anonymous**.

answer *verb*
answers
answering
answered

answerphone *noun*
answerphones

-ant and **-ent** *suffixes*
Many adjectives end in *-ant*, e.g. **abundant**, **important**. Some adjectives end in *-ent*, e.g. **dependent** (**dependant** is a noun), **permanent**, and you need to be careful not to misspell these.

antagonism *noun*

antagonistic *adjective*

antagonize *verb*
antagonizes
antagonizing
antagonized

Antarctic *adjective* & *noun*

anteater *noun*
anteaters

antelope★ *noun*
antelope *or* antelopes

antenna *noun*
antennae

anthem *noun*
anthems

anthill *noun*
anthills

anthology *noun*
anthologies

anthracite *noun*

anthropologist *noun*
anthropologists

anthropology *noun*

anti- *prefix*
anti- at the beginning of a word makes a word meaning 'against something' or 'stopping something', e.g. **antifreeze** means 'a liquid that stops water from freezing'. If the word you are adding *anti-* to begins with a vowel, you use a hyphen, e.g. **anti-aircraft**.

antibiotic *noun*
antibiotics

anticipate *verb*
anticipates
anticipating
anticipated

anticipation *noun*

anticlimax *noun*
anticlimaxes

anticlockwise *adverb* & *adjective*

antics *noun*

anticyclone *noun*
anticyclones

antidote *noun*
antidotes

antifreeze *noun*

Antipodes☆ *plural noun*

antiquated *adjective*

antique *adjective* & *noun*
antiques

antiseptic *noun*
antiseptics

antisocial *adjective*
antisocially *adverb*

antler *noun*
antlers

antonym *noun*
antonyms

anvil *noun*
anvils

anxiety *noun*
anxieties

anxious *adjective*
anxiously *adverb*

anybody *noun* & *pronoun*

anyhow *adverb*

anyone *noun* & *pronoun*

anything *noun* & *pronoun*

anyway *adverb*

anywhere *adverb*

apart *adverb*

apartment *noun*
apartments

apathetic *adjective*

apathy *noun*

ape *noun*
apes

apex *noun*
apexes

aphid *noun*
aphids

apiece *adverb*

apologetic *adjective*
apologetically *adverb*

apologize✪ *verb*
apologizes
apologizing
apologized

apology *noun*
apologies

apostle *noun*
apostles

apostrophe *noun*
apostrophes

appal *verb*
appals
appalling
appalled

appalling *adjective*
appallingly *adverb*

★ You use **antelope** when you mean a lot of animals and **antelopes** when you mean several you are thinking about separately.
☆ A word Europeans use for Australia and New Zealand.
✪ This word can also be spelled **apologise**.

a
b
c
d
e
f
g
h
i
j
k
l
m
n
o
p
q
r
s
t
u
v
w
x
y
z

apparatus *noun*
apparatuses
apparent *adjective*
apparently *adverb*
appeal *verb*
appeals
appealing
appealed
appeal *noun*
appeals
appear *verb*
appears
appearing
appeared
appearance *noun*
appearances
appease *verb*
appeases
appeasing
appeased
appeasement *noun*
appendicitis *noun*
appendix* *noun*
appendixes *or* appendices
appetite *noun*
appetites
appetizing *adjective*
applaud *verb*
applauds
applauding
applauded
applause *noun*
apple *noun*
apples
appliance *noun*
appliances
applicable *adjective*
applicant *noun*
applicants
application *noun*
applications
applied *adjective*
apply *verb*
applies
applying
applied
appoint *verb*
appoints
appointing
appointed
appointment *noun*
appointments
appraisal *noun*
appraisals
appraise *verb*
appraises
appraising
appraised
appreciate *verb*
appreciates
appreciating
appreciated
appreciation *noun*
appreciative *adjective*
apprehension *noun*
apprehensive *adjective*
apprehensively *adverb*
apprentice *noun*
apprentices
apprenticeship *noun*
approach *verb*
approaches
approaching
approached
approach *noun*
approaches
approachable *adjective*
appropriate *adjective*
appropriately *adverb*
approval *noun*
approve *verb*
approves
approving
approved
approximate *adjective*
approximately *adverb*
apricot *noun*
apricots
April *noun*
apron *noun*
aprons
aptitude *noun*
aptitudes
aquaplane *noun*
aquaplanes
aquarium *noun*
aquariums
Aquarius *noun*
aquatic *adjective*
aqueduct *noun*
aqueducts
Arab☆ *noun*
Arabs
Arabian *adjective*
Arabic✪ *noun*
arabic *adjective*
arable *adjective*
arachnophobia *noun*
arbitrary *adjective*
arbitrate *verb*
arbitrates
arbitrating
arbitrated
arbitration *noun*
arbitrator *noun*
arbitrators
arc✣ *noun*
arcs

---

* You use **appendixes** when you mean organs of the body and **appendices** when you mean parts of a book.
☆ You use **Arab** when you mean a person or the people, and **Arabian** when you mean the place, e.g. *the Arabian desert.*
✪ You use **Arabic** when you mean the language, and **arabic** when you mean numbers, e.g. *arabic numerals.*
✣ **Arc** means a curve. **! ark.**

arcade *noun*
arcades
arch *noun*
arches
arch *verb*
arches
arching
arched
archaeology *noun*
archaeological *adjective*
archaeologist *noun*
archaeologists
archbishop *noun*
archbishops
archer *noun*
archers
archery *noun*
architect *noun*
architects
architecture *noun*

> **-archy** *suffix*
> *-archy* at the end of a word means 'rule or government', e.g. **anarchy** (= a lack of rule) and **monarchy** (= rule by a king or queen). The plural forms is *-archies*, e.g. **monarchies**.

Arctic *noun*
are *verb*
area *noun*
areas
arena *noun*
arenas
aren't *verb*
arguable *adjective*
arguably *adverb*
argue *verb*
argues
arguing
argued
argument *noun*
arguments
arid *adjective*
aridity *noun*
arise *verb*
arises
arising
arose
arisen
aristocracy *noun*
aristocracies
aristocrat *noun*
aristocrats
aristocratic *adjective*
arithmetic *noun*
arithmetical *adjective*
ark* *noun*
arks
arm *noun*
arms
arm *verb*
arms
arming
armed
armada *noun*
armadas
armadillo *noun*
armadillos
armaments *plural noun*
armchair *noun*
armchairs
armful *noun*
armfuls
armistice *noun*
armistices
armour *noun*
armoured *adjective*
armpit *noun*
armpits
army *noun*
armies
aroma *noun*
aromas
aromatic *adjective*
arose SEE **arise**
around *adverb & preposition*
arouse *verb*
arouses
arousing
aroused
arrange *verb*
arranges
arranging
arranged
arrangement *noun*
arrangements
array *noun*
arrays
arrears *plural noun*
arrest *verb*
arrests
arresting
arrested
arrest *noun*
arrests
arrival *noun*
arrivals
arrive *verb*
arrives
arriving
arrived
arrogance *noun*
arrogant *adjective*
arrogantly *adverb*
arrow *noun*
arrows
arsenal *noun*
arsenals
arsenic *noun*
arson *noun*
art *noun*
artefact *noun*
artefacts
artery *noun*
arteries
artful *adjective*
artfully *adverb*
arthritic *adjective*
arthritis *noun*
article *noun*
articles

* **Ark** means a boat. **! arc.**

a
b
c
d
e
f
g
h
i
j
k
l
m
n
o
p
q
r
s
t
u
v
w
x
y
z

articulate *adjective*

articulate *verb*
articulates
articulating
articulated

artificial *adjective*
artificially *adverb*

artillery *noun*
artilleries

artist *noun*
artists

artiste *noun*
artistes

artistic *adjective*
artistically *adverb*

artistry *noun*

asbestos *noun*

ascend *verb*
ascends
ascending
ascended

ascent *noun*
ascents

ash★ *noun*
ashes

ashamed *adjective*

ashen *adjective*

ashore *adverb*

Asian *adjective* & *noun*
Asians

aside *adverb*

ask *verb*
asks
asking
asked

asleep *adverb* & *adjective*

aspect *noun*
aspects

asphalt☆ *noun*

aspirin *noun*
aspirins

ass *noun*
asses

assassin *noun*
assassins

assassinate *verb*
assassinates
assassinating
assassinated

assassination *noun*
assassinations

assault *verb*
assaults
assaulting
assaulted

assault *noun*
assaults

assemble *verb*
assembles
assembling
assembled

assembly *noun*
assemblies

assent *verb*

assert *verb*
asserts
asserting
asserted

assertion *noun*
assertions

assertive *adjective*

assess *verb*
assesses
assessing
assessed

assessment *noun*
assessments

assessor *noun*
assessors

asset *noun*
assets

assign *verb*
assigns
assigning
assigned

assignment *noun*
assignments

assist *verb*
assists
assisting
assisted

assistance *noun*

assistant *noun*
assistants

associate *verb*
associates
associating
associated

associate *noun*
associates

association *noun*
associations

assonance *noun*

assorted *adjective*

assortment *noun*

assume *verb*
assumes
assuming
assumed

assumption *noun*
assumptions

assurance *noun*
assurances

assure *verb*
assures
assuring
assured

asterisk *noun*
asterisks

asteroid *noun*
asteroids

asthma *noun*

asthmatic *adjective* & *noun*
asthmatics

astonish *verb*
astonishes
astonishing
astonished

astonishment *noun*

★ The tree and the burnt powder.
☆ Note that this word is not spelled *ash-*.

astound *verb*
astounds
astounding
astounded
astride *adverb & preposition*
astrologer *noun*
astrologers
astrological *adjective*
astrology *noun*
astronaut *noun*
astronauts
astronomer *noun*
astronomers
astronomical *adjective*
astronomy *noun*

> **-asy** *suffix*
> Not many words end in *-asy*. The most important are **ecstasy**, **fantasy**, **idiosyncrasy**. There are a lot of words ending in *-acy*, however, e.g. **accuracy**.

asylum *noun*
ate★ *verb* SEE **eat**
atheist *noun*
atheists
atheism *noun*
athlete *noun*
athletes
athletic *adjective*
athletics *plural noun*
atlas *noun*
atlases
atmosphere *noun*
atmospheres
atmospheric *adjective*
atoll *noun*
atolls
atom *noun*
atoms
atomic *adjective*
atrocious *adjective*
atrociously *adverb*
atrocity *noun*
atrocities
attach *verb*
attaches
attaching
attached
attached *verb*
attachment *noun*
attachments
attack *verb*
attacks
attacking
attacked
attack *noun*
attacks
attacker *noun*
attackers
attain *verb*
attains
attaining
attained
attainment *noun*
attempt *verb*
attempts
attempting
attempted
attempt *noun*
attempts
attend *verb*
attends
attending
attended
attendance *noun*
attendances
attendant *noun*
attendants
attention *noun*
attentive *adjective*
attic *noun*
attics
attitude *noun*
attitudes
attorney *noun*
attorneys
attract *verb*
attracts
attracting
attracted
attraction *noun*
attractions
attractive *adjective*
attractively *adverb*
auburn *adjective*
auction *noun*
auctions
auctioneer *noun*
auctioneers
audibility *adjective*
audible *adjective*
audience *noun*
audiences
audio *noun*

> **audio-** *prefix*
> *audio-* makes words with 'sound' or 'hearing' in their meaning. Some of them have hyphens, e.g. **audio-visual** (= to do with hearing and seeing).

audio-visual *adjective*
audition *noun*
auditions
auditorium *noun*
auditoriums
August *noun*
aunt *noun*
aunts
auntie☆ *noun*
aunties
au pair✪ *noun*
au pairs
aura *noun*
auras

★ **Ate** is the past tense of **eat** e.g. *I ate an apple.* **! eight**.
☆ You can also spell this word *aunty*.
✪ **Au pair** means a young person from another country who works in your house.

a b c d e f g h i j k l m n o p q r s t u v w x y z

aural★ *adjective*
austere *adjective*
austerity *noun*
Australian *adjective & noun*
Australians
authentic *adjective*
authentically *adverb*
authenticity *noun*
author *noun*
authors
authority *noun*
authorities
authorize *verb*
authorizes
authorizing
authorized
autism *noun*
autistic *adjective*

> **auto-** *prefix*
> *auto-* at the beginning of a word means 'self', e.g. **autobiography** (= a biography of yourself), **automatic** (= done by itself). But some words beginning with *auto-* are to do with cars, e.g. **autocross** (= car racing across country).

autobiographical *adjective*
autobiography *noun*
autobiographies
autograph *noun*
autographs
automate *verb*
automates
automating
automated
automatic *adjective*
automatically *adverb*
automation *noun*
automaton *noun*
automata *or* automatons
automobile *noun*
automobiles
autopsy *noun*
autopsies
autumn *noun*
autumns
autumnal *adjective*
auxiliary *adjective & noun*
auxiliaries
availability *noun*
available *adjective*
avalanche *noun*
avalanches
avenue *noun*
avenues
average *adjective & noun*
averages
average *verb*
averages
averaging
averaged
avert *verb*
averts
averting
averted
aviary *noun*
aviaries
aviation *noun*
avid *adjective*
avoid *verb*
avoids
avoiding
avoided
avoidable *adjective*
avoidance *noun*
await *verb*
awaits
awaiting
awaited
awake *adjective*
awake *verb*
awakes
awaking
awoke
awoken
awaken *verb*
awakens
awakening
awakened
award *noun*
awards
award *verb*
awards
awarding
awarded
aware *adjective*
awareness *noun*
awash *adjective*
away *adverb*
awe *noun*
awed *adjective*
awesome *adjective*
awful *adjective*
awfully *adverb*
awhile☆ *adverb*
awkward *adjective*
awkwardly *adverb*
awoke *verb* SEE **awake**
awoken *verb* SEE **awake**
axe *noun*
axes
axe *verb*
axes
axing
axed
axis *noun*
axes
axle *noun*
axles
Aztec *noun*
Aztecs
azure *adjective*

★ **Aural** means 'to do with hearing'. **! oral.**
☆ **Awhile** means 'for a short time', e.g. *Wait here awhile*. You use it as two words in e.g. *a short while*.

Bb

babble *verb*
babbles
babbling
babbled

baboon *noun*
baboons

baby *noun*
babies

babyish *adjective*

babysit *verb*
babysits
babysitting
babysat

babysitter *noun*
babysitters

bachelor *noun*
bachelors

back *noun*
backs

back *verb*
backs
backing
backed

backache *noun*
backaches

backbone *noun*
backbones

background *noun*
backgrounds

backing *verb*

backlash *noun*
backlashes

backlog *noun*
backlogs

backpack *noun*
backpacks

backside *noun*
backsides

backstage *adverb*

backstroke *noun*

backup *noun*

backward *adjective & adverb*

backwards *adverb*

backwater *noun*
backwaters

backyard *noun*
backyards

bacon *noun*

bacteria *noun*

bacterial *adjective*

bad *adjective*
worse
worst
badly *adverb*

badge *noun*
badges

badger *noun*
badgers

badger *verb*
badgers
badgering
badgered

badminton *noun*

baffle *verb*
baffles
baffling
baffled

bag *noun*
bags

bag *verb*
bags
bagging
bagged

bagel *noun*
bagels

baggage *noun*

baggy *adjective*
baggier
baggiest

bagpipes *plural noun*

bail★ *noun*
bails

bail☆ *verb*
bails
bailing
bailed

Bairam *noun*
Bairams

Baisakhi *noun*

bait *noun*

bait *verb*
baits
baiting
baited

bake *verb*
bakes
baking
baked

baker *noun*
bakers

bakery *noun*
bakeries

baking powder *noun*

balance *noun*
balances

★ **Bail** (noun) means 'money paid to let a prisoner out of prison' and 'a piece of wood put on the stumps in cricket'. **! bale.**

☆ **Bail** (verb) means 'to pay money to let a prisoner out of prison' and 'to scoop water out of a boat'. **! bale.**

balance *verb*
balances
balancing
balanced
balcony *noun*
balconies
bald *adjective*
balder
baldest
bale★ *noun*
bales
bale☆ *verb*
bales
baling
baled
ball *noun*
balls
ballad *noun*
ballads
ballerina *noun*
ballerinas
ballet *noun*
ballets
ballistic *adjective*
balloon *noun*
balloons
balloonist *noun*
balloonists
ballot *noun*
ballots
ballroom *noun*
ballrooms
balsa *noun*
bamboo *noun*
bamboos
ban *verb*
bans
banning
banned
banana *noun*
bananas
band *noun*
bands

band *verb*
bands
banding
banded
bandage *noun*
bandages
bandit *noun*
bandits
bandstand *noun*
bandstands
bandwagon *noun*
bandwagons
bandy *adjective*
bandier
bandiest
bang *noun*
bangs
bang *verb*
bangs
banging
banged
banger *noun*
bangers
banish *verb*
banishes
banishing
banished
banishment *noun*
banisters *plural noun*
banjo *noun*
banjos
bank *noun*
banks
bank *verb*
banks
banking
banked
banker *noun*
bankers
banknote *noun*
banknotes
bankrupt *adjective*
bankruptcy *noun*

banner *noun*
banners
banquet *noun*
banquets
baptism *noun*
baptisms
Baptist✪ *noun*
Baptists
baptize *verb*
baptizes
baptizing
baptized
bar *noun*
bars
bar *verb*
bars
barring
barred
barb *noun*
barbs
barbarian *noun*
barbarians
barbaric *adjective*
barbarism *noun*
barbarity *noun*
barbarities
barbarous *adjective*
barbecue *noun*
barbecues
barber *noun*
barbers
bar code *noun*
bar codes
bard *noun*
bards
bare✢ *adjective*
barer
barest
bareback *adjective & adverb*
barely *adverb*
bargain *noun*
bargains

★ **Bale** (noun) means 'a large bundle'. **! bail**.
☆ **Bale** (verb) means 'to jump out of an aircraft'. **! bail**.
✪ You use a capital B when you mean a member of the Christian Church.
✢ **Bare** means 'naked' or 'not covered'. **! bear**.

bargain *verb*
bargains
bargaining
bargained
barge *noun*
barges
barge *verb*
barges
barging
barged
baritone *noun*
baritones
bark *noun*
barks
bark *verb*
barks
barking
barked
barley *noun*
barman *noun*
barmen
bar mitzvah *noun*
bar mitzvahs
barn *noun*
barns
barnacle *noun*
barnacles
barnyard *noun*
barnyards
barometer *noun*
barometers
baron *noun*
barons
baroness *noun*
baronesses
baronial *adjective*
barrack *verb*
barracks
barracking
barracked
barracks★ *plural noun*
barrage *noun*
barrages
barrel *noun*
barrels
barren *adjective*
barricade *noun*
barricades
barricade *verb*
barricades
barricading
barricaded
barrier *noun*
barriers
barrister *noun*
barristers
barrow *noun*
barrows
barter *verb*
barters
bartering
bartered
base☆ *noun*
bases
base *verb*
bases
basing
based
baseball *noun*
baseballs
basement *noun*
basements
bash *verb*
bashes
bashing
bashed
bash *noun*
bashes
bashful *adjective*
bashfully *adverb*
basic *adjective*
basically *adverb*
basin *noun*
basins
basis *noun*
bases
bask *verb*
basks
basking
basked
basket *noun*
baskets
basketball *noun*
basketballs
basketful *noun*
basketfuls
bass✪ *noun*
basses
bassoon *noun*
bassoons
bat *noun*
bats
bat *verb*
bats
batting
batted
batch *noun*
batches
bath *noun*
baths
bath *verb*
baths
bathing
bathed
bathe *verb*
bathes
bathing
bathed
bathroom *noun*
bathrooms
baton✢ *noun*
batons
batsman *noun*
batsmen
battalion *noun*
battalions

★ **Barracks** is plural but sometimes has a singular verb, e.g. *The barracks is over there.*
☆ **Base** means 'a place where things are controlled'. **! bass.**
✪ **Bass** means 'a singer with a low voice'. **! base.**
✢ A **baton** is a stick used by a conductor in an orchestra. **! batten.**

a
b
c
d
e
f
g
h
i
j
k
l
m
n
o
p
q
r
s
t
u
v
w
x
y
z

batten⋆ *noun*
battens
batter *verb*
batters
battering
battered
batter *noun*
batters
battery *noun*
batteries
battle *noun*
battles
battlefield *noun*
battlefields
battlements *plural noun*
battleship *noun*
battleships
bawl *verb*
bawls
bawling
bawled
bay *noun*
bays
bayonet *noun*
bayonets
bazaar *noun*
bazaars
beach☆ *noun*
beaches
beacon *noun*
beacons
bead *noun*
beads
beady *adjective*
beadier
beadiest
beagle *noun*
beagles
beak *noun*
beaks
beaker *noun*
beakers

beam *noun*
beams
beam *verb*
beams
beaming
beamed
bean✪ *noun*
beans
bear⁜ *verb*
bears
bearing
bore
borne
bear *noun*
bears
bearable *adjective*
beard *noun*
beards
bearded *verb*
bearing *noun*
bearings
beast *noun*
beasts
beastly *adjective*
beat *verb*
beats
beating
beat
beaten
beat *noun*
beats
beautiful *adjective*
beautifully *adverb*
beautify *verb*
beautifies
beautifying
beautified
beauty *noun*
beauties
beaver *noun*
beavers
became *verb* SEE **become**

because *conjunction*
beckon *verb*
beckons
beckoning
beckoned
become *verb*
becomes
becoming
became
become
bed *noun*
beds
bedclothes *plural noun*
bedding *noun*
bedlam *noun*
bedraggled *adjective*
bedridden *adjective*
bedroom *noun*
bedrooms
bedside *noun*
bedspread *noun*
bedspreads
bedstead *noun*
bedsteads
bedtime *noun*
bee *noun*
bees
beech✱ *noun*
beeches
beef *noun*
beefburger *noun*
beefburgers
beefeater *noun*
beefeaters
beefy *adjective*
beefier
beefiest
beehive *noun*
beehives
beeline *noun*

⋆ A **batten** is a flat strip of wood. **! baton.**
☆ **Beach** means 'sandy part of the seashore'. **! beech.**
✪ A **bean** is a vegetable. **! been.**
⁜ To **bear** something is to carry it and a **bear** is an animal. **! bare.**
✱ **Beech** means 'a tree'. **! beach.**

been★ *verb* SEE **be**

beep *noun*
beeps

beep *verb*
beeps
beeping
beeped

beer *noun*
beers

beet *noun*
beet
beets

beetle *noun*
beetles

beetroot *noun*
beetroot

before *adverb*

beforehand *adverb*

beg *verb*
begs
begging
begged

began *verb* SEE **begin**

beggar *noun*
beggars

begin *verb*
begins
beginning
began
begun

beginner *noun*
beginners

beginning *noun*
beginnings

begrudge *verb*
begrudges
begrudging
begrudged

begun *verb* SEE **begin**

behalf *noun*

behave *verb*
behaves
behaving
behaved

behaviour *noun*

behead *verb*
beheads
beheading
beheaded

behind *adverb* & *preposition*

beige *noun*

being *noun*
beings

belfry *noun*
belfries

belief *noun*
beliefs

believe *verb*
believes
believing
believed

believable *adjective*

believer *noun*
believers

bellow *verb*
bellows
bellowing
bellowed

bellows *plural noun*

belly *noun*
bellies

belong *verb*
belongs
belonging
belonged

belongings *plural noun*

beloved *adjective*

below *adverb*

belt *noun*
belts

belt *verb*
belts
belting
belted

bench *noun*
benches

bend *verb*
bends
bending
bent

bend *noun*
bends

beneath *preposition*

benefactor *noun*
benefactors

benefit *noun*
benefits

beneficial *adjective*
beneficially *adverb*

benevolence *noun*

benevolent *adjective*

bent *adjective* SEE **bend**

bequeath *verb*
bequeaths
bequeathing
bequeathed

bequest *noun*

bereaved☆ *adjective*

bereavement *noun*

bereft✪ *adjective*

beret *noun*
berets

berry *noun*
berries

berserk *adjective*

berth *noun*
berths

beside *preposition*

besides *preposition* & *adverb*

a b c d e f g h i j k l m n o p q r s t u v w x y z

★ You use **been** in e.g. *I've been to the zoo.* **! bean.**
☆ You use **bereaved** when you mean a person whose close relative has died. **! bereft.**
✪ You use **bereft** when you mean 'deprived of something', e.g. *bereft of hope*. **! bereaved.**

besiege *verb*
besieges
besieging
besieged

best-seller *noun*
best-sellers

bet *noun*
bets

bet *verb*
bets
betting
bet
betted

betray *verb*
betrays
betraying
betrayed

betrayal *noun*

better *adjective* & *adverb*

better *verb*
betters
bettering
bettered

between *preposition* & *adverb*

beware* *verb*

bewilder *verb*
bewilders
bewildering
bewildered

bewilderment *noun*

bewitch *verb*
bewitches
bewitching
bewitched

beyond *preposition* & *adverb*

bhaji *noun*
bhajis

> **bi-** *prefix*
> *bi-* at the beginning of a word means 'two', e.g. **bicycle** (= a machine with two wheels), **bilateral** (= having two sides).

bias *noun*
biases

biased *adjective*

bib *noun*
bibs

Bible *noun*
Bibles

biblical *adjective*

bibliography *noun*
bibliographies

biceps *plural noun*

bicycle *noun*
bicycles

bid *noun*
bids

bid *verb*
bids
bidding
bid

bide *verb*
bides
biding
bided

bifocals *plural noun*

big *adjective*
bigger
biggest

bigamist *noun*
bigamists

bigamous *adjective*

bigamy *noun*

bike *noun*
bikes

bikini *noun*
bikinis

bile *noun*

bilge *noun*

bilingual *adjective*

bill *noun*
bills

billiards *noun*

billion *noun*
billions

billionth *adjective*

billow *noun*
billows

billow *verb*
billows
billowing
billowed

billy goat *noun*
billy goats

bin *noun*
bins

binary *adjective*

bind *verb*
binds
binding
bound

bingo *noun*

binoculars *plural noun*

> **bio-** *prefix*
> *bio-* at the beginning of a word means 'life', e.g. **biography** (= a story of a person's life), **biology** (= the study of living things).

biodegradable *adjective*

biodiversity *noun*

biographer *noun*
biographers

biographical *adjective*

biography *noun*
biographies

biological *adjective*
biologically *adverb*

biologist *noun*
biologists

biology *noun*

bionic *adjective*

biosphere *noun*

biped *noun*
bipeds

birch *noun*
birches

bird *noun*
birds

* **Beware** has no other forms.

birdseed *noun*
Biro *noun*
Biros
birth *noun*
births
birth control *noun*
birthday *noun*
birthdays
birthmark *noun*
birthmarks
birthplace *noun*
birthplaces
biscuit *noun*
biscuits
bisect *verb*
bisects
bisecting
bisected
bishop *noun*
bishops
bison *noun*
bison
bit *noun*
bits
bit *verb* SEE **bite**
bitch *noun*
bitches
bitchy *adjective*
bitchier
bitchiest
bite *verb*
bites
biting
bit
bitten
bite* *noun*
bites
biter *noun*
biters
bitter *adjective*
bitterly *adverb*
bizarre *adjective*
black *adjective*
blacker
blackest
black *noun*
blacks
blackberry *noun*
blackberries
blackbird *noun*
blackbirds
blackboard *noun*
blackboards
blacken *verb*
blackens
blackening
blackened
blackmail *verb*
blackmails
blackmailing
blackmailed
blackout *noun*
blackouts
blacksmith *noun*
blacksmiths
bladder *noun*
bladders
blade *noun*
blades
blame *verb*
blames
blaming
blamed
blame *noun*
blancmange *noun*
blancmanges
blank *adjective* & *noun*
blanks
blankly *adverb*
blanket *noun*
blankets
blare *verb*
blares
blaring
blared
blast *noun*
blasts
blast *verb*
blasts
blasting
blasted
blast-off *noun*
blatant *adjective*
blatantly *adverb*
blaze *noun*
blazes
blaze *verb*
blazes
blazing
blazed
blazer *noun*
blazers
bleach *noun*
bleaches
bleach *verb*
bleaches
bleaching
bleached
bleak *adjective*
bleaker
bleakest
bleary *adjective*
blearier
bleariest
blearily *adverb*
bleat *noun*
bleats
bleat *verb*
bleats
bleating
bleated
bleed *verb*
bleeds
bleeding
bled
bleep *noun*
bleeps
blemish *noun*
blemishes
blend *verb*
blends
blending
blended
blend *noun*
blends

a
b
c
d
e
f
g
h
i
j
k
l
m
n
o
p
q
r
s
t
u
v
w
x
y
z

* A **bite** is an act of biting. **! byte.**

a b c d e f g h i j k l m n o p q r s t u v w x y z

bless *verb*
blesses
blessing
blessed

blessing *noun*
blessings

blew★ *verb* SEE **blow**

blight *noun*
blights

blind *adjective*
blinder
blindest
blindly *adverb*

blind *verb*
blinds
blinding
blinded

blind *noun*
blinds

blindfold *noun*
blindfolds

blindfold *verb*
blindfolds
blindfolding
blindfolded

blindfold *noun*
blindfolds

blink *verb*
blinks
blinking
blinked

bliss *noun*

blissful *adjective*
blissfully *adverb*

blister *noun*
blisters

blitz *noun*
blitzes

blizzard *noun*
blizzards

bloated *adjective*

block *noun*
blocks

block *verb*
blocks
blocking
blocked

blockade *noun*
blockades

blockage *noun*
blockages

blog *noun*
blogs

blogger *noun*
bloggers

blond *adjective*
blonder
blondest

blonde☆ *noun*
blondes

blood *noun*

bloodhound *noun*
bloodhounds

bloodshed *noun*

bloodshot *adjective*

bloodstream *noun*

bloodthirsty *adjective*
bloodthirstier
bloodthirstiest

bloody *adjective*
bloodier
bloodiest

bloom *verb*
blooms
blooming
bloomed

bloom *noun*
blooms

blossom *noun*
blossoms

blossom *verb*
blossoms
blossoming
blossomed

blot *noun*
blots

blot *verb*
blots
blotting
blotted

blotch *noun*
blotches

blotchy *adjective*
blotchier
blotchiest

blouse *noun*
blouses

blow *noun*
blows

blow *verb*
blows
blowing
blew
blown

blowlamp *noun*
blowlamps

blowtorch *noun*
blowtorches

blue *adjective*
bluer
bluest

blue✪ *noun*
blues

bluebell *noun*
bluebells

bluebottle *noun*
bluebottles

blueprint *noun*
blueprints

bluff *verb*
bluffs
bluffing
bluffed

bluff *noun*
bluffs

blunder *verb*
blunders
blundering
blundered

★ You use **blew** in e.g. *the wind blew hard*. **! blue**.
☆ You use **blonde** when you are talking about a girl or woman.
✪ **Blue** is the colour. **! blew**.

blunder *noun*
blunders
blunt *adjective*
blunter
bluntest
blur *verb*
blurs
blurring
blurred
blur *noun*
blurs
blush *verb*
blushes
blushing
blushed
bluster *verb*
blusters
blustering
blustered
blustery *adjective*
boa constrictor *noun*
boa constrictors
boar★ *noun*
boars
board☆ *noun*
boards
board *verb*
boards
boarding
boarded
boarder *noun*
boarders
board game *noun*
board games
boast *verb*
boasts
boasting
boasted
boastful *adjective*
boastfully *adverb*
boat *noun*
boats
boating *noun*

bob *verb*
bobs
bobbing
bobbed
bobble *noun*
bobbles
bobsled *noun*
bobsleds
bobsleigh *noun*
bobsleighs
bodice *noun*
bodices
bodily *adjective*
body *noun*
bodies
bodyguard *noun*
bodyguards
boggy *adjective*
boggier
boggiest
bogus *adjective*
boil *verb*
boils
boiling
boiled
boil *noun*
boils
boiler *noun*
boilers
boisterous *adjective*
boisterously *adverb*
bold *adjective*
bolder
boldest
boldly *adverb*
bollard *noun*
bollards
bolster *verb*
bolsters
bolstering
bolstered
bolster *noun*
bolsters
bolt *noun*
bolts

bolt *verb*
bolts
bolting
bolted
bomb *noun*
bombs
bomb *verb*
bombs
bombing
bombed
bombard *verb*
bombards
bombarding
bombarded
bombardier *noun*
bombardiers
bombardment *noun*
bombastic *adjective*
bomber *noun*
bombers
bond *noun*
bonds
bondage *noun*
bone *noun*
bones
bonfire *noun*
bonfires
bongos *plural noun*
bonnet *noun*
bonnets
bonus *noun*
bonuses
bony *adjective*
bonier
boniest
boo *verb*
boos
booing
booed
book *noun*
books
book *verb*
books
booking
booked

★ A **boar** is a wild pig. **! bore.**
☆ A **board** is a piece of wood. **! bored.**

a
b
c
d
e
f
g
h
i
j
k
l
m
n
o
p
q
r
s
t
u
v
w
x
y
z

bookcase *noun*
bookcases
booklet *noun*
booklets
bookmaker *noun*
bookmakers
bookmark *noun*
bookmarks
boom *noun*
booms
boom *verb*
booms
booming
boomed
boomerang *noun*
boomerangs
boost *verb*
boosts
boosting
boosted
booster *noun*
boosters
boot *noun*
boots
boot *verb*
boots
booting
booted
booth *noun*
booths
border *noun*
borders
borderline *noun*
bore *verb*
bores
boring
bored
bore★ *noun*
bores
boredom *noun*
boring *adjective*
born☆ *verb*
borne✪ *verb* SEE **bear**
borough *noun*
boroughs
borrow *verb*
borrows
borrowing
borrowed
boss *noun*
bosses
boss *verb*
bosses
bossing
bossed
bossy *adjective*
bossier
bossiest
botanical *adjective*
botanist *noun*
botanists
botany *noun*
both *adjective* & *pronoun*
bother *verb*
bothers
bothering
bothered
bother *noun*
bottle *noun*
bottles
bottle *verb*
bottles
bottling
bottled
bottleneck *noun*
bottlenecks
bottom *noun*
bottoms
bottomless *adjective*
bough✣ *noun*
boughs
bought *verb*
boulder *noun*
boulders
bounce *verb*
bounces
bouncing
bounced
bounce *noun*
bounces
bouncing *verb*
bouncy *adjective*
bouncier
bounciest
bound *verb*
bounds
bounding
bounded
bound *adjective* & *noun*
bounds
bound *verb* SEE **bind**
boundary *noun*
boundaries
bounds *plural noun*
bountiful *adjective*
bounty *noun*
bouquet *noun*
bouquets
bout *noun*
bouts
boutique *noun*
boutiques
bow● *noun*
bows
bow✻ *verb*
bows
bowing
bowed

★ **Bore** means 'something boring'. **! boar.**
☆ You use **born** in e.g. *He was born in June*. **! borne.**
✪ You use **borne** in e.g. *She has borne three children* and *The cost is borne by the government*. **! born.**
✣ A **bough** is a part of a tree. **! bow.**
● A **bow** is a knot with loops and rhymes with 'go'. A **bow** is also the front of a ship or a bending of the body and rhymes with 'cow'.
✻ To **bow** is to bend the body and rhymes with 'cow'.

bowl *noun*
bowls

bowl *verb*
bowls
bowling
bowled

bow-legged *adjective*

bowler *noun*
bowlers

bowling *noun*

bowls *verb*

bow tie *noun*
bow ties

box *noun*
boxes

box *verb*
boxes
boxing
boxed

boxer *noun*
boxers

Boxing Day *noun*

boy *noun*
boys

boycott *verb*
boycotts
boycotting
boycotted

boyfriend *noun*
boyfriends

boyhood *noun*

boyish *adjective*

brace *noun*
braces

bracelet *noun*
bracelets

braces *plural noun*

bracken *noun*

bracket *noun*
brackets

bracket *verb*
brackets
bracketing
bracketed

brag *verb*
brags
bragging
bragged

braid *noun*
braids

braille *noun*

brain *noun*
brains

brainstorm *verb*
brainstorms
brainstorming
brainstormed

brainy *adjective*
brainier
brainiest

brake★ *noun*
brakes

bramble *noun*
brambles

branch *noun*
branches

branch *verb*
branches
branching
branched

brand *noun*
brands

brand *verb*
brands
branding
branded

brandish *verb*
brandishes
brandishing
brandished

brand new *adjective*

brandy *noun*
brandies

brass *noun*

brassy *adjective*
brassier
brassiest

brave *adjective*
braver
bravest
bravely *adverb*

bravery *noun*

brawl *noun*
brawls

brawn *noun*

brawny *adjective*
brawnier
brawniest

bray *verb*
brays
braying
brayed

brazen *adjective*

brazier *noun*
braziers

breach☆ *noun*
breaches

bread *noun*

breadth *noun*
breadths

breadwinner *noun*
breadwinners

break✪ *verb*
breaks
breaking
broke
broken

break *noun*
breaks

breakable *adjective*

breakage *noun*
breakages

breakdown *noun*
breakdowns

breaker *noun*
breakers

breakfast *noun*
breakfasts

★ A **brake** is what makes a car stop. **! break.**
☆ A **breach** is a gap or a breaking of a rule. **! breech.**
✪ To **break** something is to make it go into pieces. **! brake.**

a b c d e f g h i j k l m n o p q r s t u v w x y z

breakneck *adjective*
breakthrough *noun*
breakthroughs
breakwater *noun*
breakwaters
breast *noun*
breasts
breaststroke *noun*
breath *noun*
breaths
breathalyse *verb*
breathalyses
breathalysing
breathalysed
breathalyser *noun*
breathalysers
breathe *verb*
breathes
breathing
breathed
breather *noun*
breathers
breathless *adjective*
breathtaking *adjective*
bred *verb* SEE **breed**
breech* *noun*
breeches
breeches *plural noun*
breed *verb*
breeds
breeding
bred
breed *noun*
breeds
breeder *noun*
breeders
breeze *noun*
breezes
breezy *adjective*
breezier
breeziest
brethren *plural noun*
brevity *noun*

brew *verb*
brews
brewing
brewed
brewer *noun*
brewers
brewery *noun*
breweries
briar☆ *noun*
briars
bribe *noun*
bribes
bribe *verb*
bribes
bribing
bribed
bribery *noun*
brick *noun*
bricks
bricklayer *noun*
bricklayers
bride *noun*
brides
bridal○ *adjective*
bridegroom *noun*
bridegrooms
bridesmaid *noun*
bridesmaids
bridge *noun*
bridges
bridle✣ *noun*
bridles
brief *adjective*
briefer
briefest
briefly *adverb*
brief *noun*
briefs
brief *verb*
briefs
briefing
briefed

briefcase *noun*
briefcases
brigade *noun*
brigades
brigadier *noun*
brigadiers
brigand *noun*
brigands
bright *adjective*
brighter
brightest
brightly *adverb*
brighten *verb*
brightens
brightening
brightened
brilliance *noun*
brilliant *adjective*
brilliantly *adverb*
brim *noun*
brims
brimming *verb*
brine *noun*
bring *verb*
brings
bringing
brought
brink *noun*
brisk *adjective*
brisker
briskest
briskly *adverb*
bristle *noun*
bristles
bristly *adjective*
British *noun*
Briton *noun*
Britons
brittle *adjective*

* A **breech** is a part of a gun. **! breach**.
☆ **Briar** means 'a prickly bush' and 'a pipe'. You will sometimes see it spelled *brier*.
○ **Bridal** means 'to do with a **bride**'. **! bridle**.
✣ A **bridle** is part of a horse's harness. **! bridal**.

broach[*] *verb*
broaches
broaching
broached

broad *adjective*
broader
broadest
broadly *adverb*

broadband *noun*

broadcast *noun*
broadcasts

broadcast *verb*
broadcasts
broadcasting
broadcast

broadcaster *noun*
broadcasters

broaden *verb*
broadens
broadening
broadened

broad-minded *adjective*

brochure *noun*
brochures

brogue *noun*
brogues

broke *verb* SEE **break**

broken *adjective* SEE **break**

bronchitis *noun*

bronze *noun*

brooch[☆] *noun*
brooches

brood *noun*
broods

brood *verb*
broods
brooding
brooded

broody *adjective*
broodier
broodiest

brook *noun*
brooks

broom *noun*
brooms

broomstick *noun*
broomsticks

broth *noun*
broths

brother *noun*
brothers

brotherly *adjective*

brother-in-law *noun*
brothers-in-law

brought *verb* SEE **bring**

brow *noun*
brows

brown *adjective*
browner
brownest

brownie[✪] *noun*
brownies

Brownie[✣] *noun*
Brownies

browse *verb*
browses
browsing
browsed

bruise *noun*
bruises

bruise *verb*
bruises
bruising
bruised

brunette *noun*
brunettes

brush *noun*
brushes

brush *verb*
brushes
brushing
brushed

Brussels sprout *noun*
Brussels sprouts

brutal *adjective*
brutally *adverb*

brutality *noun*
brutalities

brute *noun*
brutes

bubble *noun*
bubbles

bubble *verb*
bubbles
bubbling
bubbled

bubblegum *noun*

bubbly *adjective*
bubblier
bubbliest

buccaneer *noun*
buccaneers

buck *noun*
bucks

buck *verb*
bucks
bucking
bucked

bucket *noun*
buckets

bucketful *noun*
bucketfuls

buckle *noun*
buckles

buckle *verb*
buckles
buckling
buckled

bud *noun*
buds

Buddhism *noun*

Buddhist *noun*
Buddhists

budding *adjective*

buddy *noun*
buddies

* **Broach** means 'to mention something'. **! brooch.**
☆ A **brooch** is an ornament you wear. **! broach.**
✪ A **brownie** is a chocolate cake.
✣ A **Brownie** is a junior Guide.

a b c d e f g h i j k l m n o p q r s t u v w x y z

budge *verb*
budges
budging
budged
budgerigar *noun*
budgerigars
budget *noun*
budgets
budget *verb*
budgets
budgeting
budgeted
budgie *noun*
budgies
buff *noun*
buffalo *noun*
buffalo *or* buffaloes
buffer *noun*
buffers
buffet *noun*
buffets
bug *noun*
bugs
bug *verb*
bugs
bugging
bugged
bugle *noun*
bugles
bugler *noun*
buglers
build *verb*
builds
building
built
builder *noun*
builders
building *noun*
buildings
built-in *adjective*
built-up *adjective*
bulb *noun*
bulbs
bulge *noun*
bulges
bulge *verb*
bulges
bulging
bulged
bulk *noun*
bulky *adjective*
bulkier
bulkiest
bull *noun*
bulls
bulldoze *verb*
bulldozes
bulldozing
bulldozed
bulldozer *noun*
bulldozers
bullet *noun*
bullets
bulletin *noun*
bulletins
bullet point *noun*
bullet points
bulletproof *adjective*
bullfight *noun*
bullfights
bullfighter *noun*
bullfighters
bullion *noun*
bullock *noun*
bullocks
bullseye *noun*
bullseyes
bully *verb*
bullies
bullying
bullied
bully *noun*
bullies
bulrush *noun*
bulrushes
bulwark* *noun*
bulwarks
bumblebee *noun*
bumblebees
bump *verb*
bumps
bumping
bumped
bump *noun*
bumps
bumper *adjective* & *noun*
bumpers
bumpy *adjective*
bumpier
bumpiest
bunch *noun*
bunches
bundle *noun*
bundles
bundle *verb*
bundles
bundling
bundled
bung *verb*
bungs
bunging
bunged
bung *noun*
bungs
bungalow *noun*
bungalows
bungee jumping *noun*
bungle *verb*
bungles
bungling
bungled
bungler *noun*
bunglers
bunk *noun*
bunks
bunk bed *noun*
bunk beds
bunker *noun*
bunkers
bunny *noun*
bunnies
Bunsen burner *noun*
Bunsen burners
buoy *noun*
buoys

* A **bulwark** is a strong wall.

buoyancy *noun*
buoyant *adjective*
burden *noun*
burdens
burdensome *adjective*
bureau★ *noun*
bureaux
bureaucracy *noun*
bureaucratic *adjective*
burger *noun*
burgers
burglar *noun*
burglars
burglary *noun*
burglaries
burgle *verb*
burgles
burgling
burgled
burial *noun*
burials
burly *adjective*
burlier
burliest
burn☆ *verb*
burns
burning
burnt *or* burned
burn *noun*
burns
burner *noun*
burners
burning *adjective*
burrow *noun*
burrows
burrow *verb*
burrows
burrowing
burrowed
burst *verb*
bursts
bursting
burst
burst *noun*
bursts
bury *verb*
buries
burying
buried
bus *noun*
buses
bus stop *noun*
bus stops
bush *noun*
bushes
bushy *adjective*
bushier
bushiest
busily *adverb*
business *noun*
businesses
businesslike *adjective*
businessman *noun*
businessmen
businesswoman *noun*
businesswomen
busker *noun*
buskers
bust *verb*
busts
busting
bust
bust *noun*
busts
bust *adjective*
bustle *verb*
bustles
bustling
bustled
busy *adjective*
busier
busiest
busybody *noun*
busybodies
but✪ *conjunction*
butcher *noun*
butchers
butchery *noun*
butler *noun*
butlers
butt✣ *noun*
butts
butt● *verb*
butts
butting
butted
butter *noun*
buttercup *noun*
buttercups
butterfingers *noun*
butterfingers
butterfly *noun*
butterflies
butterscotch *noun*
butterscotches
button *noun*
buttons
button *verb*
buttons
buttoning
buttoned
buttonhole *noun*
buttonholes
buttress *noun*
buttresses
buy *verb*
buys
buying
bought

★ **Bureau** is a French word used in English. It means 'a writing desk' or 'an office'.
☆ You use **burned** in e.g. *I burned the cakes.* You use **burnt** in e.g. *I can smell burnt cakes.* You use **burned** or **burnt** in e.g. *I have burned/burnt the cakes.*
✪ You use **but** in e.g. *I like fish but I'm not hungry.* **! butt.**
✣ A **butt** is a barrel or part of a gun. **! but.**
● **Butt** means 'to hit with your head' **! but.**

a
b
c
d
e
f
g
h
i
j
k
l
m
n
o
p
q
r
s
t
u
v
w
x
y
z

buy *noun*
buys

buyer *noun*
buyers

buzz *noun*
buzzes

buzz *verb*
buzzes
buzzing
buzzed

buzzard *noun*
buzzards

buzzer *noun*
buzzers

by★ *preposition*

bye☆ *noun*
byes

bye-bye *interjection*

by-election *noun*
by-elections

by-law *noun*
by-laws

bypass *noun*
bypasses

by-product *noun*
by-products

bystander *noun*
bystanders

byte✪ *noun*

★ You use **by** in e.g. *a book by J. K. Rowling*. **! bye**.
☆ You use **bye** in e.g *bye for now*. **! by**.
✪ A **byte** is a unit in computing. **! bite**.

For words beginning with a **k-** sound, try also **ch-**

Cc

CAB *abbreviation*
cab *noun*
cabs
cabaret *noun*
cabarets
cabbage *noun*
cabbages
cabin *noun*
cabins
cabinet *noun*
cabinets
cable *noun*
cables
cackle *verb*
cackles
cackling
cackled
cackle *noun*
cackles
cactus *noun*
cacti
caddie★ *noun*
caddies
caddy☆ *noun*
caddies
cadet *noun*
cadets
cadge *verb*
cadges
cadging
cadged
cafe *noun*
cafes
cafeteria *noun*
cafeterias
caffeine *noun*
caftan *noun*
caftans SEE **kaftan**
cage *noun*
cages
cagey *adjective*
cagier
cagiest
cagoule *noun*
cagoules
cake *noun*
cakes
caked *adjective*
calamine *noun*
calamitous *adjective*
calamity *noun*
calamities
calcium *noun*
calculate *verb*
calculates
calculating
calculated
calculation *noun*
calculations
calculator *noun*
calculators
calendar *noun*
calendars
calf✪ *noun*
calves
calico *noun*
call *noun*
calls
call *verb*
calls
calling
called
caller *noun*
callers
calligram *noun*
calligrams
calling *noun*
callings
callipers *plural noun*
callous *adjective*
calm *adjective*
calmer
calmest
calmly *adverb*
calmness *noun*
calorie *noun*
calories
calves✣ *noun* SEE **calf**
calypso *noun*
calypsos
camcorder *noun*
camcorders
came *verb* SEE **come**
camel *noun*
camels
camera *noun*
cameras
cameraman *noun*
cameramen
camouflage *noun*
camp *noun*
camps
camp *verb*
camps
camping
camped

★ A **caddie** is a person who helps a golfer. **! caddy**.
☆ A **caddy** is a container for tea. **! caddie**.
✪ **Calf** means 'a young cow' and 'a part of your leg'.
✣ **Calves** is the plural of calf. **! carves**.

For words beginning with a **k-** sound, try also **ch-**

campaign *verb*
campaigns
campaigning
campaigned

campaign *noun*
campaigns

campaigner *noun*
campaigners

camper *noun*
campers

campsite *noun*
campsites

campus *noun*
campuses

can *verb*
could

can★ *verb*
cans
canning
canned

can *noun*
cans

Canadian *adjective & noun*
Canadians

canal *noun*
canals

canary *noun*
canaries

cancel *verb*
cancels
cancelling
cancelled

cancellation *noun*
cancellations

cancer *noun*
cancers

candidate *noun*
candidates

candle *noun*
candles

candlelight *noun*

candlestick *noun*
candlesticks

candy *noun*
candies

candyfloss *noun*

cane *noun*
canes

cane *verb*
canes
caning
caned

canine *noun*
canines

cannabis *noun*

cannibal *noun*
cannibals

cannibalism *noun*

cannon☆ *noun*
cannon
cannons

cannonball *noun*
cannonballs

cannot *verb*

canoe *noun*
canoes

canoe *verb*
canoes
canoeing
canoed

canoeist *noun*
canoeists

canon✪ *noun*
canons

canopy *noun*
canopies

can't *verb*

canteen *noun*
canteens

canter *verb*
canters
cantering
cantered

canton *noun*
cantons

canvas✣ *noun*
canvases

canvass● *verb*
canvasses
canvassing
canvassed

canyon *noun*
canyons

cap *verb*
caps
capping
capped

cap *noun*
caps

capable *adjective*
capably *adverb*

capability *noun*
capabilities

capacity *noun*
capacities

cape *noun*
capes

caper *verb*
capers
capering
capered

caper *noun*
capers

capital *noun*
capitals

capitalism *noun*

capitalist *noun*
capitalists

★ This verb **can** means 'to put food in a can', and it has normal forms.
☆ A **cannon** is a gun. **! canon.** You use **cannons** in e.g. *There are ten cannons on the walls* and **cannon** in e.g. *They use all their cannon.*
✪ A **canon** is a member of the clergy. **! cannon.**
✣ **Canvas** means 'a strong cloth'. **! canvass.**
● **Canvass** means 'to ask people for their support'. **! canvas.**

For words beginning with a **k-** sound, try also **ch-**

capsize *verb*
capsizes
capsizing
capsized
capsule *noun*
capsules
captain *noun*
captains
caption *noun*
captions
captivating *adjective*
captive *adjective* & *noun*
captives
captivity *noun*
captor *noun*
captors
capture *verb*
captures
capturing
captured
capture *noun*
car *noun*
cars
caramel *noun*
caramels
carat *noun*
carats
caravan *noun*
caravans
carbohydrate *noun*
carbohydrates
carbon *noun*
carbon emissions *plural noun*
car boot sale *noun*
car boot sales
carburettor *noun*
carburettors
carcass *noun*
carcasses
card *noun*
cards
cardboard *noun*
cardiac *adjective*
cardigan *noun*
cardigans
cardinal *noun*
cardinals
cardphone *noun*
cardphones
care *noun*
cares
care *verb*
cares
caring
cared
career *noun*
careers
career *verb*
careers
careering
careered
carefree *adjective*
careful *adjective*
carefully *adverb*
careless *adjective*
carelessly *adverb*
carelessness *noun*
caress *verb*
caresses
caressing
caressed
caress *noun*
caresses
caretaker *noun*
caretakers
cargo *noun*
cargoes
Caribbean *adjective*
caricature *noun*
caricatures
carnage *noun*
carnation *noun*
carnations
carnival *noun*
carnivals
carnivore *noun*
carnivores
carnivorous *adjective*
carol *noun*
carols
carp *noun*
carp
carpenter *noun*
carpenters
carpentry *noun*
carpet *noun*
carpets
carriage *noun*
carriages
carriageway *noun*
carriageways
carrier *noun*
carriers
carrot *noun*
carrots
carry *verb*
carries
carrying
carried
cart *noun*
carts
cart *verb*
carts
carting
carted
carthorse *noun*
carthorses
cartilage *noun*
carton *noun*
cartons
cartoon *noun*
cartoons
cartoonist *noun*
cartoonists
cartridge *noun*
cartridges
cartwheel *noun*
cartwheels
carve* *verb*
carves
carving
carved

* You use **carves** in e.g. *He carves the meat with a knife.* **! calves.**

a b c d e f g h i j k l m n o p q r s t u v w x y z

cascade *noun*
cascades
case *noun*
cases
cash *verb*
cashes
cashing
cashed
cash *noun*
cashier *noun*
cashiers
cash register *noun*
cash registers
casino *noun*
casinos
cask *noun*
casks
casket *noun*
caskets
casserole *noun*
casseroles
cassette *noun*
cassettes
cast *verb*
casts
casting
cast
cast *noun*
casts
castanets *plural noun*
castaway *noun*
castaways
castle *noun*
castles
castor *noun*
castors
castor sugar *noun*
casual *adjective*
casually *adverb*
casualty *noun*
casualties
cat *noun*
cats
catalogue *noun*
catalogues
catalyst *noun*
catalysts
catamaran *noun*
catamarans
catapult *noun*
catapults
catastrophe *noun*
catastrophes
catastrophic *adjective*
catch *verb*
catches
catching
caught
catch *noun*
catches
catching *adjective*
catchphrase *noun*
catchphrases
catchy *adjective*
catchier
catchiest
category *noun*
categories
cater *verb*
caters
catering
catered
caterer *noun*
caterers
caterpillar *noun*
caterpillars
cathedral *noun*
cathedrals
Catherine wheel *noun*
Catherine wheels
cathode *noun*
cathodes
catholic* *adjective*
Catholic* *adjective* & *noun*
Catholics
catkin *noun*
catkins
catseye *noun*
catseyes
cattle *plural noun*
caught *verb* SEE **catch**
cauldron *noun*
cauldrons
cauliflower *noun*
cauliflowers
cause *verb*
causes
causing
caused
cause *noun*
causes
caution *noun*
cautions
cautionary *adjective*
cautious *adjective*
cautiously *adverb*
cavalier *noun*
cavaliers
cavalry *noun*
cavalries
cave *noun*
caves
cave *verb*
caves
caving
caved
caveman *noun*
cavemen
cavern *noun*
caverns
cavity *noun*
cavities
CCTV *noun*
CD *noun*
CDs
CD-ROM *noun*
CD-ROMs
cease *verb*
ceases
ceasing
ceased
ceasefire *noun*
ceasefires
ceaseless *adjective*
ceaselessly *adverb*

* Use a capital C when you refer to the religion.

cedar *noun*
cedars
ceiling *noun*
ceilings
celebrate *verb*
celebrates
celebrating
celebrated
celebration *noun*
celebrations
celebrity *noun*
celebrities
celery *noun*
cell★ *noun*
cells
cellar☆ *noun*
cellars
cello *noun*
cellos
cellophane *noun*
cellphone *noun*
cellphones
cellular *adjective*
celluloid *noun*
cellulose *noun*
Celsius *adjective*
Celt *noun*
Celts
Celtic *adjective*
cement *noun*
cemetery *noun*
cemeteries
censor *verb*
censors
censoring
censored
censor✪ *noun*
censors
censorship *noun*
censure *verb*
censures
censured
censuring
censure✣ *noun*
census *noun*
censuses
cent● *noun*
cents
centenary *noun*
centenaries
centigrade *adjective*
centilitre *noun*
centilitres
centimetre *noun*
centimetres
centipede *noun*
centipedes
central *adjective*
centrally *adverb*
centre *noun*
centres
centre *verb*
centres
centring
centred
centrifugal force *noun*
centurion *noun*
centurions
century *noun*
centuries
ceramic *adjective*
ceramics *plural noun*
cereal❋ *noun*
cereals
ceremony *noun*
ceremonies
ceremonial *adjective*
ceremonially *adverb*
certain *adjective*
certainly *adverb*
certainty *noun*
certainties
certificate *noun*
certificates
certify *verb*
certifies
certifying
certified
chain *noun*
chains
chair *noun*
chairs
chairlift *noun*
chairlifts
chairman *noun*
chairmen
chairperson *noun*
chairpersons
chalet *noun*
chalets
chalk *noun*
chalks
chalky *adjective*
chalkier
chalkiest
challenge *verb*
challenges
challenging
challenged
challenge *noun*
challenges
challenger *noun*
challengers
chamber *noun*
chambers
chambermaid *noun*
chambermaids
champagne *noun*

★ A **cell** is a small room or a part of an organism. **! sell.**
☆ A **cellar** is a room under a house. **! seller.**
✪ A **censor** is someone who makes sure books and films are suitable for people to see. **! censure.**
✣ **Censure** means 'harsh criticism'. **! censor.**
● A **cent** is a coin used in America. **! scent, sent.**
❋ A **cereal** is something you eat. **! serial.**

For words beginning with a **k-** sound, try also **ch-**

champion *noun*
champions
championship *noun*
championships
chance *noun*
chances
chancellor *noun*
chancellors
Chancellor of the Exchequer *noun*
chandelier *noun*
chandeliers
change *verb*
changes
changing
changed
change *noun*
changes
changeable *adjective*
channel *noun*
channels
chant *noun*
chants
chant *verb*
chants
chanting
chanted
chaos *noun*
chaotic *adjective*
chaotically *adverb*
chap *noun*
chaps
chapatti *noun*
chapattis
chapel *noun*
chapels
chapped *adjective*
chapter *noun*
chapters
char *verb*
chars
charring
charred
character *noun*
characters

characteristic *adjective*
characteristically *adverb*
characteristic *noun*
characteristics
characterize *verb*
characterizes
characterizing
characterized
charades *plural noun*
charcoal *noun*
charge *verb*
charges
charging
charged
charge *noun*
charges
chariot *noun*
chariots
charioteer *noun*
charioteers
charitable *adjective*
charitably *adverb*
charity *noun*
charities
charm *verb*
charms
charming
charmed
charm *noun*
charms
charming *adjective*
chart *noun*
charts
charter *noun*
charters
charter *verb*
charters
chartering
chartered
charwoman *noun*
charwomen
chase *verb*
chases
chasing
chased

chase *noun*
chases
chasm *noun*
chasms
chassis *noun*
chassis
chat *verb*
chats
chatting
chatted
chat *noun*
chats
chatroom *noun*
chatrooms
chatty *adjective*
chattier
chattiest
chateau★ *noun*
chateaux *or* chateaus
French château, châteaux
chatter *verb*
chatters
chattering
chattered
chauffeur *noun*
chauffeurs
chauvinism *noun*
chauvinist *noun*
chauvinists
cheap☆ *adjective*
cheaper
cheapest
cheaply *adverb*
cheat *verb*
cheats
cheating
cheated
cheat *noun*
cheats
check *verb*
checks
checking
checked
check *noun*
checks

★ **Château** is a French word. It means 'a castle or large house'.
☆ **Cheap** means 'not costing much'. **! cheep**.

For words beginning with a **k-** sound, try also **ch-**

checkmate *noun*
checkmates
checkout *noun*
checkouts
check-up *noun*
check-ups
cheek *noun*
cheeks
cheek *verb*
cheeks
cheeking
cheeked
cheeky *adjective*
cheekier
cheekiest
cheekily *adverb*
cheep★ *verb*
cheeps
cheeping
cheeped
cheer *verb*
cheers
cheering
cheered
cheer *noun*
cheers
cheerful *adjective*
cheerfully *adverb*
cheerio *interjection*
cheese *noun*
cheeses
cheesy *adjective*
cheesier
cheesiest
cheetah *noun*
cheetahs
chef *noun*
chefs
chemical *adjective*
chemically *adverb*
chemical *noun*
chemicals
chemist *noun*
chemists
chemistry *noun*
chemotherapy *noun*
cheque *noun*
cheques
chequebook *noun*
chequebooks
chequered *adjective*
cherish *verb*
cherishes
cherishing
cherished
cherry *noun*
cherries
chess *noun*
chest *noun*
chests
chestnut *noun*
chestnuts
chest of drawers *noun*
chests of drawers
chew *verb*
chews
chewing
chewed
chewy *adjective*
chewier
chewiest
chic☆ *adjective*
chick *noun*
chicks
chicken *noun*
chickens
chicken *verb*
chickens
chickening
chickened
chickenpox *noun*
chief *adjective*
chiefly *adverb*
chief *noun*
chiefs
chieftain *noun*
chieftains
chilblain *noun*
chilblains
child *noun*
children
childhood *noun*
childhoods
childish *adjective*
childishness *noun*
childless *adjective*
childlike *adjective*
childminder *noun*
childminders
childproof *adjective*
chill *noun*
chills
chill *verb*
chills
chilling
chilled
chilli✪ *noun*
chillies
chilly✣ *adjective*
chillier
chilliest
chime *noun*
chimes
chime *verb*
chimes
chiming
chimed
chimney *noun*
chimneys
chimpanzee *noun*
chimpanzees
chin *noun*
chins
china *noun*
chink *noun*
chinks
chip *noun*
chips

★ **Cheep** is the noise a bird makes. **! cheap**.
☆ **Chic** is a French word and means 'smart or elegant'. There is no word *chicly*.
✪ A **chilli** is a type of hot pepper, added to meat or vegetable dishes. **! chilly**.
✣ You use **chilly** to describe cold, bleak weather or atmosphere. **! chilli**.

a b c d e f g h i j k l m n o p q r s t u v w x y z

chip *verb*
chips
chipping
chipped
chirp *verb*
chirps
chirping
chirped
chirpy *adjective*
chirpier
chirpiest
chisel *noun*
chisels
chisel *verb*
chisels
chiselling
chiselled
chivalrous *adjective*
chivalrously *adverb*
chivalry *noun*
chlorine *noun*
chlorophyll *noun*
choc ice *noun*
choc ices
chock-a-block *adjective*
chock-full *adjective*
chocolate *noun*
chocolates
choice *noun*
choices
choir *noun*
choirs
choirboy *noun*
choirboys
choirgirl *noun*
choirgirls
choke *verb*
chokes
choking
choked
choke *noun*
chokes
cholera *noun*
cholesterol *noun*
choose *verb*
chooses
choosing
chose
chosen
choosy *adjective*
choosier
choosiest
chop *verb*
chops
chopping
chopped
chop *noun*
chops
chopper *noun*
choppers
choppy *adjective*
choppier
choppiest
chopsticks *plural noun*
choral *adjective*
chord* *noun*
chords
chore *noun*
chores
choreographer *noun*
choreographers
choreography *noun*
chorister *noun*
choristers
chorus *noun*
choruses
chose *verb* SEE **choose**
chosen *verb* SEE **choose**
christen *verb*
christens
christening
christened
christening *noun*
Christian *adjective & noun*
Christians
Christianity *noun*
Christmas *noun*
Christmases
chrome *noun*
chromium *noun*
chromosome *noun*
chromosomes
chronic *adjective*
chronically *adverb*
chronicle *noun*
chronicles
chronological *adjective*
chronologically *adverb*
chronology *noun*
chrysalis *noun*
chrysalises
chrysanthemum *noun*
chrysanthemums
chubby *adjective*
chubbier
chubbiest
chuck *verb*
chucks
chucking
chucked
chuckle *verb*
chuckles
chuckling
chuckled
chuckle *noun*
chuckles
chug *verb*
chugs
chugging
chugged
chum *noun*
chums
chummy *adjective*
chummier
chummiest
chunk *noun*
chunks
chunky *adjective*
chunkier
chunkiest
church *noun*
churches
churchyard *noun*
churchyards

* A **chord** is a number of musical notes played together. **! cord.**

churn *noun*
churns
churn *verb*
churns
churning
churned
chute* *noun*
chutes
chutney *noun*
chutneys
cider *noun*
ciders
cigar *noun*
cigars
cigarette *noun*
cigarettes
cinder *noun*
cinders
cinema *noun*
cinemas
cinnamon *noun*
cinquain *noun*
cinquains
circle *noun*
circles
circle *verb*
circles
circling
circled
circuit *noun*
circuits
circular *adjective* & *noun*
circulars
circulate *verb*
circulates
circulating
circulated
circulation *noun*
circulations
circumference *noun*
circumferences
circumnavigate *verb*
circumnavigates
circumnavigating
circumnavigated
circumstance *noun*
circumstances
circumvent *verb*
circumvents
circumventing
circumvented
circus *noun*
circuses
cistern *noun*
cisterns
citizen *noun*
citizens
citizenship *noun*
citric acid *noun*
citrus fruit *noun*
citrus fruits
city *noun*
cities
civic *adjective*
civil *adjective*
civilian *noun*
civilians
civilization *noun*
civilizations
civilize *verb*
civilizes
civilizing
civilized
clad *adjective*
claim *verb*
claims
claiming
claimed
claim *noun*
claims
claimant *noun*
claimants
clam *noun*
clams
clamber *verb*
clambers
clambering
clambered
clammy *adjective*
clammier
clammiest
clamp *noun*
clamps
clamp *verb*
clamps
clamping
clamped
clan *noun*
clans
clandestine *adjective*
clang *verb*
clangs
clanging
clanged
clanger *noun*
clangers
clank *verb*
clanks
clanking
clanked
clap *verb*
claps
clapping
clapped
clap *noun*
claps
clapper *noun*
clappers
clarification *noun*
clarify *verb*
clarifies
clarifying
clarified
clarinet *noun*
clarinets
clarinettist *noun*
clarinettists
clarity *noun*
clash *verb*
clashes
clashing
clashed
clash *noun*
clashes

* A **chute** is a funnel for sending things down. **! shoot**.

a b **c** d e f g h i j k l m n o p q r s t u v w x y z

clasp *verb*
clasps
clasping
clasped
clasp *noun*
clasps
class *noun*
classes
class *verb*
classes
classing
classed
classic *noun*
classics
classic *adjective*
classical *adjective*
classically *adverb*
classification *noun*
classifications
classified *adjective*
classify *verb*
classifies
classifying
classified
classmate *noun*
classmates
classroom *noun*
classrooms
clatter *noun*
clatter *verb*
clatters
clattering
clattered
clause★ *noun*
clauses
claustrophobia *noun*
claw☆ *noun*
claws
claw✪ *verb*
claws
clawing
clawed
clay *noun*

clean *adjective*
cleaner
cleanest
cleanly *adverb*
clean *verb*
cleans
cleaning
cleaned
cleaner *noun*
cleaners
cleanliness *noun*
cleanse *verb*
cleanses
cleansing
cleansed
cleanser *noun*
cleansers
clear *adjective*
clearer
clearest
clearly *adverb*
clear *verb*
clears
clearing
cleared
clearance *noun*
clearances
clearing *noun*
clearings
clef *noun*
clefs
clench *verb*
clenches
clenching
clenched
clergy *noun*
clergyman *noun*
clergymen
clergywoman *noun*
clergywomen
clerical *adjective*
clerihew *noun*
clerihews

clerk *noun*
clerks
clever *adjective*
cleverer
cleverest
cleverly *adverb*
cliché *noun*
clichés
click *noun*
clicks
client *noun*
clients
cliff *noun*
cliffs
cliffhanger *noun*
cliffhangers
climate *noun*
climates
climatic *adjective*
climax *noun*
climaxes
climb *verb*
climbs
climbing
climbed
climb *noun*
climbs
climber *noun*
climbers
cling *verb*
clings
clinging
clung
cling film *noun*
clinic *noun*
clinics
clink *verb*
clinks
clinking
clinked
clip *verb*
clips
clipping
clipped

★ A **clause** is a part of a sentence or contract. **! claws**.
☆ **Claws** are the hard sharp nails that some animals have on their feet. **! clause**.
✪ To **claw** is to scratch, maul, or pull a person or thing.

For words beginning with a **k-** sound, try also **ch-**

clip *noun*
clips
clipboard *noun*
clipboards
clipper *noun*
clippers
clippers *plural noun*
clipping *noun*
clippings
cloak *noun*
cloaks
cloakroom *noun*
cloakrooms
clobber *verb*
clobbers
clobbering
clobbered
clock *noun*
clocks
clockwise *adverb & adjective*
clockwork *noun*
clog *verb*
clogs
clogging
clogged
clog *noun*
clogs
cloister *noun*
cloisters
clone *noun*
clones
clone *verb*
clones
cloning
cloned
close *verb*
closes
closing
closed
close *adjective & noun*
closer
closest
closely *adverb*
close *noun*
closes
close-up *noun*
close-ups

closure *noun*
closures
clot *noun*
clots
clot *verb*
clots
clotting
clotted
cloth *noun*
cloths
clothe *verb*
clothes
clothing
clothed
clothes *plural noun*
clothing *noun*
cloud *noun*
clouds
cloud *verb*
clouds
clouding
clouded
cloudless *adjective*
cloudy *adjective*
cloudier
cloudiest
clout *verb*
clouts
clouting
clouted
clove *noun*
cloves
clover *noun*
clown *noun*
clowns
clown *verb*
clowns
clowning
clowned
club *noun*
clubs
club *verb*
clubs
clubbing
clubbed

cluck *verb*
clucks
clucking
clucked
clue *noun*
clues
clueless *adjective*
clump *noun*
clumps
clumsiness *noun*
clumsy *adjective*
clumsier
clumsiest
clumsily *adverb*
clung *verb* SEE **cling**
cluster *noun*
clusters
clutch *verb*
clutches
clutching
clutched
clutch *noun*
clutches
clutter *verb*
clutters
cluttering
cluttered
clutter *noun*

co- *prefix*
co- makes words meaning 'together', e.g. a **co-pilot** is another pilot who sits together with the chief pilot. You often need a hyphen, e.g. **co-author**, **co-driver**, but some words are spelled joined up, e.g. **cooperate**, **coordinate**.

coach *verb*
coaches
coaching
coached
coach *noun*
coaches
coal *noun*
coalition *noun*
coalitions

For words beginning with a **k-** sound, try also **ch-**

coarse★ *adjective*
coarser
coarsest
coarsely *adverb*
coast *noun*
coasts
coast *verb*
coasts
coasting
coasted
coastal *adjective*
coastguard *noun*
coastguards
coastline *noun*
coat *noun*
coats
coat *verb*
coats
coating
coated
coating *noun*
coatings
coax *verb*
coaxes
coaxing
coaxed
cobalt *noun*
cobbled *verb*
cobbler *noun*
cobblers
cobbles *plural noun*
cobblestone *noun*
cobblestones
cobra *noun*
cobras
cobweb *noun*
cobwebs
cock *noun*
cocks
cock *verb*
cocks
cocking
cocked
cockerel *noun*
cockerels
cockle *noun*
cockles
cockney *noun*
cockneys
cockpit *noun*
cockpits
cockroach *noun*
cockroaches
cocky *adjective*
cockier
cockiest
cocoa *noun*
cocoas
coconut *noun*
coconuts
cocoon *noun*
cocoons
cod☆ *noun*
cod
code *noun*
codes
code *verb*
codes
coding
coded
co-education *noun*
co-educational *adjective*
coffee *noun*
coffees
coffin *noun*
coffins
cog *noun*
cogs
cohort *noun*
cohorts
coil *verb*
coils
coiling
coiled
coil *noun*
coils
coin *noun*
coins
coin *verb*
coins
coining
coined
coinage *noun*
coinages
coincide *verb*
coincides
coinciding
coincided
coincidence *noun*
coincidences
coincidentally *adverb*
coke *noun*
cola *noun*
colas
colander *noun*
colanders
cold *adjective*
colder
coldest
coldly *adverb*
cold *noun*
colds
cold-blooded *adjective*
coldness *noun*
coleslaw *noun*
collaborate *verb*
collaborates
collaborating
collaborated
collaboration *noun*
collaborator *noun*
collaborators
collage *noun*
collages
collapse *verb*
collapses
collapsing
collapsed
collapse *noun*
collapses
collapsible *adjective*
collar *noun*
collars

★ **Coarse** means ‘rough’ or ‘crude’. **! course.**
☆ You use **cod** for the plural: *The sea is full of cod.*

collate *verb*
collates
collating
collated

colleague *noun*
colleagues

collect *verb*
collects
collecting
collected

collection *noun*
collections

collective *adjective*

collector *noun*
collectors

college *noun*
colleges

collide *verb*
collides
colliding
collided

collision *noun*
collisions

colloquial *adjective*
colloquially

colon *noun*
colons

colonel* *noun*
colonels

colonial *adjective*

colonist *noun*
colonists

colony *noun*
colonies

colossal *adjective*
colossally *adverb*

colour *noun*
colours

colour *verb*
colours
colouring
coloured

colour-blind *adjective*

coloured *adjective*

colourful *adjective*
colourfully *adverb*

colouring *noun*

colourless *adjective*

colt *noun*
colts

column *noun*
columns

coma *noun*
comas

comb *noun*
combs

comb *verb*
combs
combing
combed

combat *noun*
combats

combat *verb*
combats
combating
combated

combatant *noun*
combatants

combination *noun*
combinations

combine *verb*
combines
combining
combined

combine *noun*
combines

combustion *noun*

come *verb*
comes
coming
came

comeback *noun*
comebacks

comedian *noun*
comedians

comedy *noun*
comedies

comet *noun*
comets

comfort *verb*
comforts
comforting
comforted

comfort *noun*
comforts

comfortable *adjective*
comfortably *adverb*

comic *adjective & noun*
comics

comical *adjective*
comically *adverb*

comma *noun*
commas

command *verb*
commands
commanding
commanded

command *noun*
commands

commander *noun*
commanders

commandment *noun*
commandments

commando *noun*
commandos

commemorate *verb*
commemorates
commemorating
commemorated

commemoration *noun*

commence *verb*
commences
commencing
commenced

commencement *noun*

commend *verb*
commends
commending
commended

commendable *adjective*

commendation *noun*
commendations

* A **colonel** is an army officer. **! kernel.**

comment *verb*
comments
commenting
commented
comment *noun*
comments
commentary *noun*
commentaries
commentate *verb*
commentates
commentating
commentated
commentator *noun*
commentators
commerce *noun*
commercial *adjective*
commercially *adverb*
commercial *noun*
commercials
commercialized *adjective*
commissioner *noun*
commissioners
commit *verb*
commits
committing
committed
commitment *noun*
commitments
committee *noun*
committees
commodity *noun*
commodities
common *adjective*
commoner
commonest
commonly *adverb*
common *noun*
commons
commonplace *adjective & noun*
commonwealth *noun*
commonwealths
commotion *noun*
commotions
communal *adjective*
communally *adverb*

commune *noun*
communes
communicate *verb*
communicates
communicating
communicated
communication *noun*
communications
communicative *adjective*
communion *noun*
communions
communism *noun*
communist *noun*
communists
community *noun*
communities
commute *verb*
commutes
commuting
commuted
commuter *noun*
commuters
compact *adjective*
compact *noun*
compacts
compact disc *noun*
compact discs
companion *noun*
companions
companionship *noun*
company *noun*
companies
comparable *adjective*
comparably *adverb*
comparative *adjective*
comparatively *adverb*
comparative *noun*
comparatives
compare *verb*
compares
comparing
compared
comparison *noun*
comparisons
compartment *noun*
compartments

compass *noun*
compasses
compassion *noun*
compassionate *adjective*
compassionately *adverb*
compatible *adjective*
compel *verb*
compels
compelling
compelled
compensate *verb*
compensates
compensating
compensated
compensation *noun*
compensations
compère *noun*
compères
compete *verb*
competes
competing
competed
competence *noun*
competent *adjective*
competently *adverb*
competition *noun*
competitions
competitive *adjective*
competitively *adverb*
competitor *noun*
competitors
compilation *noun*
compilations
compile *verb*
compiles
compiling
compiled
compiler *noun*
compilers
complacent *adjective*
complacently *adverb*
complain *verb*
complains
complaining
complained
complaint *noun*
complaints

complement[*] *noun*
complements
complementary[☆] *adjective*
complete *adjective*
completely *adverb*
complete *verb*
completes
completing
completed
completion *noun*
complex *adjective* & *noun*
complexes
complexion *noun*
complexions
complexity *noun*
complexities
complicated *adjective*
complication *noun*
complications
compliment[✪] *noun*
compliments
complimentary[✣] *adjective*
component *noun*
components
compose *verb*
composes
composing
composed
composer *noun*
composers
composition *noun*
compositions
compost *noun*
compound *noun*
compounds
comprehend *verb*
comprehends
comprehending
comprehended
comprehension *noun*
comprehensions

comprehensive *adjective*
comprehensively *adverb*
comprehensive *noun*
comprehensives
compress *verb*
compresses
compressing
compressed
compression *noun*
comprise *verb*
comprises
comprising
comprised
compromise *noun*
compromises
compromise *verb*
compromises
compromising
compromised
compulsory *adjective*
computation *noun*
compute *verb*
computes
computing
computed
computer *noun*
computers
comrade *noun*
comrades
comradeship *noun*
con *verb*
cons
conning
conned
concave *adjective*
conceal *verb*
conceals
concealing
concealed
concealment *noun*

concede *verb*
concedes
conceding
conceded
conceit *noun*
conceited *adjective*
conceive *verb*
conceives
conceiving
conceived
concentrate *verb*
concentrates
concentrating
concentrated
concentrated *adjective*
concentration *noun*
concentrations
concentric *adjective*
concept *noun*
concepts
conception *noun*
conceptions
conceptual *adjective*
concern *verb*
concerns
concerning
concerned
concern *noun*
concerns
concerning *preposition*
concert *noun*
concerts
concertina *noun*
concertinas
concerto *noun*
concertos
concession *noun*
concessions
concise *adjective*
concisely *adverb*

---

[*] A **complement** is a thing that completes something. **! compliment.**
[☆] Something **complementary** completes something. **! complimentary.**
[✪] A **compliment** is something good you say about someone. **! complement.**
[✣] Something **complimentary** praises someone. **! complementary.**

a b c d e f g h i j k l m n o p q r s t u v w x y z

a b c d e f g h i j k l m n o p q r s t u v w x y z

conclude *verb*
concludes
concluding
concluded
conclusion *noun*
conclusions
concrete *adjective* & *noun*
concussion *noun*
condemn *verb*
condemns
condemning
condemned
condemnation *noun*
condensation *noun*
condense *verb*
condenses
condensing
condensed
condition *noun*
conditions
conduct *verb*
conducts
conducting
conducted
conduct *noun*
conduction *noun*
conductor *noun*
conductors
cone *noun*
cones
confectioner *noun*
confectioners
confectionery *noun*
confer *verb*
confers
conferring
conferred
conference *noun*
conferences
confess *verb*
confesses
confessing
confessed
confession *noun*
confessions

confetti *noun*
confide *verb*
confides
confiding
confided
confidence *noun*
confidences
confident *adjective*
confidently
confidential *adjective*
confidentially *adverb*
confine *verb*
confines
confining
confined
confinement *noun*
confirm *verb*
confirms
confirming
confirmed
confirmation *noun*
confirmations
confiscate *verb*
confiscates
confiscating
confiscated
confiscation *noun*
confiscations
conflict *verb*
conflicts
conflicting
conflicted
conflict *noun*
conflicts
conform *verb*
conforms
conforming
conformed
conformity *noun*
confront *verb*
confronts
confronting
confronted
confrontation *noun*
confrontations

confuse *verb*
confuses
confusing
confused
confusion *noun*
confusions
congested *adjective*
congestion *noun*
congratulate *verb*
congratulates
congratulating
congratulated
congratulations *plural noun*
congregation *noun*
congregations
congress *noun*
congresses
congruence *noun*
congruent *adjective*
conical *adjective*
conifer *noun*
conifers
coniferous *adjective*
conjunction *noun*
conjunctions
conjure *verb*
conjures
conjuring
conjured
conjuror *noun*
conjurors
conker★ *noun*
conkers
connect *verb*
connects
connecting
connected
connection *noun*
connections
conquer☆ *verb*
conquers
conquering
conquered

★ A **conker** is the fruit of a horse chestnut tree. **! conquer**.
☆ To **conquer** means 'to invade or take over'. **! conker**.

conqueror *noun*
conquerors
conquest *noun*
conquests
conscience *noun*
conscientious *adjective*
conscientiously *adverb*
conscious *adjective*
consciously *adverb*
consciousness *noun*
conscription *noun*
consecutive *adjective*
consecutively *adverb*
consensus *noun*
consent *verb*
consents
consenting
consented
consent *noun*
consequence *noun*
consequences
consequently *adverb*
conservation *noun*
conservationist *noun*
conservationists
conservative *adjective*
Conservative* *noun*
Conservatives
conservatory *noun*
conservatories
conserve *verb*
conserves
conserving
conserved
consider *verb*
considers
considering
considered
considerable *adjective*
considerably *adverb*
considerate *adjective*
considerately *adverb*
consideration *noun*
considerations

consist *verb*
consists
consisting
consisted
consistency *noun*
consistencies
consistent *adjective*
consistently *adverb*
consolation *noun*
consolations
console *verb*
consoles
consoling
consoled
consonant *noun*
consonants
conspicuous *adjective*
conspicuously *adverb*
conspiracy *noun*
conspiracies
conspirator *noun*
conspirators
conspire *verb*
conspires
conspiring
conspired
constable *noun*
constables
constancy *noun*
constant *adjective*
constantly *adverb*
constant *noun*
constants
constellation *noun*
constellations
constipated *adjective*
constipation *noun*
constituency *noun*
constituencies
constituent *noun*
constituents
constitute *verb*
constitutes
constituting
constituted

constitution *noun*
constitutions
constitutional *adjective*
construct *verb*
constructs
constructing
constructed
construction *noun*
constructions
constructive *adjective*
consul *noun*
consuls
consult *verb*
consults
consulting
consulted
consultant *noun*
consultants
consultation *noun*
consultations
consume *verb*
consumes
consuming
consumed
consumer *noun*
consumers
consumption *noun*
contact *noun*
contacts
contact *verb*
contacts
contacting
contacted
contagious *adjective*
contain *verb*
contains
containing
contained
container *noun*
containers
contaminate *verb*
contaminates
contaminating
contaminated
contamination *noun*

* Use a capital C when you mean a member of the political party.

contemplate *verb*
contemplates
contemplating
contemplated
contemplation *noun*
contemporary *adjective & noun*
contemporaries
contempt *noun*
contemptible *adjective*
contemptibly *adverb*
contemptuous *adjective*
contemptuously *adverb*
contend *verb*
contends
contending
contended
contender *noun*
contenders
content *adjective & noun*
contented *adjective*
contentedly *adverb*
contentment *noun*
contents *plural noun*
contest *verb*
contests
contesting
contested
contest *noun*
contests
contestant *noun*
contestants
context *noun*
contexts
continent *noun*
continents
continental *adjective*
continual *adjective*
continually *adverb*
continuation *noun*
continue *verb*
continues
continuing
continued
continuous *adjective*
continuously *adverb*
continuity *noun*

contour *noun*
contours
contract *verb*
contracts
contracting
contracted
contract *noun*
contracts
contraction *noun*
contractions
contractor *noun*
contractors
contradict *verb*
contradicts
contradicting
contradicted
contradiction *noun*
contradictions
contradictory *adjective*
contraflow *noun*
contraflows
contraption *noun*
contraptions
contrary *adjective & noun*
contrast *verb*
contrasts
contrasting
contrasted
contrast *noun*
contrasts
contribute *verb*
contributes
contributing
contributed
contribution *noun*
contributions
contributor *noun*
contributors
contrivance *noun*
contrivances
contrive *verb*
contrives
contriving
contrived
control *verb*
controls
controlling
controlled

control *noun*
controls
controller *noun*
controllers
controversial *adjective*
controversially *adverb*
controversy *noun*
controversies
conundrum *noun*
conundrums
convalescence *noun*
convalescent *adjective & noun*
convalescents
convection *noun*
convector *noun*
convectors
convenience *noun*
conveniences
convenient *adjective*
conveniently *adverb*
convent *noun*
convents
convention *noun*
conventions
conventional *adjective*
conventionally *adverb*
converge *verb*
converges
converging
converged
conversation *noun*
conversations
conversational *adjective*
converse *verb*
converses
conversing
conversed
converse *noun*
conversion *noun*
conversions
convert *verb*
converts
converting
converted
convert *noun*
converts

For words beginning with a **k-** sound, try also **ch-**

convertible *adjective*
convex *adjective*
convey *verb*
conveys
conveying
conveyed
conveyor belt *noun*
conveyor belts
convict *verb*
convicts
convicting
convicted
convict *noun*
convicts
conviction *noun*
convictions
convince *verb*
convinces
convincing
convinced
convoy *noun*
convoys
cook *verb*
cooks
cooking
cooked
cook *noun*
cooks
cooker *noun*
cookers
cookery *noun*
cool *adjective*
cooler
coolest
coolly *adverb*
cool *verb*
cools
cooling
cooled
cooler *noun*
coolers
coolness *noun*
coop *noun*
coops

cooperate *verb*
cooperates
cooperating
cooperated
cooperate *verb*
cooperation *noun*
cooperative *adjective*
coordinate *verb*
coordinates
coordinating
coordinated
coordinate *noun*
coordinates
coordination *noun*
coordinator *noun*
coordinators
coot *noun*
coots
cop *verb*
cops
copping
copped
cop *noun*
cops
cope *verb*
copes
coping
coped
copier *noun*
copiers
copper *noun*
coppers
copper sulphate *noun*
copy *verb*
copies
copying
copied
copy *noun*
copies
coral *noun*
cord★ *noun*
cords
cordial *adjective*
cordially *adverb*

cordial *noun*
cordials
cordiality *noun*
corduroy *noun*
core *noun*
cores
cork *noun*
corks
corkscrew *noun*
corkscrews
corn *noun*
corns
corned beef *noun*
corner *noun*
corners
corner *verb*
corners
cornering
cornered
cornet *noun*
cornets
cornflakes *plural noun*
cornflour *noun*
cornflower *noun*
cornflowers
Cornish *adjective*
Cornish pasty *noun*
Cornish pasties
corny *adjective*
cornier
corniest
coronation *noun*
coronations
coroner *noun*
coroners
corporal *noun*
corporals
corporal *adjective*
corporation *noun*
corporations
corps☆ *noun*
corps

★ A **cord** is a piece of thin rope. **! chord.**
☆ A **corps** is a unit of soldiers. **! corpse.**

For words beginning with a **k-** sound, try also **ch-**

a b c d e f g h i j k l m n o p q r s t u v w x y z

corpse★ *noun*
corpses
corpuscle *noun*
corpuscles
corral *noun*
corrals
correct *adjective*
correctly *adverb*
correct *verb*
corrects
correcting
corrected
correction *noun*
corrections
correctness *noun*
correlation *noun*
correlations
correspond *verb*
corresponds
corresponding
corresponded
correspondence *noun*
correspondent *noun*
correspondents
corridor *noun*
corridors
corrode *verb*
corrodes
corroding
corroded
corrosion *noun*
corrosive *adjective*
corrugated *adjective*
corrupt *adjective*
corruption *noun*
corset *noun*
corsets
cosmetic *adjective*
cosmetics *plural noun*
cosmic *adjective*

cosmonaut *noun*
cosmonauts
cost *verb*
costs
costing
cost
cost *noun*
costs
co-star *noun*
costly *adjective*
costlier
costliest
costume *noun*
costumes
cosy *adjective*
cosier
cosiest
cosily *adverb*
cot *noun*
cots
cottage *noun*
cottages
cotton *noun*
couch *noun*
couches
cough *verb*
coughs
coughing
coughed
cough *noun*
coughs
could *verb* SEE **can**
couldn't *verb*
council☆ *noun*
councils
councillor✪ *noun*
councillors
counsel✣ *noun*
counsels

counsel *verb*
counsels
counselling
counselled
counsellor● *noun*
counsellors
count *verb*
counts
counting
counted
count *noun*
counts
countdown *noun*
countdowns
countenance *noun*
countenances

counter- *prefix*
counter- makes words meaning 'opposite', e.g. a **counter-claim** is a claim someone makes in response to a claim from someone else. You often need a hyphen, but some words are spelled joined up, e.g. **counteract**, **counterbalance**.

counter *noun*
counters
counteract *verb*
counteracts
counteracting
counteracted
counterbalance *verb*
counterbalances
counterbalancing
counterbalanced
counterfeit *adjective*
countess *noun*
countesses
countless *adjective*

★ A **corpse** is a dead body. **! corps.**
☆ A **council** is a group of people who run the affairs of a town. **! counsel.**
✪ A **councillor** is a member of a council. **! counsellor.**
✣ **Counsel** means 'advice'. **! council.**
● A **counsellor** is someone who gives advice. **! councillor.**

country *noun*
countries
countryman *noun*
countrymen
countryside *noun*
countrywoman *noun*
countrywomen
county *noun*
counties
coup *noun*
coups
couple *noun*
couples
couple *verb*
couples
coupling
coupled
couplet *noun*
couplets
coupling *noun*
couplings
coupon *noun*
coupons
courage *noun*
courageous *adjective*
courageously *adverb*
courgette *noun*
courgettes
courier *noun*
couriers
course* *noun*
courses
court *noun*
courts
court *verb*
courts
courting
courted
courteous *adjective*
courteously *adverb*
courtesy *noun*
courtesies
court martial *noun*
courts martial
courtship *noun*
courtyard *noun*
courtyards
cousin *noun*
cousins
cove *noun*
coves
cover *verb*
covers
covering
covered
cover *noun*
covers
coverage *noun*
cover-up *noun*
cover-ups
cow *noun*
cows
coward *noun*
cowards
cowardice *noun*
cowardly *adjective*
cowboy *noun*
cowboys
co-writer *noun*
co-writers
cowslip *noun*
cowslips
cox *noun*
coxes
coxswain *noun*
coxswains
coy *adjective*
coyly *adverb*
coyness *noun*
crab *noun*
crabs
crack *verb*
cracks
cracking
cracked
crack *noun*
cracks
cracker *noun*
crackers
crackle *verb*
crackles
crackling
crackled
cradle *noun*
cradles
craft *noun*
crafts
craftsman *noun*
craftsmen
craftsmanship *noun*
crafty *adjective*
craftier
craftiest
craftily *adverb*
craftiness *noun*
crag *noun*
crags
craggy *adjective*
craggier
craggiest
cram *verb*
crams
cramming
crammed
cramp *verb*
cramps
cramping
cramped
cramp *noun*
cramps
crane *noun*
cranes
crane *verb*
cranes
craning
craned
crane fly *noun*
crane flies
crank *verb*
cranks
cranking
cranked
crank *noun*
cranks

* You use **course** in e.g. *a French course.* **! coarse**.

a b c d e f g h i j k l m n o p q r s t u v w x y z

cranky *adjective*
crankier
crankiest

cranny *noun*
crannies

crash *verb*
crashes
crashing
crashed

crash *noun*
crashes

crate *noun*
crates

crater *noun*
craters

crave *verb*
craves
craving
craved

crawl *verb*
crawls
crawling
crawled

crawl *noun*
crawls

crayon *noun*
crayons

craze *noun*
crazes

craziness *noun*

crazy *adjective*
crazier
craziest
crazily *adverb*

creak *verb*
creaks
creaking
creaked

creak *noun*
creaks

creaky *adjective*
creakier
creakiest

cream *noun*
creams

creamy *adjective*
creamier
creamiest

crease *verb*
creases
creasing
creased

crease *noun*
creases

create *verb*
creates
creating
created

creation *noun*
creations

creative *adjective*
creatively *adverb*

creativity *noun*

creator *noun*
creators

creature *noun*
creatures

crèche *noun*
crèches

credibility *noun*

credible *adjective*
credibly *adverb*

credit *verb*
credits
crediting
credited

credit *noun*

creditable *adjective*
creditably *adverb*

creditor *noun*
creditors

creed *noun*
creeds

creek *noun*
creeks

creep *verb*
creeps
creeping
crept

creep *noun*
creeps

creeper *noun*
creepers

creepy *adjective*
creepier
creepiest

cremate *verb*
cremates
cremating
cremated

cremation *noun*
cremations

crematorium *noun*
crematoria

creosote *noun*

crêpe *noun*
crêpes

crept *verb* SEE **creep**

crescendo *noun*
crescendos

crescent *noun*
crescents

cress *noun*

crest *noun*
crests

crevice *noun*
crevices

crew *noun*
crews

crib *verb*
cribs
cribbing
cribbed

crib *noun*
cribs

cricket* *noun*
crickets

cricketer *noun*
cricketers

cried *verb* SEE **cry**

crime *noun*
crimes

criminal *adjective & noun*
criminals

crimson *adjective & noun*

* **Cricket** means 'a game' and 'an insect like a grasshopper'.

crinkle *verb*
crinkles
crinkling
crinkled

crinkly *adjective*
crinklier
crinkliest

cripple *verb*
cripples
crippling
crippled

cripple *noun*
cripples

crisis *noun*
crises

crisp *adjective*
crisper
crispest

crisp *noun*
crisps

crispy *adjective*

criss-cross *adjective*

criterion *noun*
criteria

critic *noun*
critics

critical *adjective*
critically *adverb*

criticism *noun*
criticisms

criticize *verb*
criticizes
criticizing
criticized

croak *verb*
croaks
croaking
croaked

croak *noun*
croaks

crochet★

crock *noun*
crocks

crockery *noun*

crocodile *noun*
crocodiles

crocus *noun*
crocuses

croft *noun*
crofts

crofter *noun*
crofters

croissant *noun*
croissants

crook *noun*
crooks

crook *verb*
crooks
crooking
crooked

crooked *adjective*

croon *verb*
croons
crooning
crooned

crop *noun*
crops

crop *verb*
crops
cropping
cropped

> **cross-** *prefix*
> *cross-* makes words meaning 'across', e.g. a *cross-channel ferry* is one that goes across the English Channel. You usually need a hyphen, but some words are spelled joined up, e.g. **crossroads** and **crosswind**.

cross *adjective*
crosser
crossest
crossly *adverb*

cross *verb*
crosses
crossing
crossed

cross *noun*
crosses

crossbar *noun*
crossbars

crossbow *noun*
crossbows

cross-country *adjective*

cross-examine *verb*
cross-examines
cross-examining
cross-examined

cross-examination *noun*
cross-examinations

cross-eyed *adjective*

crossing *noun*
crossings

cross-legged *adjective & adverb*

crossness *noun*

crossroads *noun*
crossroads

cross section *noun*
cross sections

crosswind *noun*
crosswinds

crosswise *adverb & adjective*

crossword *noun*
crosswords

crotchet☆ *noun*
crotchets

crouch *verb*
crouches
crouching
crouched

crow *noun*
crows

★ **Crochet** is a kind of needlework. **! crotchet.**
☆ A **crotchet** is a note in music. **! crochet.**

a b c d e f g h i j k l m n o p q r s t u v w x y z

crow *verb*
crows
crowing
crowed

crowbar *noun*
crowbars

crowd *noun*
crowds

crowd *verb*
crowds
crowding
crowded

crown *noun*
crowns

crown *verb*
crowns
crowning
crowned

crow's nest *noun*
crow's nests

crucial *adjective*
crucially *adverb*

crucifix *noun*
crucifixes

crucifixion* *noun*
crucifixions

crucify *verb*
crucifies
crucifying
crucified

crude *adjective*
cruder
crudest
crudely *adverb*

cruel *adjective*
crueller
cruellest
cruelly *adverb*

cruelty *noun*
cruelties

cruise *verb*
cruises
cruising
cruised

cruise *noun*
cruises

cruiser *noun*
cruisers

crumb *noun*
crumbs

crumble *verb*
crumbles
crumbling
crumbled

crumbly *adjective*
crumblier
crumbliest

crumpet *noun*
crumpets

crumple *verb*
crumples
crumpling
crumpled

crunch *noun*
crunches

crunch *verb*
crunches
crunching
crunched

crunchy *adjective*
crunchier
crunchiest

crusade *noun*
crusades

crusader *noun*
crusaders

crush *verb*
crushes
crushing
crushed

crush *noun*
crushes

crust *noun*
crusts

crustacean *noun*
crustaceans

crutch *noun*
crutches

cry *verb*
cries
crying
cried

cry *noun*
cries

crypt *noun*
crypts

crystal *noun*
crystals

crystalline *adjective*

crystallize *verb*
crystallizes
crystallizing
crystallized

cub *noun*
cubs

cubbyhole *noun*
cubbyholes

cube *noun*
cubes

cube *verb*
cubes
cubing
cubed

cubic *adjective*

cubicle *noun*
cubicles

cuboid *noun*
cuboids

cuckoo *noun*
cuckoos

cucumber *noun*
cucumbers

cud *noun*

cuddle *verb*
cuddles
cuddling
cuddled

cuddly *adjective*

cue☆ *noun*
cues

★ Use a capital C when you are talking about Christ.
☆ A **cue** is a signal for action or a stick used in snooker. **! queue.**

For words beginning with a **k-** sound, try also **ch-**

cuff *verb*
cuffs
cuffing
cuffed
cuff *noun*
cuffs
cuisine *noun*
cul-de-sac *noun*
cul-de-sacs *or* culs-de-sac
culinary *adverb*
culminate *verb*
culminates
culminating
culminated
culmination *noun*
culprit *noun*
culprits
cult *noun*
cults
cultivate *verb*
cultivates
cultivating
cultivated
cultivation *noun*
cultivated *adjective*
culture *noun*
cultures
cultural *adjective*
culturally *adverb*
cultured *adjective*
cunning *adjective*
cunningly *adverb*
cup *noun*
cups
cup *verb*
cups
cupping
cupped
cupboard *noun*
cupboards
cupful *noun*
cupfuls
curate *noun*
curates

curator *noun*
curators
curb★ *verb*
curbs
curbing
curbed
curd *noun*
curds
curdle *verb*
curdles
curdling
curdled
cure *verb*
cures
curing
cured
cure *noun*
cures
curfew *noun*
curfews
curiosity *noun*
curiosities
curious *adjective*
curiously *adverb*
curl *verb*
curls
curling
curled
curl *noun*
curls
curly *adjective*
curlier
curliest
currant☆ *noun*
currants
currency *noun*
currencies
current✪ *noun*
currents
current *adjective*
currently *adverb*
curriculum *noun*
curriculums *or* curricula

curry *verb*
curries
currying
curried
curry *noun*
curries
curse *verb*
curses
cursing
cursed
curse *noun*
curses
cursor *noun*
cursors
curtain *noun*
curtains
curtsy *verb*
curtsies
curtsying
curtsied
curtsy *noun*
curtsies
curvature *noun*
curvatures
curve *verb*
curves
curving
curved
curve *noun*
curves
cushion *noun*
cushions
cushion *verb*
cushions
cushioning
cushioned
custard *noun*
custody *noun*
custom *noun*
customs
customary *adjective*
customarily *adverb*
customer *noun*
customers

★ To **curb** a feeling is to restrain it. **! kerb.**
☆ A **currant** is a small dried grape. **! current.**
✪ A **current** is a flow of water, air, or electricity. **! currant.**

a b c d e f g h i j k l m n o p q r s t u v w x y z

customize *noun*
customizes
customizing
customized

cut *verb*
cuts
cutting
cut

cut *noun*
cuts

cute *adjective*
cuter
cutest

cutlass *noun*
cutlasses

cutlery *noun*

cutlet *noun*
cutlets

cut-out *noun*
cut-outs

cut-price *adjective*

cutter *noun*
cutters

cutting *noun*
cuttings

cyanide *noun*

cycle *noun*
cycles

cycle *verb*
cycles
cycling
cycled

cyclist *noun*
cyclists

cyclone *noun*
cyclones

cyclonic *adjective*

cygnet* *noun*
cygnets

cylinder *noun*
cylinders

cylindrical *adjective*

cymbal *noun*
cymbals

cynic *noun*
cynics

cynical *adjective*
cynically *adverb*

cynicism *noun*

cypress *noun*
cypresses

cyst *noun*
cysts

* A **cygnet** is a young swan. **! signet**.

Dd

dab *verb*
dabs
dabbing
dabbed
dab *noun*
dabs
dabble *verb*
dabbles
dabbling
dabbled
dad *noun*
dads
daddy *noun*
daddies
daddy-long-legs *noun*
daddy-long-legs
daffodil *noun*
daffodils
daft *adjective*
dafter
daftest
dagger *noun*
daggers
dahlia *noun*
dahlias
daily *adjective* & *adverb*
daintiness
dainty *adjective*
daintier
daintiest
daintily *adverb*
dairy *noun*
dairies
daisy *noun*
daisies
dale *noun*
dales

dam *noun*
dams
dam★ *verb*
dams
damming
dammed
damage *verb*
damages
damaging
damaged
damage *noun*
damages *plural noun*
Dame☆ *noun*
Dames
dame✪ *noun*
dames
damn✣ *verb*
damns
damning
damned
damned *adjective*
damp *adjective* & *noun*
damper
dampest
dampen *verb*
dampens
dampening
dampened
dance *verb*
dances
dancing
danced
dance *noun*
dances
dancer *noun*
dancers
dandelion *noun*
dandelions

dandruff *noun*
danger *noun*
dangers
dangerous *adjective*
dangerously *adverb*
dangle *verb*
dangles
dangling
dangled
dappled *adjective*
dare *verb*
dares
daring
dared
dare *noun*
dares
daredevil *noun*
daredevils
daring *adjective*
dark *adjective* & *noun*
darker
darkest
darken *verb*
darkens
darkening
darkened
darkness *noun*
darkroom *noun*
darkrooms
darling *noun*
darlings
darn *verb*
darns
darning
darned
dart *noun*
darts

a b c d e f g h i j k l m n o p q r s t u v w x y z

★ **Dam** means 'to build a dam across water'. **! damn.**
☆ Use a capital D when it is a title, e.g. *Dame Jane Smith*.
✪ Use a small d when you mean a pantomime woman played by a man.
✣ **Damn** means 'to say that something is very bad or wrong'. **! dam.**

dartboard *noun*
dartboards

dash *verb*
dashes
dashing
dashed

dash *noun*
dashes

dashboard *noun*
dashboards

data* *plural noun*

database *noun*
databases

date *noun*
dates

date *verb*
dates
dating
dated

daughter *noun*
daughters

dawdle *verb*
dawdles
dawdling
dawdled

dawn *noun*
dawns

dawn *verb*
dawns
dawning
dawned

day *noun*
days

daybreak *noun*

daydream *verb*
daydreams
daydreaming
daydreamed

daylight *noun*

daze *verb*
dazes
dazing
dazed

daze *noun*

dazzle *verb*
dazzles
dazzling
dazzled

> **de-** *prefix*
> *de-* makes verbs with an opposite meaning, e.g. **deactivate** means 'to stop something working'. You need a hyphen when the word begins with an *e* or *i*, e.g. **de-ice**.

dead *adjective*

deaden *verb*
deadens
deadening
deadened

dead end *noun*
dead ends

deadline *noun*
deadlines

deadlock *noun*

deadly *adjective*
deadlier
deadliest

deaf *adjective*
deafer
deafest

deafness *noun*

deafen *verb*
deafens
deafening
deafened

deal *verb*
deals
dealing
dealt

deal *noun*
deals

dealer *noun*
dealers

dean *noun*
deans

dear☆ *adjective*
dearer
dearest
dearly *adverb*

death *noun*
deaths

deathly *adjective & adverb*

debatable *adjective*

debate *noun*
debates

debate *verb*
debates
debating
debated

debris *noun*

debt *noun*
debts

debtor *noun*
debtors

debug *verb*
debugs
debugging
debugged

debut *noun*
debuts
French début

decade *noun*
decades

decamp *verb*
decamps
decamping
decamped

decay *verb*
decays
decaying
decayed

decay *noun*

deceased *adjective*

deceit *noun*

deceitful *adjective*
deceitfully *adverb*

deceive *verb*
deceives
deceiving
deceived

---

* **Data** is strictly a plural noun, but is often used as a singular noun: *Here is the data.*
☆ **Dear** means 'loved' or 'expensive'. **! deer**.

December *noun*
decency *noun*
decent *adjective*
decently *adverb*
deception *noun*
deceptions
deceptive *adjective*
decibel *noun*
decibels
decide *verb*
decides
deciding
decided
decidedly *adverb*
deciduous *adjective*
decimal *noun*
decimals
decimalize *verb*
decimalizes
decimalizing
decimalized
decipher *verb*
deciphers
deciphering
deciphered
decision *noun*
decisions
decisive *adjective*
decisively *adverb*
deck *noun*
decks
deckchair *noun*
deckchairs
declaration *noun*
declarations
declare *verb*
declares
declaring
declared
decline *verb*
declines
declining
declined

decode *verb*
decodes
decoding
decoded
decompose *verb*
decomposes
decomposing
decomposed
decorate *verb*
decorates
decorating
decorated
decoration *noun*
decorations
decorative *verb*
decoratively *adverb*
decorator *noun*
decorators
decoy *noun*
decoys
decrease *verb*
decreases
decreasing
decreased
decrease *noun*
decreases
decree *noun*
decrees
decree *verb*
decrees
decreeing
decreed
decrepit *adjective*
dedicate *verb*
dedicates
dedicating
dedicated
dedication *noun*
dedications
deduce *verb*
deduces
deducing
deduced

deduct *verb*
deducts
deducting
deducted
deductible *adjective*
deduction *noun*
deductions
deed *noun*
deeds
deep *adjective*
deeper
deepest
deeply *adverb*
deepen *verb*
deepens
deepening
deepened
deep-freeze *noun*
deep-freezes
deer* *noun*
deer
deface *verb*
defaces
defacing
defaced
default *noun*
defaults
defeat *verb*
defeats
defeating
defeated
defeat *noun*
defeats
defect *noun*
defects
defect *verb*
defects
defecting
defected
defective *adjective*
defence *noun*
defences
defenceless *adjective*

* A **deer** is an animal. **! dear.**

a b c d e f g h i j k l m n o p q r s t u v w x y z

defend *verb*
defends
defending
defended
defendant *noun*
defendants
defender *noun*
defenders
defensible *adjective*
defensive *adjective*
defensively *adverb*
defer *verb*
defers
deferring
deferred
deferment *noun*
defiance *noun*
defiant *adjective*
defiantly *adverb*
deficiency *noun*
deficiencies
deficient *adjective*
deficit *noun*
deficits
defile *verb*
defiles
defiling
defiled
define *verb*
defines
defining
defined
definite *adjective*
definitely *adverb*
definition *noun*
definitions
definitive *adjective*
deflate *verb*
deflates
deflating
deflated
deflect *verb*
deflects
deflecting
deflected
deflection *noun*
deflections
deforestation *noun*
deform *verb*
deforms
deforming
deformed
deformed *adjective*
deformity *noun*
deformities
defrost *verb*
defrosts
defrosting
defrosted
deft *adjective*
defter
deftest
deftly *adverb*
defuse *verb*
defuses
defusing
defused
defy *verb*
defies
defying
defied
degenerate *verb*
degenerates
degenerating
degenerated
degeneration *noun*
degradation *noun*
degrade *verb*
degrades
degrading
degraded
degree *noun*
degrees
dehydrated *adjective*
dehydration *noun*
de-ice *verb*
de-ices
de-icing
de-iced
de-icer *noun*
deity *noun*
deities
dejected *adjective*
dejectedly *adverb*
dejection *noun*
delay *verb*
delays
delaying
delayed
delay *noun*
delays
delegate *noun*
delegates
delegate *verb*
delegates
delegating
delegated
delegation *noun*
delegations
delete *verb*
deletes
deleting
deleted
deletion *noun*
deletions
deliberate *adjective*
deliberately *adverb*
deliberate *verb*
deliberates
deliberating
deliberated
deliberation *noun*
delicacy *noun*
delicacies
delicate *adjective*
delicately *adverb*
delicatessen *noun*
delicatessens
delicious *adjective*
deliciously *adverb*
delight *verb*
delights
delighting
delighted
delight *noun*
delights
delightful *adjective*
delightfully *adverb*
delinquency *noun*
delinquent *noun*
delinquents
delirious *adjective*
deliriously *adverb*

delirium *noun*

deliver *verb*
delivers
delivering
delivered

delivery *noun*
deliveries

delta *noun*
deltas

delude *verb*
deludes
deluding
deluded

deluge *noun*
deluges

deluge *verb*
deluges
deluging
deluged

delusion *noun*
delusions

de luxe *adjective*

demand *verb*
demands
demanding
demanded

demand *noun*
demands

demanding *adjective*

dementia *noun*

demise *noun*

demist *verb*
demists
demisting
demisted

demo *noun*
demos

democracy *noun*
democracies

democrat *noun*
democrats

democratic *adjective*
democratically *adverb*

demolish *verb*
demolishes
demolishing
demolished

demolition *noun*

demon *noun*
demons

demonstrate *verb*
demonstrates
demonstrating
demonstrated

demonstration *noun*
demonstrations

demonstrator *noun*
demonstrators

demoralize *verb*
demoralizes
demoralizing
demoralized

demote *verb*
demotes
demoting
demoted

den *noun*
dens

denial *noun*
denials

denim *noun*

denominator *noun*
denominators

denote *verb*
denotes
denoting
denoted

denounce *verb*
denounces
denouncing
denounced

denunciation *noun*

dense *adjective*
denser
densest
densely *adverb*

density *noun*
densities

dent *noun*
dents

dental *adjective*

dentist *noun*
dentists

dentistry *noun*

denture *noun*
dentures

deny *verb*
denies
denying
denied

deodorant *noun*
deodorants

depart *verb*
departs
departing
departed

department *noun*
departments

departure *noun*
departures

depend *verb*
depends
depending
depended

dependable *adjective*

dependant* *noun*
dependants

dependence *noun*

dependent*☆* *adjective*

depict *verb*
depicts
depicting
depicted

deplorable *adjective*
deplorably *adverb*

deplore *verb*
deplores
deploring
deplored

deploy *verb*
deploys
deploying
deployed

a b c d e f g h i j k l m n o p q r s t u v w x y z

★ **Dependant** is a noun: *She has three dependants.* **! dependent.**
☆ **Dependent** is an adjective: *She has three dependent children.* **! dependant.**

deployment *noun*

deport *verb*
deports
deporting
deported

deportation *noun*
deportations

deposit *verb*
deposits
depositing
deposited

deposit *noun*
deposits

depot *noun*
depots

depress *verb*
depresses
depressing
depressed

depression *noun*
depressions

deprivation *noun*

deprive *verb*
deprives
depriving
deprived

depth *noun*
depths

deputize *verb*
deputizes
deputizing
deputized

deputy *noun*
deputies

derail *verb*
derails
derailing
derailed

derby *noun*
derbies

derelict *adjective*

deride *verb*
derides
deriding
derided

derision *noun*

derive *verb*
derives
deriving
derived

derrick *noun*
derricks

descant* *noun*
descants

descend *verb*
descends
descending
descended

descendant *noun*
descendants

descent☆ *noun*

describe *verb*
describes
describing
described

description *noun*
descriptions

descriptive *adjective*
descriptively *adverb*

desert✪ *noun*
deserts

desert *verb*
deserts
deserting
deserted

deserter *noun*
deserters

desertion *noun*

deserve *verb*
deserves
deserving
deserved

design *verb*
designs
designing
designed

design *noun*
designs

designate *verb*
designates
designating
designated

designer *noun*
designers

desirable *adjective*

desire *verb*
desires
desiring
desired

desire *noun*
desires

desk *noun*
desks

desktop *noun*
desktops

desolate *adjective*

desolation *noun*

despair *verb*
despairs
despairing
despaired

despair *noun*

despatch *verb* SEE **use dispatch**

desperate *adjective*
desperately *adverb*

desperation *noun*

despicable *adjective*
despicably *adverb*

despise *verb*
despises
despising
despised

despite *preposition*

* **Descant** is a term in music. **! descent.**
☆ **Descent** is a way down. **! descant.**
✪ A **desert** is a very dry area of land. **! dessert.**

dessert★ *noun*
desserts
dessertspoon *noun*
dessertspoons
destination *noun*
destinations
destined *adjective*
destiny *noun*
destinies
destroy *verb*
destroys
destroying
destroyed
destroyer *noun*
destroyers
destruction *noun*
destructive *adjective*
detach *verb*
detaches
detaching
detached
detachable *adjective*
detached *adjective*
detachment *noun*
detachments
detail *noun*
details
detain *verb*
detains
detaining
detained
detect *verb*
detects
detecting
detected
detection *noun*
detector *noun*
detectors
detective *noun*
detectives
detention *noun*
detentions

deter *verb*
deters
deterring
deterred
detergent *noun*
detergents
deteriorate *verb*
deteriorates
deteriorating
deteriorated
deterioration *noun*
determination *noun*
determine *verb*
determines
determining
determined
determined *adjective*
deterrence *noun*
deterrent *noun*
deterrents
detest *verb*
detests
detesting
detested
detestable *adjective*
detonate *verb*
detonates
detonating
detonated
detonation *noun*
detonator *noun*
detonators
detour *noun*
detours
detrimental *adjective*
deuce☆ *noun*
devastate *verb*
devastates
devastating
devastated
devastation *noun*

develop *verb*
develops
developing
developed
developer *noun*
developers
development *noun*
developments
device *noun*
devices
devil *noun*
devils
devilish *adjective*
devilment *noun*
devious *adjective*
deviously *adverb*
devise *verb*
devises
devising
devised
devolution *noun*
devote *verb*
devotes
devoting
devoted
devotee *noun*
devotees
devotion *noun*
devour *verb*
devours
devouring
devoured
devout *adjective*
dew✪ *noun*
dewy *adjective*
dhoti✢ *noun*
dhotis
diabetes *noun*
diabetic *adjective* & *noun*
diabolical *adjective*
diabolically *adverb*

★ A **dessert** is a sweet pudding. **! desert.**
☆ **Deuce** is a score in tennis. **! juice.**
✪ **Dew** is moisture on grass and plants. **! due.**
✢ A **dhoti** is a piece of clothing worn by Hindus.

a
b
c
d
e
f
g
h
i
j
k
l
m
n
o
p
q
r
s
t
u
v
w
x
y
z

diagnose *verb*
diagnoses
diagnosing
diagnosed
diagnosis *noun*
diagnoses
diagonal *adjective*
diagonally *adverb*
diagonal *noun*
diagonals
diagram *noun*
diagrams
dial *noun*
dials
dial *verb*
dials
dialling
dialled
dialect *noun*
dialects
dialogue *noun*
dialogues
diameter *noun*
diameters
diamond *noun*
diamonds
diaphragm *noun*
diaphragms
diarrhoea *noun*
diary *noun*
diaries
dice *noun*
dice
dictate *verb*
dictates
dictating
dictated
dictation *noun*
dictations
dictator *noun*
dictators
dictatorial *adjective*
dictatorship *noun*
diction *noun*
dictionary *noun*
dictionaries
did *verb* SEE **do**
diddle *verb*
diddles
diddling
diddled
didn't *verb*
die *noun* SEE **dice**
die★ *verb*
dies
dying
died
diesel *noun*
diesels
diet *noun*
diets
diet *verb*
diets
dieting
dieted
dietary *adjective*
differ *verb*
differs
differing
differed
difference *noun*
differences
different *adjective*
differently *adverb*
difficult *adjective*
difficulty *noun*
difficulties
diffusion *noun*
dig *verb*
digs
digging
dug
dig *noun*
digs
digest *verb*
digests
digesting
digested
digestible *adjective*
digestion *noun*
digestive *adjective*
digger *noun*
diggers
digit *noun*
digits
digital *adjective*
digitally *adverb*
dignified *adjective*
dignity *noun*
dike *noun* SEE **dyke**
dilemma *noun*
dilemmas
dilute *verb*
dilutes
diluting
diluted
dilution *noun*
dilutions
dim *adjective*
dimmer
dimmest
dimly *adverb*
dimension *noun*
dimensions
diminish *verb*
diminishes
diminishing
diminished
dimple *noun*
dimples
din *noun*
dins
dine *verb*
dines
dining
dined
diner☆ *noun*
diners
dingo *noun*
dingos
dinghy✪ *noun*
dinghies

★ **Die** means 'to stop living'. **! dye.**
☆ A **diner** is someone who eats dinner. **! dinner.**
✪ A **dinghy** is a small sailing boat. **! dingy.**

dingy★ *adjective*
dingier
dingiest
dinner☆ *noun*
dinners
dinosaur *noun*
dinosaurs
dioxide *noun*
dioxides
dip *verb*
dips
dipping
dipped
dip *noun*
dips
diphtheria *noun*
diploma *noun*
diplomas
diplomacy *noun*
diplomat *noun*
diplomats
diplomatic *adjective*
diplomatically *adverb*
dire *adjective*
direr
direst
direct *adjective*
directly *adverb*
direct *verb*
directs
directing
directed
direction *noun*
directions
director *noun*
directors
directory *noun*
directories
dirt *noun*
dirtiness *noun*
dirty *adjective*
dirtier
dirtiest
dirtily *adverb*

> **dis-** *prefix*
> *dis-* makes a word with an opposite meaning, e.g. **disobey** means 'to refuse to obey' and **disloyal** means 'not loyal'. These words are spelled joined up.

disability *noun*
disabilities
disabled *adjective*
disadvantage *noun*
disadvantages
disagree *verb*
disagrees
disagreeing
disagreed
disagreeable *adjective*
disagreeably *adverb*
disagreement *noun*
disagreements
disallow *verb*
disappear *verb*
disappears
disappearing
disappeared
disappearance *noun*
disappearances
disappoint *verb*
disappoints
disappointing
disappointed
disappointing *adjective*
disappointment *noun*
disappointments
disapproval *noun*
disapprove *verb*
disapproves
disapproving
disapproved
disarm *verb*
disarms
disarming
disarmed

disarmament *noun*
disaster *noun*
disasters
disastrous *adjective*
disastrously *adverb*
disbelief *noun*
disc✪ *noun*
discs
discard *verb*
discards
discarding
discarded
discern *verb*
discharge *verb*
discharges
discharging
discharged
disciple *noun*
disciples
discipline *noun*
disc jockey *noun*
disc jockeys
disclose *verb*
discloses
disclosing
disclosed
disclosure *noun*
disco *noun*
discos
discomfort *noun*
disconnect *verb*
disconnects
disconnecting
disconnected
disconnection *noun*
discontent *noun*
discontented *adjective*
discotheque *noun*
discotheques
discontinue *verb*
discontinues
discontinuing
discontinued

★ **Dingy** means 'dirty-looking, drab, dull-coloured'. **! dinghy**.
☆ **Dinner** is a meal. **! diner**.
✪ A **disc** is a flat round object. **! disk**.

a b c d e f g h i j k l m n o p q r s t u v w x y z

discount *noun*
discounts
discourage *verb*
discourages
discouraging
discouraged
discouragement *noun*
discover *verb*
discovers
discovering
discovered
discovery *noun*
discoveries
discreet *adjective*
discreetly *adverb*
discriminate *verb*
discriminates
discriminating
discriminated
discrimination *noun*
discriminatory *adjective*
discus *noun*
discuses
discuss *verb*
discusses
discussing
discussed
discussion *noun*
discussions
disease *noun*
diseases
diseased *adjective*
disembark *verb*
disembarks
disembarking
disembarked
disgrace *verb*
disgraces
disgracing
disgraced
disgrace *noun*
disgraceful *adjective*
disgracefully *adverb*
disgruntled *adjective*

disguise *verb*
disguises
disguising
disguised
disguise *noun*
disguises
disgust *verb*
disgusts
disgusting
disgusted
disgust *noun*
disgusting *adjective*
disgustingly *adverb*
dish *noun*
dishes
dish *verb*
dishes
dishing
dished
dishcloth *noun*
dishcloths
dishearten *verb*
disheartens
disheartening
disheartened
dishevelled *adjective*
dishonest *adjective*
dishonestly *adverb*
dishonesty *noun*
dishwasher *noun*
dishwashers
disinfect *verb*
disinfects
disinfecting
disinfected
disinfectant *noun*
disinfectants
disintegrate *verb*
disintegrates
disintegrating
disintegrated
disintegration *noun*
disinterested *adjective*
disk* *noun*
disks

dislike *verb*
dislikes
disliking
disliked
dislike *noun*
dislikes
dislocate *verb*
dislocates
dislocating
dislocated
dislodge *verb*
dislodges
dislodging
dislodged
disloyal *adjective*
disloyally *adverb*
disloyalty *noun*
dismal *adjective*
dismally *adverb*
dismantle *verb*
dismantles
dismantling
dismantled
dismay *noun*
dismayed *adjective*
dismiss *verb*
dismisses
dismissing
dismissed
dismissal *noun*
dismissals
dismount *verb*
dismounts
dismounting
dismounted
disobedience *noun*
disobedient *adjective*
disobediently *adverb*
disobey *verb*
disobeys
disobeying
disobeyed
disorder *noun*
disorders
disorderly *adjective*

* A **disk** is what you put in a computer. **! disc.**

disown *verb*
disowns
disowning
disowned
dispatch *verb*
dispatches
dispatching
dispatched
dispense *verb*
dispenses
dispensing
dispensed
dispenser *noun*
dispensers
dispersal *noun*
disperse *verb*
disperses
dispersing
dispersed
display *verb*
displays
displaying
displayed
display *noun*
displays
displease *verb*
displeases
displeasing
displeased
disposable *adjective*
disposal *noun*
dispose *verb*
disposes
disposing
disposed
disprove *verb*
disproves
disproving
disproved
dispute *noun*
disputes
disqualification *noun*
disqualifications
disqualify *verb*
disqualifies
disqualifying
disqualified

disregard *verb*
disregards
disregarding
disregarded
disrespect *noun*
disrespectful *adjective*
disrespectfully *adverb*
disrupt *verb*
disrupts
disrupting
disrupted
disruption *noun*
disruptive *adjective*
dissatisfaction *noun*
dissatisfied *adjective*
dissect *verb*
dissects
dissecting
dissected
dissection *noun*
dissolve *verb*
dissolves
dissolving
dissolved
dissuade *verb*
dissuades
dissuading
dissuaded
distance *noun*
distances
distant *adjective*
distantly *adverb*
distaste *noun*
distil *verb*
distils
distilling
distilled
distillery *noun*
distilleries
distinct *adjective*
distinctly *adverb*
distinction *noun*
distinctions
distinctive *adjective*
distinguish *verb*
distinguishes
distinguishing
distinguished

distinguished *adjective*
distort *verb*
distorts
distorting
distorted
distortion *noun*
distortions
distract *verb*
distracts
distracting
distracted
distraction *noun*
distractions
distraught *adjective*
distress *verb*
distresses
distressing
distressed
distress *noun*
distribute *verb*
distributes
distributing
distributed
distribution *noun*
distributor *noun*
distributors
district *noun*
districts
distrust *noun*
distrustful *adjective*
disturb *verb*
disturbs
disturbing
disturbed
disturbance *noun*
disturbances
disused *adjective*
ditch *noun*
ditches
dither *verb*
dithers
dithering
dithered
divan *noun*
divans

a b c d e f g h i j k l m n o p q r s t u v w x y z

dive *verb*
dives
diving
dived

diver *noun*
divers

diverse *adjective*

diversify *verb*
diversifies
diversifying
diversified

diversion *noun*
diversions

diversity *noun*

divert *verb*
diverts
diverting
diverted

divide *verb*
divides
dividing
divided

dividend *noun*
dividends

dividers *plural noun*

divine *adjective*
divinely *adverb*

divine *verb*
divines
divining
divined

divinity *noun*

divisible *adjective*

division *noun*
divisions

divorce *verb*
divorces
divorcing
divorced

divorce *noun*
divorces

Diwali★ *noun*

dizziness *noun*

dizzy *adjective*
dizzier
dizziest
dizzily *adverb*

DJ *noun*
DJs

do *verb*
does
doing
did
done

docile *adjective*
docilely *adverb*

dock *noun*
docks

dock *verb*
docks
docking
docked

dock *noun*
docks

docker *noun*
dockers

dockyard *noun*
dockyards

doctor *noun*
doctors

doctrine *noun*
doctrines

document *noun*
documents

documentary *noun*
documentaries

documentation *noun*

doddery *adjective*

dodge *verb*
dodges
dodging
dodged

dodge *noun*
dodges

dodgem *noun*
dodgems

dodgy *adjective*
dodgier
dodgiest

doe☆ *noun*
does

does *verb*

doesn't *verb*

dog *noun*
dogs

dog-eared *adjective*

dogged *adjective*
doggedly *adverb*

doldrums *plural noun*

dole *verb*
doles
doling
doled

dole *noun*

doll *noun*
dolls

dollar *noun*
dollars

dolly *noun*
dollies

dolphin *noun*
dolphins

> **-dom** *suffix*
> -*dom* makes nouns, e.g. **kingdom**. Other noun suffixes are **-hood**, **-ment**, **-ness**, and **-ship**.

domain *noun*
domains

dome *noun*
domes

domestic *adjective*
domestically *adverb*

domesticated *adjective*

dominance *noun*

dominant *adjective*
dominantly *adverb*

★ **Diwali** is a Hindu festival.
☆ A **doe** is a female deer. **! dough.**

dominate *verb*
dominates
dominating
dominated

domination *noun*

dominion *noun*
dominions

domino *noun*
dominoes

donate *verb*
donates
donating
donated

donation *noun*
donations

done *verb* SEE **do**

donkey *noun*
donkeys

donor *noun*
donors

don't *verb*

doodle *verb*
doodles
doodling
doodled

doodle *noun*
doodles

doom *verb*
dooms
dooming
doomed

doom *noun*

door *noun*
doors

doorstep *noun*
doorsteps

doorway *noun*
doorways

dope *noun*
dopes

dopey *adjective*
dopier
dopiest

dormant *adjective*

dormitory *noun*
dormitories

dorsal *adjective*

dose *noun*
doses

dossier *noun*
dossiers

dot *verb*
dots
dotting
dotted

dot *noun*
dots

dottiness *noun*

dotty *adjective*
dottier
dottiest
dottily *adverb*

double *adjective*
doubly *adverb*

double *noun*
doubles

double *verb*
doubles
doubling
doubled

double-cross *verb*
double-crosses
double-crossing
double-crossed

double-decker *noun*
double-deckers

doubt *verb*
doubts
doubting
doubted

doubt *noun*
doubts

doubtful *adjective*
doubtfully *adverb*

doubtless *adverb*

dough* *noun*

doughnut *noun*
doughnuts

doughy *adjective*
doughier
doughiest

dove *noun*
doves

down *adverb* & *preposition* & *adjective* & *noun*

downcast *adjective*

downfall *noun*
downfalls

downhill *adverb* & *adjective*

download *verb*
downloads
downloading
downloaded

downpour *noun*
downpours

downright *adjective*

downstairs *adverb* & *adjective*

downstream *adjective* & *adverb*

downward *adjective* & *adverb*

downwards *adverb*

downy *adjective*
downier
downiest

doze *verb*
dozes
dozing
dozed

dozen *noun*
dozens

dozy *adjective*
dozier
doziest

drab *adjective*
drabber
drabbest

draft *verb*
drafts
drafting
drafted

* **Dough** is a mixture of flour and water used for baking. **! doe.**

a b c d e f g h i j k l m n o p q r s t u v w x y z

a b c d e f g h i j k l m n o p q r s t u v w x y z

draft *noun*
drafts
drag *verb*
drags
dragging
dragged
drag *noun*
dragon *noun*
dragons
dragonfly *noun*
dragonflies
drain *verb*
drains
draining
drained
drain *noun*
drains
drainage *noun*
drake *noun*
drakes
drama *noun*
dramas
dramatic *adjective*
dramatically *adverb*
dramatist *noun*
dramatists
dramatization *noun*
dramatize *verb*
dramatizes
dramatizing
dramatized
drank *verb* SEE **drink**
drape *verb*
drapes
draping
draped
drastic *adjective*
drastically *adverb*
draught *noun*
draughts
draughty *adjective*
draughtier
draughtiest
draughts *plural noun*

draughtsman *noun*
draughtsmen
draw★ *verb*
draws
drawing
drew
drawn
draw *noun*
draws
drawback *noun*
drawbacks
drawbridge *noun*
drawbridges
drawer☆ *noun*
drawers
drawing *noun*
drawings
drawl *verb*
drawls
drawling
drawled
dread *verb*
dreads
dreading
dreaded
dread *noun*
dreadful *adjective*
dreadfully *adverb*
dreadlocks *plural noun*
dream *noun*
dreams
dream *verb*
dreams
dreaming
dreamt
dreamed
dreamer *noun*
dreamers
dreamy *adjective*
dreamier
dreamiest
dreariness *noun*

dreary *adjective*
drearier
dreariest
drearily *adverb*
dredge *verb*
dredges
dredging
dredged
dredger *noun*
dredgers
drench *verb*
drenches
drenching
drenched
dress *verb*
dresses
dressing
dressed
dress *noun*
dresses
dresser *noun*
dressers
dressing *noun*
dressings
dressmaker *noun*
dressmakers
drew *verb* SEE **draw**
dribble *verb*
dribbles
dribbling
dribbled
dried *verb* & *adjective* SEE **dry**
drier *noun*
driers
drift *verb*
drifts
drifting
drifted
drift *noun*
drifts
driftwood *noun*

★ To **draw** is to make a picture with a pencil, pen, or crayon. **! drawer**.
☆ A **drawer** is part of a cupboard. **! draw**.

drill *verb*
drills
drilling
drilled

drill *noun*
drills

drink *verb*
drinks
drinking
drank
drunk

drink *noun*
drinks

drinkable *adjective*

drinker *noun*
drinkers

drip *noun*
drips

drip *verb*
drips
dripping
dripped

drive *verb*
drives
driving
drove
driven

drive *noun*
drives

driver *noun*
drivers

drizzle *verb*
drizzles
drizzling
drizzled

drizzle *noun*

drone *verb*
drones
droning
droned

drone *noun*
drones

drool *verb*
drools
drooling
drooled

droop *verb*
droops
drooping
drooped

drop *verb*
drops
dropping
dropped

drop *noun*
drops

droplet *noun*
droplets

drought *noun*
droughts

drove *verb* SEE **drive**

drown *verb*
drowns
drowning
drowned

drowsiness *noun*

drowsy *adjective*
drowsier
drowsiest
drowsily *adverb*

drug *noun*
drugs

drug *verb*
drugs
drugging
drugged

Druid *noun*
Druids

drum *noun*
drums

drum *verb*
drums
drumming
drummed

drummer *noun*
drummers

drumstick *noun*
drumsticks

drunk *verb* SEE **drink**

drunk *adjective & noun*
drunks

drunkard *noun*
drunkards

dry *adjective*
drier
driest
drily *adverb*

dry *verb*
dries
drying
dried

dryness *noun*

dual★ *adjective*
dually *adverb*

dub *verb*
dubs
dubbing
dubbed

dubious *adjective*

duchess *noun*
duchesses

duck *noun*
ducks

duck *verb*
ducks
ducking
ducked

duckling *noun*
ducklings

duct *noun*
ducts

dud *noun*
duds

due☆ *adjective*

duel✪ *noun*
duels

duet *noun*
duets

duff *adjective*

★ **Dual** means 'having two parts'. **! duel.**
☆ **Due** means 'expected'. **! dew.**
✪ A **duel** is a fight between two people. **! dual.**

a b c **d** e f g h i j k l m n o p q r s t u v w x y z

a b c d e f g h i j k l m n o p q r s t u v w x y z

duffel coat *noun*
duffel coats
dug *verb* SEE **dig**
dugout *noun*
dugouts
duke *noun*
dukes
dull *adjective*
duller
dullest
dully *adverb*
dullness *noun*
duly *adverb*
dumb *adjective*
dumber
dumbest
dumbfounded *adjective*
dummy *noun*
dummies
dump *verb*
dumps
dumping
dumped
dump *noun*
dumps
dumpling *noun*
dumplings
dumpy *adjective*
dumpier
dumpiest
dune *noun*
dunes
dung *noun*
dungarees *plural noun*
dungeon *noun*
dungeons
duo *noun*
duos
duplicate *noun*
duplicates
duplicate *verb*
duplicates
duplicating
duplicated
duplication *noun*
durability *noun*
durable *adjective*
duration *noun*
during *preposition*
dusk *noun*
dust *noun*
dust *verb*
dusts
dusting
dusted
dustbin *noun*
dustbins
duster *noun*
dusters
dustman *noun*
dustmen
dustpan *noun*
dustpans
dusty *adjective*
dustier
dustiest
Dutch *adjective*
dutiful *adjective*
dutifully *adverb*
duty *noun*
duties
duvet *noun*
duvets
DVD *noun*
DVDs
dwarf *verb*
dwarfs
dwarfing
dwarfed
dwell *verb*
dwells
dwelling
dwelt
dwelling *noun*
dwellings
dwindle *verb*
dwindles
dwindling
dwindled
dye* *verb*
dyes
dyeing
dyed
dye *noun*
dyes
dying *verb* SEE **die**
dyke *noun*
dykes
dynamic *adjective*
dynamically
dynamite *noun*
dynamo *noun*
dynamos
dynasty *noun*
dynasties
dyslexia *noun*
dyslexic *adjective*
dystrophy *noun*

* **Dye** means 'to change the colour of something'. **! die.**

Ee

e- *prefix*
e- stands for 'electronic' and makes words about computers and the Internet, e.g. **email** (spelled joined up), **e-commerce** and **e-shopping** (spelled with hyphens).

each *adjective & pronoun*
eager *adjective*
eagerly *adverb*
eagerness *noun*
eagle *noun*
eagles
ear *noun*
ears
earache *noun*
eardrum *noun*
eardrums
earl *noun*
earls
early *adjective & adverb*
earlier
earliest
earmark *verb*
earmarks
earmarking
earmarked
earn *verb*
earns
earning
earned
earnest *adjective*
earnestly *adverb*
earnings *plural noun*
earphones *plural noun*
earring *noun*
earrings
earth *noun*
earths
earthenware *noun*
earthly *adjective*
earthquake *noun*
earthquakes
earthworm *noun*
earthworms
earthy *adjective*
earthier
earthiest
earwig *noun*
earwigs
ease *verb*
eases
easing
eased
ease *noun*
easel *noun*
easels
east *adjective & adverb*
east* *noun*
Easter *noun*
easterly *adjective & noun*
easterlies
eastern *adjective*
eastward *adjective & adverb*
eastwards *adverb*
easy *adjective & adverb*
easier
easiest
easily *adverb*
eat *verb*
eats
eating
ate
eaten
eatable *adjective*
eaves *plural noun*
ebb *verb*
ebbs
ebbing
ebbed
ebb *noun*
ebony *noun*
eccentric *adjective*
eccentricity *noun*
eccentricities
echo *verb*
echoes
echoing
echoed
echo *noun*
echoes
eclair *noun*
eclairs
French éclair
eclipse *noun*
eclipses
ecological *adjective*
ecology *noun*
economic *adjective*
economical *adjective*
economically *adverb*
economics *noun*
economist *noun*
economists
economize *verb*
economizes
economizing
economized
economy *noun*
economies
ecosystem *noun*
ecosystems
ecstasy *noun*
ecstasies

* You use a capital E in **the East**, meaning China, Japan, etc.

a b c d e f g h i j k l m n o p q r s t u v w x y z

ecstatic *adjective*
ecstatically *adverb*
ecu *noun*
ecus
eczema *noun*

> **-ed** and **-t** *suffixes*
> Some verbs ending in *l*, *m*, *n*, and *p* have past forms and past participles ending in *-ed* and *-t*, e.g. **burned/burnt, leaped/leapt**. Both forms are correct, and the *-t* form is especially common when it comes before a noun, e.g. *burnt cakes*.

edge *noun*
edges
edge *verb*
edges
edging
edged
edgeways *adverb*
edgy *adjective*
edgier
edgiest
edible *adjective*
edit *verb*
edits
editing
edited
edition *noun*
editions
editor *noun*
editors
editorial *noun*
editorials
educate *verb*
educates
educating
educated
education *noun*
educational *adjective*
educator *noun*
educators
eel *noun*
eels
eerie *adjective*
eerier
eeriest
eerily *adverb*
eeriness *noun*
effect★ *noun*
effects
effective *adjective*
effectively *adverb*
effectiveness *noun*
effeminate *adjective*
effervescence *noun*
effervescent *adjective*
efficiency *noun*
efficient *adjective*
efficiently *adverb*
effort *noun*
efforts
effortless *adjective*
effortlessly *adverb*
egg *noun*
eggs
egg *verb*
eggs
egging
egged

> **-ei-** and **-ie-**
> The rule 'i before e except after c' is true when it is pronounced -ee-, e.g. **thief, ceiling**. There are a few exceptions, of which the most important are **seize** and **protein**.

Eid☆ *noun*
eiderdown *noun*
eiderdowns
eight✪ *noun & adjective*
eighteen *noun & adjective*
eighteenth *adjective & noun*
eighth✣ *adjective & noun*
eighthly
eightieth *adjective & noun*
eighty *noun*
eighties
either *adjective & pronoun*
eject *verb*
ejects
ejecting
ejected
ejection *noun*
elaborate *adjective*
elaborately *adverb*
elaborate *verb*
elaborates
elaborating
elaborated
elaboration *noun*
elastic *adjective & noun*
elated *adjective*
elation *noun*
elbow *noun*
elbows
elbow *verb*
elbows
elbowing
elbowed
elder *adjective & noun*
elders
elderberry *noun*
elderberries
elderly *adjective*
eldest *adjective*
elect *verb*
elects
electing
elected
election *noun*
elections

★ An **effect** is something that is caused by something else. **! affect**.
☆ **Eid** is a Muslim festival.
✪ **Eight** is the number. **! ate**.
✣ Note that there are two h's in **eighth**.

electoral *adjective*
electorate *noun*
electric *adjective*
electrical *adjective*
electrically *adverb*
electrician *noun*
electricians
electricity *noun*
electrification *noun*
electrify *verb*
electrifies
electrifying
electrified
electrocute *verb*
electrocutes
electrocuting
electrocuted
electrocution *noun*
electromagnet *noun*
electromagnets
electron *noun*
electrons
electronic *adjective*
electronically *adverb*
electronics *noun*
elegance *noun*
elegant *adjective*
elegantly *adverb*
elegy *noun*
elegies
element *noun*
elements
elementary *adjective*
elephant *noun*
elephants
elevate *verb*
elevates
elevating
elevated
elevation *noun*
elevations
elevator *noun*
elevators
eleven *adjective* & *noun*
eleventh *adjective* & *noun*
elf *noun*
elves
eligibility *noun*
eligible *adjective*
eliminate *verb*
eliminates
eliminating
eliminated
elimination *noun*
elite *noun*
elites
French élites
elk *noun*
elk
elks
ellipse *noun*
ellipses
elliptical *adjective*
elliptically *adverb*
elm *noun*
elms
elocution *noun*
eloquence *noun*
eloquent *adjective*
else *adverb*
elsewhere *adverb*
elude *verb*
eludes
eluding
eluded
elusive *adjective*
elves *noun* SEE **elf**
email★ *noun*
emails
email *verb*
emails
emailing
emailed
emancipate *verb*
emancipates
emancipating
emancipated
emancipation *noun*
embankment *noun*
embankments
embark *verb*
embarks
embarking
embarked
embarkation *noun*
embarrass☆ *verb*
embarrasses
embarrassing
embarrassed
embarrassment *noun*
embassy *noun*
embassies
embedded *verb*
embers *plural noun*
emblem *noun*
emblems
embrace *verb*
embraces
embracing
embraced
embroider *verb*
embroiders
embroidering
embroidered
embroidery *noun*
embroideries
embryo *noun*
embryos
emerald *noun*
emeralds
emerge *verb*
emerges
emerging
emerged
emergence *noun*
emergency *noun*
emergencies
emery paper *noun*
emigrant *noun*
emigrants

★ **email** is short for **electronic mail**.
☆ Note that there are two ‘r’s in **embarrass** and **embarrassment**.

a b c d e f g h i j k l m n o p q r s t u v w x y z

emigrate *verb*
emigrates
emigrating
emigrated
emigration *noun*
eminence *noun*
eminent *adjective*
emission* *noun*
emissions
emit *verb*
emits
emitting
emitted
emotion *noun*
emotions
emotional *adjective*
emotionally *adverb*
empathy *noun*
emperor *noun*
emperors
emphasis *noun*
emphases
emphasize *verb*
emphasizes
emphasizing
emphasized
emphatic *adjective*
emphatically *adverb*
empire *noun*
empires
employ *verb*
employs
employing
employed
employee *noun*
employees
employer *noun*
employers
employment *noun*
empress *noun*
empresses
emptiness *noun*
empty *adjective*
emptier
emptiest
emptily *adverb*
empty *verb*
empties
emptying
emptied
emu *noun*
emus
emulsion *noun*
emulsions
enable *verb*
enables
enabling
enabled
enamel *noun*
enamels
encampment *noun*
encampments

> **-ence** *suffix*
> See the note at **-ance**.

enchant *verb*
enchants
enchanting
enchanted
enchantment *noun*
encircle *verb*
encircles
encircling
encircled
enclose *verb*
encloses
enclosing
enclosed
enclosure *noun*
enclosures
encore *noun*
encores
encounter *verb*
encounters
encountering
encountered
encourage *verb*
encourages
encouraging
encouraged
encouragement *noun*
encyclopedia *noun*
encyclopedias
encyclopedic *adjective*
end *verb*
ends
ending
ended
end *noun*
ends
endanger *verb*
endangers
endangering
endangered
endeavour *verb*
endeavours
endeavouring
endeavoured
ending *noun*
endings
endless *adjective*
endlessly *adverb*
endurance *noun*
endure *verb*
endures
enduring
endured
enemy *noun*
enemies
energetic *adjective*
energetically *adverb*
energy *noun*
energies
enforce *verb*
enforces
enforcing
enforced
enforceable *adjective*
enforcement *noun*
engage *verb*
engages
engaging
engaged
engagement *noun*
engagements
engine *noun*
engines

* An **emission** is something that escapes, like fumes. **! omission.**

engineer *noun*
engineers
engineering *noun*
engrave *verb*
engraves
engraving
engraved
engraver *noun*
engrossed *verb*
engulf *verb*
engulfs
engulfing
engulfed
enhance *verb*
enhances
enhancing
enhanced
enhancement *noun*
enjoy *verb*
enjoys
enjoying
enjoyed
enjoyable *adjective*
enjoyment *noun*
enlarge *verb*
enlarges
enlarging
enlarged
enlargement *noun*
enlargements
enlist *verb*
enlists
enlisting
enlisted
enmity *noun*
enmities
enormity★ *noun*
enormities
enormous *adjective*
enormously *adverb*
enormousness *noun*
enough *adjective* & *noun* & *adverb*

enquire *verb*
enquires
enquiring
enquired
enquiry☆ *noun*
enquiries
enrage *verb*
enrages
enraging
enraged
enrich *verb*
enriches
enriching
enriched
enrichment *noun*
enrol *verb*
enrols
enrolling
enrolled
enrolment *noun*
ensemble *noun*
ensembles
ensue *verb*
ensues
ensuing
ensued
ensure *verb*
ensures
ensuring
ensured

-ent *suffix*
See the note at **-ant**.

entangle *verb*
entangles
entangling
entangled
entanglement *noun*
enter *verb*
enters
entering
entered
enterprise *noun*
enterprises
enterprising *adjective*

entertain *verb*
entertains
entertaining
entertained
entertainer *noun*
entertainers
entertainment *noun*
entertainments
enthusiasm *noun*
enthusiasms
enthusiast *noun*
enthusiasts
enthusiastic *adjective*
enthusiastically *adverb*
entire *adjective*
entirely *adverb*
entirety *noun*
entitle *verb*
entitles
entitling
entitled
entrance *noun*
entrances
entrance *verb*
entrances
entrancing
entranced
entrant *noun*
entrants
entreat *verb*
entreats
entreating
entreated
entreaty *noun*
entreaties
entrepreneur *noun*
entrepreneurs
entrust *verb*
entrusts
entrusting
entrusted
entry *noun*
entries

★ An **enormity** is a wicked act. If you mean 'large size', use **enormousness**.
☆ An **enquiry** is a question. **! inquiry**.

envelop *verb*
envelops
enveloping
enveloped

envelope *noun*
envelopes

enviable *adjective*

envious *adjective*
enviously *adverb*

environment *noun*
environments

environmental *adjective*
environmentally *adverb*

environmentalist *noun*
environmentalists

envy *verb*
envies
envying
envied

envy *noun*

enzyme *noun*
enzymes

epic *noun*
epics

epidemic *noun*
epidemics

epilepsy *noun*

epileptic *adjective & noun*
epileptics

epilogue *noun*
epilogues

episode *noun*
episodes

epistle *noun*
epistles

epitaph *noun*
epitaphs

epoch *noun*
epochs

equal *adjective*
equally *adverb*

equal *verb*
equals
equalling
equalled

equal *noun*
equals

equality *noun*

equalize *verb*
equalizes
equalizing
equalized

equalizer *noun*
equalizers

equation *noun*
equations

equator *noun*

equatorial *adjective*

equestrian *adjective*

equilateral *adjective*

equilibrium *noun*
equilibria

equinox *noun*
equinoxes

equip *verb*
equips
equipping
equipped

equipment *noun*

equivalence *noun*

equivalent *adjective*

-er and **-est** *suffixes*
-er and *-est* make adjectives and adverbs meaning 'more' or 'most', e.g. **faster**, **slowest**. You can do this when the word has one syllable, and when a consonant comes at the end of the word after a single vowel you double it, e.g. **fatter**, **bigger**. You can use *-er* and *-est* with some two-syllable adjectives, e.g. **commoner**, **pleasantest**, and words ending in *y*, which change to *-ier* and *-iest*, e.g. **angrier**, **happiest**.

-er and **-or** *suffixes*
-er makes nouns meaning 'a person or thing that does something', e.g. a **helper** is a person who helps and an **opener** is a tool that opens things. You can make new words this way, e.g. **complainer**, **repairer**. Some words end in *-or*, e.g. **actor**, **visitor**, but you can't use *-or* to make new words.

era *noun*
eras

eradicate *verb*
eradicates
eradicating
eradicated

erase *verb*
erases
erasing
erased

eraser *noun*
erasers

erect *adjective*

erect *verb*
erects
erecting
erected

ermine *noun*
ermine

erode *verb*
erodes
eroding
eroded

erosion *noun*

errand *noun*
errands

erratic *adjective*
erratically *adverb*

erroneous *adjective*
erroneously *adverb*

error *noun*
errors

erupt *verb*
erupts
erupting
erupted
eruption *noun*
eruptions
escalate *verb*
escalates
escalating
escalated
escalation *noun*
escalator *noun*
escalators
escape *verb*
escapes
escaping
escaped
escape *noun*
escapes
escort *verb*
escorts
escorting
escorted
escort *noun*
escorts
Eskimo *noun*
Eskimos *or* Eskimo
especially *adverb*
espionage *noun*
esplanade *noun*
esplanades

> **-ess** *suffix*
> makes nouns for female people and animals, e.g. **manageress, lioness.**

essay *noun*
essays
essence *noun*
essences
essential *adjective*
essentially *adverb*
essential *noun*
essentials
establish *verb*
establishes
establishing
established
establishment *noun*
establishments
estate *noun*
estates
esteem *verb*
esteems
esteeming
esteemed
estimate *noun*
estimates
estimate *verb*
estimates
estimating
estimated
estuary *noun*
estuaries
etch *verb*
etches
etching
etched
etching *noun*
etchings
eternal *adjective*
eternally *adverb*
eternity *noun*
ether *noun*
ethical *adjective*
ethnic *adjective*
etymology *noun*
etymologies
eucalyptus *noun*
eucalyptuses
euphemism *noun*
euphemisms
euphemistic *adjective*
euphemistically *adverb*
Eurasian *adjective* & *noun*
euro *noun*
euros
Europe *noun*
European *adjective* & *noun*
Europeans
euthanasia *noun*
evacuate *verb*
evacuates
evacuating
evacuated
evacuation *noun*
evacuee *noun*
evacuees
evade *verb*
evades
evading
evaded
evaluate *verb*
evaluates
evaluating
evaluated
evaluation *noun*
evaluations
evangelical *adjective*
evangelism *noun*
evangelist *noun*
evangelists
evaporate *verb*
evaporates
evaporating
evaporated
evaporation *noun*
evasion *noun*
evasions
evasive *adjective*
eve *noun*
eves
even *adjective*
evenly *adverb*
even *adverb*
even *verb*
evens
evening
evened
evening *noun*
evenings
evenness *noun*
event *noun*
events
eventful *adjective*
eventfully *adverb*
eventual *adjective*
eventually *adverb*

a b c d e f g h i j k l m n o p q r s t u v w x y z

ever *adverb*

evergreen *adjective & noun*
evergreens

everlasting *adjective*

every *adjective*

everybody *pronoun*

everyday *adjective*

everyone *pronoun*

everything *pronoun*

everywhere *adverb*

evict *verb*
evicts
evicting
evicted

eviction *noun*
evictions

evidence *noun*

evident *adjective*
evidently *adverb*

evil *adjective*
evilly *adverb*

evil *noun*
evils

evolution *noun*

evolutionary *adjective*

evolve *verb*
evolves
evolving
evolved

ewe★ *noun*
ewes

> **ex-** *prefix*
> *ex-* makes nouns with the meaning 'former' or 'who used to be', e.g. **ex-president**, **ex-wife**. You use a hyphen to make these words.

exact *adjective*
exactly *adverb*

exactness *noun*

exaggerate *verb*
exaggerates
exaggerating
exaggerated

exaggeration *noun*

exalt *verb*
exalts
exalting
exalted

exam *noun*
exams

examination *noun*
examinations

examine *verb*
examines
examining
examined

examiner *noun*
examiners

example *noun*
examples

exasperate *verb*
exasperates
exasperating
exasperated

exasperation *noun*

excavate *verb*
excavates
excavating
excavated

excavation *noun*
excavations

excavator *noun*
excavators

exceed *verb*
exceeds
exceeding
exceeded

exceedingly *adverb*

excel *verb*
excels
excelling
excelled

excellence *noun*

excellent *adjective*
excellently *adverb*

except☆ *preposition*

exception *noun*
exceptions

exceptional *adjective*
exceptionally *adverb*

excerpt *noun*
excerpts

excess *noun*
excesses

excessive *adjective*
excessively *adverb*

exchange *verb*
exchanges
exchanging
exchanged

exchange *noun*
exchanges

excitable *adjective*
excitably *adverb*

excite *verb*
excites
exciting
excited

excitedly *adverb*

excitement *noun*
excitements

exclaim *verb*
exclaims
exclaiming
exclaimed

exclamation *noun*
exclamations

exclude *verb*
excludes
excluding
excluded

exclusion *noun*

★ A **ewe** is a female sheep. **! yew, you.**
☆ You use **except** in e.g. *everyone except me.* **! accept.**

exclusive *adjective*
exclusively
excrete *verb*
excretes
excreting
excreted
excretion *noun*
excursion *noun*
excursions
excusable *adjective*
excuse *verb*
excuses
excusing
excused
excuse *noun*
excuses
execute *verb*
executes
executing
executed
execution *noun*
executions
executioner *noun*
executioners
executive *noun*
executives
exempt *adjective*
exemption *noun*
exemptions
exercise *noun*
exercises
exercise★ *verb*
exercises
exercising
exercised
exert *verb*
exerts
exerting
exerted
exertion *noun*
exertions
exhale *verb*
exhales
exhaling
exhaled
exhalation *noun*
exhaust *verb*
exhausts
exhausting
exhausted
exhaust *noun*
exhausts
exhaustion *noun*
exhibit *verb*
exhibits
exhibiting
exhibited
exhibit *noun*
exhibits
exhibition *noun*
exhibitions
exhibitor *noun*
exhibitors
exile *verb*
exiles
exiling
exiled
exile *noun*
exiles
exist *verb*
exists
existing
existed
existence *noun*
existences
exit *verb*
exits
exiting
exited
exit *noun*
exits
exorcism *noun*
exorcist *noun*
exorcists
exorcize☆ *verb*
exorcizes
exorcizing
exorcized
exotic *adjective*
exotically *adverb*
expand *verb*
expands
expanding
expanded
expanse *noun*
expanses
expansion *noun*
expect *verb*
expects
expecting
expected
expectant *adjective*
expectantly *adverb*
expectation *noun*
expectations
expedition *noun*
expeditions
expel *verb*
expels
expelling
expelled
expenditure *noun*
expense *noun*
expenses
expensive *adjective*
expensively *adverb*
experience *verb*
experiences
experiencing
experienced
experience *noun*
experiences
experienced *adjective*
experiment *verb*
experiments
experimenting
experimented
experiment *noun*
experiments
experimental *adjective*
experimentally *adverb*

★ To **exercise** is to keep your body fit. **! exorcize.**
☆ To **exorcize** is to get rid of evil spirits. **! exercise.**

a b c d e f g h i j k l m n o p q r s t u v w x y z

experimentation *noun*

expert *adjective & noun*
experts
expertly *adverb*

expertise *noun*

expire *verb*
expires
expiring
expired

expiry *noun*

explain *verb*
explains
explaining
explained

explanation *noun*
explanations

explanatory *adjective*

explicit *adjective*
explicitly *adverb*

explode *verb*
explodes
exploding
exploded

exploit *noun*
exploits

exploit *verb*
exploits
exploiting
exploited

exploitation *noun*

exploration *noun*
explorations

exploratory *adjective*

explore *verb*
explores
exploring
explored

explorer *noun*
explorers

explosion *noun*
explosions

explosive *adjective & noun*
explosives

export *verb*
exports
exporting
exported

export *noun*
exports

exporter *noun*
exporters

expose *verb*
exposes
exposing
exposed

exposure *noun*
exposures

express *adjective & noun*
expresses

express *verb*
expresses
expressing
expressed

expression *noun*
expressions

expressive *adjective*
expressively *adverb*

expulsion *noun*
expulsions

exquisite *adjective*
exquisitely *adverb*

extend *verb*
extends
extending
extended

extension *noun*
extensions

extensive *adjective*
extensively *adverb*

extent *noun*
extents

exterior *noun*
exteriors

exterminate *verb*
exterminates
exterminating
exterminated

extermination *noun*

external *adjective*
externally *adverb*

extinct *adjective*

extinction *noun*

extinguish *verb*
extinguishes
extinguishing
extinguished

extinguisher *noun*
extinguishers

extra *adjective & noun*
extras

extract *verb*
extracts
extracting
extracted

extract *noun*
extracts

extraction *noun*
extractions

extraordinary *adjective*
extraordinarily *adverb*

extrasensory *adjective*

extraterrestrial *adjective & noun*
extraterrestrials

extravagance *noun*

extravagant *adjective*
extravagantly *adverb*

extreme *adjective*
extremely *adverb*

extreme *noun*
extremes

extremist *noun*
extremists

extremity *noun*
extremities

exuberance *noun*

exuberant *adjective*
exuberantly *adverb*

exult *verb*
exults
exulting
exulted

exultant *adjective*

exultation *noun*

eye *noun*
eyes

eye *verb*
eyes
eyeing
eyed

eyeball *noun*
eyeballs

eyebrow *noun*
eyebrows

eyelash *noun*
eyelashes

eyelid *noun*
eyelids

eyepiece *noun*
eyepieces

eyesight *noun*

eyesore *noun*
eyesores

eyewitness *noun*
eyewitnesses

Try also words beginning with **ph-**

a b c d e f g h i j k l m n o p q r s t u v w x y z

Ff

-f
Most nouns ending in *-f* have plurals ending in *-ves*, e.g. **shelf - shelves**, but some have plurals ending in *-fs*, e.g. **chiefs**. Nouns ending in *-ff* have plurals ending in *-ffs*, e.g. **cuffs**.

fable *noun*
fables
fabric *noun*
fabrics
fabricate *verb*
fabricates
fabricating
fabricated
fabulous *adjective*
fabulously *adverb*
face *noun*
faces
face *verb*
faces
facing
faced
facet *noun*
facets
facetious *adjective*
facetiously *adverb*
facial *adjective & noun*
facials
facially *adverb*
facilitate *verb*
facilitates
facilitating
facilitated
facility *noun*
facilities
fact *noun*
facts
factor *noun*
factors
factory *noun*
factories
factual *adjective*
factually *adverb*
faculty *noun*
faculties
fad *noun*
fads
fade *verb*
fades
fading
faded
fagged *adjective*
faggot *noun*
faggots
Fahrenheit *adjective*
fail *verb*
fails
failing
failed
fail *noun*
fails
failing *noun*
failings
failure *noun*
failures
faint *adjective*
fainter
faintest
faintly *adverb*
faint *verb*
faints
fainting
fainted
faint-hearted *adjective*
faintness *noun*
fair *adjective*
fairer
fairest
fairly *adverb*
fair* *noun*
fairs
fairground *noun*
fairgrounds
fairness *noun*
fairy *noun*
fairies
fairyland *noun*
faith *noun*
faiths
faithful *adjective*
faithfully *adverb*
faithfulness *noun*
fake *noun*
fakes
fake *verb*
fakes
faking
faked
faker *noun*
fakers
falcon *noun*
falcons
falconry *noun*
fall *verb*
falls
falling
fell
fallen
fall *noun*
falls
fallacious *adjective*
fallacy *noun*
fallacies
fallen *verb* SEE **fall**

* A **fair** is a group of outdoor entertainments or an exhibition. **! fare.**

Try also words beginning with **ph-**

fallout *noun*
fallow *adjective*
falls *plural noun*
false *adjective*
falser
falsest
falsely *adverb*
falsehood *noun*
falsehoods
falseness *noun*
falter *verb*
falters
faltering
faltered
fame *noun*
famed *adjective*
familiar *adjective*
familiarly *adverb*
familiarity *noun*
family *noun*
families
famine *noun*
famines
famished *adjective*
famous *adjective*
famously *adverb*
fan *verb*
fans
fanning
fanned
fan *noun*
fans
fanatic *noun*
fanatics
fanatical *adjective*
fanatically *adverb*
fanciful *adjective*
fancifully *adverb*
fancy *adjective*
fancier
fanciest
fancy *verb*
fancies
fancying
fancied
fancy *noun*
fancies
fanfare *noun*
fanfares
fang *noun*
fangs
fantastic *adjective*
fantastically *adverb*
fantasy *noun*
fantasies
far *adjective & adverb*
farther
farthest
faraway *adjective*
farce *noun*
farces
farcical *adjective*
farcically *adverb*
fare *verb*
fares
faring
fared
fare★ *noun*
fares
farewell *interjection & noun*
farewells
far-fetched *adjective*
farm *noun*
farms
farm *verb*
farms
farming
farmed
farmer *noun*
farmers
farmhouse *noun*
farmhouses
farmyard *noun*
farmyards
farther☆ *adverb & adjective*
farthest✪ *adverb & adjective*
farthing *noun*
farthings
fascinate *verb*
fascinates
fascinating
fascinated
fascination *noun*
fascism *noun*
fascist *noun*
fascists
fashion *noun*
fashions
fashion *verb*
fashions
fashioning
fashioned
fashionable *adjective*
fashionably *adverb*
fast *adjective & adverb*
faster
fastest
fast *verb*
fasts
fasting
fasted
fasten *verb*
fastens
fastening
fastened
fastener *noun*
fasteners
fastening *noun*
fastenings
fat *adjective*
fatter
fattest
fat *noun*
fats
fatal *adjective*
fatally *adverb*

★ A **fare** is money you pay, for example on a bus. **! fair.**
☆ You can use **farther** or **further** in e.g. *farther up the road.* SEE **further**.
✪ You can use **farthest** or **furthest** in e.g. *the place farthest from here.* SEE **furthest**.

fatality *noun*
fatalities
fate★ *noun*
fates
father *noun*
fathers
fatherhood *noun*
father-in-law *noun*
fathers-in-law
fathom *noun*
fathoms
fathom *verb*
fathoms
fathoming
fathomed
fatigue *noun*
fatigued *adjective*
fatten *verb*
fattens
fattening
fattened
fattening *adjective*
fatty *adjective*
fattier
fattiest
fault *noun*
faults
fault *verb*
faults
faulting
faulted
faultless *adjective*
faultlessly *adverb*
faulty *adjective*
faultier
faultiest
fauna *noun*
favour *noun*
favours
favour *verb*
favours
favouring
favoured
favourable *adjective*
favourably *adverb*
favourite *adjective* & *noun*
favourites
favouritism *noun*
fawn *noun*
fawns
fax *noun*
faxes
fax *verb*
faxes
faxing
faxed

-fe
Most nouns ending in *-fe* have plurals ending in *-ves*, e.g. **life - lives.**

fear *noun*
fears
fear *verb*
fears
fearing
feared
fearful *adjective*
fearfully *adverb*
fearless *adjective*
fearlessly *adverb*
fearsome *adjective*
feasible *adjective*
feast *noun*
feasts
feast *verb*
feasts
feasting
feasted
feat☆ *noun*
feats
feather *noun*
feathers
feathery *adjective*
feature *noun*
features
feature *verb*
features
featuring
featured
February✪ *noun*
Februaries
fed *verb* SEE **feed**
federal *adjective*
federation *noun*
fee *noun*
fees
feeble *adjective*
feebler
feeblest
feebly
feed *verb*
feeds
feeding
fed
feed *noun*
feeds
feedback *noun*
feel *verb*
feels
feeling
felt
feel *noun*
feeler *noun*
feelers
feeling *noun*
feelings
feet✢ *plural noun* SEE **foot**
feline *adjective*
fell *verb* SEE **fall**
fell *verb*
fells
felling
felled
fell *noun*
fells
fellow *noun*
fellows

★ **Fate** is a power that is thought to make things happen. **! fête.**
☆ A **feat** is an achievement. **! feet.**
✪ Note that **February** has two 'r's.
✢ **Feet** is the plural of foot. **! feat.**

Try also words beginning with **ph-**

fellowship *noun*
fellowships
felt *verb* SEE **feel**
felt *noun*
felt-tip pen *or* **felt-tipped pen** *noun*
felt-tip pens *or* felt-tipped pens
female *adjective* & *noun*
females
feminine *adjective*
femininity *noun*
feminism *noun*
feminist *noun*
feminists
fen *noun*
fens
fence *noun*
fences
fence *verb*
fences
fencing
fenced
fencer *adjective*
fencers
fencing *noun*
fend *verb*
fends
fending
fended
fender *noun*
fenders
ferment *verb*
ferments
fermenting
fermented
fermentation *noun*
ferment *verb*
fern *noun*
ferns
ferocious *adjective*
ferociously *adverb*
ferocity *noun*
ferret *noun*
ferrets
ferret *verb*
ferrets
ferreting
ferreted
ferry *noun*
ferries
ferry *verb*
ferries
ferrying
ferried
fertile *adjective*
fertility *noun*
fertilization *noun*
fertilize *verb*
fertilizes
fertilizing
fertilized
fertilizer *noun*
fertilizers
fervent *adjective*
fervently *adverb*
fervour *noun*
festival *noun*
festivals
festive *adjective*
festivity *noun*
festivities
festoon *verb*
festoons
festooning
festooned
fetal *adjective*
fetch *verb*
fetches
fetching
fetched
fête★ *noun*
fêtes
fetlock *noun*
fetlocks
fetters *plural noun*
fetus☆ *noun*
fetuses
feud *noun*
feuds
feudal *adjective*
feudalism *noun*
fever *noun*
fevers
fevered *adjective*
feverish *adjective*
feverishly *adverb*
few *adjective*
fewer
fewest
fiancé✪ *noun*
fiancés
fiancée✢ *noun*
fiancées
fiasco *noun*
fiascos
fib *noun*
fibs
fibber *noun*
fibbers
fibre *noun*
fibres
fibreglass *noun*
fibrous *adjective*
fickle *adjective*
fiction *noun*
fictions
fictional *adjective*
fictionally *adverb*
fictitious *adjective*
fiddle *verb*
fiddles
fiddling
fiddled
fiddle *noun*
fiddles

★ A **fête** is an outdoor entertainment with stalls. **! fate.**
☆ You will also see this word spelled **foetus.**
✪ A woman's **fiancé** is the man who is going to marry her.
✢ A man's **fiancée** is the woman who is going to marry him.

Try also words beginning with **ph-**

fiddler *noun*
fiddlers

fiddly *adjective*

fidelity *noun*

fidget *verb*
fidgets
fidgeting
fidgeted

fidgety *adjective*

field *noun*
fields

field *verb*
fields
fielding
fielded

fielder *noun*
fielders

Field Marshal *noun*
Field Marshals

fieldwork *noun*

fiend *noun*
fiends

fiendish *adjective*
fiendishly *adverb*

fierce *adjective*
fiercer
fiercest
fiercely *adverb*

fierceness *noun*

fiery *adjective*
fierier
fieriest

fiesta *noun*
fiestas

fife *noun*
fifes

fifteen *noun & adjective*

fifteenth *adjective & noun*

fifth *adjective & noun*

fifthly *adverb*

fiftieth *adjective & noun*

fifty *noun*
fifties

fig *noun*
figs

fight *verb*
fights
fighting
fought

fight *noun*
fights

fighter *noun*
fighters

figurative *adjective*
figuratively *adverb*

figure *noun*
figures

figure *verb*
figures
figuring
figured

filament *noun*
filaments

file *verb*
files
filing
filed

file *noun*
files

filings *plural noun*

fill *verb*
fills
filling
filled

fill *noun*
fills

filler *noun*
fillers

fillet *noun*
fillets

filling *noun*
fillings

filly *noun*
fillies

film *noun*
films

film *verb*
films
filming
filmed

filter *noun*
filters

filter *verb*
filters
filtering
filtered

filth *noun*

filthy *adjective*
filthier
filthiest

fin *noun*
fins

final *adjective*
finally *adverb*

final *noun*
finals

finale *noun*
finales

finalist *noun*
finalists

finality *noun*

finance *noun*

finance *verb*
finances
financing
financed

finances *plural noun*

financial *adjective*
financially *adverb*

financier *noun*
financiers

finch *noun*
finches

find *verb*
finds
finding
found

finder *noun*
finders

findings *plural noun*

fine *adjective*
finer
finest
finely *adverb*

fine *noun*
fines

fine *verb*
fines
fining
fined

finger *noun*
fingers
finger *verb*
fingers
fingering
fingered
fingernail *noun*
fingernails
fingerprint *noun*
fingerprints
finicky *adjective*
finish *verb*
finishes
finishing
finished
finish *noun*
finishes
finite *adjective*
fir★ *noun*
firs
fire *noun*
fires
fire *verb*
fires
firing
fired
firearm *noun*
firearms
firefighter *noun*
firefighters
fireman *noun*
firemen
fireplace *noun*
fireplaces
fireproof *adjective*
fireside *noun*
firesides
firewood *noun*
firework *noun*
fireworks
firm *adjective*
firmer
firmest
firmly *adverb*
firm *noun*
firms
firmness *noun*
first *adjective & adverb*
firstly *adverb*
first class *adjective*
first floor *noun*
first floors
first hand *adjective*
first rate *adjective*
fish *noun*
fish
fishes
fish *verb*
fishes
fishing
fished
fisherman *noun*
fishermen
fishmonger *noun*
fishmongers
fishy *adjective*
fishier
fishiest
fission *noun*
fist *noun*
fists
fit *adjective*
fitter
fittest
fit *verb*
fits
fitting
fitted
fit *noun*
fits
fitness *noun*
fitter *noun*
fitters
fitting *adjective*
fitting *noun*
fittings
five *noun & adjective*
fiver *noun*
fivers
fix *verb*
fixes
fixing
fixed
fix *noun*
fixes
fixture *noun*
fixtures
fizz *verb*
fizzes
fizzing
fizzed
fizzy *adjective*
fizzier
fizziest
fizzle *verb*
fizzles
fizzling
fizzled
fjord *noun*
fjords
flabbergasted *adjective*
flabby *adjective*
flabbier
flabbiest
flag *noun*
flags
flag *verb*
flags
flagging
flagged
flagpole *noun*
flagpoles
flagship *noun*
flagships
flagstaff *noun*
flagstaffs
flagstone *noun*
flagstones
flair☆ *noun*
flake *noun*
flakes

★ A **fir** is a tree. **! fur.**
☆ **Flair** is a special talent. **! flare.**

a b c d e f g h i j k l m n o p q r s t u v w x y z

flake *verb*
flakes
flaking
flaked

flaky *adjective*
flakier
flakiest

flame *noun*
flames

flame *verb*
flames
flaming
flamed

flamingo *noun*
flamingos *or* flamingoes

flan *noun*
flans

flank *noun*
flanks

flannel *noun*
flannels

flap *noun*
flaps

flap *verb*
flaps
flapping
flapped

flapjack *noun*
flapjacks

flare★ *noun*
flares

flare *verb*
flares
flaring
flared

flash *noun*
flashes

flash *verb*
flashes
flashing
flashed

flashback *noun*
flashbacks

flashy *adjective*
flashier
flashiest

flask *noun*
flasks

flat *adjective*
flatter
flattest
flatly *adverb*

flat *noun*
flats

flatness *noun*

flatten *verb*
flattens
flattening
flattened

flatter *verb*
flatters
flattering
flattered

flatterer *noun*
flatterers

flattery *noun*

flaunt *verb*
flaunts
flaunting
flaunted

flavour *noun*
flavours

flavour *verb*
flavours
flavouring
flavoured

flavouring *noun*

flaw *noun*
flaws

flawed *adjective*

flawless *adjective*
flawlessly *adverb*

flax *noun*

flea☆ *noun*
fleas

fleck *noun*
flecks

flee✪ *verb*
flees
fleeing
fled

fleece *noun*
fleeces

fleece *verb*
fleeces
fleecing
fleeced

fleecy *adjective*
fleecier
fleeciest

fleet *noun*
fleets

fleeting *adjective*

flesh *noun*

fleshy *adjective*
fleshier
fleshiest

flew✣ *verb* SEE **fly**

flex *noun*
flexes

flex *verb*
flexes
flexing
flexed

flexibility *noun*

flexible *adjective*
flexibly *adverb*

flick *verb*
flicks
flicking
flicked

flick *noun*
flicks

flicker *verb*
flickers
flickering
flickered

★ A **flare** is a bright light. **! flair.**
☆ A **flea** is an insect. **! flee.**
✪ To **flee** is to run away. **! flea.**
✣ **Flew** is the past of **fly. ! flu, flue.**

Try also words beginning with **ph-**

flight *noun*
flights
flimsy *adjective*
flimsier
flimsiest
flinch *verb*
flinches
flinching
flinched
fling *verb*
flings
flinging
flung
flint *noun*
flints
flinty *adjective*
flintier
flintiest
flip *verb*
flips
flipping
flipped
flippancy *noun*
flippant *adjective*
flippantly *adverb*
flipper *noun*
flippers
flirt *verb*
flirts
flirting
flirted
flirtation *noun*
flirtations
flit *verb*
flits
flitting
flitted
float *verb*
floats
floating
floated
float *noun*
floats

flock *verb*
flocks
flocking
flocked
flock *noun*
flocks
flog *verb*
flogs
flogging
flogged
flood *verb*
floods
flooding
flooded
flood *noun*
floods
floodlight *noun*
floodlights
floodlit *adjective*
floor *noun*
floors
floor *verb*
floors
flooring
floored
floorboard *noun*
floorboards
flop *verb*
flops
flopping
flopped
flop *noun*
flops
floppy *adjective*
floppier
floppiest
floppy disk *noun*
floppy disks
flora *noun*
floral *adjective*
florist *noun*
florists
floss *noun*

flounder *verb*
flounders
floundering
floundered
flour★ *noun*
flourish *verb*
flourishes
flourishing
flourished
floury *adjective*
flourier
flouriest
flow *verb*
flows
flowing
flowed
flow *noun*
flows
flower☆ *noun*
flowers
flower *verb*
flowers
flowering
flowered
flowerpot *noun*
flowerpots
flowery *adjective*
flown *verb* SEE **fly**
flu✪ *noun*
fluctuate *verb*
fluctuates
fluctuating
fluctuated
fluctuation *noun*
flue✣ *noun*
flues
fluency *noun*
fluent *adjective*
fluently
fluff *noun*
fluffy *adjective*
fluffier
fluffiest

★ **Flour** is powder used in making bread. **! flower.**
☆ A **flower** is a part of a plant. **! flour.**
✪ **Flu** is an illness. **! flew, flue.**
✣ A **flue** is a pipe for smoke and fumes. **! flew, flu.**

Try also words beginning with **ph-**

a b c d e f g h i j k l m n o p q r s t u v w x y z

fluid *noun*
fluids
fluke *noun*
flukes
flung *verb* SEE **fling**
fluorescent *adjective*
fluoridation *noun*
fluoride *noun*
flurry *noun*
flurries
flush *verb*
flushes
flushing
flushed
flush *noun*
flushes
flush *adjective*
flustered *adjective*
flute *noun*
flutes
flutter *verb*
flutters
fluttering
fluttered
flutter *noun*
flutters
fly *verb*
flies
flying
flew
flown
fly *noun*
flies
flyleaf *noun*
flyleaves
flyover *noun*
flyovers
flywheel *noun*
flywheels
foal *noun*
foals
foam *noun*
foam *verb*
foams
foaming
foamed
foamy *adjective*
foamier
foamiest
focal *adjective*
focus *verb*
focuses
focusing
focused
focus *noun*
focuses *or* foci
fodder *noun*
foe *noun*
foes
foetus *noun* SEE **fetus**
fog *noun*
fogs
foggy★ *adjective*
foggier
foggiest
foghorn *noun*
foghorns
fogy☆ *noun*
fogies
foil *verb*
foils
foiling
foiled
foil *noun*
foils
fold *verb*
folds
folding
folded
fold *noun*
folds
folder *noun*
folders
foliage *noun*
folk *plural noun*
folklore *noun*
follow *verb*
follows
following
followed
follower *noun*
followers
fond *adjective*
fonder
fondest
fondly
fondness *noun*
font *noun*
fonts
food *noun*
foods
fool *noun*
fools
fool *verb*
fools
fooling
fooled
foolhardiness *noun*
foolhardy *adjective*
foolhardier
foolhardiest
foolish *adjective*
foolishly *adverb*
foolishness *noun*
foolproof *adjective*
foot✪ *noun*
feet
footage *noun*
football *noun*
footballs
footballer *noun*
footballers
foothill *noun*
foothills
foothold *noun*
footholds
footing *noun*
footlights *plural noun*

★ **Foggy** means 'covered in fog'. **! fogy.**
☆ A **fogy** is someone with old-fashioned ideas. **! foggy.**
✪ The plural is **foot** in e.g. *a six-foot pole.*

Try also words beginning with **ph-**

footnote *noun*
footnotes
footpath *noun*
footpaths
footprint *noun*
footprints
footstep *noun*
footsteps
for* *preposition* & *conjunction*
forbid *verb*
forbids
forbidding
forbade
forbidden
force *verb*
forces
forcing
forced
force *noun*
forces
forceful *adjective*
forcefully *adverb*
forceps *plural noun*
forcible *adjective*
forcibly *adverb*
ford *verb*
fords
fording
forded
ford *noun*
fords
fore☆ *adjective* & *noun*
forecast *verb*
forecasts
forecasting
forecast
forecasted
forecast *noun*
forecasts
forecourt *noun*
forecourts
forefathers *plural noun*
forefinger *noun*
forefingers
foregone✪ *adjective*
foreground *noun*
foregrounds
forehead *noun*
foreheads
foreign *adjective*
foreigner *noun*
foreigners
foreman *noun*
foremen
foremost *adjective* & *adverb*
forename *noun*
forenames
forensic *adjective*
forensics *plural noun*
foresee *verb*
foresees
foreseeing
foresaw
foreseen
foreseeable *adjective*
foresight *noun*
forest *noun*
forests
forester *noun*
foresters
forestry *noun*
foretell *verb*
foretells
foretelling
foretold
forever✣ *adverb*
forfeit *verb*
forfeits
forfeiting
forfeited
forfeit *noun*
forfeits
forgave *verb* SEE **forgive**
forge *verb*
forges
forging
forged
forge *noun*
forges
forgery *noun*
forgeries
forget *verb*
forgets
forgetting
forgot
forgotten
forgetful *adjective*
forgetfulness *noun*
forget-me-not *noun*
forget-me-nots
forgivable *adjective*
forgive *verb*
forgives
forgiving
forgave
forgiven
forgiveness *noun*
fork *noun*
forks
fork *verb*
forks
forking
forked
fork-lift truck *noun*
fork-lift trucks
forlorn *adjective*
form *verb*
forms
forming
formed
form *noun*
forms
formal *adjective*
formally *adverb*

* You use **for** in phrases like *a present for you.* **! fore.**
☆ You use **fore** in phrases like *come to the fore.* **! for.**
✪ You can use **foregone** in *a foregone conclusion.*
✣ You use **forever** in e.g. *They are forever complaining*. You can also use **for ever** in e.g. *The rain seemed to go on for ever.*

a b c d e f g h i j k l m n o p q r s t u v w x y z

formality *noun*
formalities

format *noun*
formats

formation *noun*
formations

former *adjective*
formerly *adverb*

formidable *adjective*
formidably *adverb*

formula *noun*
formulas *or* formulae

formulate *verb*
formulates
formulating
formulated

forsake *verb*
forsakes
forsaking
forsook
forsaken

fort *noun*
forts

forth★ *adverb*

fortieth *adjective* & *noun*

fortification *noun*
fortifications

fortify *verb*
fortifies
fortifying
fortified

fortnight *noun*
fortnights

fortnightly *adverb* & *adjective*

fortress *noun*
fortresses

fortunate *adjective*
fortunately *adverb*

fortune *noun*
fortunes

fortune-teller *noun*
fortune-tellers

forty *noun*
forties

forum *noun*
forums

forward *adjective* & *adverb*

forward *noun*
forwards

forwards *adverb*

fossil *noun*
fossils

fossilized *adjective*

foster *verb*
fosters
fostering
fostered

foster-child *noun*
foster-children

foster-parent *noun*
foster-parents

fought *verb* SEE **fight**

foul☆ *adjective*
fouler
foulest
foully *adverb*

foul✪ *verb*
fouls
fouling
fouled

foul✣ *noun*
fouls

foulness *noun*

found *verb*
founds
founding
founded

found *verb* SEE **find**

foundation *noun*
foundations

founder *noun*
founders

founder *verb*
founders
foundering
foundered

foundry *noun*
foundries

fountain *noun*
fountains

four *noun*
fours

fourteen *noun*
fourteens

fourteenth *adjective* & *noun*

fourth● *adjective*

fourthly *adverb*

fowl✱ *noun*
fowl *or* fowls

fox *noun*
foxes

fox *verb*
foxes
foxing
foxed

foxglove *noun*
foxgloves

foxy *adjective*
foxier
foxiest

foyer *noun*
foyers

fraction *noun*
fractions

fractionally *adverb*

fracture *verb*
fractures
fracturing
fractured

★ You use **forth** in e.g. *to go forth.* **! fourth.**
☆ **Foul** means 'dirty' or 'disgusting'. **! fowl.**
✪ To **foul** is to break a rule in a game. **! fowl.**
✣ A **foul** is breaking a rule in a game. **! fowl.**
● You use **fourth** in e.g. *for the fourth time.* **! forth.**
✱ A **fowl** is a kind of bird. **! foul.**

fracture *noun*
fractures
fragile *adjective*
fragility *noun*
fragment *noun*
fragments
fragmentary *adjective*
fragmentation *noun*
fragrance *noun*
fragrances
fragrant *adjective*
frail *adjective*
frailer
frailest
frailty *noun*
frailties
frame *verb*
frames
framing
framed
frame *noun*
frames
framework *noun*
frameworks
franchise *noun*
franchises
frank *adjective*
franker
frankest
frankly *adverb*
frank *verb*
franks
franking
franked
frankness *noun*
frantic *adjective*
frantically *adverb*
fraud *noun*
frauds
fraudulent *adjective*
fraudulently *adverb*
fraught *adjective*
frayed *verb*

freak *noun*
freaks
freakish *adjective*
freckle *noun*
freckles
freckled *adjective*
free *adjective*
freer
freest
freely *adverb*
free *verb*
frees
freeing
freed
freedom *noun*
freedoms
freehand *adjective*
freewheel *verb*
freewheels
freewheeling
freewheeled
freeze★ *verb*
freezes
freezing
froze
frozen
freezer *noun*
freezers
freight *noun*
freighter *noun*
freighters
frenzied *adjective*
frenzy *noun*
frenzies
frequency *noun*
frequencies
frequent *adjective*
frequently *adverb*
frequent *verb*
frequents
frequenting
frequented

fresh *adjective*
fresher
freshest
freshly *adverb*
freshness *noun*
freshen *verb*
freshens
freshening
freshened
freshwater *noun*
fret *verb*
frets
fretting
fretted
fretful *adjective*
fretfully *adverb*
friar *noun*
friars
friary *noun*
friaries
friction *noun*
Friday *noun*
Fridays
fridge *noun*
fridges
friend *noun*
friends
friendless *adjective*
friendliness *noun*
friendly *adjective*
friendlier
friendliest
friendly *noun*
friendlies
friendship *noun*
friendships
frieze☆ *noun*
friezes
frigate *noun*
frigates
fright *noun*
frights

★ To **freeze** is to be very cold. **! frieze.**
☆ A **frieze** is a strip of designs along a wall. **! freeze.**

a b c d e **f** g h i j k l m n o p q r s t u v w x y z

frighten *verb*
frightens
frightening
frightened
frightful *adjective*
frightfully *adverb*
frill *noun*
frills
frilled *adjective*
frilly *adjective*
frillier
frilliest
fringe *noun*
fringes
fringed *adjective*
frisk *verb*
frisks
frisking
frisked
friskiness *noun*
frisky *adjective*
friskier
friskiest
friskily *adverb*
fritter *verb*
fritters
frittering
frittered
fritter *noun*
fritters
frivolous *adjective*
frivolously *adverb*
frivolity *noun*
frivolities
frizzy *adjective*
frizzier
frizziest
fro★ *adverb*
frock *noun*
frocks
frog *noun*
frogs
frogman *noun*
frogmen
frolic *noun*
frolics

frolicsome *adjective*
frolic *verb*
frolics
frolicking
frolicked
from *preposition*
front *noun*
fronts
frontier *noun*
frontiers
frost *noun*
frosts
frost *verb*
frosts
frosting
frosted
frostbite *noun*
frostbitten *adjective*
frosty *adjective*
frostier
frostiest
froth *noun*
froth *verb*
froths
frothing
frothed
frothy *adjective*
frothier
frothiest
frown *verb*
frowns
frowning
frowned
frown *noun*
frowns
froze *verb* SEE **freeze**
frozen *adjective* SEE **freeze**
frugal *adjective*
frugally *adverb*
frugality *noun*
fruit *noun*
fruit *or* fruits
fruitful *adjective*
fruitless *adjective*
fruitlessly *adverb*

fruity *adjective*
fruitier
fruitiest

frustrate *verb*
frustrates
frustrating
frustrated

frustration *noun*
frustrations

fry *verb*
fries
frying
fried

fudge *noun*

fuel *noun*
fuels

fuel *verb*
fuels
fuelling
fuelled

fug *noun*
fugs

fuggy *adjective*
fuggier
fuggiest

fugitive *noun*
fugitives

-ful *suffix*
-ful makes nouns for amounts, e.g. **handful**, **spoonful**. The plural of these words ends in *-fuls*, e.g. **handfuls**. *-ful* also makes adjectives, e.g. **graceful**, and when the adjective ends in *-y* following a consonant, you change the *y* to *i*, e.g. **beauty - beautiful**.

fulcrum *noun*
fulcra *or* fulcrums

★ You use **fro** in *to and fro*.

Try also words beginning with **ph-**

fulfil *verb*
fulfils
fulfilling
fulfilled
fulfilment *noun*
full *adjective*
fully *adverb*
fullness *noun*
fumble *verb*
fumbles
fumbling
fumbled
fume *verb*
fumes
fuming
fumed
fumes *plural noun*
fun *noun*
function *verb*
functions
functioning
functioned
function *noun*
functions
functional *adjective*
functionally *adverb*
fund *noun*
funds
fundamental *adjective*
fundamentally *adverb*
fundamentalist *noun*
fundamentalists
fundraising *noun*
funeral *noun*
funerals
fungus *noun*
fungi
funnel *noun*
funnels
funny *adjective*
funnier
funniest
funnily *adverb*
fur★ *noun*
furs
furious *adjective*
furiously *adverb*
furl *verb*
furls
furling
furled
furlong *noun*
furlongs
furnace *noun*
furnaces
furnish *verb*
furnishes
furnishing
furnished
furniture *noun*
furrow *noun*
furrows
furry *adjective*
furrier
furriest
further☆ *adjective*
further✪ *verb*
furthers
furthering
furthered
furthermore *adverb*
furthest✣ *adverb & adjective*
furtive *adjective*
furtively *adverb*
fury *noun*
furies
fuse *verb*
fuses
fusing
fused
fuse *noun*
fuses
fuselage *noun*
fuselages
fusion *noun*
fusions
fuss *verb*
fusses
fussing
fussed
fuss *noun*
fusses
fussiness *noun*
fussy *adjective*
fussier
fussiest
fussily *adverb*
futile *adjective*
futilely *adverb*
futility *noun*
futon *noun*
futons
future *noun*
futuristic *adjective*
fuzz *noun*
fuzziness *noun*
fuzzy *adjective*
fuzzier
fuzziest
fuzzily *adverb*

★ **Fur** is the hair of animals. **! fir**.
☆ You use **further** in e.g. *We need further information.* SEE **farther**.
✪ To **further** something is to make it progress.
✣ You use **furthest** in e.g. *Who has read the furthest?* SEE **farthest**.

Try also words beginning with **gh-** or **gu-**

Gg

gabble *verb*
gabbles
gabbling
gabbled
gable *noun*
gables
gabled *adjective*
gadget *noun*
gadgets
Gaelic *noun*
gag *verb*
gags
gagging
gagged
gag *noun*
gags
gaiety *noun*
gaily *adverb*
gain *verb*
gains
gaining
gained
gain *noun*
gains
gala *noun*
galas
galactic *adjective*
galaxy *noun*
galaxies
gale *noun*
gales
gallant *adjective*
gallantly *adverb*
gallantry *noun*
galleon* *noun*
galleons
gallery *noun*
galleries
galley *noun*
galleys
gallon☆ *noun*
gallons
gallop *verb*
gallops
galloping
galloped
gallop *noun*
gallops
gallows *noun*
galore *adverb*
galvanize *verb*
galvanizes
galvanizing
galvanized
gamble *verb*
gambles
gambling
gambled
gamble *noun*
gambles
gambler *noun*
gamblers
game *noun*
games
gamekeeper *noun*
gamekeepers
gammon *noun*
gander *noun*
ganders
gang *noun*
gangs
gang *verb*
gangs
ganging
ganged
gangplank *noun*
gangplanks
gangster *noun*
gangsters
gangway *noun*
gangways
gaol *noun* SEE **jail**
gaoler *noun* SEE **jailer**
gap *noun*
gaps
gape *verb*
gapes
gaping
gaped
garage *noun*
garages
garbage *noun*
garden *noun*
gardens
gardener *noun*
gardeners
gardening *noun*
gargle *verb*
gargles
gargling
gargled
gargoyle *noun*
gargoyles
garland *noun*
garlands
garlic *noun*
garment *noun*
garments
garnish *verb*
garnishes
garnishing
garnished
garrison *noun*
garrisons
garter *noun*
garters

* A **galleon** is a type of ship. **! gallon**.
☆ A **gallon** is a measurement of liquid. **! galleon**.

gas *noun*
gases
gas *verb*
gasses
gassing
gassed
gaseous *adjective*
gash *noun*
gashes
gasket *noun*
gaskets
gasoline *noun*
gasometer *noun*
gasometers
gasp *verb*
gasps
gasping
gasped
gasp *noun*
gasps
gastric *adjective*
gate *noun*
gates
gateau* *noun*
gateaux
gateway *noun*
gateways
gather *verb*
gathers
gathering
gathered
gathering *noun*
gatherings
gaudy *adjective*
gaudier
gaudiest
gauge *verb*
gauges
gauging
gauged
gauge *noun*
gauges
gaunt *adjective*
gauntlet *noun*
gauntlets

gauze *noun*
gave *verb* SEE **give**
gaze *verb*
gazes
gazing
gazed
gaze *noun*
gazes
gazetteer *noun*
gazetteers
gear *noun*
gears
gecko *noun*
geckos
geese *plural noun* SEE **goose**
Geiger counter *noun*
Geiger counters
gel *noun*
gels
gelatine *noun*
gelding *noun*
geldings
gem *noun*
gems
gender *noun*
genders
gene *noun*
genes
genealogy *noun*
genealogies
general *adjective*
generally *adverb*
general *noun*
generals
generalization *noun*
generalizations
generalize *verb*
generalizes
generalizing
generalized
generate *verb*
generates
generating
generated

generation *noun*
generations
generator *noun*
generators
generosity *noun*
generous *adjective*
generously *adverb*
genetic *adjective*
genetically *adverb*
genetics *plural noun*
genial *adjective*
genially *adverb*
genie *noun*
genies
genius *noun*
geniuses
genocide *noun*
gent *noun*
gents
gentle *adjective*
gentler
gentlest
gently *adverb*
gentleman *noun*
gentlemen
gentlemanly *adjective*
gentleness *noun*
genre *noun*
genres
genuine *adjective*
genuinely *adverb*
genus *noun*
genera

> **geo-** *prefix*
> *geo-* means 'earth', e.g. **geography** (the study of the earth).

geographer *noun*
geographers
geographical *adjective*
geographically *adverb*
geography *noun*
geological *adjective*
geologically *adverb*

* **Gateau** is a French word used in English. It means 'a rich cream cake'.

Try also words beginning with **gh-** or **gu-**

a b c d e f g h i j k l m n o p q r s t u v w x y z

geologist *noun*
geologists
geology *noun*
geometric *adjective*
geometrical *adjective*
geometry *noun*
geranium *noun*
geraniums
gerbil *noun*
gerbils
germ *noun*
germs
germinate *verb*
germinates
germinating
germinated
germination *noun*
gesticulate *verb*
gesticulates
gesticulating
gesticulated
gesture *noun*
gestures
get *verb*
gets
getting
got
getaway *noun*
getaways
geyser *noun*
geysers
ghastly *adjective*
ghastlier
ghastliest
ghetto *noun*
ghettos
ghost *noun*
ghosts
ghostly *adjective*
ghostlier
ghostliest
ghoulish *adjective*
ghoulishly *adverb*
giant *noun*
giants
giddiness *noun*
giddy *adjective*
giddier
giddiest
giddily *adverb*
gift *noun*
gifts
gifted *adjective*
gig *noun*
gigs
gigabyte *noun*
gigabytes
gigantic *adjective*
gigantically *adverb*
giggle *verb*
giggles
giggling
giggled
giggle *noun*
giggles
gild* *verb*
gilds
gilding
gilded
gills *plural noun*
gimmick *noun*
gimmicks
gin *noun*
ginger *noun*
gingerbread *noun*
gingerly *adverb*
gingery *adjective*
gipsy *noun* SEE **gypsy**
giraffe *noun*
giraffes
girder *noun*
girders
girdle *noun*
girdles
girl *noun*
girls
girlfriend *noun*
girlfriends
girlhood *noun*
girlish *adjective*
girth *noun*
girths
gist *noun*
give *verb*
gives
giving
gave
given
given *adjective* SEE **give**
giver *noun*
givers
glacial *adjective*
glacier *noun*
glaciers
glad *adjective*
gladder
gladdest
gladly *adverb*
gladden *verb*
gladdens
gladdening
gladdened
gladiator *noun*
gladiators
gladness *noun*
glamorize *verb*
glamorizes
glamorizing
glamorized
glamorous *adjective*
glamorously *adverb*
glamour *noun*
glance *verb*
glances
glancing
glanced
glance *noun*
glances
gland *noun*
glands
glandular *adjective*
glare *verb*
glares
glaring
glared

* To **gild** something is to cover it with gold. **! guild.**

glare *noun*
glares
glass *noun*
glasses
glassful *noun*
glassfuls
glassy *adjective*
glassier
glassiest
glaze *verb*
glazes
glazing
glazed
glaze *noun*
glazes
glazier *noun*
glaziers
gleam *noun*
gleams
gleam *verb*
gleams
gleaming
gleamed
glee *noun*
gleeful *adjective*
gleefully *adverb*
glen *noun*
glens
glide *verb*
glides
gliding
glided
glider *noun*
gliders
glimmer *verb*
glimmers
glimmering
glimmered
glimmer *noun*
glimmers
glimpse *verb*
glimpses
glimpsing
glimpsed
glimpse *noun*
glimpses
glint *verb*
glints
glinting
glinted
glint *noun*
glints
glisten *verb*
glistens
glistening
glistened
glitter *verb*
glitters
glittering
glittered
gloat *verb*
gloats
gloating
gloated
global *adjective*
globally *adverb*
globalization *noun*
globe *noun*
globes
gloom *noun*
gloominess *noun*
gloomy *adjective*
gloomier
gloomiest
gloomily *adverb*
glorification *noun*
glorify *verb*
glorifies
glorifying
glorified
glorious *adjective*
gloriously *adverb*
glory *noun*
glories
gloss *noun*
glosses
glossary *noun*
glossaries
glossy *adjective*
glossier
glossiest
glove *noun*
gloves
glow *verb*
glows
glowing
glowed
glow *noun*
glows
glower *verb*
glowers
glowering
glowered
glow-worm *noun*
glow-worms
glucose *noun*
glue *noun*
glues
glue *verb*
glues
gluing
glued
gluey *adjective*
glum *adjective*
glummer
glummest
glumly *adverb*
glutton *noun*
gluttons
gluttonous *adjective*
gluttony *noun*
GM *adjective*
gnarled* *adjective*
gnash* *verb*
gnashes
gnashing
gnashed
gnat* *noun*
gnats
gnaw* *verb*
gnaws
gnawing
gnawed
gnome* *noun*
gnomes
gnu *noun*
gnus

* In these words beginning with **gn-** the 'g' is silent.

Try also words beginning with **gh-** or **gu-**

a b c d e f g h i j k l m n o p q r s t u v w x y z

go *verb*
goes
going
went
gone
go *noun*
goes
goal *noun*
goals
goalie *noun*
goalies
goalkeeper *noun*
goalkeepers
goalpost *noun*
goalposts
goat *noun*
goats
gobble *verb*
gobbles
gobbling
gobbled
gobbledegook *noun*
goblet *noun*
goblets
goblin *noun*
goblins
God★ *noun*
god☆ *noun*
gods
godchild *noun*
godchildren
goddess *noun*
goddesses
godparent *noun*
godparents
goggles *plural noun*
gold *noun*
golden *adjective*
goldfinch *noun*
goldfinches
goldfish *noun*
goldfish
golf *noun*
golfer *noun*
golfers
golfing *noun*
gondola *noun*
gondolas
gondolier *noun*
gondoliers
gone *verb* SEE **go**
gong *noun*
gongs
good *adjective*
better
best
goodbye *interjection*
Good Friday *noun*
good-looking *adjective*
good-natured *adjective*
goodness *noun*
goodnight *noun*
goods *plural noun*
goodwill *noun*
gooey *adjective*
gooier
gooiest
goose *noun*
geese
gooseberry *noun*
gooseberries
gore *verb*
gores
goring
gored
gorge *noun*
gorges
gorgeous *adjective*
gorgeously *adverb*
gorilla✪ *noun*
gorillas
gorse *noun*
gory *adjective*
gorier
goriest
gosling *noun*
goslings
gospel *noun*
gospels
gossip *verb*
gossips
gossiping
gossiped
gossip *noun*
gossips
got *verb* SEE **get**
gouge *verb*
gouges
gouging
gouged
gourd *noun*
gourds
govern *verb*
governs
governing
governed
government *noun*
governments
governor *noun*
governors
gown *noun*
gowns
GP *noun*
GPs
grab *verb*
grabs
grabbing
grabbed
grace *noun*
graces
graceful *adjective*
gracefully *adverb*
gracefulness *noun*
gracious *adjective*
graciously *adverb*
grade *noun*
grades

★ You use a capital G when you mean the Christian, Jewish, and Muslim creator.
☆ You use a small g when you mean any male divine being.
✪ A **gorilla** is a large ape. **! guerrilla**.

Try also words beginning with **gh-** or **gu-**

grade *verb*
grades
grading
graded

gradient *noun*
gradients

gradual *adjective*
gradually *adverb*

graduate *noun*
graduates

graduate *verb*
graduates
graduating
graduated

graduation *noun*

graffiti *noun*

grain *noun*
grains

grainy *adjective*
grainier
grainiest

gram *noun*
grams

grammar *noun*
grammars

grammatical *adjective*
grammatically *adverb*

gramophone *noun*
gramophones

grand *adjective*
grander
grandest
grandly *adverb*

grandad *noun*
grandads

grandchild *noun*
grandchildren

granddaughter *noun*
granddaughters

grandeur *noun*

grandfather *noun*
grandfathers

grandma *noun*
grandmas

grandmother *noun*
grandmothers

grandpa *noun*
grandpas

grandparent *noun*
grandparents

grandson *noun*
grandsons

grandstand *noun*
grandstands

granite *noun*

granny *noun*
grannies

grant *verb*
grants
granting
granted

grant *noun*
grants

granulated *adjective*

grape *noun*
grapes

grapefruit *noun*
grapefruit

grapevine *noun*
grapevines

graph *noun*
graphs

graphic *adjective*
graphically

graphics *plural noun*

graphite *noun*

-graphy *suffix*
-graphy makes words for subjects of study, e.g. **geography** (the study of the earth). A **bibliography** is a list of books on a subject, and the plural is **bibliographies**.

grapple *verb*
grapples
grappling
grappled

grasp *verb*
grasps
grasping
grasped

grasp *noun*
grasps

grass *noun*
grasses

grasshopper *noun*
grasshoppers

grassy *adjective*
grassier
grassiest

grate★ *verb*
grates
grating
grated

grate☆ *noun*
grates

grateful *adjective*
gratefully *adverb*

grating *noun*
gratings

gratitude *noun*

grave *noun*
graves

grave *adjective*
graver
gravest
gravely *adverb*

gravel *noun*

gravelled *adjective*

gravestone *noun*
gravestones

graveyard *noun*
graveyards

gravitation *noun*

gravitational *adjective*

gravity *noun*

gravy *noun*

★ To **grate** something is to shred it. **! great.**
☆ A **grate** is a replace. **! great.**

Try also words beginning with **gh-** or **gu-**

graze *verb*
grazes
grazing
grazed
graze *noun*
grazes
grease *noun*
greasy *adjective*
greasier
greasiest
great *adjective*
greater
greatest
greatly *adverb*
greatness *noun*
greed *noun*
greediness *noun*
greedy *adjective*
greedier
greediest
greedily *adverb*
green *adjective* & *noun*
greener
greenest
greenery *noun*
greengage *noun*
greengages
greengrocer *noun*
greengrocers
greenhouse *noun*
greenhouses
greens *plural noun*
greet *verb*
greets
greeting
greeted
greeting *noun*
greetings
grenade *noun*
grenades
grew *verb* SEE **grow**
grey *adjective* & *noun*
greyer
greyest

greyhound *noun*
greyhounds
grid *noun*
grids
grief *noun*
grievance *noun*
grievances
grieve *verb*
grieves
grieving
grieved
grievous★ *adjective*
grievously *adverb*
grill *verb*
grills
grilling
grilled
grill *noun*
grills
grim *adjective*
grimmer
grimmest
grimly *adverb*
grimace *noun*
grimaces
grime *noun*
grimness *noun*
grimy *adjective*
grimier
grimiest
grin *noun*
grins
grin *verb*
grins
grinning
grinned
grind *verb*
grinds
grinding
ground
grinder *noun*
grinders
grindstone *noun*
grindstones

grip *verb*
grips
gripping
gripped
grip *noun*
grips
grisly☆ *adjective*
grislier
grisliest
gristle *noun*
gristly *adjective*
grit *verb*
grits
gritting
gritted
grit *noun*
gritty *adjective*
grittier
grittiest
grizzly✪ *adjective*
groan *verb*
groans
groaning
groaned
groan *noun*
groans
grocer *noun*
grocers
grocery *noun*
groceries
groggy *adjective*
groggier
groggiest
groin *noun*
groins
groom *verb*
grooms
grooming
groomed
groom *noun*
grooms
groove *noun*
grooves

★ Note that this word does not end *-ious*.
☆ **Grisly** means 'revolting' or 'horrible'. **! grizzly**.
✪ You use **grizzly** in *grizzly bear*. **! grisly**.

Try also words beginning with **gh-** or **gu-**

grope *verb*
gropes
groping
groped
gross *adjective*
grosser
grossest
grossly *adverb*
gross *noun*
gross
grossness *noun*
grotesque★ *adjective*
grotesquely *adverb*
grotty *adjective*
grottier
grottiest
ground *noun*
grounds
ground *verb* SEE **grind**
grounded *adjective*
grounds *plural noun*
groundsheet *noun*
groundsheets
groundsman *noun*
groundsmen
group *noun*
groups
group *verb*
groups
grouping
grouped
grouse *verb*
grouses
grousing
groused
grouse *noun*
grouse
grove *noun*
groves
grovel *verb*
grovels
grovelling
grovelled

grow *verb*
grows
growing
grew
grown
grower *noun*
growers
growl *verb*
growls
growling
growled
growl *noun*
growls
grown-up *noun*
grown-ups
growth *noun*
growths
grub *noun*
grubs
grubby *adjective*
grubbier
grubbiest
grudge *verb*
grudges
grudging
grudged
grudge *noun*
grudges
grudgingly *adverb*
gruelling *adjective*
gruesome *adjective*
gruff *adjective*
gruffer
gruffest
gruffly *adverb*
grumble *verb*
grumbles
grumbling
grumbled
grumbler *noun*
grumblers
grumpiness *noun*

grumpy *adjective*
grumpier
grumpiest
grumpily *adverb*
grunt *verb*
grunts
grunting
grunted
grunt *noun*
grunts
guarantee *noun*
guarantees
guarantee *verb*
guarantees
guaranteeing
guaranteed
guard *verb*
guards
guarding
guarded
guard *noun*
guards
guardian *noun*
guardians
guardianship *noun*
guerrilla☆ *noun*
guerrillas
guess *verb*
guesses
guessing
guessed
guess *noun*
guesses
guesswork
guest *noun*
guests
guidance *noun*
guide *verb*
guides
guiding
guided
guide *noun*
guides
guidelines *plural noun*

★ **Grotesque** means ‘strange’ and ‘ugly’. It sounds like ‘grotesk’.
☆ A **guerrilla** is a member of a small army. **! gorilla**.

a b c d e f g h i j k l m n o p q r s t u v w x y z

guild★ *noun*
guilds

guillotine *noun*
guillotines

guilt *noun*

guilty *adjective*
guiltier
guiltiest

guinea *noun*
guineas

guinea pig *noun*
guinea pigs

guitar *noun*
guitars

guitarist *noun*
guitarists

gulf *noun*
gulfs

gull *noun*
gulls

gullet *noun*
gullets

gullible *adjective*

gully *noun*
gullies

gulp *verb*
gulps
gulping
gulped

gulp *noun*
gulps

gum *noun*
gums

gum *verb*
gums
gumming
gummed

gummy *adjective*

gun *noun*
guns

gun *verb*
guns
gunning
gunned

gunboat *noun*
gunboats

gunfire

gunman *noun*
gunmen

gunner *noun*
gunners

gunpowder *noun*

gunshot *noun*
gunshots

gurdwara☆ *noun*
gurdwaras

gurgle *verb*
gurgles
gurgling
gurgled

guru *noun*
gurus

Guru Granth Sahib✪
noun

gush *verb*
gushes
gushing
gushed

gust *noun*
gusts

gusty *adjective*
gustier
gustiest

gut *noun*
guts

gut *verb*
guts
gutting
gutted

gutter *noun*
gutters

guy *noun*
guys

guzzle *verb*
guzzles
guzzling
guzzled

gym *noun*
gyms

gymkhana *noun*
gymkhanas

gymnasium *noun*
gymnasiums

gymnast *noun*
gymnasts

gymnastics *plural noun*

gypsy *noun*
gypsies

gyro *noun*
gyros

gyroscope *noun*
gyroscopes

★ A **guild** is an organization of people. **! gild**.
☆ A Sikh place of worship.
✪ The holy book of Sikhs.

Hh

habit *noun*
habits
habitat *noun*
habitats
habitual *adjective*
habitually *adverb*
hack *verb*
hacks
hacking
hacked
hacker *noun*
hackers
hacksaw *noun*
hacksaws
had *verb* SEE **have**
haddock *noun*
haddock
hadn't *verb*
hag *noun*
hags
haggard *adjective*
haggis *noun*
haggises
haggle *verb*
haggles
haggling
haggled
haiku★ *noun*
haiku *or* haikus
hail *verb*
hails
hailing
hailed
hail *noun*
hailstone *noun*
hailstones
hair☆ *noun*
hairs
hairbrush *noun*
hairbrushes
haircut *noun*
haircuts
hairdresser *noun*
hairdressers
hairpin *noun*
hairpins
hair-raising *adjective*
hairstyle *noun*
hairstyles
hairy *adjective*
hairier
hairiest
hajj *noun*
hake *noun*
hake
halal *noun*
half *adjective & noun*
halves
half-baked *adjective*
half-hearted *adjective*
half-heartedly *adverb*
half-life *noun*
half-lives *or* half-lifes
half mast *noun*
halfpenny✪ *noun*
halfpennies *or* halfpence
half-term *noun*
half-terms
half-time *noun*
half-times
halfway *adjective & adverb*
halibut *noun*
halibut
hall✣ *noun*
halls
hallo *interjection*
Halloween● *noun*
hallucination *noun*
hallucinations
halo *noun*
haloes
halt *verb*
halts
halting
halted
halt *noun*
halts
halter *noun*
halters
halting *adjective*
haltingly *adverb*
halve *verb*
halves
halving
halved
halves *plural noun* SEE **half**
ham *noun*
hams
hamburger *noun*
hamburgers
hammer *noun*
hammers

★ A Japanese poem.
☆ **Hair** is the covering on the head. **! hare.**
✪ You use **halfpennies** when you mean several coins and **halfpence** for a sum of money.
✣ A **hall** is a large space in a building. **! haul.**
● You will also see this word spelled *Hallowe'en*.

Try also words beginning with **wh-**

hammer *verb*
hammers
hammering
hammered
hammock *noun*
hammocks
hamper *verb*
hampers
hampering
hampered
hamper *noun*
hampers
hamster *noun*
hamsters
hand *noun*
hands
hand *verb*
hands
handing
handed
handbag *noun*
handbags
handbook *noun*
handbooks
handcuff *verb*
handcuffs
handcuffing
handcuffed
handcuffs *plural noun*
handful *noun*
handfuls
handicap *noun*
handicaps
handicapped *adjective*
handicraft *noun*
handicrafts
handiwork *noun*
handkerchief *noun*
handkerchiefs
handle *noun*
handles
handle *verb*
handles
handling
handled
handlebars *plural noun*
handler *noun*
handrail *noun*
handrails
handsome *adjective*
handsomer
handsomest
handsomely *adverb*
hands-on *adjective*
handstand *noun*
handstands
handwriting *noun*
handwritten *adjective*
handy *adjective*
handier
handiest
handyman *noun*
handymen
hang *verb*
hangs
hanging
hung
hangar★ *noun*
hangars
hanger☆ *noun*
hangers
hang-glider *noun*
hang-gliders
hang-gliding *noun*
hangman *noun*
hangmen
hangover *noun*
hangovers
hank *noun*
hanks
hanker *verb*
hankers
hankering
hankered
hanky *noun*
hankies
Hanukkah✪ *noun*
haphazard *adjective*
haphazardly *adverb*
happen *verb*
happens
happening
happened
happening *noun*
happenings
happiness *noun*
happy *adjective*
happier
happiest
happily *adverb*
happy-go-lucky *adjective*
harass✢ *verb*
harasses
harassing
harassed
harassment *noun*
harbour *noun*
harbours
harbour *verb*
harbours
harbouring
harboured
hard *adjective*
harder
hardest
hard *adverb*
harder
hardest
hardboard *noun*
hard-boiled *adjective*
hard disk *noun*
hard disks
harden *verb*
hardens
hardening
hardened
hardly *adverb*
hardness *noun*
hardship *noun*
hardships
hardware *noun*

★ A **hangar** is a shed for aircraft. **! hanger**.
☆ A **hanger** is a thing for hanging clothes on. **! hangar**.
✪ A Jewish festival.
✢ Note that there is only one 'r' in **harass** and **harassment**.

hardwood *noun*
hardwoods
hardy *adjective*
hardier
hardiest
hare★ *noun*
hares
hark *verb*
harks
harking
harked
harm *verb*
harms
harming
harmed
harm *noun*
harmful *adjective*
harmfully *adverb*
harmless *adjective*
harmlessly *adverb*
harmonic *adjective*
harmonica *noun*
harmonicas
harmonious *adjective*
harmoniously *adverb*
harmonization *noun*
harmonize *verb*
harmonizes
harmonizing
harmonized
harmony *noun*
harmonies
harness *verb*
harnesses
harnessing
harnessed
harness *noun*
harnesses
harp *noun*
harps
harp *verb*
harps
harping
harped

harpist *noun*
harpists
harpoon *noun*
harpoons
harpsichord *noun*
harpsichords
harrow *noun*
harrows
harsh *adjective*
harsher
harshest
harshly *adverb*
harshness *noun*
harvest *noun*
harvests
harvest *verb*
harvests
harvesting
harvested
has *verb* SEE **have**
hash *noun*
hashes
hasn't *verb*
hassle *noun*
hassles
haste *noun*
hasten *verb*
hastens
hastening
hastened
hastiness *noun*
hasty *adjective*
hastier
hastiest
hastily *adverb*
hat *noun*
hats
hatch *verb*
hatches
hatching
hatched
hatch *noun*
hatches
hatchback *noun*
hatchbacks

hatchet *noun*
hatchets
hate *verb*
hates
hating
hated
hate *noun*
hates
hateful *adjective*
hatred *noun*
hat-trick *noun*
hat-tricks
haughtiness *noun*
haughty *adjective*
haughtier
haughtiest
haughtily *adverb*
haul☆ *verb*
hauls
hauling
hauled
haul *noun*
hauls
haunt *verb*
haunts
haunting
haunted
have *verb*
has
having
had
haven *noun*
havens
haven't *verb*
haversack *noun*
haversacks
havoc *noun*
hawk *noun*
hawks
hawk *verb*
hawks
hawking
hawked
hawthorn *noun*
hawthorns

★ A **hare** is an animal like a large rabbit. **! hair.**
☆ To **haul** is to pull something heavy. **! hall.**

a b c d e f g **h** i j k l m n o p q r s t u v w x y z

hay *noun*
hay fever *noun*
haymaking *noun*
haystack *noun*
haystacks
hazard *noun*
hazards
hazardous *adjective*
haze *noun*
hazes
hazel *noun*
hazels
haziness *noun*
hazy *adjective*
hazier
haziest
hazily *adverb*
H-bomb *noun*
H-bombs
he *pronoun*
head *noun*
heads
head *verb*
heads
heading
headed
headache *noun*
headaches
headdress *noun*
headdresses
header *noun*
headers
heading *noun*
headings
headland *noun*
headlands
headless *adjective*
headlight *noun*
headlights
headline *noun*
headlines
headlong *adverb* & *adjective*
headmaster *noun*
headmasters
headmistress *noun*
headmistresses
head-on *adverb* & *adjective*
headphones *plural noun*
headquarters *noun*
headquarters
headteacher *noun*
headteachers
headway *noun*
heal *verb*
heals
healing
healed
healer *noun*
healers
health *noun*
healthiness *noun*
healthy *adjective*
healthier
healthiest
healthily *adverb*
heap *verb*
heaps
heaping
heaped
heap *noun*
heaps
hear★ *verb*
hears
hearing
heard
hearing *noun*
hearings
hearse *noun*
hearses
heart *noun*
hearts
hearth *noun*
hearths
heartiness *noun*
heartless *adjective*
hearty *adjective*
heartier
heartiest
heartily *adverb*
heat *verb*
heats
heating
heated
heat *noun*
heats
heater *noun*
heaters
heath *noun*
heaths
heathen *noun*
heathens
heather *noun*
heatwave *noun*
heatwaves
heave☆ *verb*
heaves
heaving
heaved
hove
heaven *noun*
heavenly *adjective*
heaviness
heavy *adjective*
heavier
heaviest
heavily *adverb*
heavyweight *noun*
heavyweights
Hebrew *noun*
hectare *noun*
hectares
hectic *adjective*
hectically *adverb*
he'd *verb*
hedge *noun*
hedges
hedge *verb*
hedges
hedging
hedged

★ You use **hear** in e.g. *I can't hear you.* **! here.**
☆ You use **hove** in e.g. *the ship hove to.*

hedgehog *noun*
hedgehogs
hedgerow *noun*
hedgerows
heed *verb*
heeds
heeding
heeded
heed *noun*
heedless *adjective*
heel *noun*
heels
heel *verb*
heels
heeling
heeled
hefty *adjective*
heftier
heftiest
heifer *noun*
heifers
height *noun*
heights
heighten *verb*
heightens
heightening
heightened
heir★ *noun*
heirs
heiress *noun*
heiresses
held *verb* SEE **hold**
helicopter *noun*
helicopters
helium *noun*
helix *noun*
helices
hell *noun*
he'll *verb*
hellish *adjective*
hellishly *adverb*
hello *interjection*
helm *noun*
helms
helmsman *noun*
helmsmen
helmet *noun*
helmets
helmeted *adjective*
help *verb*
helps
helping
helped
help *noun*
helps
helper *noun*
helpers
helpful *adjective*
helpfully *adverb*
helping *noun*
helpings
helpless *adjective*
helplessly *adverb*
helter-skelter *noun*
helter-skelters
hem *noun*
hems
hem *verb*
hems
hemming
hemmed
hemisphere *noun*
hemispheres
hemp *noun*
hence *adverb*
henceforth *adverb*
henceforward *adverb*
heptagon *noun*
heptagons
her *pronoun*
herald *noun*
heralds
herald *verb*
heralds
heralding
heralded
heraldic *adjective*
heraldry *noun*
herb *noun*
herbs
herbal *adjective*
herbicide *noun*
herbicides
herbivore *noun*
herbivores
herd *noun*
herds
herd☆ *verb*
herds
herding
herded
here✪ *adverb*
hereditary *adjective*
heredity *noun*
heritage *noun*
heritages
hermit *noun*
hermits
hermitage *noun*
hero *noun*
heroes
heroic *adjective*
heroically *adverb*
heroin✣ *noun*
heroine● *noun*
heroines
heroism *noun*
heron *noun*
herons
herring *noun*
herring *or* herrings
hers✱ *posessive pronoun*

★ You do not pronounce the 'h' in **heir** (sounds like *air*).
☆ A **herd** is a group of sheep. **! heard**.
✪ You use **here** in e.g. *come here*. **! hear**.
✣ **Heroin** is a drug. **! heroine**.
● A **heroine** is a woman or girl in a story. **! heroin**.
✱ You use **hers** in e.g. *the book is hers*. Note that there is no apostrophe in this word.

Try also words beginning with **wh-**

herself *pronoun*
he's *verb*
hesitant *adjective*
hesitantly *adverb*
hesitate *verb*
hesitates
hesitating
hesitated
hesitation *noun*
hexagon *noun*
hexagons
hexagonal *adjective*
hibernate *verb*
hibernates
hibernating
hibernated
hibernation *noun*
hiccup *noun*
hiccups
hide *verb*
hides
hiding
hidden
hid
hidden
hide-and-seek *noun*
hideous *adjective*
hideously *adverb*
hideout *noun*
hideouts
hiding *noun*
hidings
hierarchy *noun*
hierarchies
hieroglyphics *plural noun*
higgledy-piggledy *adjective*
high *adjective*
higher
highest
highland *adjective*
highlands *plural noun*
highlander *noun*
highlanders
highlight *noun*
highlights
highlight *verb*
highlights
highlighting
highlighted
highlighter *noun*
highlighters
highly *adverb*
Highness *noun*
Highnesses
high-rise *adjective*
highway *noun*
highways
highwayman *noun*
highwaymen
hijack *verb*
hijacks
hijacking
hijacked
hijacker *noun*
hijackers
hike *verb*
hikes
hiking
hiked
hike *noun*
hikes
hiker *noun*
hikers
hilarious *adjective*
hilariously *adverb*
hilarity *noun*
hill *noun*
hills
hillside *noun*
hillsides
hilly *adjective*
hillier
hilliest
hilt *noun*
hilts
him *pronoun*
himself *pronoun*
hind *adjective*
hind *noun*
hinds
hinder *verb*
hinders
hindering
hindered
Hindi *noun*
hindrance *noun*
hindrances
hindsight *noun*
Hindu *noun*
Hindus
Hinduism *noun*
hinge *noun*
hinges
hinge *verb*
hinges
hinging
hinged
hint *noun*
hints
hint *verb*
hints
hinting
hinted
hip *noun*
hips
hippo *noun*
hippos
hippopotamus *noun*
hippopotamuses
hire *verb*
hires
hiring
hired
his *posessive pronoun*
hiss *verb*
hisses
hissing
hissed
histogram *noun*
histograms
historian *noun*
historians
historic *adjective*
historical *adjective*
historically *adverb*
history *noun*
histories

Try also words beginning with **wh-**

hit *verb*
hits
hitting
hit

hit *noun*
hits

hitch *verb*
hitches
hitching
hitched

hitch *noun*
hitches

hitch-hike *verb*
hitch-hikes
hitch-hiking
hitch-hiked

hitch-hiker *noun*
hitch-hikers

hi-tech *adjective*

hither *adverb*

hitherto *adverb*

HIV *noun*

hive *noun*
hives

hoard *verb*
hoards
hoarding
hoarded

hoard★ *noun*
hoards

hoarder *noun*
hoarders

hoarding *noun*
hoardings

hoar frost *noun*

hoarse☆ *adjective*
hoarser
hoarsest
hoarsely *adverb*

hoax *verb*
hoaxes
hoaxing
hoaxed

hoax *noun*
hoaxes

hobble *verb*
hobbles
hobbling
hobbled

hobby *noun*
hobbies

hockey *noun*

hoe *noun*
hoes

hoe *verb*
hoes
hoeing
hoed

hog *noun*
hogs

hog *verb*
hogs
hogging
hogged

Hogmanay *noun*

hoist *verb*
hoists
hoisting
hoisted

hold *verb*
holds
holding
held

hold *noun*
holds

holdall *noun*
holdalls

holder *noun*
holders

hold-up *noun*
hold-ups

hole✪ *noun*
holes

holey✣ *adjective*

Holi● *noun*

holiday *noun*
holidays

holiness *noun*

hollow *adjective & adverb*

hollow *verb*
hollows
hollowing
hollowed

hollow *noun*
hollows

holly *noun*

holocaust *noun*
holocausts

hologram *noun*
holograms

holster *noun*
holsters

holy✱ *adjective*
holier
holiest

home *noun*
homes

home *verb*
homes
homing
homed

homeless *adjective*

homely *adverb*

home-made *adjective*

homesick *adjective*

homesickness *noun*

homestead *noun*
homesteads

homeward *adjective*

homewards *adjective & adverb*

★ A **hoard** is a secret store. **! horde.**
☆ A **hoarse** voice is rough or croaking. **! horse.**
✪ A **hole** is a gap or opening. **! whole.**
✣ **Holey** means 'full of holes'. **! holy.**
● A Hindu festival.
✱ You use **holy** in e.g. *a holy man.* **! holey.**

a b c d e f g **h** i j k l m n o p q r s t u v w x y z

homework *noun*
homicide *noun*
homicides
homing *adjective*
homosexual *adjective & noun*
homosexuals
honest *adjective*
honestly *adverb*
honesty *noun*
honey *noun*
honeys
honeycomb *noun*
honeycombs
honeymoon *noun*
honeymoons
honeysuckle *noun*
honk *verb*
honks
honking
honked
honk *noun*
honks
honour *verb*
honours
honouring
honoured
honour *noun*
honours
honourable *adjective*
honourably *adverb*
hood *noun*
hoods

> **-hood** *suffix*
> *-hood* makes nouns, e.g. **childhood**. Other noun suffixes are **-dom**, **-ment**, **-ness**, and **-ship**.

hooded *adjective*
hoof *noun*
hoofs
hook *noun*
hooks
hook *verb*
hooks
hooking
hooked
hooligan *noun*
hooligans
hoop *noun*
hoops
hoopla *noun*
hooray *interjection*
hoot *verb*
hoots
hooting
hooted
hoot *noun*
hoots
hooter *noun*
hooters
hop *verb*
hops
hopping
hopped
hop *noun*
hops
hope *verb*
hopes
hoping
hoped
hope *noun*
hopes
hopeful *adjective*
hopefully *adverb*
hopeless *adjective*
hopelessly *adverb*
hopscotch *noun*
horde* *noun*
hordes
horizon *noun*
horizons
horizontal *adjective*
horizontally *adverb*
hormone *noun*
hormones
horn *noun*
horns
hornet *noun*
hornets
horoscope *noun*
horoscopes
horrendous *adjective*
horrendously *adverb*
horrible *adjective*
horribly *adverb*
horrid *adjective*
horrific *adjective*
horrifically *adverb*
horrify *verb*
horrifies
horrifying
horrified
horror *noun*
horrors
horse *noun*
horses
horseback *noun*
horseman *noun*
horsemen
horsemanship *noun*
horsepower *noun*
horsepower
horseshoe *noun*
horseshoes
horsewoman *noun*
horsewomen
horticulture *noun*
hose *noun*
hoses
hospitable *adjective*
hospitably
hospital *noun*
hospitals
hospitality *noun*
host *noun*
hosts
host *verb*
hosts
hosting
hosted
hostage *noun*
hostages

* A **horde** is a large crowd. **! hoard**.

Try also words beginning with **wh-**

hostel *noun*
hostels
hostess *noun*
hostesses
hostile *adjective*
hostility *noun*
hostilities
hot *adjective*
hotter
hottest
hotly *adverb*
hot *verb*
hots
hotting
hotted
hotel *noun*
hotels
hothouse *noun*
hothouses
hotpot *noun*
hotpots
hound *noun*
hounds
hound *verb*
hounds
hounding
hounded
hour* *noun*
hours
hourglass *noun*
hourglasses
hourly *adjective* & *adverb*
house *noun*
houses
house *verb*
houses
housing
housed
houseboat *noun*
houseboats
household *noun*
households
householder *noun*
householders
housekeeper *noun*
housekeepers
housekeeping *noun*
housewife *noun*
housewives
housework *noun*
housing *noun*
hove *verb* SEE **heave**
hover *verb*
hovers
hovering
hovered
hovercraft *noun*
hovercraft
however *adverb*
howl *verb*
howls
howling
howled
howl *noun*
howls
howler *noun*
howlers
hub *noun*
hubs
huddle *verb*
huddles
huddling
huddled
hue *noun*
hues
huff *noun*
huffs
hug *verb*
hugs
hugging
hugged
hug *noun*
hugs
huge *adjective*
huger
hugest
hugely *adverb*
hugeness *noun*
hulk *noun*
hulks
hulking *adjective*
hull *noun*
hulls
hullabaloo *noun*
hullabaloos
hullo *interjection*
hum *verb*
hums
humming
hummed
hum *noun*
hums
human *adjective* & *noun*
humans
humane *adjective*
humanely *adverb*
humanitarian *adjective*
humanity *noun*
humanities
humble *adjective*
humbler
humblest
humbly *adverb*
humid *adjective*
humidity *noun*
humiliate *verb*
humiliates
humiliating
humiliated
humiliation *noun*
humility *noun*
hummingbird *noun*
hummingbirds
humorous *adjective*
humorously *adverb*
humour *noun*
humour *verb*
humours
humouring
humoured
hump *noun*
humps
hump *verb*
humps
humping
humped

* An **hour** is a measure of time. **! our**.

Try also words beginning with **wh-**

a
b
c
d
e
f
g
h
i
j
k
l
m
n
o
p
q
r
s
t
u
v
w
x
y
z

humpback *noun*

humus *noun*

hunch *verb*
hunches
hunching
hunched

hunch *noun*
hunches

hundred *noun*
hundreds

hundredth *adjective & noun*

hundredweight *noun*
hundredweights

hung *verb* SEE **hang**

hunger *noun*

hungriness *noun*

hungry *adjective*
hungrier
hungriest
hungrily *adverb*

hunk *noun*
hunks

hunt *verb*
hunts
hunting
hunted

hunt *noun*
hunts

hunter *noun*
hunters

hurdle *noun*
hurdles

hurdler *noun*
hurdlers

hurdling *noun*

hurl *verb*
hurls
hurling
hurled

hurrah *or* **hurray** *interjection*

hurricane *noun*
hurricanes

hurriedly *adverb*

hurry *verb*
hurries
hurrying
hurried

hurry *noun*
hurries

hurt *verb*
hurts
hurting
hurt

hurt *noun*

hurtful *adjective*

hurtle *verb*
hurtles
hurtling
hurtled

husband *noun*
husbands

hush *verb*
hushes
hushing
hushed

hush *noun*

husk *noun*
husks

huskiness *noun*

husky *adjective*
huskier
huskiest
huskily *adverb*

husky *noun*
huskies

hustle *verb*
hustles
hustling
hustled

hutch *noun*
hutches

hyacinth *noun*
hyacinths

hybrid *noun*
hybrids

hydrangea *noun*
hydrangeas

hydrant *noun*
hydrants

hydraulic *adjective*
hydraulically *adverb*

hydroelectric *adjective*

hydrofoil *noun*
hydrofoils

hydrogen *noun*

hydrophobia *noun*

hyena *noun*
hyenas

hygiene *noun*

hygienic *adjective*
hygienically *adverb*

hymn *noun*
hymns

hyperactive *adjective*

hypermarket *noun*
hypermarkets

hyphen *noun*
hyphens

hyphenated *verb*

hypnosis *noun*

hypnotism *noun*

hypnotist *noun*
hypnotists

hypnotize *verb*
hypnotizes
hypnotizing
hypnotized

hypocrisy *noun*

hypocrite *noun*
hypocrites

hypocritical *adjective*
hypocritically *adverb*

hypodermic *adjective*

hypotenuse *noun*
hypotenuses

hypothermia *noun*

hypothesis *noun*
hypotheses

hypothetical *adjective*
hypothetically *adverb*

hysteria *noun*

hysterical *adjective*
hysterically *adverb*

hysterics *plural noun*

Ii

-i
Most nouns ending in *-i*, e.g. **ski**, **taxi**, have plurals ending in *-is*, e.g. **skis**, **taxis**.

-ible *suffix*
See the note at **-able**.

-ic and **-ically**
Most adjectives ending in *-ic* have adverbs ending in *-ically*, e.g. **heroic** – **heroically**, **scientific** – **scientifically**. An exception is **public**, which has an adverb – **publicly**.

ice *noun*
ices
ice *verb*
ices
icing
iced
iceberg *noun*
icebergs
ice cream *noun*
ice creams
icicle *noun*
icicles
icing *noun*
icon *noun*
icons
ICT *noun*
icy *adjective*
icier
iciest
icily *adverb*
ID *noun*
I'd *verb*
idea *noun*
ideas
ideal *adjective*
ideally *adverb*
ideal *noun*
ideals
identical *adjective*
identically *adverb*
identifiable *adjective*
identification *noun*
identify *verb*
identifies
identifying
identified
identity *noun*
identities
ideology *noun*
ideologies
idiocy *noun*
idiocies
idiom *noun*
idioms
idiomatic *adjective*
idiot *noun*
idiots
idiotic *adjective*
idiotically
idle★ *adjective*
idler
idlest
idly *adverb*
idle *verb*
idles
idling
idled
idol☆ *noun*
idols
idolatry *noun*
idolize *verb*
idolizes
idolizing
idolized

-ie-
See the note at **-ei-**.

igloo *noun*
igloos
igneous *adjective*
ignite *verb*
ignites
igniting
ignited
ignition *noun*
ignorance *noun*
ignorant *adjective*
ignore *verb*
ignores
ignoring
ignored
I'll *verb*
ill *adjective* & *adverb*
illegal *adjective*
illegally *adverb*
illegible *adjective*
illegibly *adverb*
illegitimate *adjective*
illiteracy *noun*
illiterate *adjective*
illness *noun*
illnesses
illogical *adjective*
illogically *adverb*

★ **Idle** means 'lazy'. **! idol.**
☆ An **idol** is someone people admire. **! idle.**

illuminate *verb*
illuminates
illuminating
illuminated

illumination *noun*
illuminations

illusion *noun*
illusions

illustrate *verb*
illustrates
illustrating
illustrated

illustration *noun*
illustrations

illustrious *adjective*

I'm *verb*

image *noun*
images

imagery *noun*

imaginable *adjective*

imaginary *adjective*

imagination *noun*
imaginations

imaginative *adjective*
imaginatively *adverb*

imagine *verb*
imagines
imagining
imagined

imam★ *noun*
imams

imbalance *noun*

imbecile *noun*
imbeciles

imitate *verb*
imitates
imitating
imitated

imitation *noun*
imitations

imitator *noun*
imitators

immature *adjective*

immaturity *noun*

immediate *adjective*
immediately *adverb*

immense *adjective*
immensely

immensity *noun*

immerse *verb*
immerses
immersing
immersed

immersion *noun*

immigrant *noun*
immigrants

immigrate *verb*
immigrates
immigrating
immigrated

immigration *noun*

immobile *adjective*

immobility *noun*

immobilize *verb*
immobilizes
immobilizing
immobilized

immoral *adjective*
immorally *adverb*

immorality *noun*

immortal *adjective*

immortality *noun*

immune *adjective*

immunity *noun*
immunities

immunization *noun*

immunize *verb*
immunizes
immunizing
immunized

imp *noun*
imps

impish *adjective*

impact *noun*
impacts

impair *verb*
impairs
impairing
impaired

impairment *noun*
impairments

impale *verb*
impales
impaling
impaled

impartial *adjective*
impartially *adverb*

impartiality *noun*

impassable *adjective*

impatience *noun*

impatient *adjective*
impatiently *adverb*

impeccable *adjective*
impeccably *adverb*

impede *verb*
impedes
impeding
impeded

imperative *noun & adjective*

imperceptible *adjective*
imperceptibly *adverb*

imperfect *adjective*
imperfectly *adverb*

imperfection *noun*
imperfections

imperial *adjective*

impersonal *adjective*
impersonally *adverb*

impersonate *verb*
impersonates
impersonating
impersonated

impersonation *noun*
impersonations

impersonator *noun*
impersonators

★ A Muslim religious leader.

impertinence *noun*
impertinent *adjective*
impertinently *adverb*
implement *verb*
implements
implementing
implemented
implement *noun*
implements
implication *noun*
implications
implore *verb*
implores
imploring
implored
imply *verb*
implies
implying
implied
impolite *adjective*
impolitely *adverb*
import *verb*
imports
importing
imported
import *noun*
imports
importance *noun*
important *adjective*
importantly *adverb*
importer *noun*
importers
impose *verb*
imposes
imposing
imposed
imposition *noun*
impositions
impossibility *noun*
impossible *adjective*
impossibly *adverb*
impostor *noun*
impostors
impracticable *adjective*
impractical *adjective*
impress *verb*
impresses
impressing
impressed
impression *noun*
impressions
impressive *adjective*
impressively *adverb*
imprison *verb*
imprisons
imprisoning
imprisoned
imprisonment *noun*
improbability *noun*
improbable *adjective*
improbably *adverb*
impromptu *adjective & adverb*
improper *adjective*
improperly *adverb*
impropriety *noun*
improprieties
improve *verb*
improves
improving
improved
improvement *noun*
improvements
improvisation *noun*
improvisations
improvise *verb*
improvises
improvising
improvised
impudence *noun*
impudent *adjective*
impudently *adverb*
impulse *noun*
impulses
impulsive *adjective*
impulsively *adverb*
impure *adjective*
impurity *adjective*
impurities

in- *prefix*
in- makes words with the meaning 'not', e.g. **inedible**, **infertile**. There is a fixed number of these, and you cannot freely add *in-* as you can with *un-*. *in-* changes to *il-* or *im-* before certain sounds, e.g. **illogical**, **impossible**.

inability *noun*
inaccessible *adjective*
inaccuracy *noun*
inaccuracies
inaccurate *adjective*
inaccurately *adverb*
inaction *noun*
inactive *adjective*
inactivity *noun*
inadequacy *noun*
inadequate *adjective*
inadequately *adverb*
inanimate *adjective*
inappropriate *adjective*
inappropriately *adverb*
inattention *noun*
inattentive *adjective*
inaudible *adjective*
inaudibly *adverb*
incapable *adjective*
incapacity *noun*
incendiary *adjective*
incense *noun*
incense *verb*
incenses
incensing
incensed
incentive *noun*
incentives
incessant *adjective*
incessantly *adverb*

inch *noun*
inches

incident *noun*
incidents

incidental *adjective*
incidentally *adverb*

incinerator *noun*
incinerators

incisor *noun*
incisors

inclination *noun*
inclinations

incline *verb*
inclines
inclining
inclined

incline *noun*
inclines

include *verb*
includes
including
included

inclusion *noun*

inclusive *adjective*

income *noun*
incomes

incompatible *adjective*

incompetence *noun*

incompetent *adjective*
incompetently *adverb*

incomplete *adjective*
incompletely *adverb*

incomprehensible *adjective*
incomprehensibly *adverb*

incongruity *noun*

incongruous *adjective*
incongruously *adverb*

inconsiderate *adjective*
inconsiderately *adverb*

inconsistency *noun*
inconsistencies

inconsistent *adjective*

inconspicuous *adjective*
inconspicuously *adverb*

inconvenience *noun*

inconvenient *adjective*
inconveniently *adverb*

incorporate *verb*
incorporates
incorporating
incorporated

incorporation *noun*

incorrect *adjective*
incorrectly *adverb*

increase *verb*
increases
increasing
increased

increase *noun*
increases

increasingly *adverb*

incredible *adjective*
incredibly *adverb*

incredulity *noun*

incredulous *adjective*

incubate *verb*
incubates
incubating
incubated

incubation *noun*

incubator *noun*
incubators

indebted *adjective*

indecency *noun*

indecent *adjective*
indecently *adverb*

indeed *adverb*

indefinite *adjective*
indefinitely *adverb*

indelible *adjective*
indelibly *adverb*

indent *verb*
indents
indenting
indented

indentation *noun*

independence *noun*

independent *adjective*
independently *adverb*

index *noun*
indexes

Indian *adjective & noun*
Indians

indicate *verb*
indicates
indicating
indicated

indication *noun*
indications

indicative *adjective*

indicator *noun*
indicators

indifference *noun*

indifferent *adjective*
indifferently *adverb*

indigestible *adjective*

indigestion *noun*

indiginous *adjective*

indignant *adjective*
indignantly *adverb*

indignation *noun*

indigo *noun*

indirect *adjective*
indirectly *adverb*

indispensable *adjective*

indistinct *adjective*
indistinctly *adverb*

indistinguishable *adjective*

individual *adjective*
individually *adverb*

individual *noun*
individuals

individuality *noun*

indoctrinate *verb*
indoctrinates
indoctrinating
indoctrinated

indoctrination *noun*

indoor *adjective*

indoors *adverb*

induce *verb*
induces
inducing
induced

inducement *noun*
inducements

indulge *verb*
indulges
indulging
indulged

indulgence *noun*
indulgences

indulgent *adjective*

industrial *adjective*

industrialist *noun*
industrialists

industrialization *noun*

industrialize *verb*
industrializes
industrializing
industrialized

industrious *adjective*
industriously *adverb*

industry *noun*
industries

ineffective *adjective*
ineffectively *adverb*

ineffectual *adjective*
ineffectually *adverb*

inefficiency *noun*
inefficiencies

inefficient *adjective*
inefficiently *adverb*

inequality *noun*
inequalities

inert *adjective*

inertia *noun*

inevitability *noun*

inevitable *adjective*
inevitably *adverb*

inexhaustible *adjective*

inexpensive *adjective*
inexpensively *adverb*

inexperience *noun*

inexperienced *adjective*

inexplicable *adjective*
inexplicably *adverb*

infallibility *noun*

infallible *adjective*

infamous *adjective*

infamy *noun*

infancy *noun*

infant *noun*
infants

infantile *adjective*

infantry *noun*

infect *verb*
infects
infecting
infected

infection *noun*
infections

infectious *adjective*
infectiously *adverb*

infer *verb*
infers
inferring
inferred

inference *noun*
inferences

inferior *adjective* & *noun*
inferiors

inferiority *noun*

infernal *adjective*
infernally *adverb*

inferno *noun*
infernos

infested *adjective*

infiltrate *verb*
infiltrates
infiltrating
infiltrated

infiltration *noun*

infinite *adjective*
infinitely *adverb*

infinitive *noun*
infinitives

infinity *noun*

infirm *adjective*

infirmary *noun*
infirmaries

infirmity *noun*

inflame *verb*
inflames
inflaming
inflamed

inflammable *adjective*

inflammation *noun*
inflammations

inflammatory *adjective*

inflatable *adjective*

inflate *verb*
inflates
inflating
inflated

inflation *noun*

inflect *verb*
inflects
inflecting
inflected

inflection *noun*
inflections

inflexibility *noun*

inflexible *adjective*
inflexibly *adverb*

inflict *verb*
inflicts
inflicting
inflicted

influence *verb*
influences
influencing
influenced

influence *noun*
influences

influential *adjective*

influenza *noun*

influx *noun*

inform *verb*
informs
informing
informed

informal *adjective*
informally *adverb*

informality *noun*

informant *noun*
informants

information *noun*

informative *adjective*

informed *adjective & verb*

informer *noun*
informers

infrastructure *noun*

infrequency *noun*

infrequent *adjective*
infrequently *adverb*

infuriate *verb*
infuriates
infuriating
infuriated

infusion *noun*
infusions

> **-ing** *suffix*
> -*ing* makes present participles and nouns, e.g. **hunt - hunting**. You normally drop an *e* at the end, e.g. **change - changing, smoke - smoking**. An exception is **ageing**. Words ending in a consonant following a single vowel double the consonant, e.g. **run - running**.

ingenious *adjective*
ingeniously *ingeniously*

ingenuity *noun*

ingot *noun*
ingots

ingrained *adjective*

ingredient *noun*
ingredients

inhabit *verb*
inhabits
inhabiting
inhabited

inhabitant *noun*
inhabitants

inhale *verb*
inhales
inhaling
inhaled

inhaler *noun*
inhalers

inherent *adjective*
inherently *adverb*

inherit *verb*
inherits
inheriting
inherited

inheritance *noun*

inhibited *adjective*

inhospitable *adjective*

inhuman *adjective*

inhumanity *noun*

initial *adjective*
initially *adverb*

initial *noun*
initials

initiate *verb*
initiates
initiating
initiated

initiation *noun*

initiative *noun*
initiatives

inject *verb*
injects
injecting
injected

injection *noun*
injections

injure *verb*
injures
injuring
injured

injurious *adjective*

injury *noun*
injuries

injustice *noun*
injustices

ink *noun*
inks

inkling *noun*
inklings

inky *adjective*
inkier
inkiest

inland *adjective & adverb*

inlet *noun*
inlets

inn *noun*
inns

innkeeper *noun*
innkeepers

inner *adjective*

innermost *adjective*

innings *noun*
innings

innocence *noun*

innocent *adjective*
innocently *adverb*

innocuous *adjective*
innocuously *adverb*

innovation *noun*
innovations

innovative *adjective*

innovator *noun*
innovators

innumerable *adjective*

inoculate *verb*
inoculates
inoculating
inoculated

inoculation *noun*
innoculations

input *verb*
inputs
inputting
input

input *noun*
inputs

inquest *noun*
inquests

inquire *verb*
inquires
inquiring
inquired

inquiry* *noun*
inquiries
inquisitive *adjective*
inquisitively *adverb*
insane *adjective*
insanely *adverb*
insanitary *adjective*
insanity *noun*
inscribe *verb*
inscribes
inscribing
inscribed
inscription *noun*
inscriptions
insect *noun*
insects
insecticide *noun*
insecticides
insecure *adjective*
insecurely *adverb*
insecurity *noun*
insensitive *adjective*
insensitively *adverb*
insensitivity *noun*
inseparable *adjective*
inseparably *adverb*
insert *verb*
inserts
inserting
inserted
insertion *noun*
insertions
inshore *adjective* & *adverb*
inside *noun*
insides
inside *adverb, adjective, and preposition*
insider *noun*
insiders
insight *noun*
insights
insignificance *noun*
insignificant *adjective*
insignificantly *adverb*
insincere *adjective*
insincerely *adverb*
insincerity *noun*
insist *verb*
insists
insisting
insisted
insistence *noun*
insistent *adjective*
insistently *adverb*
insolence *noun*
insolent *adjective*
insolently *adverb*
insolubility *noun*
insoluble *adjective*
insomnia *noun*
inspect *verb*
inspects
inspecting
inspected
inspection *noun*
inspections
inspector *noun*
inspectors
inspiration *noun*
inspirational *adjective*
inspire *verb*
inspires
inspiring
inspired
install *verb*
installs
installing
installed
installation *noun*
installations
instalment *noun*
instalments
instance *noun*
instances
instant *adjective*
instantly *adverb*
instant *noun*
instants
instantaneous *adjective*
instantaneously *adverb*
instead *adverb*
instep *noun*
insteps
instinct *noun*
instincts
instinctive *adjective*
instinctively *adverb*
institute *verb*
institutes
instituting
instituted
institute *noun*
institutes
institution *noun*
institutions
instruct *verb*
instructs
instructing
instructed
instruction *noun*
instructions
instructor *noun*
instructors
instrument *noun*
instruments
instrumental *adjective*
instrumentalist *noun*
instrumentalists
insufficient *adjective*
insufficiently *adverb*
insulate *verb*
insulates
insulating
insulated
insulation *noun*
insulin *noun*

* An **inquiry** is an official investigation. **! enquiry**.

insult *verb*
insults
insulting
insulted

insult *noun*
insults

insurance *noun*

insure *verb*
insures
insuring
insured

insurgent *noun*
insurgents

intact *adjective*

intake *noun*
intakes

integer *noun*
integers

integral *adjective*

integrate *verb*
integrates
integrating
integrated

integration *noun*

integrity *noun*

intellect *noun*
intellects

intellectual *adjective*
intellectually *adverb*

intellectual *noun*
intellectuals

intelligence *noun*

intelligent *adjective*
intelligently *adverb*

intelligibility *noun*

intelligible *adjective*
intelligibly *adverb*

intend *verb*
intends
intending
intended

intense *adjective*
intensely *adverb*

intensification *noun*

intensify *verb*
intensifies
intensifying
intensified

intensity *noun*
intensities

intensive *adjective*
intensively *adverb*

intent *adjective*
intently *adverb*

intent *noun*
intents

intention *noun*
intentions

intentional *adjective*
intentionally *adverb*

interact *verb*
interacts
interacting
interacted

interaction *noun*

interactive *adjective*

intercept *verb*
intercepts
intercepting
intercepted

interception *noun*

interchange *noun*
interchanges

interchangeable *adjective*

intercom *noun*
intercoms

interdependent *adjective*

interest *verb*
interests
interesting
interested

interest *noun*
interests

interface *noun*
interfaces

interfere *verb*
interferes
interfering
interfered

interference *noun*

interior *noun*
interiors

interjection *noun*
interjections

interlock *verb*
interlocks
interlocking
interlocked

interlude *noun*
interludes

intermediate *adjective*

interminable *adjective*
interminably *adverb*

intermission *noun*
intermissions

intermittent *adjective*
intermittently *adverb*

intern *verb*
interns
interning
interned

internal *adjective*
internally *adverb*

international *adjective*
internationally *adverb*

internee *noun*
internees

internment *noun*

internet *noun*

interplanetary *adjective*

interpret *verb*
interprets
interpreting
interpreted

interpretation *noun*
interpretations

interpreter *noun*
interpreters

interrogate *verb*
interrogates
interrogating
interrogated

interrogation *noun*
interrogations

interrogative *adjective*

interrogator *noun*
interrogators

interrupt *verb*
interrupts
interrupting
interrupted

interruption *noun*
interruptions

intersect *verb*
intersects
intersecting
intersected

intersection *noun*
intersections

interval *noun*
intervals

intervene *verb*
intervenes
intervening
intervened

intervention *noun*
interventions

interview *noun*
interviews

interview *verb*
interviews
interviewing
interviewed

interviewer *noun*
interviewers

intestinal *adjective*

intestine *noun*
intestines

intimacy *noun*

intimate *adjective*
intimately *adverb*

intimate *verb*
intimates
intimating
intimated

intimation *noun*
intimations

intimidate *verb*
intimidates
intimidating
intimidated

intimidation *noun*

into *preposition*

intolerable *adjective*
intolerably *adverb*

intolerance *noun*

intolerant *adjective*

intonation *noun*
intonations

intoxicate *verb*
intoxicates
intoxicating
intoxicated

intoxication *noun*

intransitive *adjective*

intrepid *adjective*
intrepidly *adverb*

intricacy *noun*
intricacies

intricate *adjective*
intricately *adverb*

intrigue *verb*
intrigues
intriguing
intrigued

introduce *verb*
introduces
introducing
introduced

introduction *noun*
introductions

introductory *adjective*

intrude *verb*
intrudes
intruding
intruded

intruder *noun*
intruders

intrusion *noun*
intrusions

intrusive *adjective*

intuition *noun*

intuitive *adjective*
intuitively *adverb*

Inuit *noun*
Inuit
Inuits

inundate *verb*
inundates
inundating
inundated

inundation *noun*
inundations

invade *verb*
invades
invading
invaded

invader *noun*
invaders

invalid *noun*
invalids

invalid *adjective*

invaluable *adjective*

invariable *adjective*
invariably *adverb*

invasion *noun*
invasions

invent *verb*
invents
inventing
invented

invention *noun*
inventions

inventive *adjective*
inventively *adverb*

inventor *noun*
inventors

inverse *noun* & *adjective*
inversely *adverb*

inversion *noun*
inversions

invert *verb*
inverts
inverting
inverted

invertebrate *noun*
invertebrates
invest *verb*
invests
investing
invested
investigate *verb*
investigates
investigating
investigated
investigation *noun*
investigations
investigative *adjective*
investigator *noun*
investigators
investiture *noun*
investitures
investment *noun*
investments
investor *noun*
investors
invigilate *verb*
invigilates
invigilating
invigilated
invigilation *noun*
invigilations
invigilator *noun*
invigilators
invigorate *verb*
invigorates
invigorating
invigorated
invincible *adjective*
invisibility *noun*
invisible *adjective*
invisibly *adverb*
invitation *noun*
invitations
invite *verb*
invites
inviting
invited
invoice *noun*
invoices
involuntary *adjective*
involve *verb*
involves
involving
involved
involvement
inward *adjective*
inwardly *adverb*
inwards *adverb*
iodine *noun*
ion *noun*
ions
iPod® *noun*
iPods®
IQ *noun*
iris *noun*
irises
iron *noun*
irons
iron *verb*
irons
ironing
ironed
ironic *adjective*
ironically *adverb*
ironmonger *noun*
ironmongers
ironmongery *noun*
irony *noun*
ironies
irrational *adjective*
irrationally *adverb*
irregular *adjective*
irregularly *adverb*
irregularity *noun*
irregularities
irrelevance *noun*
irrelevant *adjective*
irresistible *adjective*
irresistibly *adverb*
irresponsible *adjective*
irresponsibly *adverb*
irresponsibility *noun*
irreverence *noun*
irreverent *adjective*
irrigate *verb*
irrigates
irrigating
irrigated
irrigation *noun*
irritability *noun*
irritable *adjective*
irritably *adverb*
irritant *adjective* & *noun*
irritants
irritate *verb*
irritates
irritating
irritated
irritation *noun*
irritations

> **-ish** *suffix*
> -*ish* makes words meaning 'rather' or 'fairly', e.g. **soft - softish**. You normally drop an *e* at the end, e.g. **blue - bluish**. Words ending in a consonant following a single vowel double the consonant, e.g. **fat - fattish**.

Islam *noun*
Islamic *adjective*
island *noun*
islands
islander *noun*
islanders
isle* *noun*
isles
isn't *verb*
isobar *noun*
isobars
isolate *verb*
isolates
isolating
isolated

* An **isle** is a small island. **! aisle**.

isolation *noun*

isosceles *adjective*

isotope *noun*
isotopes

issue *verb*
issues
issuing
issued

issue *noun*
issues

isthmus *noun*
isthmuses

italics *adjective*

itch *verb*
itches
itching
itched

itch *noun*
itches

itchy *adjective*
itchier
itchiest

item *noun*
items

itinerary *noun*
itineraries

it'll *verb*

its★ *possessive pronoun*

it's☆ *verb*

itself *pronoun*

I've *verb*

ivory *adjective* & *noun*
ivories

ivy *noun*

-ize and **-ise**
You can use -*ize* or -*ise* at the end of many verbs, e.g. **realize** or **realise**, **privatize** or **privatise**. This book prefers -*ize*, but some words have to be spelled -*ise*, e.g. **advertise**, **exercise**, **supervise**. Check each spelling if you are not sure.

★ You use **its** in e.g. *the cat licked its paw*. **! it's.**
☆ You use **it's** in *it's* (it is) *raining* and *it's* (it has) *been raining*. **! its.**

Try also words beginning with **ge-**, **gi-**, or **gy-**

Jj

jab *verb*
jabs
jabbing
jabbed
jab *noun*
jabs
jabber *verb*
jabbers
jabbering
jabbered
jack *noun*
jacks
jack *verb*
jacks
jacking
jacked
jackal *noun*
jackals
jackass *noun*
jackasses
jackdaw *noun*
jackdaws
jacket *noun*
jackets
jack-in-the-box *noun*
jack-in-the-boxes
jackknife *verb*
jackknifes
jackknifing
jackknifed
jackpot *noun*
jackpots
jacuzzi *noun*
jacuzzis
jade *noun*
jaded *adjective*
jagged *adjective*
jaguar *noun*
jaguars

jail *noun*
jails
jail *verb*
jails
jailing
jailed
jailer *noun*
jailers
Jain* *noun*
Jains
jam *noun*
jams
jam *verb*
jams
jamming
jammed
jamboree *noun*
jamborees
jammy *adjective*
jammier
jammiest
jangle *verb*
jangles
jangling
jangled
January *noun*
Januaries
Japanese *adjective*
jar *noun*
jars
jar *verb*
jars
jarring
jarred
jargon *noun*
jaundice *noun*
jaunt *noun*
jaunts
jauntiness *noun*

jaunty *adjective*
jauntier
jauntiest
jauntily *adverb*
javelin *noun*
javelins
jaw *noun*
jaws
jay *noun*
jays
jazz *noun*
jazzy *adjective*
jazzier
jazziest
jealous *adjective*
jealously *adverb*
jealousy *noun*
jeans *plural noun*
Jeep *noun*
Jeeps
jeer *verb*
jeers
jeering
jeered
jelly *noun*
jellies
jellyfish *noun*
jellyfish
jeopardy *noun*
jerk *verb*
jerks
jerking
jerked
jerk *noun*
jerks
jerky *adjective*
jerkier
jerkiest
jerkily

* A member of an Indian religion.

Try also words beginning with **ge-**, **gi-**, or **gy-**

jersey *noun*
jerseys
jest *verb*
jests
jesting
jested
jest *noun*
jests
jester *noun*
jesters
jet *noun*
jets
jet *verb*
jets
jetting
jetted
jet-propelled *adjective*
jetty *noun*
jetties
Jew *noun*
Jews
jewel *noun*
jewels
jewelled *adjective*
jeweller *noun*
jewellers
jewellery *noun*
Jewish *adjective*
jib *noun*
jibs
jiffy *noun*
jig *noun*
jigs
jig *verb*
jigs
jigging
jigged
jigsaw *noun*
jigsaws
jihad *noun*
jihads
jingle *verb*
jingles
jingling
jingled
jingle *noun*
jingles

job *noun*
jobs
jobcentre *noun*
jobcentres
jobless *adjective*
jockey *noun*
jockeys
jodhpurs *plural noun*
jog *verb*
jogs
jogging
jogged
jogger *noun*
joggers
jogtrot *noun*
jogtrots
join *verb*
joins
joining
joined
join *noun*
joins
joiner *noun*
joiners
joinery *noun*
joint *noun*
joints
joint *adjective*
jointly *adverb*
joist *noun*
joists
jojoba *noun*
joke *verb*
jokes
joking
joked
joke *noun*
jokes
joker *noun*
jokers
jokingly *adverb*
jollity *noun*
jolly *adjective*
jollier
jolliest

jolly *verb*
jollies
jollying
jollied
jolt *verb*
jolts
jolting
jolted
jolt *noun*
jolts
jostle *verb*
jostles
jostling
jostled
jot *verb*
jots
jotting
jotted
jot *noun*
jots
jotter *noun*
jotters
joule *noun*
joules
journal *noun*
journals
journalism *noun*
journalist *noun*
journalists
journey *noun*
journeys
journey *verb*
journeys
journeying
journeyed
joust *verb*
jousts
jousting
jousted
jovial *adjective*
jovially *adverb*
joviality *noun*
joy *noun*
joys
joyful *adjective*
joyfully *adverb*
joyous *adjective*
joyously *adverb*

a b c d e f g h i **j** k l m n o p q r s t u v w x y z

joyride *noun*
joyrides
joystick *noun*
joysticks
jubilant *adjective*
jubilantly *adverb*
jubilation *noun*
jubilee *noun*
jubilees
Judaism *noun*
judge *verb*
judges
judging
judged
judge *noun*
judges
judgement *noun*
judgements
judicial *adjective*
judicious *adjective*
judo *noun*
jug *noun*
jugs
juggernaut *noun*
juggernauts
juggle *verb*
juggles
juggling
juggled
juggler *noun*
jugglers
juice★ *noun*
juices
juicy *adjective*
juicier
juiciest
jukebox *noun*
jukeboxes
July *noun*
Julys
jumble *verb*
jumbles
jumbling
jumbled
jumble *noun*
jumbo jet *noun*
jumbo jets
jumbo *noun*
jumbos
jump *verb*
jumps
jumping
jumped
jump *noun*
jumps
jumper *noun*
jumpers
jumpy *adjective*
jumpier
jumpiest
junction *noun*
junctions
June *noun*
Junes
jungle *noun*
jungles
jungly *adjective*
junior *adjective* & *noun*
juniors
junk *noun*
junks
juror *noun*
jurors
jury *noun*
juries
just *adjective*
justly *adverb*
just *adverb*
justice *noun*
justices
justifiable *adjective*
justifiably *adverb*
justification *noun*
justify *verb*
justifies
justifying
justified
jut *verb*
juts
jutting
jutted
juvenile *adjective*

★ **Juice** is the liquid from fruit. **! deuce**.

Try also words beginning with **c-**, **ch-**, **kh-**, or **qu-**

Kk

kaleidoscope *noun*
kaleidoscopes

kangaroo *noun*
kangaroos

karaoke *noun*

karate *noun*

karma *noun*

kayak *noun*
kayaks

kebab *noun*
kebabs

keel *noun*
keels

keel *verb*
keels
keeling
keeled

keen *adjective*
keener
keenest
keenly *adverb*

keenness *noun*

keep *verb*
keeps
keeping
kept

keep *noun*
keeps

keeper *noun*
keepers

keg *noun*
kegs

kennel *noun*
kennels

kenning *noun*
kennings

kept *verb* SEE **keep**

kerb★ *noun*
kerbs

kerbstone *noun*
kerbstones

kernel☆ *noun*
kernels

kestrel *noun*
kestrels

ketchup *noun*

kettle *noun*
kettles

kettledrum *noun*
kettledrums

key✪ *noun*
keys

key *verb*
keys
keying
keyed

keyboard *noun*
keyboards

keyhole *noun*
keyholes

khaki *noun*

kibbutz *noun*
kibbutzim

kick *verb*
kicks
kicking
kicked

kick *noun*
kicks

kick-off *noun*
kick-offs

kid *noun*
kids

kid *verb*
kids
kidding
kidded

kidnap *verb*
kidnaps
kidnapping
kidnapped

kidnapper *noun*
kidnappers

kidney *noun*
kidneys

kill *verb*
kills
killing
killed

killer *noun*
killers

kiln *noun*
kilns

kilo *noun*
kilos

kilogram *noun*
kilograms

kilometre *noun*
kilometres

kilowatt *noun*
kilowatts

kilt *noun*
kilts

kimono *noun*
kimonos

★ A **kerb** is the edge of a pavement. **! curb.**
☆ **Kernel** is part of a nut. **! colonel.**
✪ A **key** is a device for opening a lock. **! quay.**

Try also words beginning with **c-**, **ch-**, **kh-**, or **qu-**

a b c d e f g h i j **k** l m n o p q r s t u v w x y z

kin *noun*

kind *adjective*
kinder
kindest
kindly *adverb*

kind *noun*
kinds

kindergarten *noun*
kindergartens

kind hearted *adjective*

kindle *verb*
kindles
kindling
kindled

kindliness *noun*

kindling *noun*

kindly *adjective*
kindlier
kindliest

kindness *noun*

kinetic *adjective*

king *noun*
kings

kingdom *noun*
kingdoms

kingfisher *noun*
kingfishers

kingly *adjective*

kink *noun*
kinks

kiosk *noun*
kiosks

kipper *noun*
kippers

kiss *verb*
kisses
kissing
kissed

kiss *noun*
kisses

kit *noun*
kits

kitchen *noun*
kitchens

kitchenette *noun*

kite *noun*
kites

kitten *noun*
kittens

kitty *noun*
kitties

kiwi *noun*
kiwis

knack *noun*
knacks

knapsack *noun*
knapsacks

knave *noun*
knaves

knead★ *verb*
kneads
kneading
kneaded

knee *noun*
knees

kneecap *noun*
kneecaps

kneel *verb*
kneels
kneeling
knelt

knew☆ *verb* SEE **know**

knife *noun*
knives

knife *verb*
knifes
knifing
knifed

knight✪ *noun*
knights

knight *verb*
knights
knighting
knighted

knighthood *noun*
knighthoods

knit *verb*
knits
knitting
knitted

knives *noun* SEE **knife**

knob *noun*
knobs

knobbly *adjective*
knobblier
knobbliest

knock *verb*
knocks
knocking
knocked

knock *noun*
knocks

knocker *noun*
knockers

knockout *noun*
knockouts

knot *noun*
knots

knot *verb*
knots
knotting
knotted

knotty *adjective*
knottier
knottiest

★ To **knead** is to work a mixture into a dough. **! need**.
☆ **Knew** is the past tense of know. **! new**.
✪ A **knight** is a soldier in old times. **! night**.

Try also words beginning with **c-**, **ch-**, **kh-**, or **qu-**

know *verb*
knows
knowing
knew
known

know-all *noun*
know-alls

know-how *noun*

knowing *adjective*
knowingly *adverb*

knowledge *noun*

knowledgeable *adjective*
knowledgeably *adverb*

knuckle *noun*
knuckles

koala *noun*
koalas

kookaburra *noun*
kookaburras

Koran *noun*

kosher *adjective*

kung fu *noun*

Ll

label *noun*
labels
label *verb*
labels
labelling
labelled
laboratory *noun*
laboratories
laborious *adjective*
laboriously *adverb*
labour *noun*
labours
labourer *noun*
labourers
labyrinth *noun*
labyrinths
lace *noun*
laces
lace *verb*
laces
lacing
laced
lack *verb*
lacks
lacking
lacked
lack *noun*
lacquer *noun*
lacrosse *noun*
lacy *adjective*
lad *noun*
lads
ladder *noun*
ladders
laden *adjective*
ladle *noun*
ladles
lady *noun*
ladies
ladybird *noun*
ladybirds
ladylike *adjective*
ladyship *noun*
ladyships
lag *verb*
lags
lagging
lagged
lager *noun*
lagers
lagoon *noun*
lagoons
laid *verb* SEE **lay**
lain *verb* SEE **lie**
lair *noun*
lairs
lake *noun*
lakes
lama *noun*
lamas
lamb *noun*
lambs
lame *adjective*
lamer
lamest
lamely *adverb*
lameness *noun*
lament *verb*
laments
lamenting
lamented
lament *noun*
laments
lamentation *noun*
lamentations
laminated *adjective*
lamp *noun*
lamps
lamp post *noun*
lamp posts
lampshade *noun*
lampshades
lance *noun*
lances
lance corporal *noun*
lance corporals
land *noun*
lands
land *verb*
lands
landing
landed
landing *noun*
landings
landlady *noun*
landladies
landlord *noun*
landlords
landmark *noun*
landmarks
landowner *noun*
landowners
landscape *noun*
landscapes
landslide *noun*
landslides
lane *noun*
lanes
language *noun*
languages
lankiness *noun*
lanky *adjective*
lankier
lankiest
lantern *noun*
lanterns
lap *verb*
laps
lapping
lapped
lap *noun*
laps

a b c d e f g h i j k l m n o p q r s t u v w x y z

lapel *noun*
lapels
lapse *verb*
lapses
lapsing
lapsed
lapse *noun*
lapses
laptop *noun*
laptops
lard *noun*
larder *noun*
larders
large *adjective*
larger
largest
largely *adverb*
largeness *noun*
lark *noun*
larks
lark *verb*
larks
larking
larked
larva *noun*
larvae
lasagne *noun*
lasagnes
laser *noun*
lasers
lash *verb*
lashes
lashing
lashed
lash *noun*
lashes
lass *noun*
lasses
lasso *noun*
lassos
lasso *verb*
lassoes
lassoing
lassoed
last *adjective* & *adverb*
lastly *adverb*

last *verb*
lasts
lasting
lasted
last *noun*
latch *noun*
latches
late *adjective* & *adverb*
later
latest
lately *adverb*
lateness *noun*
latent *adjective*
lateral *adjective*
lathe *noun*
lathes
lather *noun*
lathers
Latin *noun*
latitude *noun*
latitudes
latter *adjective*
lattice *noun*
lattices
laugh *verb*
laughs
laughing
laughed
laugh *noun*
laughs
laughable *adjective*
laughably *adverb*
laughter *noun*
launch *verb*
launches
launching
launched
launch *noun*
launches
launder *verb*
launders
laundering
laundered
launderette *noun*
launderettes
laundry *noun*
laundries

lava *noun*
lavender
lavish *adjective*
lavishly *adverb*
law *noun*
laws
law court *noun*
law courts
lawful *adjective*
lawfully *adverb*
lawless *adjective*
lawlessly *adverb*
lawn *noun*
lawns
lawnmower *noun*
lawnmowers
lawsuit *noun*
lawsuits
lawyer *noun*
lawyers
lax *adjective*
lay *verb*
lays
laying
laid
lay *verb* SEE **lie**
layabout *noun*
layabouts
layer *noun*
layers
layman *noun*
laymen
layout *noun*
layouts
laze *verb*
lazes
lazing
lazed
laziness *noun*
lazy *adjective*
lazier
laziest
lazily *adverb*
lead *verb*
leads
leading
led

a b c d e f g h i j k l m n o p q r s t u v w x y z

lead★ *noun*
leads
leader *noun*
leaders
leadership *noun*
leaf *noun*
leaves
leaflet *noun*
leaflets
leafy *adjective*
leafier
leafiest
league *noun*
leagues
leak *verb*
leaks
leaking
leaked
leak☆ *noun*
leaks
leakage *noun*
leakages
leaky *adjective*
leakier
leakiest
lean *verb*
leans
leaning
leaned
leant
lean *adjective*
leaner
leanest
leap *verb*
leaps
leaping
leapt
leaped
leap *noun*
leaps
leapfrog *noun*
leap year *noun*
leap years
learn *verb*
learns
learning
learnt
learned
learned✪ *adjective*
learner *noun*
learners
lease *noun*
leases
leash *noun*
leashes
least *adjective* & *noun*
leather *noun*
leathers
leathery *adjective*
leave *verb*
leaves
leaving
left
leave *noun*
leaves *plural noun* SEE **leaf**
lectern *noun*
lecterns
lecture *verb*
lectures
lecturing
lectured
lecture *noun*
lectures
lecturer *noun*
lecturers
led *verb* SEE **lead**
ledge *noun*
ledges
lee *noun*
leek✣ *noun*
leeks
leer *verb*
leers
leering
leered
left *adjective* & *noun*
left *verb* SEE **leave**
left-handed *adjective*
left-handedness *noun*
leftovers *plural noun*
leg *noun*
legs
legacy *noun*
legacies
legal *adjective*
legally *adverb*
legality *noun*
legalize *verb*
legalizes
legalizing
legalized
legend *noun*
legends
legendary *adjective*
legibility *noun*
legible *adjective*
legibly *adverb*
legion *noun*
legions
legislate *verb*
legislates
legislating
legislated
legislation *noun*
legislator *noun*
legislators
legitimacy *noun*
legitimate *adjective*
legitimately *adverb*
leisure *noun*
leisurely *adjective*
lemon *noun*
lemons
lemonade *noun*
lemonades

★ A **lead** (pronounced *leed*) is a cord for leading a dog. **Lead** (pronounced *led*) is a metal.
☆ A **leak** is a hole or crack that liquid or gas can get through. **! leek**.
✪ Pronounced *ler-nid*.
✣ A **leek** is a vegetable. **! leak**.

lend *verb*
lends
lending
lent
length *noun*
lengths
lengthen *verb*
lengthens
lengthening
lengthened
lengthways *adverb*
lengthwise *adverb*
lengthy *adjective*
lengthier
lengthiest
lenience *noun*
lenient *adjective*
leniently *adverb*
lens *noun*
lenses
Lent★ *noun*
lent *verb* SEE **lend**
lentil *noun*
lentils
leopard *noun*
leopards
leotard *noun*
leotards
leper *noun*
lepers
leprosy *noun*
less *noun* & *preposition*
lessen☆ *verb*
lessens
lessening
lessened
lesser *adjective*
lesson✪ *noun*
lessons
lest *conjunction*
let *verb*
lets
letting
let

> **-let** *suffix*
> -*let* makes nouns meaning 'a small version of', e.g. **booklet**, **piglet**. It also makes words for pieces of jewellery, e.g. **anklet** (worn on the ankle), **bracelet** (from a French word *bras* meaning 'arm')

lethal *adjective*
lethally *adverb*
let's *verb*
letter *noun*
letters
letter box *noun*
letter boxes
lettering *noun*
lettuce *noun*
lettuces
leukaemia *noun*
level *verb*
levels
levelling
levelled
level *adjective* & *noun*
levels
lever *noun*
levers
leverage *noun*
liability *noun*
liabilities
liable *adjective*
liar *noun*
liars
liberal *adjective*
liberally *adverb*
liberate *verb*
liberates
liberating
liberated
liberation *noun*
liberty *noun*
liberties
librarian *noun*
librarians
library *noun*
libraries
licence *noun*
licences
license *verb*
licenses
licensing
licensed
lichen *noun*
lichens
lick *verb*
licks
licking
licked
lick *noun*
licks
lid *noun*
lids
lie✢ *verb*
lies
lying
lay
lain
lie● *verb*
lies
lying
lied
lie *noun*
lies
lieutenant *noun*
lieutenants
life *noun*
lives

★ **Lent** is the Christian time of fasting. **! lent**.
☆ To **lessen** something is to make it less. SEE **lesson**.
✪ A **lesson** is a period of learning. **! lessen**.
✢ As in *to lie on the bed*.
● Meaning 'to say something untrue'.

lifebelt *noun*
lifebelts
lifeboat *noun*
lifeboats
life cycle *noun*
life cycles
lifeguard *noun*
lifeguards
lifeless *adjective*
lifelessly *adverb*
lifelike *adjective*
lifelong *adjective*
lifestyle *noun*
lifestyles
lifetime *noun*
lifetimes
lift *verb*
lifts
lifting
lifted
lift *noun*
lifts
lift-off *noun*
lift-offs
ligament *noun*
ligaments
light *adjective*
lighter
lightest
lightly *adverb*
light *verb*
lights
lighting
lit
lighted
light *noun*
lights
lighten *verb*
lightens
lightening
lightened
lighter *noun*
lighters
lighthouse *noun*
lighthouses
lighting *noun*
lightning *noun*
lightweight *adjective*

like *verb*
likes
liking
liked
like *preposition*
likeable *adjective*
likelihood *noun*
likely *adjective*
likelier
likeliest
liken *verb*
likens
likening
likened
likeness *noun*
likenesses
likewise *adverb*
liking *noun*
likings
lilac *noun*
lilacs
lily *noun*
lilies
limb *noun*
limbs
limber *verb*
limbers
limbering
limbered
lime *noun*
limes
limelight
limerick *noun*
limericks
limestone *noun*
limit *noun*
limits
limit *verb*
limits
limiting
limited
limitation *noun*
limitations
limited *adjective*
limitless *adjective*
limp *adjective*
limply *adverb*

limp *verb*
limps
limping
limped
limp *noun*
limps
limpet *noun*
limpets
line *noun*
lines
line *verb*
lines
lining
lined
linen *noun*
liner *noun*
liners
linesman *noun*
linesmen
line-up *noun*
line-ups

-ling *suffix*
-ling makes words for small things, e.g. **duckling**.

linger *verb*
lingers
lingering
lingered
lingerie *noun*
linguist *noun*
linguists
linguistic *adjective*
linguistics *noun*
lining *noun*
linings
link *verb*
links
linking
linked
link *noun*
links
lino *noun*
linoleum *noun*
lint *noun*

lion *noun*
lions
lioness *noun*
lionesses
lip *noun*
lips
lip-read *verb*
lip-reads
lip-reading
lip-read
lipstick *noun*
lipsticks
liquid *adjective & noun*
liquids
liquidizer *noun*
liquidizers
liquor *noun*
liquors
liquorice *noun*
lisp *noun*
lisps
lisp *verb*
lisps
lisping
lisped
list *noun*
lists
list *verb*
lists
listing
listed
listen *verb*
listens
listening
listened
listener *noun*
listeners
listless *adjective*
listlessly *adverb*
lit *verb* SEE **light**
literacy *noun*
literal *adjective*
literally *adverb*
literary *adjective*
literate *adjective*
literature *noun*
litmus *noun*
litre *noun*
litres
litter *noun*
litters
litter *verb*
litters
littering
littered
little★ *adjective & adverb*
less
least
live *verb*
lives
living
lived
live *adjective*
livelihood *noun*
livelihoods
liveliness *noun*
lively *adjective*
livelier
liveliest
liver *noun*
livers
livery *noun*
liveries
lives *plural noun* SEE **life**
livestock *noun*
livid *adjective*
living *noun*
livings
lizard *noun*
lizards
llama *noun*
llamas
load *verb*
loads
loading
loaded
load *noun*
loads
loaf *noun*
loaves
loaf *verb*
loafs
loafing
loafed
loafer *noun*
loafers
loam *noun*
loamy *adjective*
loamier
loamiest
loan☆ *noun*
loans
loan *verb*
loans
loaning
loaned
loath✪ *adjective*
loathe✣ *verb*
loathes
loathing
loathed
loathsome *adjective*
loaves *plural noun* SEE **loaf**
lob *verb*
lobs
lobbing
lobbed
lobby *noun*
lobbies
lobby *verb*
lobbies
lobbying
lobbied
lobe *noun*
lobes
lobster *noun*
lobsters

★ You can also use **littler** and **littlest** when you are talking about size.
☆ A **loan** is a thing that is lent to someone. **! lone.**
✪ **Loath** means 'unwilling'. **! loathe.**
✣ To **loathe** is to dislike very much. **! loath.**

a b c d e f g h i j k **l** m n o p q r s t u v w x y z

local *adjective*
locally *adverb*

local *noun*
locals

locality *noun*
localities

locate *verb*
locates
locating
located

location *noun*
locations

loch* *noun*
lochs

lock☆ *noun*
locks

lock *verb*
locks
locking
locked

locker *noun*
lockers

locket *noun*
lockets

locomotive *noun*
locomotives

locust *noun*
locusts

lodge *noun*
lodges

lodge *verb*
lodges
lodging
lodged

lodger *noun*
lodgers

lodgings *plural noun*

loft *noun*
lofts

lofty *adjective*
loftier
loftiest

log *noun*
logs

log *verb*
logs
logging
logged

logarithm *noun*
logarithms

logbook *noun*
logbooks

logic *noun*

logical *adjective*
logically *adverb*

logistics *plural noun*

logo *noun*
logos

-logy *suffix*
-logy makes words for subjects of study, e.g. **archaeology** (the study of ancient remains). Most of these words end in *-ology*, but an important exception is **genealogy**. Some words have plurals, e.g. **genealogies**.

loiter *verb*
loiters
loitering
loitered

loiterer *noun*
loiterers

loll *verb*
lolls
lolling
lolled

lollipop *noun*
lollipops

lolly *noun*
lollies

Londoner *noun*
Londoners

lone✪ *adjective*

loneliness *noun*

lonely *adjective*
lonelier
loneliest

long *adjective & adverb*
longer
longest

long *verb*
longs
longing
longed

longitude *noun*
longitudes

longitudinal *adjective*
longitudinally *adverb*

look *verb*
looks
looking
looked

look *noun*
looks

lookout *noun*
lookouts

loom *noun*
looms

loom *verb*
looms
looming
loomed

loop *noun*
loops

loop *verb*
loops
looping
looped

loophole *noun*
loopholes

loose *adjective*
looser
loosest
loosely *adverb*

loosen *verb*
loosens
loosening
loosened

looseness *noun*

* A **loch** is a lake in Scotland. **! lock.**
☆ A **lock** is a mechanism for keeping something closed. **! loch.**
✪ **Lone** means 'alone'. **! loan.**

loot *verb*
loots
looting
looted
loot *noun*
looter *noun*
looters
lopsided *adjective*
lord *noun*
lords
lordly *adjective*
lordship *noun*
lorry *noun*
lorries
lose *verb*
loses
losing
lost
loser *noun*
losers
loss *noun*
losses
lot *noun*
lots
lotion *noun*
lotions
lottery *noun*
lotteries
lotto *noun*
loud *adjective*
louder
loudest
loudly *adverb*
loudness *noun*
loudspeaker *noun*
loudspeakers
lounge *noun*
lounges
lounge *verb*
lounges
lounging
lounged
louse *noun*
lice
lousy *adjective*
lousier
lousiest
lousily *adverb*

lout *noun*
louts
lovable *adjective*
lovably *adverb*
love *verb*
loves
loving
loved
love *noun*
loves
loveliness *noun*
lovely *adjective*
lovelier
loveliest
loving *adjective*
lovingly *adverb*
low *adjective*
lower
lowest
low *verb*
lows
lowing
lowed
lower *verb*
lowers
lowering
lowered
lowland *adjective*
lowlands *plural nouns*
lowliness *noun*
lowly *adjective*
lowlier
lowliest
lowness *noun*
loyal *adjective*
loyally *adverb*
loyalty *noun*
loyalties
lozenge *noun*
lozenges
lubricant *noun*
lubricants
lubricate *verb*
lubricates
lubricating
lubricated
lubrication *noun*

lucid *adjective*
lucidly *adverb*
lucidity *noun*
luck *noun*
lucky *adjective*
luckier
luckiest
luckily *adverb*
lucrative *adjective*
ludicrous *adjective*
ludicrously *adverb*
ludo *noun*
lug *verb*
lugs
lugging
lugged
luggage *noun*
lukewarm *adjective*
lull *verb*
lulls
lulling
lulled
lull *noun*
lulls
lullaby *noun*
lullabies
lumber *verb*
lumbers
lumbering
lumbered
lumber *noun*
lumberjack *noun*
lumberjacks
luminosity *noun*
luminous *adjective*
lump *noun*
lumps
lump *verb*
lumps
lumping
lumped
lumpy *adjective*
lumpier
lumpiest
lunacy *noun*
lunacies
lunar *adjective*

lunatic *noun*
lunatics

lunch *noun*
lunches

lung *noun*
lungs

lunge *verb*
lunges
lunging
lungeing
lunged

lupin *noun*
lupins

lurch *verb*
lurches
lurching
lurched

lurch *noun*
lurches

lure *verb*
lures
luring
lured

lurk *verb*
lurks
lurking
lurked

luscious *adjective*
lusciously *adverb*

lush *adjective*
lusher
lushest
lushly *adverb*

lushness *noun*

lustre *noun*
lustres

lustrous *adjective*

lute *noun*
lutes

luxury *noun*
luxuries

luxurious *adjective*
luxuriously *adverb*

Lycra *noun*

-ly *suffix*
-ly makes adverbs from adjectives, e.g. **slow – slowly**. When the adjective ends in *-y* following a consonant, you change the *y* to *i*, e.g. **happy – happily**. *-ly* is also used to make some adjectives, e.g. **lovely**, and some words that are adjectives and adverbs, e.g. **kindly, hourly**.

lying *verb* SEE **lie**

lynch *verb*
lynches
lynching
lynched

lyre *noun*
lyres

lyrical *adjective*
lyrically *adverb*

lyrics *plural noun*

Mm

mac *noun*
macs
macabre *adjective*
macaroni *noun*
machine *noun*
machines
machinery *noun*
machinist *noun*
machinists
mackerel *noun*
mackerel
mackintosh *noun*
mackintoshes
mad *adjective*
madder
maddest
madly *adverb*
madam *noun*
madden *verb*
maddens
maddening
maddened
made★ *verb* SEE **make**
madman *noun*
madmen
madness *noun*
mafia *noun*
magazine *noun*
magazines
maggot *noun*
maggots
magic *noun* & *adjective*
magical *adjective*
magically *adverb*
magician *noun*
magicians
magistrate *noun*
magistrates
magma *noun*
magnesium *noun*
magnet *noun*
magnets
magnetism *noun*
magnetic *adjective*
magnetically *adverb*
magnetize *verb*
magnetizes
magnetizing
magnetized
magnificent *adjective*
magnificently *adverb*
magnificence *noun*
magnification *noun*
magnifier *noun*
magnifiers
magnify *verb*
magnifies
magnifying
magnified
magnitude *noun*
magnitudes
magnolia *noun*
magnolias
magpie *noun*
magpies
mahogany
maid☆ *noun*
maids
maiden *noun*
maidens
mail✪ *noun*
mail *verb*
mails
mailing
mailed
maim *verb*
maims
maiming
maimed
main✢ *adjective*
mainly *adverb*
mainland *noun*
mainly *adverb*
mains *plural noun*
mainstream *adjective*
maintain *verb*
maintains
maintaining
maintained
maintenance *noun*
maisonette *noun*
maisonettes
maize *noun*
majestic *adjective*
majestically *adverb*
majesty *noun*
majesties
major *adjective*
major *noun*
majors
majorette *noun*
majorettes
majority *noun*
majorities
make *verb*
makes
making
made

★ You use **made** in e.g. *I made a cake*. **! maid**.
☆ A **maid** is a female servant. **! made**.
✪ **Mail** is letters and parcels sent by post. **! male**.
✢ **Main** means 'most important'. **! mane**.

make *noun*
makes
make-believe *noun*
maker *noun*
makers
make-up *noun*
maladjusted *adjective*
malaria *noun*
male★ *adjective & noun*
males
malevolence *noun*
malevolent *adjective*
malevolently *adverb*
malice *noun*
malicious *adjective*
maliciously *adverb*
mallet *noun*
mallets
malnourished *adjective*
malnutrition *noun*
malt *noun*
malted *adjective*
mammal *noun*
mammals
mammoth *adjective & noun*
mammoths
man *noun*
men
man *verb*
mans
manning
manned
manage *verb*
manages
managing
managed
manageable *adjective*
management *noun*
manager *noun*
managers
manageress *noun*
manageresses
mane☆ *noun*
manes
manger *noun*
mangers
mangle *verb*
mangles
mangling
mangled
mango *noun*
mangoes
manhandle *verb*
manhandles
manhandling
manhandled
manhole *noun*
manholes
mania *noun*
manias
maniac *noun*
maniacs
manic *adjective*
manically *adverb*
manifesto *noun*
manifestos
manipulate *verb*
manipulates
manipulating
manipulated
manipulation *noun*
manipulator *noun*
manipulators
mankind *noun*
manliness *noun*
manly *adjective*
manlier
manliest
manner✪ *noun*
manners
manoeuvrable *adjective*
manoeuvre *verb*
manoeuvres
manoeuvring
manoeuvred
manoeuvre *noun*
manoeuvres
man-of-war *noun*
men-of-war
manor✢ *noun*
manors
mansion *noun*
mansions
manslaughter *noun*
mantelpiece *noun*
mantelpieces
mantle *noun*
mantles
manual *adjective*
manually *adverb*
manual *noun*
manuals
manufacture *verb*
manufactures
manufacturing
manufactured
manufacture *noun*
manufacturer *noun*
manufacturers
manure *noun*
manuscript *noun*
manuscripts
Manx *adjective*
many *adjective & noun*
more
most
Maori *noun*
Maoris
map *noun*
maps
map *verb*
maps
mapping
mapped

★ A **male** is a man or an animal of the same gender as a man. **! mail**.
☆ A **mane** is the long piece of hair on a horse or lion. **! main**.
✪ You use **manner** in e.g. *a friendly manner*. **! manor**.
✢ A **manor** is a big house in the country. **! manner**.

maple *noun*
maples
mar *verb*
mars
marring
marred
marathon *noun*
marathons
marauder *noun*
marauders
marauding *adjective*
marble *noun*
marbles
March *noun*
Marches
march *verb*
marches
marching
marched
march *noun*
marches
marcher *noun*
marchers
mare★ *noun*
mares
margarine *noun*
margin *noun*
margins
marginal *adjective*
marginally *adverb*
marigold *noun*
marigolds
marijuana *noun*
marina *noun*
marinas
marine *adjective & noun*
marines
mariner *noun*
mariners
marionette *noun*
marionettes
mark *verb*
marks
marking
marked
mark *noun*
marks
marker *noun*
markers
market *noun*
markets
market *verb*
markets
marketing
marketed
marksman *noun*
marksmen
marksmanship *noun*
marmalade *noun*
maroon *verb*
maroons
marooning
marooned
maroon *adjective & noun*
marquee *noun*
marquees
marriage *noun*
marriages
marrow *noun*
marrows
marry *verb*
marries
marrying
married
marsh *noun*
marshes
marshal *noun*
marshals
marshmallow *noun*
marshmallows
marshy *adjective*
marshier
marshiest
marsupial *noun*
marsupials
martial *adjective*
Martian *noun*
Martians
martyr *noun*
martyrs
martyrdom *noun*
marvel *verb*
marvels
marvelling
marvelled
marvel *noun*
marvels
marvellous *adjective*
marvellously *adverb*
Marxism *noun*
Marxist *noun & adjective*
marzipan *noun*
mascot *noun*
mascots
masculine *adjective*
masculinity *noun*
mash *verb*
mashes
mashing
mashed
mash *noun*
mask *noun*
masks
mask *verb*
masks
masking
masked
mason *noun*
masons
masonry *noun*
Mass☆ *noun*
Masses
mass *noun*
masses
mass *verb*
masses
massing
massed
massacre *verb*
massacres
massacring
massacred
massacre *noun*
massacres

★ A **mare** is a female horse. **! mayor**.
☆ Use a capital M when you mean the Roman Catholic service.

massage *verb*
massages
massaging
massaged
massage *noun*
massive *adjective*
massively *adverb*
mast *noun*
masts
master *noun*
masters
master *verb*
masters
mastering
mastered
masterly *adjective*
mastermind *noun*
masterminds
masterpiece *noun*
masterpieces
mastery *noun*
mysteries
mat* *noun*
mats
matador *noun*
matadors
match *verb*
matches
matching
matched
match *noun*
matches
mate *noun*
mates
mate *verb*
mates
mating
mated
material *noun*
materials
materialistic *adjective*
maternal *adjective*
maternally *adverb*

maternity *noun & adjective*
mathematical *adjective*
mathematically *adverb*
mathematician *noun*
mathematicians
mathematics *noun*
maths *noun*
matinee *noun*
matinees
French matinée
matrimonial *adjective*
matrimony *noun*
matrix *noun*
matrices
matron *noun*
matrons
matt☆ *adjective*
matted *adjective*
matter *verb*
matters
mattering
mattered
matter *noun*
matters
matting *noun*
mattress *noun*
mattresses
mature *adjective*
maturity *noun*
matzo *noun*
matzos
mauve *noun*
maximize *verb*
miximizes
maximizing
maximized
maximum *adjective & noun*
maxima *or* maximums
May *noun*
Mays

may *verb*
might
maybe *adverb*
May Day
Mayday✪ *noun*
Maydays
mayhem *noun*
mayonnaise *noun*
mayor⁺ *noun*
mayors
mayoress *noun*
mayoresses
maypole *noun*
maypoles
maze *noun*
mazes
meadow *noun*
meadows
meagre *adjective*
meal *noun*
meals
mean *adjective*
meaner
meanest
meanly
mean *verb*
means
meaning
meant
meander *verb*
meanders
meandering
meandered
meaning *noun*
meanings
meaningful *adjective*
meaningfully *adverb*
meaningless *adjective*
meaninglessly *adverb*
meanness *noun*
means *plural noun*

* A **mat** is a covering for a floor. **! matt**.
☆ **Matt** means 'not shiny'. **! mat**.
✪ An international radio signal.
⁺ You use **mayor** in e.g. *the Mayor of London*. **! mare**.

meantime *noun*
meanwhile *adverb*
measles *plural noun*
measly *adjective*
measlier
measliest
measure *verb*
measures
measuring
measured
measure *noun*
measures
measurement *noun*
measurements
meat★ *noun*
meats
meaty *adjective*
meatier
meatiest
mechanic *noun*
mechanics
mechanical *adjective*
mechanically *adverb*
mechanics *noun*
mechanism *noun*
mechanisms
medal *noun*
medals
medallist *noun*
medallists
meddle *verb*
meddles
meddling
meddled
meddler *noun*
meddlers
meddlesome *adjective*
media *plural noun*
median *noun*
medians
medic *noun*
medical *adjective*
medically *adverb*
medical *noun*
medicals
medication *noun*
medicine *noun*
medicines
medicinal *adjective*
medieval *adjective*
mediocre *adjective*
mediocrity *noun*
meditate *verb*
meditates
meditating
meditated
meditation *noun*
Mediterranean *adjective*
medium *adjective*
medium *noun*
media
mediums
meek *adjective*
meeker
meekest
meekly *adverb*
meekness *noun*
meet☆ *verb*
meets
meeting
met
meeting *noun*
meetings
megabyte *noun*
megabytes
megaphone *noun*
megaphones
melancholy *adjective & noun*
mellow *adjective*
melodious *adjective & adverb*
melodrama *noun*
melodramas
melodramatic *adjective*
melodramatically *adverb*
melody *noun*
melodies
melodic *adjective*
melon *noun*
melons
melt *verb*
melts
melting
melted
member *noun*
members
membership *noun*
Member of Parliament *noun*
Members of Parliament
membrane *noun*
membranes
memo *noun*
memos
memoirs *plural noun*
memorable *adjective*
memorably *adverb*
memorial *noun*
memorials
memorize *verb*
memorizes
memorizing
memorized
memory *noun*
memories
men *plural noun* SEE **man**
menace *verb*
menaces
menacing
menaced
menace *noun*
menaces
menagerie *noun*
menageries
mend *verb*
mends
mending
mended
mender *noun*
menders

★ **Meat** is the flesh of an animal. **! meet.**
☆ People **meet** when they come together. **! meat.**

menstrual *adjective*

menstruation *noun*

> **-ment** *suffix*
> *-ment* makes nouns from adjectives e.g. **contentment**. There is a fixed number of these, and you cannot freely add *-ment* as you can with *-ness*. When the adjective ends in *-y* following a consonant, you change the *y* to *i*, e.g. **merry – merriment**.

mental *adjective*
mentally *adverb*

mention *verb*
mentions
mentioning
mentioned

mention *noun*
mentions

mentor *noun*
mentors

menu *noun*
menus

mercenary *adjective & noun*
mercenaries

merchandise *noun*

merchant *noun*
merchants

merciful *adjective*
mercifully *adverb*

merciless *adjective*
mercilessly *adverb*

mercury *noun*

mercy *noun*
mercies

mere *adjective*

merely *adverb*

merge *verb*
merges
merging
merged

merger *noun*
mergers

meridian *noun*
meridians

meringue *noun*
meringues

merit *noun*
merits

merit *verb*
merits
meriting
merited

mermaid *noun*
mermaids

merriment *noun*

merry *adjective*
merrier
merriest
merrily *adverb*

merry-go-round *noun*
merry-go-rounds

mesh *noun*
meshes

mess *noun*
messes

mess *verb*
messes
messing
messed

message *noun*
messages

messenger *noun*
messengers

Messiah *noun*

messiness *noun*

messy *adjective*
messier
messiest
messily *adverb*

met *verb* SEE **meet**

metabolism *noun*

metal★ *noun*
metals

metallic *adjective*

metallurgical *adjective*

metallurgist *noun*
metallurgists

metallurgy *noun*

metamorphosis *noun*
metamorphoses

metaphor *noun*
metaphors

metaphorical *adjective*
metaphorically *adverb*

meteor *noun*
meteors

meteoric *adjective*

meteorite *noun*
meteorites

meteorological *adjective*

meteorologist *noun*
meteorologists

meteorology *noun*

meter☆ *noun*
meters

methane *noun*

method *noun*
methods

methodical *adjective*
methodically *adverb*

Methodist *noun*
Methodists

meths *noun*

methylated spirit *noun*

meticulous *adjective*
meticulously *adverb*

metre✪ *noun*
metres

metric *adjective*

metrical *adjective*
metrically *adverb*

★ **Metal** is a hard substance used to make things. **! mettle**.
☆ A **meter** is a device that shows how much of something has been used. **! metre**.
✪ A **metre** is a unit of length. **! meter**.

metronome *noun*
metronomes
mettle★ *noun*
mew *verb*
mews
mewing
mewed
miaow *verb*
miaows
miaowing
miaowed
mice *plural noun* SEE **mouse**

micro- *prefix*
micro- makes words meaning 'small', e.g. **microwave**. When the word begins with a vowel you add a hyphen, e.g. **micro-organism**.

microbe *noun*
microbes
microchip *noun*
microchips
microcomputer *noun*
microcomputers
microcosm *noun*
microfilm *noun*
microfilms
microlight *noun*
microphone *noun*
microphones
microprocessor *noun*
microprocessors
microscope *noun*
microscopes
microscopic *adjective*
microscopically *adverb*
microwave *noun*
microwaves
microwave *verb*
microwaves
microwaving
microwaved
mid☆ *adjective*
midday *noun*
middle *noun*
middles
Middle Ages *noun*
Middle East *noun*
midfield *noun*
midfielder *noun*
midfielders
midge *noun*
midges
midget *noun*
midgets
midnight *noun*
midst *noun*
midsummer *noun*
midway *adverb*
midwife *noun*
midwives
midwifery *noun*
might✪ *noun*
might *verb* SEE **may**
mightiness *noun*
mighty *adjective*
mightier
mightiest
mightily *adverb*
migraine *noun*
migraines
migrant *noun*
migrants
migrate *verb*
migrates
migrating
migrated
migration *noun*
migrations
migratory *adjective*
mike *noun*
mikes
mild *adjective*
milder
mildest
mildly *adverb*
mildness *noun*
mile *noun*
miles
mileage *noun*
mileages
milestone *noun*
milestones
militancy *noun*
militant *noun*
militants
militarism *noun*
militaristic *adjective*
military *adjective*
milk *noun*
milk *verb*
milks
milking
milked
milkman *noun*
milkmen
milky *adjective*
milkier
milkiest
Milky Way *noun*
mill *noun*
mills
mill *verb*
mills
milling
milled
millennium *noun*
millenniums
miller *noun*
millers
millet *noun*
milligram *noun*
milligrams

★ As in *to be on your mettle*. **! metal**.
☆ You use a hyphen, e.g. *mid-August*.
✪ **Might** means 'force' or 'strength'. **! mite**.

a b c d e f g h i j k l m n o p q r s t u v w x y z

millilitre *noun*
millilitres
millimetre *noun*
millimetres
million *noun*
millions
millionth *adjective & noun*
millionaire *noun*
millionaires
millstone *noun*
millstones
milometer *noun*
milometers
mime *verb*
mimes
miming
mimed
mime *noun*
mimes
mimic *verb*
mimics
mimicking
mimicked
mimic *noun*
mimics
mimicry *noun*
minaret *noun*
minarets
mince *verb*
minces
mincing
minced
mince *noun*
mincemeat *noun*
mincer *noun*
mincers
mind *noun*
minds
mind *verb*
minds
minding
minded
mindless *adjective*
mindlessly *adverb*
mine *adjective*
mine *verb*
mines
mining
mined
mine *noun*
mines
minefield *noun*
minefields
miner *noun*
miners
mineral *noun*
minerals
mingle *verb*
mingles
mingling
mingled

> **mini-** *prefix*
> *mini-* makes words meaning 'small', e.g. **miniskirt**. You do not normally need a hyphen.

mingy *adjective*
mingier
mingiest
miniature *adjective & noun*
miniatures
minibeast *noun*
minibeasts
minibus *noun*
minibuses
minim *noun*
minims
minimal *adjective*
minimally *adverb*
minimize *verb*
minimizes
minimizing
minimized
minimum *adjective & noun*
minima *or* minimums
miniskirt *noun*
miniskirts
minister *noun*
ministers
ministry *noun*
ministries
mink *noun*
minks
minnow *noun*
minnows
minor *adjective & noun*
minors
minority *noun*
minorities
minstrel *noun*
minstrels
mint *noun*
mints
mint *verb*
mints
minting
minted
minus *preposition*
minuscule *adjective*
minute *adjective*
minutely *adverb*
minute *noun*
minutes
miracle *noun*
miracles
miraculous *adjective*
miraculously *adverb*
mirage *noun*
mirages
mirror *noun*
mirrors
mirth *noun*
misbehave *verb*
misbehaves
misbehaving
misbehaved
misbehaviour *noun*
miscalculate *verb*
miscarriage *noun*
miscarriages
miscellaneous *adjective*
miscellany *noun*
miscellanies
mischief *noun*
mischievous *adjective*
mischievously *adverb*

miscount *verb*
miscounts
miscounting
miscounted

misdeal *verb*
misdeals
misdealing
misdealt

miser *noun*
misers

miserable *adjective*
miserably

miserly *adjective*

misery *noun*
miseries

misfire *verb*
misfires
misfiring
misfired

misfit *noun*
misfits

misfortune *noun*
misfortunes

misguided *adjective*

mishap *noun*
mishaps

mishear *verb*

misinform *verb*

misjudge *verb*
misjudges
misjudging
misjudged

misplace *verb*
misplaces
misplacing
misplaced

misread *verb*
misreads
misreading
misread

mislay *verb*
mislays
mislaying
mislaid

mislead *verb*
misleads
misleading
misled

misprint *noun*
misprints

miss *verb*
misses
missing
missed

miss *noun*
misses

missile *noun*
missiles

missing *adjective*

mission *noun*
missions

missionary *noun*
missionaries

misspell *verb*
misspells
misspelling
misspelled *or* misspelt

mist★ *noun*
mists

mistake *noun*
mistakes

mistake *verb*
mistakes
mistaking
mistook
mistaken

mister *noun*

mistiness *noun*

mistletoe *noun*

mistreat *verb*
mistreats
mistreating
mistreated

mistreatment *noun*

mistress *noun*
mistresses

mistrust *verb*
mistrusts
mistrusting
mistrusted

misty *adjective*
mistier
mistiest

misunderstand *verb*
misunderstands
misunderstanding
misunderstood

misunderstanding *noun*
misunderstandings

misuse *verb*
misuses
misusing
misused

misuse *noun*
misuses

mite☆ *noun*
mites

mitre *noun*
mitres

mitten *noun*
mittens

mix *verb*
mixes
mixing
mixed

mixer *noun*
mixers

mixture *noun*
mixtures

mix-up *noun*
mix-ups

mnemonic *noun*
mnemonics

moan *verb*
moans
moaning
moaned

moan *noun*
moans

★ **Mist** is damp air that is difficult to see through. **! missed**.
☆ A **mite** is a tiny insect. **! might**.

a b c d e f g h i j k l m n o p q r s t u v w x y z

moat *noun*
moats

mob *noun*
mobs

mob *verb*
mobs
mobbing
mobbed

mobile *adjective & noun*
mobiles

mobility *noun*

mobilization *noun*

mobilize *verb*
mobilizes
mobilizing
mobilized

moccasin *noun*
moccasins

mock *adjective*

mock *verb*
mocks
mocking
mocked

mockery *noun*
mockeries

mock-up *noun*
mock-ups

mode *noun*
modes

model *noun*
models

model *verb*
models
modelling
modelled

modem *noun*
modems

moderate *adjective*
moderately *adverb*

moderate *verb*
moderates
moderating
moderated

moderation *noun*

modern *adjective*

modernity *noun*

modernization *noun*

modernize *verb*
modernizes
modernizing
modernized

modest *adjective*
modestly *adverb*

modesty *noun*

modification *noun*
modifications

modify *verb*
modifies
modifying
modified

module *noun*
modules

moist *adjective*
moister
moistest

moisture *noun*

moisten *verb*
moistens
moistening
moistened

molar *noun*
molars

mole *noun*
moles

molecular *adjective*

molecule *noun*
molecules

molehill *noun*
molehills

mollusc *noun*
molluscs

molten *adjective*

moment *noun*
moments

momentary *adjective*
momentarily

momentous *adjective*
momentously *adverb*

momentum *noun*

monarch *noun*
monarchs

monarchy *noun*
monarchies

monastery *noun*
monasteries

monastic *adjective*

Monday *noun*
Mondays

money *noun*

mongoose *noun*
mongooses

mongrel *noun*
mongrels

monitor *verb*
monitors
monitoring
monitored

monitor *noun*
monitors

monk *noun*
monks

monkey *noun*
monkeys

monogram *noun*
monograms

monologue *noun*
monologues

monopolize *verb*
monopolizes
monopolizing
monopolized

monopoly *noun*
monopolies

monorail *noun*
monorails

monotonous *adjective*
monotonously *adverb*

monotony *noun*

monsoon *noun*
monsoons

monster *noun*
monsters

monstrosity *noun*
monstrosities

monstrous *adjective*
monstrously *adverb*
month *noun*
months
monthly *adjective & adverb*
monument *noun*
monuments
monumental *adjective*
monumentally *adverb*
moo *verb*
moos
mooing
mooed
mood *noun*
moods
moodiness *noun*
moody *adjective*
moodier
moodiest
moodily *adverb*
moon *noun*
moons
moonlight *noun*
moonlit *adjective*
moor★ *verb*
moors
mooring
moored
moor☆ *noun*
moors
moorhen *noun*
moorhens
mooring *noun*
moorings
moose✪ *noun*
moose
mop *noun*
mops
mop *verb*
mops
mopping
mopped
mope *verb*
mopes
moping
moped
moped *noun*
mopeds
moraine *noun*
moraines
moral *adjective*
morally *adverb*
moral *noun*
morals
morale *noun*
morality *noun*
morals *plural noun*
morbid *adjective*
morbidly *adverb*
more✣ *adjective, adverb, & noun*
moreover *adverb*
Mormon *noun*
Mormons
morning *noun*
mornings
moron *noun*
morons
moronic *adjective*
moronically *adverb*
morose *adjective*
morosely *adverb*
morphine *noun*
Morse code *noun*
morsel *noun*
morsels
mortal *adjective*
mortally *adverb*
mortality *noun*
mortar *noun*
mortgage *noun*
mortgages
mortuary *noun*
mortuaries
mosaic *noun*
mosaics
mosque *noun*
mosques
mosquito *noun*
mosquitoes
moss *noun*
mosses
mossy *adjective*
mossier
mossiest
most *adjective, adverb, & noun*
mostly *adverb*
motel *noun*
motels
moth *noun*
moths
mother *noun*
mothers
motherhood *noun*
mother-in-law *noun*
mothers-in-law
motherly *adjective*
motion *noun*
motions
motionless *adjective*
motivate *verb*
motivates
motivating
motivated
motive *noun*
motives
motor *noun*
motors
motorbike *noun*
motorbikes
motor boat *noun*
motor boats

★ To **moor** a boat is to tie it up. **! more.**
☆ A **moor** is an area of rough land. **! more.**
✪ A **moose** is an American elk. **! mouse, mousse.**
✣ You use **more** in e.g. *I'd like more to eat.* **! moor.**

a b c d e f g h i j k l **m** n o p q r s t u v w x y z

a b c d e f g h i j k l **m** n o p q r s t u v w x y z

motor car *noun*
motor cars
motorcycle *noun*
motorcycles
motorcyclist *noun*
motorcyclists
motorist *noun*
motorists
motorway *noun*
motorways
mottled *adjective*
motto *noun*
mottoes
mould *verb*
moulds
moulding
moulded
mould *noun*
moulds
mouldy *adjective*
mouldier
mouldiest
moult *verb*
moults
moulting
moulted
mound *noun*
mounds
mount *verb*
mounts
mounting
mounted
mount *noun*
mounts
mountain *noun*
mountains
mountaineer *noun*
mountaineers
mountaineering *noun*
mountainous *adjective*
mourn *verb*
mourns
mourning
mourned
mourner *noun*
mourners
mournful *adjective*
mournfully *adverb*
mouse★ *noun*
mice
mousetrap *noun*
mousetraps
mousse☆ *noun*
mousses
moustache *noun*
moustaches
mousy *adjective*
mousier
mousiest
mouth *noun*
mouths
mouthful *noun*
mouthfuls
mouthpiece *noun*
mouthpieces
movable *adjective*
move *verb*
moves
moving
moved
move *noun*
moves
movement *noun*
movements
movie *noun*
movies
mow *verb*
mows
mowing
mowed
mown
mower *noun*
mowers
MP *noun*
MPs
MP3 player *noun*
MP3 players
much *adjective, adverb, & noun*
muck *noun*
muck *verb*
mucks
mucking
mucked
mucky *adjective*
muckier
muckiest
mud *noun*
muddle *verb*
muddles
muddling
muddled
muddle *noun*
muddles
muddy *adjective*
muddier
muddiest
mudguard *noun*
mudguards
muesli *noun*
muezzin✪ *noun*
muezzins
muffle *verb*
muffles
muffling
muffled
mug *noun*
mugs
mug *verb*
mugs
mugging
mugged
mugger *noun*
muggers
muggy *adjective*
muggier
muggiest
mule *noun*
mules

★ A **mouse** is a small animal. **! moose, mousse.**
☆ A **mousse** is a creamy pudding. **! moose, mouse.**
✪ A man who calls Muslims to prayer.

multi- *prefix*
multi- makes words with the meaning 'many', e.g. **multicultural**. You do not normally need a hyphen.

multicultural *adjective*

multimedia *noun*

multinational *adjective*

multiple *adjective & noun*
multiples

multiplication *noun*

multiply *verb*
multiplies
multiplying
multiplied

multiracial *adjective*

multitude *noun*
multitudes

mumble *verb*
mumbles
mumbling
mumbled

mummify *verb*
mummifies
mummifying
mummified

mummy *noun*
mummies

mumps *noun*

munch *verb*
munches
munching
munched

mundane *adjective*

municipal *adjective*

mural *noun*
murals

murder *verb*
murders
murdering
murdered

murder *noun*
murders

murderer *noun*
murderers

murderous *adjective*
murderously *adverb*

murky *adjective*
murkier
murkiest

murmur *verb*
murmurs
murmuring
murmured

murmur *noun*
murmurs

muscle★ *noun*
muscles

muscle *verb*
muscles
muscling
muscled

muscular *adjective*

museum *noun*
museums

mushroom *noun*
mushrooms

mushroom *verb*
mushrooms
mushrooming
mushroomed

music *noun*

musical *adjective*
musically *adverb*

musical *noun*
musicals

musician *noun*
musicians

musket *noun*
muskets

musketeer *noun*
musketeers

Muslim *noun*
Muslims

muslin *noun*

mussel☆ *noun*
mussels

must *auxiliary verb*

mustard *noun*

muster *verb*
musters
mustering
mustered

mustiness *noun*

musty *adjective*
mustier
mustiest

mutant *noun*
mutants

mutation *noun*
mutations

mute *adjective*
mutely *adverb*

mute *noun*
mutes

muted *adjective*

mutilate *verb*
mutilates
mutilating
mutilated

mutilation *noun*

mutineer *noun*
mutineers

mutiny *noun*
mutinies

mutinous *adjective*
mutinously *adverb*

mutiny *verb*
mutinies
mutinying
mutinied

★ A **muscle** is a part of the body. **! mussel**.
☆ A **mussel** is a shellfish. **! muscle**.

a b c d e f g h i j k l m n o p q r s t u v w x y z

mutter *verb*
mutters
muttering
muttered

mutton *noun*

mutual *adjective*
mutually *adverb*

muzzle *verb*
muzzles
muzzling
muzzled

muzzle *noun*
muzzles

my *posessive pronoun*

myself *pronoun*

mysterious *adjective*
mysteriously *adverb*

mystery *noun*
mysteries

mystification *noun*

mystify *verb*
mystifies
mystifying
mystified

myth *noun*
myths

mythical *adjective*

mythological *adjective*

mythology *noun*

Try also words beginning with **gn-**, **kn-**, or **pn-**

Nn

nab *verb*
nabs
nabbing
nabbed
nag *verb*
nags
nagging
nagged
nag *noun*
nags
nail *noun*
nails
nail *verb*
nails
nailing
nailed
naive *adjective*
naively *adverb*
naivety *noun*
naked *adjective*
nakedness *noun*
name *noun*
names
name *verb*
names
naming
named
nameless *adjective*
namely *adverb*
nanny *noun*
nannies
nap *noun*
naps
napkin *noun*
napkins
nappy *noun*
nappies
narcissus *noun*
narcissi

narrate *verb*
narrates
narrating
narrated
narration *noun*
narrations
narrative *noun*
narratives
narrator *noun*
narrators
narrow *adjective*
narrower
narrowest
narrowly *adverb*
nasal *adjective*
nasally *adverb*
nastiness *noun*
nasturtium *noun*
nasturtiums
nasty *adjective*
nastier
nastiest
nastily *adverb*
nation *noun*
nations
national *adjective*
nationally *adverb*
nationalism *noun*
nationalist *noun*
nationalists
nationality *noun*
nationalities
nationalization *noun*
nationalize *verb*
nationalizes
nationalizing
nationalized
nationwide *adjective*

Native American *noun*
Native Americans
nativity *noun*
nativities
natural *adjective*
naturally *adverb*
natural *noun*
naturals
naturalist *noun*
naturalists
naturalization *noun*
naturalize *verb*
naturalizes
naturalizing
naturalized
nature *noun*
natures
naughtiness *noun*
naughty *adjective*
naughtier
naughtiest
naughtily *adverb*
nausea *noun*
nautical *adjective*
naval★ *adjective*
nave *noun*
naves
navel☆ *noun*
navels
navigable *adjective*
navigate *verb*
navigates
navigating
navigated
navigation *noun*
navigator *noun*
navigators

★ **Naval** means 'to do with a navy'. **! navel.**
☆ A **navel** is a small hollow in your stomach. **! naval.**

Try also words beginning with **gn-**, **kn-**, or **pn-**

navy *noun*
navies

Nazi *noun*
Nazis

Nazism *noun*

near *adjective & adverb*
nearer
nearest

near *preposition*

near *verb*
nears
nearing
neared

nearby *adjective*

nearly *adverb*

neat *adjective*
neater
neatest
neatly *adverb*

neatness *noun*

necessarily *adverb*

necessary *adjective*

necessity *noun*
necessities

neck *noun*
necks

neckerchief *noun*
neckerchiefs

necklace *noun*
necklaces

nectar *noun*

nectarine *noun*
nectarines

need* *verb*
needs
needing
needed

need *noun*
needs

needle *noun*
needles

needless *adjective*
needlessly *adverb*

needlework *noun*

needy *adjective*
needier
neediest

negative *adjective*
negatively *adverb*

negative *noun*
negatives

neglect *verb*
neglects
neglecting
neglected

neglect *noun*

neglectful *adjective*
neglectfully *adverb*

negligence *noun*

negligent *adjective*
negligently *adverb*

negligible *adjective*
negligibly *adverb*

negotiate *verb*
negotiates
negotiating
negotiated

negotiation *noun*
negotiations

negotiator *noun*
negotiators

neigh *verb*
neighs
neighing
neighed

neigh *noun*
neighs

neighbour *noun*
neighbours

neighbouring *adjective*

neighbourhood *noun*
neighbourhoods

neighbourly *adjective*

neither *adjective & conjunction*

neon *noun*

nephew *noun*
nephews

nerve *noun*
nerves

nerve-racking *adjective*

nervous *adjective*
nervously *adverb*

nervousness *noun*

> **-ness** *suffix*
> *-ness* makes nouns from adjectives, e.g. **soft - softness**. When the adjective ends in *-y* following a consonant, you change the *y* to *i*, e.g. **lively - liveliness**.

nest *noun*
nests

nest *verb*
nests
nesting
nested

nestle *verb*
nestles
nestling
nestled

nestling *noun*
nestlings

net *noun*
nets

net *adjective*

netball *noun*

nettle *noun*
nettles

network *noun*
networks

neuter *adjective*

neuter *verb*
neuters
neutering
neutered

neutral *adjective*
neutrally

neutrality *noun*

* To **need** is to require something. **! knead.**

neutralize *verb*
neutralizes
neutralizing
neutralized

neutron *noun*
neutrons

never *adverb*

nevertheless *conjunction*

new★ *adjective*
newer
newest
newly *adverb*

newcomer *noun*
newcomers

newness *noun*

news *noun*

newsagent *noun*
newsagents

newsletter *noun*
newsletters

newspaper *noun*
newspapers

newt *noun*
newts

newton *noun*
newtons

next *adjective & adverb*

next door *adverb & adjective*

nib *noun*
nibs

nibble *verb*
nibbles
nibbling
nibbled

nice *adjective*
nicer
nicest
nicely *adverb*

niceness *noun*

nicety *noun*
niceties

nick *verb*
nicks
nicking
nicked

nick *noun*
nicks

nickel *noun*
nickels

nickname *noun*
nicknames

nicotine *noun*

niece *noun*
nieces

night☆ *noun*
nights

nightclub *noun*
nightclubs

nightdress *noun*
nightdresses

nightfall *noun*

nightingale *noun*
nightingales

nightly *adjective & adverb*

nightmare *noun*
nightmares

nightmarish *adjective*

nil *noun*

nimble *adjective*
nimbler
nimblest
nimbly *adverb*

nine *noun*
nines

nineteen *noun*
nineteens

nineteenth *adjective & noun*

ninetieth *adjective & noun*

ninety *noun*
nineties

ninth *adjective*
ninthly *adverb*

nip *verb*
nips
nipping
nipped

nip *noun*
nips

nipple *noun*
nipples

nippy *adjective*
nippier
nippiest

nit *noun*
nits

nitrate *noun*
nitrates

nitric acid *noun*

nitrogen *noun*

nitty-gritty *noun*

nitwit *noun*
nitwits

nobility *noun*

noble *adjective*
nobler
noblest
nobly *adverb*

noble *noun*
nobles

nobleman *noun*
noblemen

noblewoman *noun*
noblewomen

nobody *noun*
nobodies

nocturnal *adjective*
nocturnally *adverb*

nod *verb*
nods
nodding
nodded

noise *noun*
noises

noiseless *adjective*
noiselessly *adverb*

noisiness *noun*

★ You use **new** in e.g *She has a new bike*. **! knew.**
☆ **Night** is the opposite of day. **! knight.**

Try also words beginning with **gn-**, **kn-**, or **pn-**

noisy *adjective*
noisier
noisiest
noisily *adverb*

nomad *noun*
nomads

nomadic *adjective*

no-man's-land *noun*

nominate *verb*
nominates
nominating
nominated

nomination *noun*
nominations

nominee *noun*
nominees

> **-nomy** *suffix*
> *-nomy* makes words for subjects of study, e.g. **astronomy** (the study of the stars). Most of these words end in *-onomy*.

nonchalent *adjective*
nonchalently *adverb*

none★ *pronoun* & *adverb*

> **non-** *prefix*
> *non-* makes words meaning 'not', e.g. **non-existent**, **non-smoker**. You use a hyphen to make these words. When an *un-* word has a special meaning, e.g. **unprofessional**, you can use *non-* to make a word without the special meaning, e.g. **non-professional**.

non-drip *adjective*

nonetheless *adverb*

non-existent *adjective*

non-fiction *noun*

non-flammable *adjective*

nonsense *noun*

nonsensical *adjective*
nonsensically *adverb*

non-smoker *noun*

non-starter *noun*

non-stick *adjective*

non-stop *adjective* & *adverb*

non-violent *adjective*

noodle *noun*

nook *noun*

noon *noun*

no one *noun*

noose *noun*
nooses

normal *adjective*
normally *adverb*

normality *noun*

north *adjective* & *adverb*

north☆ *noun*

north-east *noun*, *adjective*, & *adverb*

northerly *adjective* & *noun*
northerlies

northern *adjective*

northerner *noun*
northerners

northward *adjective* & *adverb*

northwards *adverb*

north-west *noun*, *adjective*, & *adverb*

nose *noun*
noses

nose *verb*
noses
nosing
nosed

nosedive *verb*
nosedives
nosediving
nosedived

nosedive *noun*
nosedives

nosiness *noun*

nostalgia *noun*

nostalgic *adjective*
nostalgically *adverb*

nostril *noun*
nostrils

nosy *adjective*
nosier
nosiest
nosily *adverb*

not *adverb*

notable *adjective*
notably *adverb*

notch *noun*
notches

note *noun*
notes

note *verb*
notes
noting
noted

notebook *noun*
notebooks

notepaper *noun*

nothing *noun*

notice *verb*
notices
noticing
noticed

notice *noun*
notices

noticeable *adjective*
noticeably *adverb*

noticeboard *noun*
noticeboards

notify *verb*

notion *noun*
notions

notoriety *noun*

notorious *adjective*
notoriously *adverb*

★ You use **none** in e.g. *none of us went.* **! nun.**
☆ You use a capital N in **the North**, when you mean a particular region.

notwithstanding *adverb*

nougat *noun*

nought *noun*
noughts

noun *noun*
nouns

nourish *verb*
nourishes
nourishing
nourished

nourishment *noun*

novel *adjective*

novel *noun*
novels

novelist *noun*
novelists

novelty *noun*
novelties

November *noun*
Novembers

novice *noun*
novices

nowadays *adverb*

nowhere *noun*

nozzle *noun*
nozzles

nuclear *adjective*

nucleus *noun*
nuclei

nude *adjective* & *noun*
nudes

nudge *verb*
nudges
nudging
nudged

nugget *noun*
nuggets

nuisance *noun*
nuisances

numb *adjective*
numbly *adverb*

number *noun*
numbers

number *verb*
numbers
numbering
numbered

numbness *noun*

numeracy *noun*

numeral *noun*
numerals

numerate *adjective*

numerator *noun*
numerators

numerical *adjective*
numerically *adverb*

numerous *adjective*

nun* *noun*
nuns

nunnery *noun*
nunneries

nurse *noun*
nurses

nurse *verb*
nurses
nursing
nursed

nursery *noun*
nurseries

nurture *verb*
nurtures
nurturing
nurtured

nut *noun*
nuts

nutcrackers *plural noun*

nutmeg *noun*
nutmegs

nutrient *noun*
nutrients

nutrition *noun*

nutritional *adjective*
nutritionally *adverb*

nutritious *adjective*

nutshell *noun*
nutshells

nutty *adjective*
nuttier
nuttiest

nuzzle *verb*
nuzzles
nuzzling
nuzzled

nylon *adjective* & *noun*
nylons

nymph *noun*
nymphs

---

* A **nun** is a member of a convent. **! none**.

a b c d e f g h i j k l m n o p q r s t u v w x y z

Oo

-o
Most nouns ending in *-o*, e.g. **hero**, **potato**, have plurals ending in *-oes*, e.g. **heroes**, **potatoes**, but a few end in *-os*. The most important are **kilos**, **photos**, **pianos**, **radios**, **ratios**, **solos**, **videos**, **zeros**. Verbs ending in *-o* usually have the forms *-oes* and *-oed*, e.g. **video** - **videoes** - **videoed**.

oak *noun*
oaks
oar* *noun*
oars
oarsman *noun*
oarsmen
oarswoman *noun*
oarswomen
oasis *noun*
oases
oath *noun*
oaths
oatmeal *noun*
oats *plural noun*
obedience *noun*
obedient *adjective*
obediently *adverb*
obese *adjective*
obesity *noun*
obey *verb*
obeys
obeying
obeyed
obituary *noun*
obituaries
object *noun*
objects
object *verb*
objects
objecting
objected
objection *noun*
objections
objectionable *adjective*
objective *adjective*
objectively *adverb*
objective *noun*
objectives
objector *noun*
objectors
obligation *noun*
obligations
obligatory *adjective*
oblige *verb*
obliges
obliging
obliged
oblique *adjective*
obliquely *adverb*
oblivious *adjective*
oblong *adjective & noun*
oblongs
obnoxious *adjective*
obnoxiously *adverb*
oboe *noun*
oboes
oboist *noun*
oboists
obscure *adjective*
obscurer
obscurest
obscurely *adverb*
obscurity *noun*
observance *noun*
observances
observant *adjective*
observantly *adverb*
observation *noun*
observations
observatory *noun*
observatories
observe *verb*
observes
observing
observed
observer *noun*
observers
obsessed *adjective*
obsession *noun*
obsessions
obsolete *adjective*
obstacle *noun*
obstacles
obstinacy *noun*
obstinate *adjective*
obstinately *adverb*
obstruct *verb*
obstructs
obstructing
obstructed
obstruction *noun*
obstructions
obstructive *adjective*
obstructively *adverb*
obtain *verb*
obtains
obtaining
obtained
obtainable *adjective*
obtuse *adjective*

* An **oar** is used for rowing a boat. **! or**, **ore**.

obvious *adjective*
obviously *adverb*
occasion *noun*
occasions
occasional *adjective*
occasionally *adverb*
occupant *noun*
occupants
occupation *noun*
occupations
occupy *verb*
occupies
occupying
occupied
occur *verb*
occurs
occurring
occurred
occurrence *noun*
occurrences
ocean *noun*
oceans
o'clock *adverb*
octagon *noun*
octagons
octagonal *adjective*
octave *noun*
octaves
October *noun*
Octobers
octopus *noun*
octopuses
odd *adjective*
odder
oddest
oddly *adverb*
oddity *noun*
oddities
oddments *plural noun*
oddness *noun*
odds *plural noun*
ode *noun*
odes

odour *noun*
odours
odorous *adjective*
oesophagus *noun*
oesophagi *or*
oesophaguses
of★ *preposition*
off☆ *preposition*
offence *noun*
offences
offend *verb*
offends
offending
offended
offender *noun*
offenders
offensive *adjective*
offensively *adverb*
offer *verb*
offers
offering
offered
offer *noun*
offers
offhand *adjective*
office *noun*
offices
officer *noun*
officers
official *adjective*
officially *adverb*
official *noun*
officials
officious *adjective*
officiously *adverb*
off-licence *noun*
off-licences
offset *verb*
offsets
offsetting
offset
offshore *adjective* & *adverb*
offside *adjective* & *adverb*

offspring *noun*
offspring
often *adverb*
ogre *noun*
ogres
ohm *noun*
ohms
oil *noun*
oils
oil *verb*
oils
oiling
oiled
oilfield *noun*
oilfields
oilskin *noun*
oilskins
oil well *noun*
oil wells
oily *adjective*
oilier
oiliest
ointment *noun*
ointments
old *adjective*
older
oldest
olive *noun*
olives
Olympic Games *plural noun*
Olympics *plural noun*
ombudsman *noun*
ombudsmen
omelette *noun*
omelettes
omen *noun*
omens
ominous *adjective*
ominously *adverb*
omission✪ *noun*
omissions

★ You use **of** in e.g. *a box of matches*. **! off.**
☆ You use **off** in e.g. *turn off the light*. **! of.**
✪ An **omission** is something left out. **! emission.**

a b c d e f g h i j k l m n o p q r s t u v w x y z

omit *verb*
omits
omitting
omitted
omnivore *noun*
omnivores
omnivorous *adjective*
on *preposition*
once *adverb*
one★ *adjective & noun*
ones
oneself *pronoun*
one-sided *adjective*
one-way *adjective*
ongoing *adjective*
onion *noun*
onions
online *adjective & adverb*
onlooker *noun*
onlookers
only *adjective*
onomatopoeia *noun*
onshore *adjective & adverb*
onslaught *noun*
onslaughts
onto *preposition*
onward *adjective & adverb*
onwards *adverb*
ooze *verb*
oozes
oozing
oozed
opaque *adjective*
open *adjective*
openly *adverb*
open *verb*
opens
opening
opened
opener *noun*
openers

opening *noun*
openings
opera *noun*
operas
operate *verb*
operates
operating
operated
operatic *adjective*
operation *noun*
operations
operator *noun*
operators
opinion *noun*
opinions
opium *noun*
opponent *noun*
opponents
opportunity *noun*
opportunities
oppose *verb*
opposes
opposing
opposed
opposite *adjective*
opposite *noun*
opposites
opposition *noun*
oppress *verb*
oppresses
oppressing
oppressed
oppression *noun*
oppressive *adjective*
oppressively *adverb*
oppressor *noun*
oppressors
opt *verb*
opts
opting
opted
optical *adjective*
optically *adverb*

optician *noun*
opticians
optimism *noun*
optimist *noun*
optimists
optimistic *adjective*
optimistically *adverb*
option *noun*
options
optional *adjective*
optionally *adverb*
opulence *noun*
opulent *adjective*
opulently *adverb*
or☆ *conjunction*
oral✪ *adjective*
orally *adverb*
orange *adjective & noun*
oranges
orangeade *noun*
orangeades
orang-utan *noun*
orang-utans
oration *noun*
orations
orator *noun*
orators
oratorical *adjective*
oratorio *noun*
oratorios
oratory *noun*
orbit *noun*
orbits
orbit *verb*
orbits
orbiting
orbited
orbital *adjective*
orchard *noun*
orchards
orchestra *noun*
orchestras
orchestral *adjective*

★ You use **one** in e.g. *one more time.* **! won.**
☆ You use **or** in e.g. *Do you want a cake or a biscuit?* **! oar, ore.**
✪ **Oral** means spoken aloud. **! aural.**

orchid *noun*
orchids
ordeal *noun*
ordeals
order *noun*
orders
order *verb*
orders
ordering
ordered
orderliness *noun*
orderly *adjective* & *noun*
ordinal number *noun*
ordinal numbers
ordinary *adjective*
ordinarily *adverb*
ore* *noun*
ores
organ *noun*
organs
organic *adjective*
organically *adverb*
organism *noun*
organisms
organist *noun*
organists
organization *noun*
organizations
organize *verb*
organizes
organizing
organized
organizer *noun*
organizers
oriental *adjective*
orienteering *noun*
origami *noun*
origin *noun*
origins
original *adjective*
originally *adverb*
originality *noun*

originate *verb*
originates
originating
originated
origination *noun*
originator *noun*
originators
ornament *noun*
ornaments
ornamental *adjective*
ornamentally *adverb*
ornamentation *noun*
ornithological *adjective*
ornithologist *noun*
ornithology *noun*
orphan *noun*
orphans
orphanage *noun*
orphanages
orthodox *adjective*
Orthodox Church
orthodoxy *noun*
oscillate *verb*
oscillates
oscillating
oscillated
oscillation *noun*
oscillations
ostrich *noun*
ostriches
other *adjective* & *noun*
others
otherwise *adverb*
otter *noun*
otters
ought *auxiliary verb*
ounce *noun*
ounces
our *posessive pronoun*
ours *posessive pronoun*
ourselves *pronoun*
out *adverb*
outback *noun*

outboard motor *noun*
outboard motors
outbreak *noun*
outbreaks
outburst *noun*
outbursts
outcast *noun*
outcasts
outcome *noun*
outcomes
outcry *noun*
outcries
outdated *adjective*
outdo *verb*
outdoes
outdoing
outdid
outdone
outdoor *adjective*
outdoors *adverb*
outer *adjective*
outfit *noun*
outfits
outgoing *adjective*
outgrow *verb*
outgrows
outgrowing
outgrew
outgrown
outhouse *noun*
outhouses
outing *noun*
outings
outlast *verb*
outlasts
outlasting
outlasted
outlaw *noun*
outlaws
outlaw *verb*
outlaws
outlawing
outlawed
outlet *noun*
outlets

* **Ore** is rock with metal in it. **! oar, or.**

outline *noun*
outlines
outline *verb*
outlines
outlining
outlined
outlook *noun*
outlooks
outlying *adjective*
outnumber *verb*
outnumbers
outnumbering
outnumbered
outpatient *noun*
outpatients
outpost *noun*
outposts
output *verb*
outputs
outputting
output
output *noun*
outputs
outrage *noun*
outrages
outrage *verb*
outrages
outraging
outraged
outrageous *adjective*
outrageously *adverb*
outright *adverb*
outset *noun*
outside *adverb & preposition*
outside *noun*
outsides
outsider *noun*
outsiders
outskirts *plural noun*
outspoken *adjective*
outstanding *adjective*
outstandingly *adverb*
outward *adjective*
outwardly *adverb*
outwards *adverb*

outweigh *verb*
outweighs
outweighing
outweighed
outwit *verb*
outwits
outwitting
outwitted
oval *adjective & noun*
ovals
ovary *noun*
ovaries
oven *noun*
ovens
over *adverb & preposition*
over *noun*
overs

> **over-** *prefix*
> *over-* makes words meaning 'too' or 'too much', e.g. **overactive** and **overcook**. You do not need a hyphen, except in some words beginning with *e*, e.g. **over-eager**.

overall *adjective*
overalls *plural noun*
overarm *adjective*
overboard *adverb*
overcast *adjective*
overcoat *noun*
overcoats
overcome *verb*
overcomes
overcoming
overcame
overcome
overdo *verb*
overdoes
overdoing
overdid
overdone
overdose *noun*
overdoses
overdue *adjective*

overflow *verb*
overflows
overflowing
overflowed
overgrown *adjective*
overhang *verb*
overhangs
overhanging
overhung
overhaul *verb*
overhauls
overhauling
overhauled
overhead *adjective*
overheads *plural noun*
overhear *verb*
overhears
overhearing
overheard
overland *adjective*
overlap *verb*
overlaps
overlapping
overlapped
overlook *verb*
overlooks
overlooking
overlooked
overly *adverb*
overnight *adjective & adverb*
overpower *verb*
overpowers
overpowering
overpowered
overrun *verb*
overruns
overrunning
overran
overrun
overseas *adjective & adverb*
oversight *noun*
oversights
oversleep *verb*
oversleeps
oversleeping
overslept

overtake *verb*
overtakes
overtaking
overtook
overtaken

overthrow *verb*
overthrows
overthrowing
overthrew
overthrown

overthrow *noun*
overthrows

overtime *noun*

overture *noun*
overtures

overturn *verb*
overturns
overturning
overturned

overwhelm *verb*
overwhelms
overwhelming
overwhelmed

overwork *verb*
overworks
overworking
overworked

overwork *noun*

ovum *noun*
ova

owe *verb*
owes
owing
owed

owl *noun*
owls

own *adjective*

own *verb*
owns
owning
owned

owner *noun*
owners

ownership *noun*

ox *noun*
oxen

oxidation *noun*

oxide *noun*
oxides

oxidize *verb*
oxidizes
oxidizing
oxidized

oxygen *noun*

oyster *noun*
oysters

ozone *noun*

Pp

pace *noun*
paces
pace *verb*
paces
pacing
paced
pacemaker *noun*
pacemakers
pacification *noun*
pacifism *noun*
pacifist *noun*
pacifists
pacify *verb*
pacifies
pacifying
pacified
pack *verb*
packs
packing
packed
pack *noun*
packs
package *noun*
packages
packet *noun*
packets
pad *noun*
pads
pad *verb*
pads
padding
padded
padding *noun*
paddle *verb*
paddles
paddling
paddled
paddle *noun*
paddles
paddock *noun*
paddocks
paddy *noun*
paddies
padlock *noun*
padlocks
paella *noun*
paellas
pagan *adjective & noun*
pagans
page *noun*
pages
pageant *noun*
pageants
pageantry *noun*
pagoda *noun*
pagodas
paid *verb* SEE **pay**
pail★ *noun*
pails
pain☆ *noun*
pains
pain *verb*
pains
paining
pained
painful *adjective*
painfully *adverb*
painkiller *noun*
painkillers
painless *adjective*
painlessly *adverb*
painstaking *adjective*
paint *noun*
paints
paint *verb*
paints
painting
painted
paintbox *noun*
paintboxes
paintbrush *noun*
paintbrushes
painter *noun*
painters
painting *noun*
paintings
pair✪ *noun*
pairs
pair *verb*
pairs
pairing
paired
pal *noun*
pals
palace *noun*
palaces
palate *noun*
palates
pale✣ *adjective*
paler
palest
paleness *noun*
palette *noun*
palettes
paling *noun*
palings
palisade *noun*
palisades

★ A **pail** is a bucket. **! pale**.
☆ A **pain** is an unpleasant feeling caused by injury or disease. **! pane**.
✪ A **pair** is a set of two. **! pear**.
✣ **Pale** means 'almost white'. **! pail**.

pall *verb*
palls
palling
palled
pallid *adjective*
pallor *noun*
palm *noun*
palms
palm *verb*
palms
palming
palmed
palmistry *noun*
paltry *adjective*
paltrier
paltriest
pampas *plural noun*
pamper *verb*
pampers
pampering
pampered
pamphlet *noun*
pamphlets
pan *noun*
pans
pancake *noun*
pancakes
panda *noun*
pandas
pandemonium *noun*
pander *verb*
panders
pandering
pandered
pane* *noun*
panes
panel *noun*
panels
pang *noun*
pangs
panic *noun*
panic *verb*
panics
panicking
panicked

panicky *adjective*
pannier *noun*
panniers
panorama *noun*
panoramas
panoramic *adjective*
pansy *noun*
pansies
pant *verb*
pants
panting
panted
panther *noun*
panthers
pantomime *noun*
pantomimes
pantry *noun*
pantries
paper *noun*
papers
paper *verb*
papers
papering
papered
paperback *noun*
paperbacks
papier mâché *noun*
papyrus *noun*
papyri
parable *noun*
parables
parachute *noun*
parachutes
parachutist *noun*
parade *noun*
parades
parade *verb*
parades
parading
paraded
paradise *noun*
paradox *noun*
paradoxes
paradoxical *adjective*
paradoxically *adverb*

paraffin *noun*
paragraph *noun*
paragraphs
parallel *adjective & noun*
parallelogram *noun*
parallelograms
paralyse *verb*
paralyses
paralysing
paralysed
paralysis *noun*
paralyses
paralytic *adjective*
paranoid *adjective*
paranormal *adjective & noun*
parapet *noun*
parapets
paraphernalia *noun*
paraphrase *verb*
paraphrases
paraphrasing
paraphrased
parasite *noun*
parasites
parasitic *adjective*
parasitically *adverb*
parasol *noun*
parasols
paratrooper *noun*
paratroops *plural noun*
parcel *noun*
parcels
parched *adjective*
parchment *noun*
pardon *verb*
pardons
pardoning
pardoned
pardon *noun*
pardons
pardonable *adjective*

* A **pane** is a piece of glass in a window. **! pain**.

a b c d e f g h i j k l m n o p q r s t u v w x y z

parent *noun*
parents
parentage *noun*
parental *adjective*
parenthood *noun*
parenthesis *noun*
parentheses
parish *noun*
parishes
parishioner *noun*
parishioners
park *noun*
parks
park *verb*
parks
parking
parked
parka *noun*
parkas
parliament *noun*
parliaments
parliamentary *adjective*
parody *noun*
parodies
parole *noun*
parrot *noun*
parrots
parsley *noun*
parsnip *noun*
parsnips
parson *noun*
parsons
parsonage *noun*
parsonages
part *noun*
parts
part *verb*
parts
parting
parted
partake *verb*
partial *adjective*
partially *adverb*
partiality *noun*
participant *noun*
participants
participate *verb*
participates
participating
participated
participation *noun*
participle *noun*
participles
particle *noun*
particles
particular *adjective*
particularly *adverb*
particulars *plural noun*
parting *noun*
partings
partition *noun*
partitions
partly *adverb*
partner *noun*
partners
partnership *noun*
partnerships
partridge *noun*
partridges
part-time *adjective*
party *noun*
parties
pass *verb*
passes
passing
passed
pass *noun*
passes
passable *adjective*
passage *noun*
passages
passageway *noun*
passageways
passed* *verb* SEE **pass**
passenger *noun*
passengers
passer-by *noun*
passers-by
passion *noun*
passions
passionate *adjective*
passionately *adverb*
passive *adjective*
passively *adverb*
Passover *noun*
passport *noun*
passports
password *noun*
passwords
past☆ *noun, adjective, & adverb*
pasta *noun*
pastas
paste *noun*
pastes
paste *verb*
pastes
pasting
pasted
pastel *noun*
pastels
pasteurization *noun*
pasteurize *verb*
pasteurizes
pasteurizing
pasteurized
pastille *noun*
pastilles
pastime *noun*
pastimes
pastoral *adjective*
pastry *noun*
pastries
pasture *noun*
pastures
pasty *noun*
pasties
pasty *adjective*
pastier
pastiest

* You use **passed** in e.g. *We passed the house.* **! past.**
☆ You use **past** in e.g. *We went past the house.* **! passed.**

pat *verb*
pats
patting
patted

pat *noun*
pats

patch *noun*
patches

patch *verb*
patches
patching
patched

patchwork *noun*

patchy *adjective*
patchier
patchiest

patent *adjective*
patently *adverb*

patent *verb*
patents
patenting
patented

patent *noun*
patents

paternal *adjective*

path *noun*
paths

pathetic *adjective*
pathetically *adverb*

patience

patient *adjective*
patiently *adverb*

patient *noun*
patients

patio *noun*
patios

patriot *noun*
patriots

patriotic *adjective*
patriotically *adverb*

patriotism *noun*

patrol *verb*
patrols
patrolling
patrolled

patrol *noun*
patrols

patron *noun*
patrons

patronage *noun*

patronize *verb*
patronizes
patronizing
patronized

patter *verb*
patters
pattering
pattered

patter *noun*
patters

pattern *noun*
patterns

pause *verb*
pauses
pausing
paused

pause *noun*
pauses

pave *verb*
paves
paving
paved

pavement *noun*
pavements

pavilion *noun*
pavilions

paw *noun*
paws

paw *verb*
paws
pawing
pawed

pawn *noun*
pawns

pawn *verb*
pawns
pawning
pawned

pawnbroker *noun*
pawnbrokers

pay *verb*
pays
paying
paid

pay *noun*

payment *noun*
payments

PC *noun*
PCs

pea *noun*
peas

peace★ *noun*

peaceful *adjective*
peacefully *adverb*

peach *noun*
peaches

peacock *noun*
peacocks

peak☆ *noun*
peaks

peak✪ *verb*
peaks
peaking
peaked

peaked *adjective*

peal✥ *verb*
peals
pealing
pealed

peal● *noun*
peals

peanut *noun*
peanuts

★ **Peace** is a time when there is no war. **! piece.**
☆ A **peak** is the top of something. **! peek.**
✪ To **peak** is to reach the highest point. **! peek.**
✥ To **peal** is to make a ringing sound of bells. **! peel.**
● A **peal** is a ringing of bells. **! peel.**

a b c d e f g h i j k l m n o p q r s t u v w x y z

pear★ *noun*
pears
pearl *noun*
pearls
pearly *adjective*
pearlier
pearliest
peasant *noun*
peasants
peasantry *noun*
peat *noun*
pebble *noun*
pebbles
pebbly *adjective*
pebblier
pebbliest
peck *verb*
pecks
pecking
pecked
peck *noun*
pecks
peckish *adjective*
peculiar *adjective*
peculiarly *adverb*
peculiarity *noun*
peculiarities
pedal *noun*
pedals
pedal *verb*
pedals
pedalling
pedalled
peddle☆ *verb*
peddles
peddling
peddled
pedestal *noun*
pedestals
pedestrian *noun*
pedestrians
pedestrian *adjective*
pedigree *noun*
pedigrees
pedlar *noun*
pedlars
peek✪ *verb*
peeks
peeking
peeked
peel✣ *noun*
peels
peel● *verb*
peels
peeling
peeled
peep *verb*
peeps
peeping
peeped
peep *noun*
peeps
peer✱ *verb*
peers
peering
peered
peer *noun*
peers
peerless *adjective*
peewit *noun*
peewits
peg *noun*
pegs
peg *verb*
pegs
pegging
pegged
pelican *noun*
pelicans
pellet *noun*
pellets
pelt *verb*
pelts
pelting
pelted
pelt *noun*
pelts
pen *noun*
pens
penalize *verb*
penalizes
penalizing
penalized
penalty *noun*
penalties
pence *plural noun* SEE **penny**
pencil *noun*
pencils
pencil *verb*
pencils
pencilling
pencilled
pendant *noun*
pendants
pending *adjective* & *preposition*
pendulum *noun*
pendulums
penetrate *verb*
penetrates
penetrating
penetrated
penetration *noun*
penfriend *noun*
penfriends
penguin *noun*
penguins
penicillin *noun*
peninsula *noun*
peninsulas
peninsular *adjective*

★ A **pear** is a fruit. **! pair**.
☆ To **peddle** is to sell things on the street. **! pedal**.
✪ To **peek** is to look secretly at something. **! peak**.
✣ **Peel** is the skin of fruit and vegetables. **! peal**.
● To **peel** something is to take the skin off it. **! peal**.
✱ To **peer** is to look closely at something. **! pier**.

penitence *noun*
penitent *adjective*
penknife *noun*
penknives
pennant *noun*
pennants
pennies *noun* SEE **penny**
penniless *adjective*
penny *noun*
pennies *or* pence
pension *noun*
pensions
pensioner *noun*
pensioners
pentagon *noun*
pentagons
pentathlon *noun*
pentathlons
peony *noun*
peonies
people *plural noun*
people *noun*
peoples
pepper *noun*
peppers
peppermint *noun*
peppermints
peppery *adjective*
perceive *verb*
perceives
perceiving
perceived
per cent *adverb*
percentage *noun*
percentages
perceptible *adjective*
perceptibly *adverb*
perception *noun*
perceptions
perceptive *adjective*
perceptively *adverb*
perch *verb*
perches
perching
perched
perch *noun*
perch

percolator *noun*
percolators
percussion *noun*
percussive *adjective*
perennial *adjective*
perennially *adverb*
perennial *noun*
perennials
perfect *adjective*
perfectly *adverb*
perfect *verb*
perfects
perfecting
perfected
perfection *noun*
perforate *verb*
perforates
perforating
perforated
perforation *noun*
perforations
perform *verb*
performs
performing
performed
performance *noun*
performances
performer *noun*
performers
perfume *noun*
perfumes
perhaps *adverb*
peril *noun*
perils
perilous *adjective*
perilously *adverb*
perimeter *noun*
perimeters
period *noun*
periods
periodic *adjective*
periodically *adverb*
periodical *noun*
periodicals
periscope *noun*
periscopes

perish *verb*
perishes
perishing
perished
perishable *adjective*
perm *noun*
perms
perm *verb*
perms
perming
permed
permanence *noun*
permanent *adjective*
permanently *adverb*
permissible *adjective*
permission *noun*
permissive *adjective*
permissiveness *noun*
permit *verb*
permits
permitting
permitted
permit *noun*
permits
perpendicular *adjective*
perpetual *adjective*
perpetually *adverb*
perpetuate *verb*
perpetuates
perpetuating
perpetuated
perplex *verb*
perplexes
perplexing
perplexed
perplexity *noun*
persecute *verb*
persecutes
persecuting
persecuted
persecution *noun*
persecutions
persecutor *noun*
persecutors
perseverance *noun*

persevere *verb*
perseveres
persevering
persevered

persist *verb*
persists
persisting
persisted

persistence *noun*

persistent *adjective*
persistently *adverb*

person★ *noun*
persons *or* people

personal *adjective*
personally *adverb*

personality *noun*
personalities

personification *noun*

personnel *plural noun*

perspective *noun*
perspectives

perspiration *noun*

perspire *verb*
perspires
perspiring
perspired

persuade *verb*
persuades
persuading
persuaded

persuasion *noun*

persuasive *adjective*
persuasively *adverb*

Pesach☆ *noun*

pessimism *noun*

pessimist *noun*
pessimists

pessimistic *adjective*
pessimistically *adverb*

pest *noun*
pests

pester *verb*
pesters
pestering
pestered

pesticide *noun*
pesticides

pestle *noun*
pestles

pet *noun*
pets

petal *noun*
petals

petite *adjective*

petition *noun*
petitions

petrify *verb*
petrifies
petrifying
petrified

petrochemical *noun*
petrochemicals

petrol *noun*

petroleum *noun*

petticoat *noun*
petticoats

pettiness *noun*

petty *adjective*
pettier
pettiest
pettily *adverb*

pew *noun*
pews

pewter *noun*

pH *noun*

pharmacy *noun*
pharmacies

phase *noun*
phases

phase *verb*
phases
phasing
phased

pheasant *noun*
pheasants

phenomenal *adjective*
phenomenally *adverb*

phenomenon *noun*
phenomena

philatelist *noun*
philatelists

philately *noun*

philosopher *noun*
philosophers

philosophical *adjective*
philosophically *adverb*

philosophy *noun*
philosophies

phobia *noun*
phobias

-phobia *suffix*
-phobia makes words meaning 'a strong fear or dislike', e.g. **xenophobia** (a dislike of strangers). It comes from a Greek word and is only used with other Greek or Latin words.

phoenix *noun*
phoenixes

phone *noun*
phones

phone *verb*
phones
phoning
phoned

-phone *suffix*
-phone makes words to do with sound, e.g. **telephone**, **saxophone**. You can sometimes make adjectives by using *-phonic*, e.g. **telephonic**, and nouns by using *-phony*, e.g. **telephony**.

phonecard *noun*
phonecards

★ The normal plural is **people**: *three people came*. **Persons** is formal, e.g. in official reports.

☆ The Hebrew name for Passover. Pronounced *pay-sahk*.

phone-in *noun*
phone-ins
phosphorescence *noun*
phosphorescent *adjective*
phosphoric *adjective*
phosphorus *noun*
photo *noun*
photos

> **photo-** *prefix*
> *photo-* makes words to do with light, e.g. **photograph**, **photocopy**. It is also used in more technical words such as **photochemistry** (the chemistry of light) and as a separate word in **photo** (photograph) and **photo finish** (close finish to a race).

photocopier *noun*
photocopiers
photocopy *noun*
photocopies
photocopy *verb*
photocopies
photocopying
photocopied
photoelectric *adjective*
photograph *noun*
photographs
photograph *verb*
photographs
photographing
photographed
photographer *noun*
photographers
photographic *adjective*
photographically *adverb*
photography *noun*
photosynthesis *noun*
phrase *noun*
phrases
phrase *verb*
phrases
phrasing
phrased
physical *adjective*
physically *adverb*
physician *noun*
physicians
physicist *noun*
physicists
physics *noun*
physiological *adjective*
physiologist *noun*
physiologists
physiology *noun*
pi★ *noun*
pianist *noun*
pianists
piano *noun*
pianos
piazza *noun*
piazzas
piccolo *noun*
piccolos
pick *verb*
picks
picking
picked
pick *noun*
picks
pickaxe *noun*
pickaxes
picket *noun*
pickets
picket *verb*
pickets
picketing
picketed
pickle *noun*
pickles
pickle *verb*
pickles
pickling
pickled
pickpocket *noun*
pickpockets
pickup *noun*
pickups
picnic *noun*
picnics
picnic *verb*
picnics
picnicking
picnicked
picnicker *noun*
picnickers
pictogram *noun*
pictograms
pictorial *adjective*
pictorially *adverb*
picture *noun*
pictures
picture *verb*
pictures
picturing
pictured
picturesque *adjective*
pie☆ *noun*
pies
piece✪ *noun*
pieces
piece *verb*
pieces
piecing
pieced
piecemeal *adjective & adverb*
pie chart *noun*
pie charts
pier✣ *noun*
piers

★ **Pi** is a Greek letter, used in mathematics. **! pie**.
☆ A **pie** is a food with pastry. **! pi**.
✪ You use **piece** in e.g. *a piece of cake*. **! peace**.
✣ A **pier** is a long building on stilts going into the sea. **! peer**.

pierce *verb*
pierces
piercing
pierced

pig *noun*
pigs

pigeon *noun*
pigeons

pigeonhole *noun*
pigeonholes

piggy *noun*
piggies

piggyback *noun*
piggybacks

piglet *noun*
piglets

pigment *noun*
pigments

pigmy *noun* SEE **pygmy**

pigsty *noun*
pigsties

pigtail *noun*
pigtails

pike *noun*
pikes

pilchard *noun*
pilchards

pile *noun*
piles

pile *verb*
piles
piling
piled

pilfer *verb*
pilfers
pilfering
pilfered

pilgrim *noun*
pilgrims

pilgrimage *noun*
pilgrimages

pill *noun*
pills

pillage *verb*
pillages
pillaging
pillaged

pillar *noun*
pillars

pillion *noun*
pillions

pillow *noun*
pillows

pillowcase *noun*
pillowcases

pilot *noun*
pilots

pilot *verb*
pilots
piloting
piloted

pimple *noun*
pimples

pimply *adjective*
pimplier
pimpliest

pin *noun*
pins

pin *verb*
pins
pinning
pinned

pinafore *noun*
pinafores

pincer *noun*
pincers

pinch *verb*
pinches
pinching
pinched

pinch *noun*
pinches

pincushion *noun*
pincushions

pine *noun*
pines

pine *verb*
pines
pining
pined

pineapple *noun*
pineapples

ping-pong *noun*

pink *adjective*
pinker
pinkest

pink *noun*
pinks

pint *noun*
pints

pioneer *noun*
pioneers

pious *adjective*
piously *adverb*

pip *noun*
pips

pipe *noun*
pipes

pipe *verb*
pipes
piping
piped

pipeline *noun*
pipelines

piper *noun*
pipers

piracy *noun*

pirate *noun*
pirates

pistil★ *noun*
pistils

pistol☆ *noun*
pistols

piston *noun*
pistons

pit *noun*
pits

pit *verb*
pits
pitting
pitted

★ A **pistil** is a part of a flower. **! pistol**.
☆ A **pistol** is a gun. **! pistil**.

pitch *noun*
pitches
pitch *verb*
pitches
pitching
pitched
pitch-black *adjective*
pitcher *noun*
pitchers
pitchfork *noun*
pitchforks
pitfall *noun*
pitfalls
pitiful *adjective*
pitifully *adverb*
pitiless *adjective*
pitilessly *adverb*
pity *verb*
pities
pitying
pitied
pity *noun*
pivot *noun*
pivots
pivot *verb*
pivots
pivoting
pivoted
pixie *noun*
pixies
pizza *noun*
pizzas
pizzicato *adjective & adverb*
placard *noun*
placards
place★ *noun*
places
place *verb*
places
placing
placed
placid *adjective*
placidly *adverb*
plague *noun*
plagues
plague *verb*
plagues
plaguing
plagued
plaice☆ *noun*
plaice
plaid *noun*
plaids
plain✪ *adjective*
plainer
plainest
plainly *adverb*
plain *noun*
plains
plain clothes *noun*
plainness *noun*
plaintiff *noun*
plaintiffs
plaintive *adjective*
plaintively *adverb*
plait *noun*
plaits
plait *verb*
plaits
plaiting
plaited
plan *noun*
plans
plan *verb*
plans
planning
planned
plane✣ *noun*
planes
plane● *verb*
planes
planing
planed
planet *noun*
planets
planetary *adjective*
plank *noun*
planks
plankton *noun*
planner *noun*
planners
plant *noun*
plants
plant *verb*
plants
planting
planted
plantation *noun*
plantations
planter *noun*
planters
plaque *noun*
plaques
plasma *noun*
plaster *noun*
plasters
plaster *verb*
plasters
plastering
plastered
plasterer *noun*
plasterers
plaster of Paris *noun*
plastic *adjective & noun*
plastics
Plasticine® *noun*
plate *noun*
plates
plate *verb*
plates
plating
plated
plateau *noun*
plateaux

★ You use **place** in e.g. *a place in the country.* **! plaice.**
☆ A **plaice** is a fish. **! place.**
✪ **Plain** means 'not pretty or decorated'. **! plane.**
✣ A **plane** is an aeroplane, a level surface, a tool, or a tree. **! plain.**
● To **plane** wood is to make it smooth with a tool. **! plain.**

plateful *noun*
platefuls
platform *noun*
platforms
platinum *noun*
platoon *noun*
platoons
platypus *noun*
platypuses
play *verb*
plays
playing
played
play *noun*
plays
playback *noun*
playbacks
player *noun*
players
playful *adjective*
playfully *adverb*
playfulness *noun*
playground *noun*
playgrounds
playgroup *noun*
playgroups
playmate *noun*
playmates
play-off *noun*
play-offs
playtime *noun*
playtimes
playwright *noun*
playwrights
plea *noun*
pleas
plead *verb*
pleads
pleading
pleaded
pleasant *adjective*
pleasanter
pleasantest
pleasantly *adverb*

please *verb*
pleases
pleasing
pleased
pleasurable *adjective*
pleasurably *adverb*
pleasure *noun*
pleasures
pleat *noun*
pleats
pleated *adjective*
pledge *verb*
pledges
pledging
pledged
pledge *noun*
pledges
plentiful *adjective*
plentifully *adverb*
plenty *noun & adverb*
pliable *adjective*
pliers *plural noun*
plight *noun*
plights
plod *verb*
plods
plodding
plodded
plodder *noun*
plodders
plop *verb*
plops
plopping
plopped
plop *noun*
plops
plot *noun*
plots
plot *verb*
plots
plotting
plotted
plotter *noun*
plotters

plough *noun*
ploughs
plough *verb*
ploughs
ploughing
ploughed
ploughman *noun*
ploughmen
plover *noun*
plovers
pluck *verb*
plucks
plucking
plucked
pluck *noun*
plucky *adjective*
pluckier
pluckiest
pluckily *adverb*
plug *noun*
plugs
plug *verb*
plugs
plugging
plugged
plum★ *noun*
plums
plumage
plumb☆ *verb*
plumbs
plumbing
plumbed
plumber *noun*
plumbers
plumbing *noun*
plume *noun*
plumes
plumed *adjective*
plump *adjective*
plumper
plumpest
plump *verb*
plumps
plumping
plumped

★ A **plum** is a fruit. **! plumb.**
☆ To **plumb** water is to see how deep it is. **! plum.**

plunder *verb*
plunders
plundering
plundered
plunder *noun*
plunderer *noun*
plunderers
plunge *verb*
plunges
plunging
plunged
plunge *noun*
plunges
plural *adjective & noun*
plurals
plus *preposition*
plus *noun*
pluses
plutonium *noun*
plywood *noun*
pneumatic *adjective*
pneumonia *noun*
poach *verb*
poaches
poaching
poached
poacher *noun*
poachers
pocket *noun*
pockets
pocket *verb*
pockets
pocketing
pocketed
pocketful *noun*
pocketfuls
pod *noun*
pods
podgy *adjective*
podgier
podgiest
poem *noun*
poems
poet *noun*
poets

poetic *adjective*
poetically *adverb*
poetry *noun*
point *noun*
points
point *verb*
points
pointing
pointed
point-blank *adjective*
pointed *adjective*
pointedly *adverb*
pointer *noun*
pointers
pointless *adjective*
pointlessly *adverb*
poise *noun*
poise *verb*
poises
poising
poised
poison *noun*
poisons
poison *verb*
poisons
poisoning
poisoned
poisoner *noun*
poisoners
poisonous *adjective*
poisonously *adverb*
poke *verb*
pokes
poking
poked
poke *noun*
pokes
poker *noun*
pokers
polar *adjective*
Polaroid® *noun*
pole★ *noun*
poles
police *plural noun*

policeman *noun*
policemen
police officer *noun*
police officers
policewoman *noun*
policewomen
policy *noun*
policies
polio *noun*
polish *verb*
polishes
polishing
polished
polish *noun*
polishes
polished *adjective*
polite *adjective*
politer
politest
politely *adverb*
politeness *noun*
political *adjective*
politically *adverb*
politician *noun*
politicians
politics *noun*
polka *noun*
polkas
poll☆ *noun*
polls
pollen *noun*
pollinate *verb*
pollute *verb*
pollutes
polluting
polluted
pollution *noun*
polo *noun*
polo neck *noun*
polo necks
poltergeist *noun*
poltergeists
polygon *noun*
polygons

★ A **pole** is a long thin stick. **! poll.**
☆ A **poll** is a vote in an election. **! pole.**

a b c d e f g h i j k l m n o p q r s t u v w x y z

polyhedron *noun*
polyhedrons
polystyrene *noun*
polythene *noun*
pomp *noun*
pomposity *noun*
pompous *adjective*
pompously *adverb*
pond *noun*
ponds
ponder *verb*
ponders
pondering
pondered
ponderous *adjective*
ponderously *adverb*
pony *noun*
ponies
ponytail *noun*
ponytails
pony-trekking *noun*
poodle *noun*
poodles
pool *noun*
pools
pool *verb*
pools
pooling
pooled
poor *adjective*
poorer
poorest
poorly *adverb*
poorly *adjective & adverb*
pop *verb*
pops
popping
popped
pop *noun*
pops
popcorn *noun*
Pope *noun*
Popes
poplar *noun*
poplars
poppadom *noun*
poppadoms
poppy *noun*
poppies
popular *adjective*
popularly *adverb*
popularity *noun*
popularize *verb*
popularizes
popularizing
popularized
populated *adjective*
population *noun*
populations
populous *adjective*
porcelain *noun*
porch *noun*
porches
porcupine *noun*
porcupines
pore *noun*
pores
pore* *verb*
pores
poring
pored
pork *noun*
porosity *noun*
porous *adjective*
porpoise *noun*
porpoises
porridge *noun*
port *noun*
ports
portable *adjective*
portcullis *noun*
portcullises
porter *noun*
porters
portfolio *noun*
portfolios
porthole *noun*
portholes
portion *noun*
portions
portly *adjective*
portlier
portliest
portrait *noun*
portraits
portray *verb*
portrays
portraying
portrayed
portrayal *noun*
portrayals
pose *verb*
poses
posing
posed
pose *noun*
poses
poser *noun*
posers
posh *adjective*
posher
poshest
position *noun*
positions
positive *adjective*
positively *adverb*
positive *noun*
positives
posse *noun*
posses
possess *verb*
possesses
possessing
possessed
possession *noun*
possessions
possessive *adjective*
possessively *adverb*
possessor *noun*
possessors
possibility *noun*
possibilities
possible *adjective*
possibly *adverb*

* To **pore** over something is to study it closely. **! pour**.

post *verb*
posts
posting
posted

post *noun*
posts

postage *noun*

postal *adjective*

postbox *noun*
postboxes

postcard *noun*
postcards

postcode *noun*
postcodes

poster *noun*
posters

postman *noun*
postmen

postmark *noun*
postmarks

post-mortem *noun*
post-mortems

postpone *verb*
postpones
postponing
postponed

postponement *noun*
postponements

postscript *noun*
postscripts

posture *noun*
postures

posy *noun*
posies

pot *noun*
pots

pot *verb*
pots
potting
potted

potassium *noun*

potato *noun*
potatoes

potency *noun*

potent *adjective*
potently *adverb*

potential *adjective*
potentially *adverb*

potential *noun*
potentials

pothole *noun*
potholes

potholer *noun*
potholer

potholing *noun*

potion *noun*
potions

potter *noun*
potters

potter *verb*
potters
pottering
pottered

pottery *noun*
potteries

potty *adjective*
pottier
pottiest

potty *noun*
potties

pouch *noun*
pouches

poultry *noun*

pounce *verb*
pounces
pouncing
pounced

pound *noun*
pounds

pound *verb*
pounds
pounding
pounded

pour* *verb*
pours
pouring
poured

pout *verb*
pouts
pouting
pouted

poverty *noun*

powder *noun*
powders

powder *verb*
powders
powdering
powdered

powdery *adjective*

power *noun*
powers

powered *adjective*

powerful *adjective*
powerfully *adverb*

powerhouse *noun*
powerhouses

powerless *adjective*

practicable *adjective*

practical *adjective*
practically *adverb*

practical *noun*
practicals

practice *noun*
practices

practise *verb*
practises
practising
practised

prairie *noun*
prairies

praise *verb*
praises
praising
praised

praise *noun*
praises

pram *noun*
prams

prance *verb*
prances
prancing
pranced

* To **pour** a liquid is to tip it from a jug etc. **! pore.**

a b c d e f g h i j k l m n o **p** q r s t u v w x y z

prank *noun*
pranks
prawn *noun*
prawns
pray* *verb*
prays
praying
prayed
prayer *noun*
prayers

> **pre-** *prefix*
> *pre-* makes words meaning 'before', e.g. **pre-date** (to exist before something else), **prefabricated** (made in advance). Many are spelled joined up, but not all.

preach *verb*
preaches
preaching
preached
preacher *noun*
preachers
precarious *adjective*
precariously *adverb*
precaution *noun*
precautions
precede *verb*
precedes
preceding
preceded
precedence *noun*
precedent *noun*
precedents
precinct *noun*
precincts
precious *adjective*
preciously *adverb*
precipice *noun*
precipices
precis *noun*
precis
French précis
precise *adjective*
precisely *adverb*
precision *noun*
predator *noun*
predators
predatory *adjective*
predecessor *noun*
predecessors
predict *verb*
predicts
predicting
predicted
predictable *adjective*
predictably *adverb*
prediction *noun*
predictions
predictive text *noun*
predominance *noun*
predominant *adjective*
predominantly *adverb*
predominate *verb*
predominates
predominating
predominated
preface *noun*
prefaces
prefect *noun*
prefects
prefer *verb*
prefers
preferring
preferred
preferable *adjective*
preferably *adverb*
preference *noun*
preferences
prefix *noun*
prefixes
pregnancy *noun*
pregnancies
pregnant *adjective*
prehistoric *adjective*
prehistory *noun*
prejudice *noun*
prejudices
prejudiced *adjective*
preliminary *adjective & noun*
preliminaries
prelude *noun*
preludes
premature *adjective*
premier *noun*
premiers
premiere *noun*
premieres
French première
premises *plural noun*
premium *noun*
premiums
Premium Bond *noun*
Premium Bonds
preoccupation *noun*
preoccupations
preoccupied *adjective*
prep *noun*
preparation *noun*
preparations
preparatory *adjective*
prepare *verb*
prepares
preparing
prepared
preposition *noun*
prepositions
prescribe *verb*
prescribes
prescribing
prescribed
prescription *noun*
prescriptions
presence *noun*
present *adjective*
presently *adverb*
present *noun*
presents
present *verb*
presents
presenting
presented

* To **pray** is to say prayers. **! prey.**

presentation *noun*
presentations
presenter *noun*
presenters
preservation *noun*
preservative *noun*
preservatives
preserve *verb*
preserves
preserving
preserved
preside *verb*
presides
presiding
presided
presidency *noun*
presidencies
president *noun*
presidents
presidential *adjective*
press *verb*
presses
pressing
pressed
press *noun*
presses
press-up *noun*
press-ups
pressure *noun*
pressures
pressurize *verb*
pressurizes
pressurizing
pressurized
prestige *noun*
prestigious *adjective*
presumably *adverb*
presume *verb*
presumes
presuming
presumed
presumption *noun*
presumptions
presumptuous *adjective*
presumptuously *adverb*

pretence *noun*
pretences
pretend *verb*
pretends
pretending
pretended
pretender *noun*
pretenders
pretentious *adjective*
pretentiously *adverb*
pretext *noun*
pretexts
prettiness *noun*
pretty *adjective & adverb*
prettier
prettiest
prettily *adverb*
prevail *verb*
prevails
prevailing
prevailed
prevalent *adjective*
prevent *verb*
prevents
preventing
prevented
prevention *noun*
preventive *adjective*
preview *noun*
previews
previous *adjective*
previously *adverb*
prey* *verb*
preys
preying
preyed
prey *noun*
price *noun*
prices
price *verb*
prices
pricing
priced
priceless *adjective*

prick *verb*
pricks
pricking
pricked
prick *noun*
pricks
prickle *noun*
prickles
prickly *adjective*
pricklier
prickliest
pride *noun*
prides
priest *noun*
priests
priestess *noun*
priestesses
priesthood *noun*
prig *noun*
prigs
priggish *adjective*
priggishly *adverb*
prim *adjective*
primmer
primmest
primly *adverb*
primary *adjective*
primarily *adverb*
primate *noun*
primates
prime *adjective*
prime *verb*
primes
priming
primed
prime *noun*
primes
prime minister *noun*
prime ministers
primer *noun*
primers
primeval
primitive *adjective*
primitively *adverb*
primness *noun*

* To **prey** on animals is to hunt and kill them. **! pray.**

primrose *noun*
primroses
prince *noun*
princes
princely *adjective*
princess *noun*
princesses
principal★ *adjective*
principally *adverb*
principal☆ *noun*
principals
principle✪ *noun*
principles
print *verb*
prints
printing
printed
print *noun*
prints
printer *noun*
printers
printout *noun*
printouts
priority *noun*
priorities
prise✣ *verb*
prises
prising
prised
prism *noun*
prisms
prison *noun*
prisons
prisoner *noun*
prisoners
prestine *adjective*
privacy *noun*
private *adjective*
privately *adverb*
private *noun*
privates
privatization *noun*
privatize *verb*
privatizes
privatizing
privatized
privet *noun*
privilege *noun*
privileges
privileged *adjective*
prize *noun*
prizes
prize● *verb*
prizes
prizing
prized
pro *noun*
pros

pro- *prefix*
pro- makes words meaning 'in favour of', e.g. **pro-choice**. In this type of word you use a hyphen.

proactive *adjective*
probability *noun*
probabilities
probable *adjective*
probably *adverb*
probation *noun*
probationary *adjective*
probe *verb*
probes
probing
probed
probe *noun*
probes
problem *noun*
problems
procedure *noun*
procedures
proceed *verb*
proceeds
proceeding
proceeded
proceedings *plural noun*
proceeds *plural noun*
process *noun*
processes
process *verb*
processes
processing
processed
procession *noun*
processions
processor *noun*
processors
proclaim *verb*
proclaims
proclaiming
proclaimed
proclamation *noun*
proclamations
prod *verb*
prods
prodding
prodded
prodigal *adjective*
produce *verb*
produces
producing
produced
produce *noun*
producer *noun*
producers
product *noun*
products
production *noun*
productions
productive *adjective*
productively *adverb*
productivity

★ **Principal** means 'chief' or 'main'. **! principle.**
☆ A **principal** is a head of a college. **! principle.**
✪ A **principle** is a rule or belief. **! principal.**
✣ To **prise** something is to open it. **! prize.**
● To **prize** something is to value it highly. **! prise.**

profession *noun*
professions

professional *adjective*
professionally *adverb*

professional *noun*
professionals

professor *noun*
professors

proficiency *noun*

proficient *adjective*
proficiently *adverb*

profile *noun*
profiles

profit★ *noun*
profits

profit *verb*
profits
profiting
profited

profitable *adjective*
profitably *adverb*

profound *adjective*
profoundly *adverb*

profundity *noun*

profuse *adjective*
profusely *adverb*

profusion *noun*

program☆ *noun*
programs

program *verb*
programs
programming
programmed

programme☆ *noun*
programmes

progress *noun*

progress *verb*
progresses
progressing
progressed

progression *noun*

progressive *adjective*
progressively *adverb*

prohibit *verb*
prohibits
prohibiting
prohibited

prohibition *noun*
prohibitions

project *noun*
projects

project *verb*
projects
projecting
projected

projection *noun*
projections

projectionist *noun*
projectionists

projector *noun*
projectors

prologue *noun*
prologues

prolong *verb*
prolongs
prolonging
prolonged

promenade *noun*
promenades

prominence *noun*

prominent *adjective*
prominently *adverb*

promise *verb*
promises
promising
promised

promise *noun*
promises

promontory *noun*
promontories

promote *verb*
promotes
promoting
promoted

promoter *noun*
promoters

promotion *noun*
promotions

prompt *adjective*
prompter
promptest
promptly *adverb*

prompt *verb*
prompts
prompting
prompted

prompter *noun*
prompters

promptness *noun*

prone *adjective*

prong *noun*
prongs

pronoun *noun*
pronouns

pronounce *verb*
pronounces
pronouncing
pronounced

pronouncement *noun*
pronouncements

pronunciation *noun*
pronunciations

proof *adjective & noun*
proofs

prop *verb*
props
propping
propped

prop *noun*
props

propaganda *noun*

propel *verb*
propels
propelling
propelled

propellant *noun*
propellants

propeller *noun*
propellers

★ A **profit** is extra money made by selling something. **! prophet**.
☆ You use **program** when you are talking about computers. In other meanings you use **programme**.

a b c d e f g h i j k l m n o p q r s t u v w x y z

proper *adjective*
properly *adverb*
property *noun*
properties
prophecy *noun*
prophecies
prophesy *verb*
prophesies
prophesying
prophesied
prophet* *noun*
prophets
prophetic *adjective*
prophetically *adverb*
proportion *noun*
proportions
proportional *adjective*
proportionally *adverb*
proportionate *adjective*
proportionately *adverb*
propose *verb*
proposes
proposing
proposed
proposal *noun*
proposals
proprietor *noun*
proprietors
propulsion *noun*
prose *noun*
prosecute *verb*
prosecutes
prosecuting
prosecuted
prosecution *noun*
prosecutions
prosecutor *noun*
prosecutors
prospect *noun*
prospects
prospect *verb*
prospects
prospecting
prospected
prospector *noun*
prospectors

prosper *verb*
prospers
prospering
prospered
prosperity *noun*
prosperous *adjective*
prosperously *adverb*
protect *verb*
protects
protecting
protected
protection *noun*
protective *adjective*
protectively *adverb*
protector *noun*
protectors
protein *noun*
proteins
protest *verb*
protests
protesting
protested
protest *noun*
protests
protester *noun*
protesters
Protestant *noun*
Protestants
proton *noun*
protons
protoplasm *noun*
prototype *noun*
prototypes
protractor *noun*
protractors
protrude *verb*
protrudes
protruding
protruded
protrusion *noun*
protrusions
proud *adjective*
prouder
proudest
proudly *adverb*

prove *verb*
proves
proving
proved
proverb *noun*
proverbs
proverbial *adjective*
proverbially *adverb*
provide *verb*
provides
providing
provided
province *noun*
provinces
provincial *adjective*
provision *noun*
provisions
provisional *adjective*
provisionally *adverb*
provocative *adjective*
provocatively *adverb*
provoke *verb*
provokes
provoking
provoked
provocation *noun*
provocations
prow *noun*
prows
prowl *verb*
prowls
prowling
prowled
prowler *noun*
prowlers
proximity *noun*
prudence *noun*
prudent *adjective*
prudently *adverb*
prune *noun*
prunes
prune *verb*
prunes
pruning
pruned

* A **prophet** is someone who makes predictions about the future. **! profit.**

pry *verb*
pries
prying
pried

psalm *noun*
psalms

pseudonym *noun*
pseudonyms

psychiatric *adjective*

psychiatrist *noun*
psychiatrists

psychiatry *noun*

psychic *adjective*

psychological *adjective*
psychologically *adverb*

psychologist *noun*
psychologists

psychology *noun*

pub *noun*
pubs

puberty *noun*

public *adjective* & *noun*
publicly *adverb*

publication *noun*
publications

publicity *noun*

publicize *verb*
publicizes
publicizing
publicized

publish *verb*
publishes
publishing
published

publisher *noun*
publishers

puck *noun*
pucks

pucker *verb*
puckers
puckering
puckered

pudding *noun*
puddings

puddle *noun*
puddles

puff *verb*
puffs
puffing
puffed

puff *noun*
puffs

puffin *noun*
puffins

pull *verb*
pulls
pulling
pulled

pull *noun*
pulls

pulley *noun*
pulleys

pullover *noun*
pullovers

pulp *noun*
pulps

pulp *verb*
pulps
pulping
pulped

pulpit *noun*
pulpits

pulse *noun*
pulses

pulverize *verb*
pulverizes
pulverizing
pulverized

puma *noun*
pumas

pumice *noun*

pump *verb*
pumps
pumping
pumped

pump *noun*
pumps

pumpkin *noun*
pumpkins

pun *noun*
puns

pun *verb*
puns
punning
punned

punch *verb*
punches
punching
punched

punch *noun*
punches

punchline *noun*
punchlines

punch-up *noun*
punch-ups

punctual *adjective*
punctually *adverb*

punctuality *noun*

punctuate *verb*
punctuates
punctuating
punctuated

punctuation *noun*

puncture *noun*
punctures

punish *verb*
punishes
punishing
punished

punishment *noun*
punishments

punk *noun*
punks

punt *noun*
punts

punt *verb*
punts
punting
punted

puny *adjective*
punier
puniest

pup *noun*
pups

pupa *noun*
pupae

pupil *noun*
pupils

a b c d e f g h i j k l m n o p q r s t u v w x y z

puppet *noun*
puppets
puppy *noun*
puppies
purchase *verb*
purchases
purchasing
purchased
purchase *noun*
purchases
purchaser *noun*
purchasers
purdah *noun*
pure *adjective*
purer
purest
purely *adverb*
purge *verb*
purges
purging
purged
purge *noun*
purges
purification
purifier *noun*
purifiers
purify *verb*
purifies
purifying
purified
Puritan★ *noun*
Puritans

puritan *noun*
puritans
purity *noun*
purple *noun*
purpose *noun*
purposes
purposely *adverb*
purr *verb*
purrs
purring
purred
purse *noun*
purses
pursue *verb*
pursues
pursuing
pursued
pursuer *noun*
pursuers
pursuit *noun*
pursuits
pus☆ *noun*
push *verb*
pushes
pushing
pushed
push *noun*
pushes
pushchair *noun*
pushchairs

puss✪ *or* **pussy** *noun*
pusses *or* pussies
put✢ *verb*
puts
putting
put
putt● *verb*
putts
putting
putted
putter *noun*
putters
putty *noun*
puzzle *verb*
puzzles
puzzling
puzzled
puzzle *noun*
puzzles
pygmy *noun*
pygmies
pyjamas *plural noun*
pylon *noun*
pylons
pyramid *noun*
pyramids
pyramidal *adjective*
python *noun*
pythons

★ You use a capital P when you are talking about people in history, and a small p when you mean anyone who is morally strict.
☆ **Pus** is yellow stuff produced in sore places on the body. **! puss.**
✪ **Puss** is a word for a cat. **! pus.**
✢ To **put** something somewhere is to place it there. **! putt.**
● To **putt** a ball is to tap it gently. **! put.**

Qq

quack *verb*
quacks
quacking
quacked

quack *noun*
quacks

quad *noun*
quads

quadrangle *noun*
quadrangles

quadrant *noun*
quadrants

quadrilateral *noun*
quadrilaterals

quadruple *adjective & noun*

quadruple *verb*
quadruples
quadrupling
quadrupled

quadruplet *noun*
quadruplets

quail *verb*
quails
quailing
quailed

quail *noun*
quail
quails

quaint *adjective*
quainter
quaintest
quaintly *adverb*

quaintness *noun*

quake *verb*
quakes
quaking
quaked

Quaker *noun*
Quakers

qualification *noun*
qualifications

qualify *verb*
qualifies
qualifying
qualified

quality *noun*
qualities

quantity *noun*
quantities

quarantine *noun*

quarrel *noun*
quarrels

quarrel *verb*
quarrels
quarrelling
quarrelled

quarrelsome *adjective*

quarry *noun*
quarries

quart *noun*
quarts

quarter *noun*
quarters

quartet *noun*
quartets

quartz *noun*

quaver *verb*
quavers
quavering
quavered

quaver *noun*
quavers

quay★ *noun*
quays

queasy *adjective*
queasier
queasiest

queen *noun*
queens

queer *adjective*
queerer
queerest

quench *verb*
quenches
quenching
quenched

query *verb*
queries
querying
queried

query *noun*
queries

quest *noun*
quests

question *noun*
questions

question *verb*
questions
questioning
questioned

questionable *adjective*
questionably *adverb*

questioner *noun*
questioner

questionnaire *noun*
questionnaires

queue☆ *noun*
queues

queue *verb*
queues
queueing
queued

★ A **quay** is a place where ships tie up. **! key**.
☆ A **queue** is a line of people waiting for something. **! cue**.

quibble *verb*
quibbles
quibbling
quibbled

quibble *noun*
quibbles

quiche *noun*
quiches

quick *adjective*
quicker
quickest
quickly *adverb*

quicken *verb*
quickens
quickening
quickened

quicksand *noun*
quicksands

quid *noun*
quid

quiet *adjective*
quieter
quietest
quietly *adverb*

quieten *verb*
quietens
quietening
quietened

quill *noun*
quills

quilt *noun*
quilts

quintet *noun*
quintets

quirky *adjective*
quirkier
quirkiest

quit *verb*
quits
quitting
quitted
quit

quitter *noun*
quitters

quite *adverb*

quiver *verb*
quivers
quivering
quivered

quiver *noun*
quivers

quiz *noun*
quizzes

quiz *verb*
quizzes
quizzing
quizzed

quoit *noun*
quoits

quota *noun*
quotas

quotation *noun*
quotations

quote *verb*
quotes
quoting
quoted

quotient *noun*
quotients

Try also words beginning with **rh-** or **wr-**

Rr

rabbi *noun*
rabbis
rabbit *noun*
rabbits
rabid *adjective*
rabies *noun*
raccoon *noun*
raccoons
race *noun*
races
race *verb*
races
racing
raced
race *noun*
races
racecourse *noun*
racecourses
racer *noun*
racers
racial *adjective*
racially *adverb*
racism *noun*
racist *noun*
racists
rack *noun*
racks
rack *verb*
racks
racking
racked
racket *noun*
rackets
radar *noun*
radial *adjective*
radially *adverb*
radiance *noun*
radiant *adjective*
radiantly *adverb*

radiate *verb*
radiates
radiating
radiated
radiation *noun*
radiator *noun*
radiators
radical *adjective*
radically *adverb*
radical *noun*
radicals
radii *plural noun* SEE **radius**
radio *noun*
radios
radio *verb*
radios
radioing
radioed
radioactive *adjective*
radioactivity *noun*
radish *noun*
radishes
radium *noun*
radius *noun*
radii
raffle *noun*
raffles
raffle *verb*
raffles
raffling
raffled
raft *noun*
rafts
rafter *noun*
rafters
rag *noun*
rags
rage *noun*
rages

rage *verb*
rages
raging
raged
ragged *adjective*
ragtime *noun*
raid *noun*
raids
raid *verb*
raids
raiding
raided
raider *noun*
raiders
rail *noun*
rails
railings *plural noun*
railway *noun*
railways
rain *verb*
rains
raining
rained
rain *noun*
rains
rainbow *noun*
rainbows
raincoat *noun*
raincoats
raindrop *noun*
raindrops
rainfall *noun*
rainforest *noun*
rainforests
rainy *adjective*
rainier
rainiest
raise *verb*
raises
raising
raised

raisin *noun*
raisins

rake *verb*
rakes
raking
raked

rake *noun*
rakes

rally *verb*
rallies
rallying
rallied

rally *noun*
rallies

RAM *noun*

ram *verb*
rams
ramming
rammed

ram *noun*
rams

Ramadan *noun*

ramble *noun*
rambles

ramble *verb*
rambles
rambling
rambled

rambler *noun*
ramblers

ramp *noun*
ramps

rampage *verb*
rampages
rampaging
rampaged

rampage *noun*

ran *verb* SEE **run**

ranch *noun*
ranches

random *adjective*
randomly *adverb*

rang *verb* SEE **ring**

range *noun*
ranges

range *verb*
ranges
ranging
ranged

ranger *noun*
rangers

rank *noun*
ranks

rank *verb*
ranks
ranking
ranked

ransack *verb*
ransacks
ransacking
ransacked

ransom *verb*
ransoms
ransoming
ransomed

ransom *noun*
ransoms

rap* *verb*
raps
rapping
rapped

rap *noun*
raps

rapid *adjective*
rapidly *adverb*

rapidity *noun*

rapids *plural noun*

rare *adjective*
rarer
rarest
rarely *adverb*

rarity *noun*
rarities

rascal *noun*
rascals

rash *adjective*
rasher
rashest
rashly *adverb*

rash *noun*
rashes

rasher *noun*
rashers

raspberry *noun*
raspberries

Rastafarian *noun*
Rastafarians

rat *noun*
rats

rate *noun*
rates

rate *verb*
rates
rating
rated

rather *adverb*

ratio *noun*
ratios

ration *noun*
rations

ration *verb*
rations
rationing
rationed

rational *adjective*
rationally *adverb*

rationalize *verb*
rationalizes
rationalizing
rationalized

rattle *verb*
rattles
rattling
rattled

rattle *noun*
rattles

rattlesnake *noun*
rattlesnakes

rave *verb*
raves
raving
raved

* To **rap** is to knock loudly. **! wrap**.

rave *noun*
raves

raven *noun*
ravens

ravenous *adjective*
ravenously *adverb*

ravine *noun*
ravines

ravioli *noun*

raw *adjective*
rawer
rawest

ray *noun*
rays

razor *noun*
razors

re- *prefix*
re- makes words meaning 'again', e.g. **reproduce**. These words are normally spelled joined up, but a few need a hyphen so you don't confuse them with other words, e.g. **re-cover** (to put a new cover on); **recover** has another meaning. You also need a hyphen in words beginning with *e*, e.g. **re-enter**.

reach *verb*
reaches
reaching
reached

reach *noun*
reaches

react *verb*
reacts
reacting
reacted

reaction *noun*
reactions

reactor *noun*
reactors

read* *verb*
reads
reading
read

readable *adjective*

reader *noun*
readers

readily *adverb*

readiness *noun*

reading *noun*
readings

ready *adjective*
readier
readiest

real☆ *adjective*

realism *noun*

realist *noun*
realists

realistic *adjective*
realistically *adverb*

reality *noun*
realities

realization *noun*

realize *verb*
realizes
realizing
realized

really *adverb*

realm *noun*
realms

reap *verb*
reaps
reaping
reaped

reaper *noun*
reapers

reappear *verb*
reappears
reappearing
reappeared

reappearance *noun*
reappearances

rear *adjective & noun*
rears

rear *verb*
rears
rearing
reared

rearrange *verb*
rearranges
rearranging
rearranged

rearrangement *noun*
rearrangements

reason *noun*
reasons

reason *verb*
reasons
reasoning
reasoned

reasonable *adjective*
reasonably *adverb*

reassurance *noun*
reassurances

reassure *verb*
reassures
reassuring
reassured

rebel *verb*
rebels
rebelling
rebelled

rebel *noun*
rebels

rebellion *noun*
rebellions

rebellious *adjective*
rebelliously *adverb*

rebound *verb*
rebounds
rebounding
rebounded

rebuild *verb*
rebuilds
rebuilding
rebuilt

* To **read** is to look at something written or printed. **! reed**.
☆ **Real** means 'true' or 'existing'. **! reel**.

recall *verb*
recalls
recalling
recalled

recap *verb*
recaps
recapping
recapped

recapture *verb*
recaptures
recapturing
recaptured

recede *verb*
recedes
receding
receded

receipt *noun*
receipts

receive *verb*
receives
receiving
received

receiver *noun*
receivers

recent *adjective*
recently *adverb*

receptacle *noun*
receptacles

reception *noun*
receptions

receptionist *noun*
receptionists

receptive *adjective*

receptor *noun*
receptors

recess *noun*
recesses

recession *noun*
recessions

recipe *noun*
recipes

reciprocal *adjective*
reciprocally *adverb*

reciprocal *noun*
reciprocals

recital *noun*
recitals

recitation *noun*
recitations

recite *verb*
recites
reciting
recited

reckless *adjective*
recklessly *adverb*

recklessness *noun*

reckon *verb*
reckons
reckoning
reckoned

reclaim *verb*
reclaims
reclaiming
reclaimed

reclaimable *adjective*

reclamation *noun*
reclamations

recline *verb*
reclines
reclining
reclined

recognition *noun*

recognizable *adjective*
recognizably *adverb*

recognize *verb*
recognizes
recognizing
recognized

recoil *verb*
recoils
recoiling
recoiled

recollect *verb*
recollects
recollecting
recollected

recollection *noun*
recollections

recommend *verb*
recommends
recommending
recommended

recommendation *noun*
recommendations

reconcile *verb*
reconciles
reconciling
reconciled

reconciliation *noun*
reconciliations

reconsider *verb*

reconstruction *noun*
reconstructions

record *noun*
records

record *verb*
records
recording
recorded

recorder *noun*
recorders

recover *verb*
recovers
recovering
recovered

recovery *noun*
recoveries

recreation *noun*
recreations

recreational *adjective*
recreationally *adverb*

recruit *noun*
recruits

recruit *verb*
recruits
recruiting
recruited

rectangle *noun*
rectangles

rectangular *adjective*

recur *verb*
recurs
recurring
recurred

recurrence *noun*
recurrences

recycle *verb*
recycles
recycling
recycled

red *adjective*
redder
reddest

red *noun*
reds

redden *verb*
reddens
reddening
reddened

reddish *adjective*

redeem *verb*
redeems
redeeming
redeemed

redemption *noun*
redemptions

redhead *noun*
redheads

reduce *verb*
reduces
reducing
reduced

reduction *noun*
reductions

redundancy *noun*
redundancies

redundant *adjective*

reed★ *noun*
reeds

reedy *adjective*

reef *noun*
reefs

reef knot *noun*
reef knots

reek *verb*
reeks
reeking
reeked

reel☆ *noun*
reels

reel *verb*
reels
reeling
reeled

refer *verb*
refers
referring
referred

referee *noun*
referees

referee *verb*
referees
refereeing
refereed

reference *noun*
references

referendum *noun*
referendums

refill *verb*
refills
refilling
refilled

refill *noun*
refills

refine *verb*
refines
refining
refined

refinement *noun*
refinements

refinery *noun*
refineries

reflect *verb*
reflects
reflecting
reflected

reflection *noun*
reflections

reflective *adjective*
reflectively *adverb*

reflex *noun*
reflexes

reflexive *adjective*
reflexively *adverb*

reform *verb*
reforms
reforming
reformed

reform *noun*
reforms

reformation *noun*
reformations

Reformation✪ *noun*

reformer *noun*
reformers

refract *verb*
refracts
refracting
refracted

refraction *noun*

refrain *verb*
refrains
refraining
refrained

refrain *noun*
refrains

refresh *verb*
refreshes
refreshing
refreshed

refreshment *noun*
refreshments

refrigerate *verb*
refrigerates
refrigerating
refrigerated

refrigeration *noun*

refrigerator *noun*
refrigerators

refuel *verb*
refuels
refuelling
refuelled

★ A **reed** is a plant or a thin strip. **! read.**
☆ A **reel** is a cylinder on which something is wound. **! real.**
✪ You use a capital R when you mean the historical religious movement.

a b c d e f g h i j k l m n o p q r s t u v w x y z

refuge *noun*
refuges

refugee *noun*
refugees

refund *verb*
refunds
refunding
refunded

refund *noun*
refunds

refusal *noun*

refuse *verb*
refuses
refusing
refused

refuse *noun*

regain *verb*
regains
regaining
regained

regard *verb*
regards
regarding
regarded

regard *noun*
regards

regarding *preposition*

regardless *adverb*

regatta *noun*
regattas

reggae *noun*

regime *noun*
regimes

regiment *noun*
regiments

regimental *adjective*

region *noun*
regions

regional *adjective*
regionally *adverb*

register *noun*
registers

register *verb*
registers
registering
registered

registration *noun*
registrations

regret *noun*
regrets

regret *verb*
regrets
regretting
regretted

regretful *adjective*
regretfully *adverb*

regrettable *adjective*
regrettably *adverb*

regular *adjective*
regularly *adverb*

regularity *noun*

regulate *verb*
regulates
regulating
regulated

regulation *noun*
regulations

regulator *noun*
regulators

rehearsal *noun*
rehearsals

rehearse *verb*
rehearses
rehearsing
rehearsed

reign★ *verb*
reigns
reigning
reigned

reign *noun*
reigns

rein☆ *noun*
reins

reindeer *noun*
reindeer

reinforce *verb*
reinforces
reinforcing
reinforced

reinforcement *noun*
reinforcements

reject *verb*
rejects
rejecting
rejected

reject *noun*
rejects

rejection *noun*
rejections

rejoice *verb*
rejoices
rejoicing
rejoiced

relate *verb*
relates
relating
related

relation *noun*
relations

relationship *noun*
relationships

relative *adjective*
relatively *adverb*

relative *noun*
relatives

relax *verb*
relaxes
relaxing
relaxed

relaxation *noun*

relay *verb*
relays
relaying
relayed

relay *noun*
relays

★ To **reign** is to rule as a king or queen. **! rein.**
☆ A **rein** is a strap used to guide a horse. **! reign.**

release *verb*
releases
releasing
released

release *noun*
releases

relegate *verb*
relegates
relegating
relegated

relegation *noun*

relent *verb*
relents
relenting
relented

relentless *adjective*
relentlessly *adverb*

relevance *noun*

relevant *adjective*

reliability *noun*

reliable *adjective*
reliably *adverb*

reliance *noun*

reliant *adjective*

relic *noun*
relics

relief *noun*
reliefs

relieve *verb*
relieves
relieving
relieved

religion *noun*
religions

religious *adjective*
religiously *adverb*

reluctance *noun*

reluctant *adjective*
reluctantly *adverb*

rely *verb*
relies
relying
relied

remain *verb*
remains
remaining
remained

remainder *noun*
remainders

remains *noun*

remark *verb*
remarks
remarking
remarked

remark *noun*
remarks

remarkable *adjective*
remarkably *adverb*

remedial *adjective*

remedy *noun*
remedies

remember *verb*
remembers
remembering
remembered

remembrance *noun*

remind *verb*
reminds
reminding
reminded

reminder *noun*
reminders

reminisce *verb*
reminisces
reminiscing
reminisced

reminiscence *noun*
reminiscences

reminiscent *adjective*

remnant *noun*
remnants

remorse *noun*

remorseful *adjective*
remorsefully *adverb*

remorseless *adjective*
remorselessly *adverb*

remote *adjective*
remoter
remotest
remotely *adverb*

remoteness *noun*

removal *noun*
removals

remove *verb*
removes
removing
removed

Renaissance* *noun*

render *verb*
renders
rendering
rendered

rendezvous *noun*
rendezvous

renew *verb*
renews
renewing
renewed

renewable *adjective*

renewal *noun*
renewals

renown *noun*

renowned *adjective*

rent *noun*
rents

rent *verb*
rents
renting
rented

repair *verb*
repairs
repairing
repaired

repair *noun*
repairs

repay *verb*
repays
repaying
repaid

repayment *noun*
repayments

* You use a capital R when you mean the historical period.

a b c d e f g h i j k l m n o p q r s t u v w x y z

repeat *verb*
repeats
repeating
repeated
repeat *noun*
repeats
repeatedly *adverb*
repel *verb*
repels
repelling
repelled
repellent *adjective & noun*
repent *verb*
repents
repenting
repented
repentance *noun*
repentant *adjective*
repertoire *noun*
repertoires
repetition *noun*
repetitions
repetitive *adjective*
repetitively *adverb*
replace *verb*
replaces
replacing
replaced
replacement *noun*
replacements
replay *noun*
replays
replica *noun*
replicas
replicate *verb*
replication *noun*
reply *verb*
replies
replying
replied
reply *noun*
replies
report *verb*
reports
reporting
reported
report *noun*
reports
reporter *noun*
reporters
repossess *verb*
repossesses
repossessing
repossessed
represent *verb*
represents
representing
represented
representation *noun*
representations
representative *adjective & noun*
representatives
repress *verb*
represses
repressing
repressed
repression *noun*
repressions
repressive *adjective*
reprieve *verb*
reprieves
reprieving
reprieved
reprieve *noun*
reprieves
reprimand *verb*
reprimands
reprimanding
reprimanded
reprisal *noun*
reprisals
reproach *verb*
reproaches
reproaching
reproached
reproduce *verb*
reproduces
reproducing
reproduced
reproduction *noun*
reproduction
reproductive *adjective*
reptile *noun*
reptiles
republic *noun*
republics
republican* *adjective & noun*
republicans
repulsion *noun*
repulsive *adjective*
repulsively *adverb*
reputation *noun*
reputations
request *verb*
requests
requesting
requested
request *noun*
requests
require *verb*
requires
requiring
required
requirement *noun*
requirements
reread *verb*
rereads
rereading
reread
rescue *verb*
rescues
rescuing
rescued
rescue *noun*
rescues
rescuer *noun*
rescuers
research *noun*
researches
researcher *noun*
researchers
resemblance *noun*
resemblances

* You use a capital R when you mean the political party in the USA.

resemble *verb*
resembles
resembling
resembled
resent *verb*
resents
resenting
resented
resentful *adjective*
resentfully *adverb*
resentment *noun*
reservation *noun*
reservations
reserve *verb*
reserves
reserving
reserved
reserve *noun*
reserves
reservoir *noun*
reservoirs
reshuffle *noun*
reshuffles
reside *verb*
resides
residing
resided
residence *noun*
residences
resident *noun*
residents
residential *adjective*
resign *verb*
resigns
resigning
resigned
resignation *noun*
resignations
resin *noun*
resins
resinous *adjective*
resist *verb*
resists
resisting
resisted
resistance *noun*
resistances
resistant *adjective*

resolute *adjective*
resolutely *adverb*
resolution *noun*
resolutions
resolve *verb*
resolves
resolving
resolved
resort *noun*
resorts
resort *verb*
resorts
resorting
resorted
resound *verb*
resounds
resounding
resounded
resource *noun*
resources
respect *verb*
respects
respecting
respected
respect *noun*
respects
respectability *noun*
respectable *adjective*
respectably *adverb*
respectful *adjective*
respectfully *adverb*
respective *adjective*
respectively *adverb*
respiration *noun*
respirator *noun*
respirators
respiratory *adjective*
respond *verb*
responds
responding
responded
response *noun*
responses
responsibility *noun*
responsibilities
responsible *adjective*
responsibly *adverb*

rest *verb*
rests
resting
rested
rest *noun*
rests
restaurant *noun*
restaurants
restful *adjective*
restfully *adverb*
restless *adjective*
restlessly *adverb*
restlessness *noun*
restoration *noun*
restorations
restore *verb*
restores
restoring
restored
restrain *verb*
restrains
restraining
restrained
restraint *noun*
restraints
restrict *verb*
restricts
restricting
restricted
restriction *noun*
restrictions
restrictive *adjective*
restrictively *adverb*
result *verb*
results
resulting
resulted
result *noun*
results
resume *verb*
resumes
resuming
resumed
resumption *noun*
resumptions
resurrection *noun*

Try also words beginning with **rh-** or **wr-**

a b c d e f g h i j k l m n o p q r s t u v w x y z

resuscitate *verb*
resuscitates
resuscitating
resuscitated

retail *verb*
retails
retailing
retailed

retail *noun*

retailer *noun*
retailers

retain *verb*
retains
retaining
retained

retina *noun*
retinas

retire *verb*
retires
retiring
retired

retirement *noun*

retort *verb*
retorts
retorting
retorted

retort *noun*
retorts

retrace *verb*
retraces
retracing
retraced

retreat *verb*
retreats
retreating
retreated

retrievable *adjective*

retrieval *noun*
retrievals

retrieve *verb*
retrieves
retrieving
retrieved

retrospect *noun*

return *verb*
returns
returning
returned

return *noun*
returns

reunion *noun*
reunions

rev *verb*
revs
revving
revved

rev *noun*
revs

reveal *verb*
reveals
revealing
revealed

revelation *noun*
revelations

revenge *noun*

revenue *noun*
revenues

revere *verb*
reveres
revering
revered

reverence *noun*

Reverend★ *noun*

reverent★ *adjective*
reverently *adverb*

reversal *noun*
reversals

reverse *verb*
reverses
reversing
reversed

reverse *noun*
reverses

reversible *adjective*

review *verb*
reviews
reviewing
reviewed

review☆ *noun*
reviews

reviewer *noun*
reviewers

revise *verb*
revises
revising
revised

revision *noun*
revisions

revisit *verb*

revival *noun*
revivals

revive *verb*
revives
reviving
revived

revolt *verb*
revolts
revolting
revolted

revolt *noun*
revolts

revolution *noun*
revolutions

revolutionary *adjective & noun*
revolutionaries

revolutionize *verb*
revolutionizes
revolutionizing
revolutionized

revolve *verb*
revolves
revolving
revolved

revolver *noun*
revolvers

★ You use **Reverend** as a title of a member of the clergy, and **reverent** as an ordinary word meaning 'showing respect'.
☆ A **review** is a piece of writing about a film, play, etc. **! revue**.

revue★ *noun*
revues
reward *verb*
rewards
rewarding
rewarded
reward *noun*
rewards
rewind *verb*
rewinds
rewinding
rewound
rewrite *verb*
rewrites
rewriting
rewrote
rewritten
rhetorical *adjective*
rheumatic *adjective*
rheumatism *noun*
rhino *noun*
rhinoceros *noun*
rhinoceroses *or*
rhinoceros
rhododendron *noun*
rhododendrons
rhombus *noun*
rhombuses
rhubarb *noun*
rhyme *verb*
rhymes
rhyming
rhymed
rhyme *noun*
rhymes
rhythm *noun*
rhythms
rhythmic *or*
rhythmical *adjective*
rhythmically *adverb*

rib *noun*
ribs
ribbon *noun*
ribbons
rice *noun*
rich *adjective*
richer
richest
richly *adverb*
riches *plural noun*
richness *noun*
rick *noun*
ricks
rickety *adjective*
rickshaw *noun*
rickshaws
ricochet *verb*
ricochets
ricocheting
ricocheted
rid *verb*
rids
ridding
rid
riddance *noun*
riddle *noun*
riddles
ride *verb*
rides
riding
rode
ridden
ride *noun*
rides
rider *noun*
riders
ridge *noun*
ridges
ridicule *verb*
ridicules
ridiculing
ridiculed

ridiculous *adjective*
ridiculously *adverb*
rifle *noun*
rifles
rift *noun*
rifts
rig *verb*
rigs
rigging
rigged
rigging *noun*
right *adjective*
rightly *adverb*
right☆ *noun*
rights
right✪ *verb*
rights
righting
righted
righteous *adjective*
righteously *adverb*
righteousness *noun*
rightful *adjective*
rightfully *adverb*
right-handed *adjective*
rigid *adjective*
rigidly *adverb*
rigidity *noun*
rim *noun*
rims
rind *noun*
rinds
ring *noun*
rings
ring✣ *verb*
rings
ringing
rang
rung

★ A **revue** is an entertainment of short sketches. **! review**.
☆ A **right** is something you are entitled to. **! rite**, **write**.
✪ To **right** something is to make it right. **! rite**, **write**.
✣ The past tense is **rang** and the past participle is **rung** when you mean 'to make a sound like a bell'. **! wring**.

a b c d e f g h i j k l m n o p q r s t u v w x y z

ring★ *verb*
rings
ringing
ringed
ring *noun*
rings
ringleader *noun*
ringleaders
ringlet *noun*
ringlets
ringmaster *noun*
ringmasters
rink *noun*
rinks
rinse *verb*
rinses
rinsing
rinsed
rinse *noun*
rinses
riot *verb*
riots
rioting
rioted
riot *noun*
riots
riotous *adjective*
riotously *adverb*
rip *verb*
rips
ripping
ripped
rip *noun*
rips
ripe *adjective*
riper
ripest
ripen *verb*
ripens
ripening
ripened
ripeness *noun*
rip-off *noun*
rip-offs
ripple *noun*
ripples
ripple *verb*
ripples
rippling
rippled
rise *verb*
rises
rising
rose
risen
rise *noun*
rises
risk *verb*
risks
risking
risked
risk *noun*
risks
risky *adjective*
riskier
riskiest
riskily *adverb*
risotto *noun*
risottos
rissole *noun*
rissoles
rite☆ *noun*
rites
ritual *noun*
rituals
rival *noun*
rivals
rival *verb*
rivals
rivalling
rivalled
rivalry *noun*
rivalries
river *noun*
rivers
rivet *noun*
rivets
rivet *verb*
rivets
riveting
riveted
road✪ *noun*
roads
roadside *noun*
roadsides
roadway *noun*
roadways
roam *verb*
roams
roaming
roamed
roar *verb*
roars
roaring
roared
roar *noun*
roars
roast *verb*
roasts
roasting
roasted
rob *verb*
robs
robbing
robbed
robber *noun*
robbers
robbery *noun*
robberies
robe *noun*
robes
robin *noun*
robins
robot *noun*
robots
robotic *adjective*
robust *adjective*
rock *verb*
rocks
rocking
rocked

★ The past tense and past participle is **ringed** when you mean 'to put a ring round something'. **! wring**.
☆ A **rite** is a ceremony or ritual. **! right**, **write**.
✪ A **road** is a hard surface for traffic to use. **! rode**.

Try also words beginning with **rh-** or **wr-**

rock *noun*
rocks
rocker *noun*
rockers
rockery *noun*
rockeries
rocket *noun*
rockets
rocky *adjective*
rockier
rockiest
rod *noun*
rods
rode★ *verb* SEE **ride**
rodent *noun*
rodents
rodeo *noun*
rodeos
rogue *noun*
rogues
roguish *adjective*
role☆ *noun*
roles
roll *verb*
rolls
rolling
rolled
roll✪ *noun*
rolls
roller *noun*
rollers
Rollerblade® *noun*
Rollerblades®
ROM *noun*
Roman *adjective & noun*
Romans
Roman Catholic *noun*
Roman Catholics
romance *noun*
romances
Roman numeral
romantic *adjective*
romantically *adverb*
Romany *noun*
romp *verb*
romps
romping
romped
romp *noun*
romps
rompers *plural noun*
roof *noun*
roofs
rook *noun*
rooks
room *noun*
rooms
roomful *noun*
roomfuls
roomy *adjective*
roomier
roomiest
roost *noun*
roosts
root✣ *noun*
roots
root *verb*
roots
rooting
rooted
rope *noun*
ropes
rose *noun*
roses
rose *verb* SEE **rise**
rosette *noun*
rosettes
rosy *adjective*
rosier
rosiest
rot *verb*
rots
rotting
rotted
rot *noun*
rota *noun*
rotas
rotary *adjective*
rotate *verb*
rotates
rotating
rotated
rotation *noun*
rotations
rotor *noun*
rotors
rotten *adjective*
rottenness *noun*
rough *adjective*
rougher
roughest
roughly *adverb*
roughness *noun*
roughage *noun*
roughen *verb*
roughens
roughening
roughened
round *adjective, adverb, & preposition*
rounder
roundest
roundly *adverb*
round *noun*
rounds
round *verb*
rounds
rounding
rounded
roundabout *adjective & noun*
roundabouts
rounders *noun*
Roundhead *noun*
Roundheads

a b c d e f g h i j k l m n o p q r s t u v w x y z

★ **Rode** is the past tense of **ride**. **! road**.
☆ A **role** is a part in a play or film. **! roll**.
✪ A **roll** is a small loaf of bread or an act of rolling. **! role**.
✣ A **root** is the part of a plant that grows underground. **! route**.

a b c d e f g h i j k l m n o p q r s t u v w x y z

rouse *verb*
rouses
rousing
roused

rout *verb*
routs
routing
routed

rout *noun*
routs

route★ *noun*
routes

routine *noun*
routines

routine *adjective*
routinely *adverb*

rove *verb*
roves
roving
roved

rover *noun*
rovers

row☆ *noun*
rows

row✪ *verb*
rows
rowing
rowed

rowdiness *noun*

rowdy *adjective*
rowdier
rowdiest
rowdily *adverb*

rower *noun*
rowers

rowlock *noun*
rowlocks

royal *adjective*
royally *adverb*

royalty *noun*

rub *verb*
rubs
rubbing
rubbed

rub *noun*
rubs

rubber *noun*
rubbers

rubbery *adjective*

rubbish *noun*

rubble *noun*

ruby *noun*
rubies

rucksack *noun*
rucksacks

rudder *noun*
rudders

ruddy *adjective*
ruddier
ruddiest

rude *adjective*
ruder
rudest
rudely *adverb*

rudeness *noun*

ruffian *noun*
ruffians

ruffle *verb*
ruffles
ruffling
ruffled

rug *noun*
rugs

rugby *noun*

rugged *adjective*
ruggedly *adverb*

rugger *noun*

ruin *verb*
ruins
ruining
ruined

ruin *noun*
ruins

ruinous *adjective*

rule *noun*
rules

rule *verb*
rules
ruling
ruled

ruler *noun*
rulers

ruling *noun*
rulings

rum *noun*
rums

rumble *verb*
rumbles
rumbling
rumbled

rumble *noun*
rumbles

rummage *verb*
rummages
rummaging
rummaged

rummy *noun*

rumour *noun*
rumours

rump *noun*
rumps

run *verb*
runs
running
ran
run

run *noun*
runs

★ A **route** is the way you go to get to a place. **! root**.
☆ A **row** is a line of people or things and rhymes with 'go'. A **row** is also a noise or argument and rhymes with 'cow'.
✪ To **row** means to use oars to make a boat move and rhymes with 'go'.

Try also words beginning with **rh-** or **wr-**

runaway *noun*
runaways

rung *noun*
rungs

rung *verb* SEE **ring**

runner *noun*
runners

runner-up *noun*
runners-up

runny *adjective*
runnier
runniest

runway *noun*
runways

rural *adjective*

rush *verb*
rushes
rushing
rushed

rush *noun*
rushes

rusk *noun*
rusks

Russian *noun*

rust *noun*

rust *verb*
rusts
rusting
rusted

rustic *adjective*

rustle *verb*
rustles
rustling
rustled

rustler *noun*
rustlers

rusty *adjective*
rustier
rustiest

rut *noun*
ruts

ruthless *adjective*
ruthlessly *adverb*

ruthlessness *noun*

rutted *adjective*

rye★ *noun*

★ **Rye** is a type of cereal or bread. **! wry.**

a b c d e f g h i j k l m n o p q r s t u v w x y z

Ss

sabbath *noun*
sabbaths
sabotage *noun*
sabotage *verb*
sabotages
sabotaging
sabotaged
saboteur *noun*
saboteurs
sac★ *noun*
sacs
saccharin *noun*
sachet *noun*
sachets
sack☆ *noun*
sacks
sack *verb*
sacks
sacking
sacked
sacred *adjective*
sacrifice *noun*
sacrifices
sacrificial *adjective*
sacrifice *verb*
sacrifices
sacrificing
sacrificed
sad *adjective*
sadder
saddest
sadly *adverb*
sadness *noun*
sadden *verb*
saddens
saddening
saddened
saddle *noun*
saddles
saddle *verb*
saddles
saddling
saddled
safari *noun*
safaris
safe *adjective*
safer
safest
safely *adverb*
safe *noun*
safes
safeguard *noun*
safeguards
safeguard *verb*
safeguards
safeguarding
safeguarded
safety *noun*
sag *verb*
sags
sagging
sagged
saga *noun*
sagas
sago *noun*
said *verb* SEE **say**
sail *verb*
sails
sailing
sailed
sail✪ *noun*
sails
sailboard *noun*
sailboards
sailor *noun*
sailors
saint *noun*
saints
saintly *adjective*
saintlier
saintliest
sake *noun*
sakes
salaam *interjection*
salad *noun*
salads
salami *noun*
salamis
salary *noun*
salaries
sale✢ *noun*
sales
salesman *noun*
salesmen
salesperson *noun*
salespersons
saleswoman *noun*
saleswomen
saline *adjective*
saliva *noun*
sally *verb*
sallies
sallying
sallied
salmon *noun*
salmon
salon *noun*
salons
saloon *noun*
saloons
salt *noun*

★ A **sac** is a bag-like part of an animal or plant. **! sack**.
☆ A **sack** is a large bag. **! sac**.
✪ A **sail** is a sheet that catches the wind to make a boat go. **! sale**.
✢ You use **sale** in e.g. *The house is for sale.* **! sail**.

salt *verb*
salts
salting
salted
salty *adjective*
saltier
saltiest
salute *verb*
salutes
saluting
saluted
salute *noun*
salutes
salvage *verb*
salvages
salvaging
salvaged
salvation *noun*
samba *noun*
sambas
same *adjective*
samosa *noun*
samosas
sample *noun*
samples
sample *verb*
samples
sampling
sampled
sanction *noun*
sanctions
sanctuary *noun*
sanctuaries
sand *noun*
sands
sand *verb*
sands
sanding
sanded
sander *noun*
sanders
sandal *noun*
sandals
sandbag *noun*
sandbags
sandpaper *noun*
sands *plural noun*
sandstone *noun*
sandwich *noun*
sandwiches
sandy *adjective*
sandier
sandiest
sane *adjective*
saner
sanest
sang *verb* SEE **sing**
sanitary *adjective*
sanitation *noun*
sanity *noun*
sank *verb* SEE **sink**
Sanskrit *noun*
sap *noun*
sap *verb*
saps
sapping
sapped
sapling *noun*
saplings
sapphire *noun*
sapphires
sarcasm *noun*
sarcastic *adjective*
sarcastically *adverb*
sardine *noun*
sardines
sari *noun*
saris
sash *noun*
sashes
sat *verb* SEE **sit**
satchel *noun*
satchels
satellite *noun*
satellites
satin *noun*
satire *noun*
satires
satirical *adjective*
satirically *adverb*
satirist *noun*
satirists
satisfaction *noun*
satisfactory *adjective*
satisfactorily *adverb*
satisfy *verb*
satisfies
satisfying
satisfied
saturate *verb*
saturates
saturating
saturated
saturation *noun*
Saturday *noun*
Saturdays
sauce* *noun*
sauces
saucepan *noun*
saucepans
saucer *noun*
saucers
saucy *adjective*
saucier
sauciest
saucily *adverb*
sauna *noun*
saunas
saunter *verb*
saunters
sauntering
sauntered
sausage *noun*
sausages
savage *adjective*
savagely *adverb*
savage *noun*
savages
savage *verb*
savages
savaging
savaged
savagery *noun*
savannah *noun*
savannahs

* A **sauce** is a liquid you put on food. **! source**.

a b c d e f g h i j k l m n o p q r s t u v w x y z

save *verb*
saves
saving
saved
saver *noun*
savers
savings *plural noun*
saviour *noun*
saviours
savoury *adjective*
saw *noun*
saws
saw *verb*
saws
sawing
sawed
sawn
saw *verb* SEE **see**
sawdust *noun*
saxophone *noun*
saxophones
say *verb*
says
saying
said
say *noun*
saying *noun*
sayings
scab *noun*
scabs
scabbard *noun*
scabbards
scaffold *noun*
scaffolds
scaffolding *noun*
scald *verb*
scalds
scalding
scalded
scale *noun*
scales
scale *verb*
scales
scaling
scaled
scales *plural noun*
scaly *adjective*
scalier
scaliest
scalp *noun*
scalps
scalp *verb*
scalps
scalping
scalped
scam *noun*
scams
scamper *verb*
scampers
scampering
scampered
scampi *plural noun*
scan *verb*
scans
scanning
scanned
scan *noun*
scans
scandal *noun*
scandals
scandalous *adjective*
scandalous
scanner *noun*
scanners
scanty *adjective*
scantier
scantiest
scantily *adverb*
scapegoat *noun*
scapegoats
scar *noun*
scars
scar *verb*
scars
scarring
scarred
scarce *adjective*
scarcer
scarcest
scarcely *adverb*
scarcity *noun*
scarcities
scare *verb*
scares
scaring
scared
scare *noun*
scares
scarecrow *noun*
scarecrows
scarf *noun*
scarves
scarlet *adjective*
scary *adjective*
scarier
scariest
scarily *adverb*
scatter *verb*
scatters
scattering
scattered
scenario *noun*
scenarios
scene★ *noun*
scenes
scenery *noun*
scent☆ *noun*
scents
scent *verb*
scents
scenting
scented
sceptic *noun*
sceptics
sceptical *adjective*
sceptically *adverb*
scepticism *noun*
schedule *noun*
schedules
scheme *noun*
schemes
scheme *verb*
schemes
scheming
schemed

★ A **scene** is a place or part of a play. **! seen**.
☆ A **scent** is a smell or perfume. **! cent**, **sent**.

schemer *noun*
schemers
schizophrenia *noun*
scholar *noun*
scholars
scholarly *adjective*
scholarship *noun*
scholarships
school *noun*
schools
schoolboy *noun*
schoolboys
schoolchild *noun*
schoolchildren
schoolgirl *noun*
schoolgirls
schoolteacher *noun*
schoolteachers
schooner *noun*
schooners
science *noun*
sciences
scientific *adjective*
scientifically *adverb*
scientist *noun*
scientists
scissors *plural noun*
scoff *verb*
scoffs
scoffing
scoffed
scold *verb*
scolds
scolding
scolded
scone *noun*
scones
scoop *noun*
scoops
scoop *verb*
scoops
scooping
scooped
scooter *noun*
scooters
scope *noun*
scorch *verb*
scorches
scorching
scorched
score *noun*
scores
score *verb*
scores
scoring
scored
scorer *noun*
scorers
scorn *noun*
scorn *verb*
scorns
scorning
scorned
scornful *adjective*
scorpion *noun*
scorpions
Scot *noun*
Scots
scoundrel *noun*
scoundrels
scour *verb*
scours
scouring
scoured
scout *noun*
scouts
scowl *verb*
scowls
scowling
scowled
scramble *verb*
scrambles
scrambling
scrambled
scramble *noun*
scrambles
scrap *verb*
scraps
scrapping
scrapped
scrap *noun*
scraps
scrape *verb*
scrapes
scraping
scraped
scrape *noun*
scrapes
scraper *noun*
scrapers
scrappy *adjective*
scrappier
scrappiest
scrappily *adverb*
scratch *verb*
scratches
scratching
scratched
scratch *noun*
scratches
scrawl *verb*
scrawls
scrawling
scrawled
scrawl *noun*
scrawls
scream *verb*
screams
screaming
screamed
scream *noun*
screams
screech *verb*
screeches
screeching
screeched
screech *noun*
screeches
screen *noun*
screens
screen *verb*
screens
screening
screened
screw *noun*
screws
screw *verb*
screws
screwing
screwed

screwdriver *noun*
screwdrivers
scribble *verb*
scribbles
scribbling
scribbled
scribble *noun*
scribbles
scribbler *noun*
scribblers
script *noun*
scripts
scripture *noun*
scriptures
scroll *noun*
scrolls
scrounge *verb*
scrounges
scrounging
scrounged
scrounger *noun*
scroungers
scrub *verb*
scrubs
scrubbing
scrubbed
scrub *noun*
scruffy *adjective*
scruffier
scruffiest
scruffily *adverb*
scrum *noun*
scrums
scrummage *noun*
scrummages
scrutinize *verb*
scrutinizes
scrutinizing
scrutinized
scrutiny *noun*
scrutinies
scuba-diving *noun*
scuff *verb & noun*
scuffle *noun*
scuffles
scuffle *verb*
scuffles
scuffling
scuffled
scullery *noun*
sculleries
sculptor *noun*
sculptors
sculpture *noun*
sculptures
scum *noun*
scurry *verb*
scurries
scurrying
scurried
scurvy *noun*
scuttle *verb*
scuttles
scuttling
scuttled
scuttle *noun*
scuttles
scythe *noun*
scythes
sea★ *noun*
seas
seabed *noun*
seafarer *noun*
seafarers
seafaring *adjective & noun*
seafood *noun*
seagull *noun*
seagulls
sea horse *noun*
sea horses
seal *verb*
seals
sealing
sealed
seal *noun*
seals
sea lion *noun*
sea lions
seam☆ *noun*
seams
seaman *noun*
seamen
seamanship *noun*
seaplane *noun*
seaplanes
seaport *noun*
seaports
search *verb*
searches
searching
searched
search *noun*
searches
search engine *noun*
search engines
searcher *noun*
searchers
searchlight *noun*
searchlights
seashore *noun*
seashores
seasick *adjective*
seasickness *noun*
seaside *noun*
season *noun*
seasons
season *verb*
seasons
seasoning
seasoned
seasonal *adjective*
seasonally *adverb*
seasoning *noun*
seasonings
seat *noun*
seats
seat *verb*
seats
seating
seated
seat belt *noun*
seat belts
seaward *adjective & adverb*

★ A **sea** is an area of salt water. **! see.**
☆ A **seam** is a line of stitching in cloth. **! seem.**

Try also words beginning with **ce-**, **ci-**, **cy-**, **ps-**, or **sc-**

seawards *adverb*
seaweed *noun*
seaweeds
secateurs *plural noun*
secluded *adjective*
seclusion *noun*
second *adjective*
secondly *adverb*
second *noun*
seconds
second *verb*
seconds
seconding
seconded
secondary *adjective*
second-hand *adjective*
secrecy *noun*
secret *adjective*
secretly *adverb*
secret *noun*
secrets
secretary *noun*
secretaries
secrete *verb*
secretes
secreting
secreted
secretion *noun*
secretions
secretive *adjective*
secretively *adverb*
secretiveness *noun*
sect *noun*
sects
section *noun*
sections
sectional *adjective*
sector *noun*
sectors
secular *adjective*
secure *adjective*
securely *adverb*
secure *verb*
secures
securing
secured
security *noun*
sedate *adjective*
sedately *adverb*
sedation *noun*
sedative *noun*
sedatives
sediment *noun*
sedimentary *adjective*
see★ *verb*
sees
seeing
saw
seen
seed *noun*
seeds
seedling *noun*
seedlings
seek *verb*
seeks
seeking
sought
seem☆ *verb*
seems
seeming
seemed
seemingly *adverb*
seen✪ *verb* SEE **see**
seep *verb*
seeps
seeping
seeped
seepage *noun*
see-saw *noun*
see-saws
seethe *verb*
seethes
seething
seethed
segment *noun*
segments
segmented *adjective*
segregate *verb*
segregates
segregating
segregated
segregation *noun*
seismograph *noun*
seismographs
seize *verb*
seizes
seizing
seized
seizure *noun*
seizures
seldom *adverb*
select *verb*
selects
selecting
selected
select *adjective*
selective *adjective*
selectively *adverb*
self *noun*
selves
self-confidence *noun*
self-confident *adjective*
self-confidently *adverb*
self-conscious *adjective*
self-consciously *adverb*
self-contained *adjective*
selfish *adjective*
selfishly *adverb*
selfishness *noun*
selfless *adjective*
selflessly *adverb*
self-service *noun*
sell✣ *verb*
sells
selling
sold

★ You use **see** in e.g. *I can't see anything.* **! sea.**
☆ You use **seem** in e.g. *they seem tired.* **! seam.**
✪ **Seen** is the past participle of **see. ! scene.**
✣ To **sell** something means 'to exchange it for money'. **! cell.**

Try also words beginning with ce-, ci-, cy-, ps-, or sc-

a b c d e f g h i j k l m n o p q r s t u v w x y z

seller★ *noun*
sellers

semaphore *noun*

> **semi-** *prefix*
> *semi-* makes words meaning 'half', e.g. **semi-automatic, semi-skimmed.** A few words are spelled joined up, e.g. **semicircle, semicolon,** but most of them have hyphens.

semibreve *noun*
semibreves

semicircle *noun*
semicircles

semicircular *adjective*

semicolon *noun*
semicolons

semi-detached *adjective*

semi-final *noun*
semi-finals

semi-finalist *noun*
semi-finalists

semitone *noun*
semitones

semolina *noun*

senate *noun*

senator *noun*
senators

send *verb*
sends
sending
sent

senior *adjective* & *noun*
seniors

seniority *noun*

sensation *noun*
sensations

sensational *adjective*
sensationally *adverb*

sense *noun*
senses

sense *verb*
senses
sensing
sensed

senseless *adjective*
senselessly *adverb*

sensible *adjective*
sensibly

sensitive *adjective*
sensitively *adverb*

sensitivity *noun*
sensitivities

sensitize *verb*
sensitizes
sensitizing
sensitized

sensor *noun*
sensors

sent☆ *verb* SEE **send**

sentence *noun*
sentences

sentence *verb*
sentences
sentencing
sentenced

sentiment *noun*
sentiments

sentimental *adjective*
sentimentally *adverb*

sentimentality *noun*

sentinel *noun*
sentinels

sentry *noun*
sentries

separable *adjective*

separate *adjective*
separately *adverb*

separate *verb*
separates
separating
separated

separation *noun*
separations

September *noun*
Septembers

septic *adjective*

sequel *noun*
sequels

sequence *noun*
sequences

sequin *noun*
sequins

serene *adjective*
serenely *adverb*

serenity *noun*

sergeant *noun*
sergeants

sergeant major *noun*
sergeant majors

serial✪ *noun*
serials

series *noun*
series

serious *adjective*
seriously *adverb*

seriousness *noun*

sermon *noun*
sermons

serpent *noun*
serpents

servant *noun*
servants

serve *verb*
serves
serving
served

server *noun*
servers

serve *noun*
serves

service *noun*
services

★ A **seller** is someone who sells something. **! cellar.**
☆ You use **sent** in e.g. *he was sent home.* **! cent, scent.**
✪ A **serial** is a story or programme in separate parts. **! cereal.**

Try also words beginning with **ce-**, **ci-**, **cy-**, **ps-**, or **sc-**

service *verb*
services
servicing
serviced
serviette *noun*
serviettes
session *noun*
sessions
set *verb*
sets
setting
set
set *noun*
sets
set square *noun*
set squares
sett★ *noun*
setts
settee *noun*
settees
setting *noun*
settings
settle *verb*
settles
settling
settled
settlement *noun*
settlements
settler *noun*
settlers
set-up *noun*
set-ups
seven *noun & adjective*
seventeen *noun & adjective*
seventeenth *adjective & noun*
seventh *adjective & noun*
seventhly *adverb*
seventieth *adjective & noun*
seventy *adjective & noun*
seventies

sever *verb*
severs
severing
severed
several *adjective*
severally *adverb*
severe *adjective*
severer
severest
severely *adverb*
severity *noun*
sew☆ *verb*
sews
sewing
sewed
sewn
sewage *noun*
sewer *noun*
sewers
sex *noun*
sexes
sextet *noun*
sextets
shabbiness *noun*
shabby *adjective*
shabbier
shabbiest
shabbily *adverb*
shack *noun*
shacks
shade *noun*
shades
shade *verb*
shades
shading
shaded
shadow *noun*
shadows
shadow *verb*
shadows
shadowing
shadowed
shadowy *adjective*

shady *adjective*
shadier
shadiest
shaft *noun*
shafts
shaggy *adjective*
shaggier
shaggiest
shake *verb*
shakes
shaking
shook
shaken
shake✪ *noun*
shakes
shaky *adjective*
shakier
shakiest
shakily *adverb*
shall *verb*
should
shallow *adjective*
shallower
shallowest
shallowly *adverb*
sham *noun*
shams
shamble *verb*
shambles
shambling
shambled
shambles *noun*
shame *verb*
shames
shaming
shamed
shame *noun*
shameful *adjective*
shamefully *adverb*
shameless *adjective*
shamelessly *adverb*
shampoo *noun*
shampoos

★ A **sett** is a badger's burrow.
☆ To **sew** is to work with a needle and thread. **! sow.**
✪ To **shake** is to tremble or quiver. **! sheikh.**

a b c d e f g h i j k l m n o p q r s t u v w x y z

shampoo *verb*
shampoos
shampooing
shampooed

shamrock *noun*

shandy *noun*
shandies

shan't *verb*

shanty *noun*
shanties

shape *noun*
shapes

shape *verb*
shapes
shaping
shaped

shapeless *adjective*
shapelessly *adverb*

shapely *adjective*
shapelier
shapeliest

share *noun*
shares

share *verb*
shares
sharing
shared

shark *noun*
sharks

sharp *adjective*
sharper
sharpest
sharply *adverb*

sharp *noun*
sharps

sharpen *verb*
sharpens
sharpening
sharpened

sharpener *noun*
sharpeners

sharpness *noun*

shatter *verb*
shatters
shattering
shattered

shave *verb*
shaves
shaving
shaved

shave *noun*
shaves

shaver *noun*
shavers

shavings *plural noun*

shawl *noun*
shawls

she *pronoun*

sheaf *noun*
sheaves

shear* *verb*
shears
shearing
sheared
shorn

shearer *noun*
shearers

shears *plural noun*

sheath *noun*
sheaths

sheathe *verb*
sheathes
sheathing
sheathed

shed *noun*
sheds

shed *verb*
sheds
shedding
shed

she'd *verb*

sheen *noun*

sheep *noun*
sheep

sheepdog *noun*
sheepdogs

sheepish *adjective*
sheepishly *adverb*

sheer☆ *adjective*
sheerer
sheerest

sheet *noun*
sheets

sheikh *noun*
sheikhs

shelf *noun*
shelves

shell *noun*
shells

shell *verb*
shells
shelling
shelled

she'll *verb*

shellfish *noun*
shellfish

shelter *noun*
shelters

shelter *verb*
shelters
sheltering
sheltered

shelve *verb*
shelves
shelving
shelved

shepherd *noun*
shepherds

sherbet *noun*
sherbets

sheriff *noun*
sheriffs

sherry *noun*
sherries

she's *verb*

shield *noun*
shields

shield *verb*
shields
shielding
shielded

* To **shear** is to cut wool from a sheep. **! sheer**.
☆ You use **sheer** in e.g. *sheer joy*. **! shear**.

Try also words beginning with ce-, ci-, cy-, ps-, or sc-

shift *noun*
shifts
shift *verb*
shifts
shifting
shifted
shilling *noun*
shillings
shimmer *verb*
shimmers
shimmering
shimmered
shin *noun*
shins
shine *verb*
shines
shining
shone
shined
shine *noun*
shingle *noun*
shiny *adjective*
shinier
shiniest

> **-ship** *suffix*
> *-ship* makes nouns, e.g. **friendship**. Other noun suffixes are **-dom**, **-hood**, **-ment**, and **-ness**.

ship *noun*
ships
ship *verb*
ships
shipping
shipped
shipping *noun*
shipwreck *noun*
shipwrecks
shipwrecked *adjective*
shipyard *noun*
shipyards
shire *noun*
shires

shirk *verb*
shirks
shirking
shirked
shirt *noun*
shirts
shiver *verb*
shivers
shivering
shivered
shiver *noun*
shivers
shivery *adjective*
shoal *noun*
shoals
shock *verb*
shocks
shocking
shocked
shock *noun*
shocks
shoddy *adjective*
shoddier
shoddiest
shoddily *adverb*
shoe *noun*
shoes
shoelace *noun*
shoelaces
shoestring *noun*
shoestrings
shone *verb* SEE **shine**
shook *verb* SEE **shake**
shoot *verb*
shoots
shooting
shot
shoot* *noun*
shoots
shooter *noun*
shooters
shop *noun*
shops

shop *verb*
shops
shopping
shopped
shopkeeper *noun*
shopkeepers
shoplifter *noun*
shoplifters
shoplifting *noun*
shopper *noun*
shoppers
shopping *noun*
shore *noun*
shores
shorn *verb* SEE **shear**
short *adjective*
shorter
shortest
shortly *adverb*
shortness *noun*
shortage *noun*
shortages
shortbread *noun*
shortcake *noun*
shortcakes
shortcoming *noun*
shortcomings
shorten *verb*
shortens
shortening
shortened
shorthand *noun*
short-handed *adjective*
shortly *adverb*
shorts *plural noun*
short-sighted *adjective*
shot *noun*
shots
shot *verb* SEE **shoot**
shotgun *noun*
shotguns
should *auxiliary verb*
shoulder *noun*
shoulders

* To **shoot** is to fire at someone with a gun. **! chute.**

a b c d e f g h i j k l m n o p q r **s** t u v w x y z

shoulder *verb*
shoulders
shouldering
shouldered

shout *verb*
shouts
shouting
shouted

shout *noun*
shouts

shove *verb*
shoves
shoving
shoved

shovel *noun*
shovels

shovel *verb*
shovels
shovelling
shovelled

show *verb*
shows
showing
showed
shown

show *noun*
shows

shower *noun*
showers

shower *verb*
showers
showering
showered

showery *adjective*

showjumper *noun*
showjumpers

showjumping *noun*

showman *noun*
showmen

showmanship *noun*

showroom *noun*
showrooms

showiness *noun*

showy *adjective*
showier
showiest
showily *adverb*

shrank *verb* SEE **shrink**

shrapnel *noun*

shred *noun*
shreds

shred *verb*
shreds
shredding
shredded

shrew *noun*
shrews

shrewd *adjective*
shrewder
shrewdest
shrewdly *adverb*

shrewdness *noun*

shriek *verb*
shrieks
shrieking
shrieked

shriek *noun*
shrieks

shrill *adjective*
shrilly *adverb*

shrillness *noun*

shrimp *noun*
shrimps

shrine *noun*
shrines

shrink *verb*
shrinks
shrinking
shrank
shrunk

shrinkage *noun*

shrivel *verb*
shrivels
shrivelling
shrivelled

shroud *noun*
shrouds

shroud *verb*
shrouds
shrouding
shrouded

shrub *noun*
shrubs

shrubbery *noun*
shrubberies

shrug *verb*
shrugs
shrugging
shrugged

shrug *noun*
shrugs

shrunk *verb* SEE **shrink**

shrunken *adjective*

shudder *verb*
shudders
shuddering
shuddered

shudder *noun*
shudders

shuffle *verb*
shuffles
shuffling
shuffled

shuffle *noun*
shuffles

shunt *verb*
shunts
shunting
shunted

shut *verb*
shuts
shutting
shut

shutter *noun*
shutters

shuttle *noun*
shuttles

shuttlecock *noun*
shuttlecocks

shy *adjective*
shyer
shyest
shyly *adverb*

sibling *noun*
siblings

sick *adjective*
sicker
sickest

sicken *verb*
sickens
sickening
sickened

Try also words beginning with ce-, ci-, cy-, ps-, or sc-

sickly *adjective*
sicklier
sickliest

sickness *noun*
sicknesses

side *noun*
sides

side *verb*
sides
siding
sided

sideboard *noun*
sideboards

sidecar *noun*
sidecars

side effects *plural noun*

sideline *noun*
sidelines

sideshow *noun*
sideshows

sideways *adverb & adjective*

siding *noun*
sidings

siege *noun*
sieges

siesta *noun*
siestas

sieve *noun*
sieves

sift *verb*
sifts
sifting
sifted

sigh *verb*
sighs
sighing
sighed

sigh *noun*
sighs

sight★ *noun*
sights

sight *verb*
sights
sighting
sighted

sightseer *noun*
sightseers

sightseeing *noun*

sign *verb*
signs
signing
signed

sign *noun*
signs

signal *noun*
signals

signal *verb*
signals
signalling
signalled

signaller *noun*
signallers

signalman *noun*
signalmen

signature *noun*
signatures

signet☆ *noun*
signets

significance *noun*

significant *adjective*
significantly *adverb*

signify *verb*
signifies
signifying
signified

signing *noun*

signpost *noun*
signposts

Sikh *noun*
Sikhs

silence *noun*
silences

silence *verb*
silences
silencing
silenced

silencer *noun*
silencers

silent *adjective*
silently *adverb*

silhouette *noun*
silhouettes

silicon *noun*

silk *noun*

silken *adjective*

silkworm *noun*
silkworms

silky *adjective*
silkier
silkiest
silkily *adverb*

sill *noun*
sills

silliness *noun*

silly *adjective*
sillier
silliest

silver *noun*

silvery *adjective*

similar *adjective*
similarly *adverb*

similarity *noun*
similarities

simile *noun*
similes

simmer *verb*
simmers
simmering
simmered

simple *adjective*
simpler
simplest

simplicity *noun*

simplification *noun*

simplify *verb*
simplifies
simplifying
simplified

simplistic *adjective*

simply *adverb*

★ A **sight** is something you see. **! site**.
☆ A **signet** is a seal worn in a ring. **! cygnet**.

simulate *verb*
simulates
simulating
simulated

simulation *noun*
simulations

simulator *noun*
simulators

simultaneous *adjective*
simultaneously *adverb*

sin *noun*
sins

sin *verb*
sins
sinning
sinned

since *preposition, adverb, & conjunction*

sincere *adjective*
sincerer
sincerest
sincerely *adverb*

sincerity *noun*

sinew *noun*
sinews

sinful *adjective*
sinfully *adverb*

sinfulness *noun*

sing *verb*
sings
singing
sang
sung

singer *noun*
singers

singe *verb*
singes
singeing
singed

single *adjective*
singly *adverb*

single *noun*
singles

single *verb*
singles
singling
singled

single-handed *adjective*

singular *adjective*
singularly *adverb*

singular *noun*
singulars

sinister *adjective*
sinisterly *adverb*

sink *verb*
sinks
sinking
sank
sunk

sink *noun*
sinks

sinkable *adjective*

sinner *noun*
sinners

sinus *noun*
sinuses

sip *verb*
sips
sipping
sipped

siphon *noun*
siphons

siphon *verb*
siphons
siphoning
siphoned

sir *noun*

siren *noun*
sirens

sister *noun*
sisters

sisterly *adjective*

sister-in-law *noun*
sisters-in-law

sit *verb*
sits
sitting
sat

sitcom *noun*
sitcoms

sitter *noun*
sitters

sitting *noun*
sittings

site* *noun*
sites

site *verb*
sites
siting
sited

situated *adjective*

situation *noun*
situations

six *noun*
sixes

sixpence *noun*
sixpences

sixteen *noun*
sixteens

sixteenth *adjective & noun*

sixth *adjective & noun*

sixthly *adverb*

sixtieth *adjective & noun*

sixty *noun*
sixties

size *noun*
sizes

size *verb*
sizes
sizing
sized

sizeable *adjective*

sizzle *verb*
sizzles
sizzling
sizzled

skate *verb*
skates
skating
skated

* A **site** is a place where something will be built. **! sight**.

Try also words beginning with **ce-**, **ci-**, **cy-**, **ps-**, or **sc-**

skate* *noun*
skates *or* skate

skateboard *noun*
skateboards

skater *noun*
skaters

skeletal *adjective*
skeletally *adverb*

skeleton *noun*
skeletons

sketch *noun*
sketches

sketch *verb*
sketches
sketching
sketched

sketchy *adjective*
sketchier
sketchiest
sketchily *adverb*

skewer *noun*
skewers

ski *verb*
skis
skiing
skied

ski *noun*
skis

skid *verb*
skids
skidding
skidded

skid *noun*
skids

skier *noun*
skiers

skilful *adjective*
skilfully *adverb*

skill *noun*
skills

skilled *adjective*

skim *verb*
skims
skimming
skimmed

skimp *verb*
skimps
skimping
skimped

skimpy *adjective*
skimpier
skimpiest

skin *noun*
skins

skin *verb*
skins
skinning
skinned

skinny *adjective*
skinnier
skinniest

skint *adjective*

skip *verb*
skips
skipping
skipped

skip *noun*
skips

skipper *noun*
skippers

skirt *noun*
skirts

skirt *verb*
skirts
skirting
skirted

skirting *noun*
skirtings

skit *noun*
skits

skittish *adjective*
skittishly *adverb*

skittle *noun*
skittles

skull *noun*
skulls

skunk *noun*
skunks

sky *noun*
skies

skylark *noun*
skylarks

skylight *noun*
skylights

skyscraper *noun*
skyscrapers

slab *noun*
slabs

slack *adjective*
slacker
slackest
slackly *adverb*

slacken *verb*
slackens
slackening
slackened

slackness *noun*

slacks *plural noun*

slag heap *noun*
slag heaps

slain *verb* SEE **slay**

slam *verb*
slams
slamming
slammed

slang *noun*

slant *verb*
slants
slanting
slanted

slant *noun*
slants

slap *verb*
slaps
slapping
slapped

slap *noun*
slaps

slapstick *noun*

slash *verb*
slashes
slashing
slashed

slash *noun*
slashes

* The plural is **skate** when you mean the fish.

a b c d e f g h i j k l m n o p q r s t u v w x y z

slat *noun*
slats
slate *noun*
slates
slaughter *verb*
slaughters
slaughtering
slaughtered
slaughter *noun*
slaughterhouse *noun*
slaughterhouses
slave *noun*
slaves
slave *verb*
slaves
slaving
slaved
slavery *noun*
slay* *verb*
slays
slaying
slew
slain
sled *noun*
sleds
sledge *noun*
sledges
sledgehammer *noun*
sledgehammers
sleek *adjective*
sleeker
sleekest
sleekly *adverb*
sleep *verb*
sleeps
sleeping
slept
sleep *noun*
sleeper *noun*
sleepers
sleepiness *noun*
sleepless *adjective*
sleepwalker *noun*
sleepwalkers
sleepwalking *noun*
sleepy *adjective*
sleepier
sleepiest
sleepily *adverb*
sleet *noun*
sleeve *noun*
sleeves
sleeveless *adjective*
sleigh☆ *noun*
sleighs
slender *adjective*
slenderer
slenderest
slept *verb* SEE **sleep**
slew *verb* SEE **slay**
slice *noun*
slices
slice *verb*
slices
slicing
sliced
slick *adjective*
slicker
slickest
slickly *adverb*
slick *noun*
slicks
slide *verb*
slides
sliding
slid
slide *noun*
slides
slight *adjective*
slighter
slightest
slightly *adverb*
slim *adjective*
slimmer
slimmest
slim *verb*
slims
slimming
slimmed
slime *noun*
slimmer *noun*
slimmers
slimy *adjective*
slimier
slimiest
sling *verb*
slings
slinging
slung
sling *noun*
slings
slink *verb*
slinks
slinking
slunk
slip *verb*
slips
slipping
slipped
slip *noun*
slips
slipper *noun*
slippers
slippery *adjective*
slipshod *adjective*
slit *noun*
slits
slit *verb*
slits
slitting
slit
slither *verb*
slithers
slithering
slithered
sliver *noun*
slivers
slog *verb*
slogs
slogging
slogged
slog *noun*
slogs
slogan *noun*
slogans

* To **slay** people is to kill them. **! sleigh**.
☆ A **sleigh** is a vehicle for sliding on snow. **! slay**.

slop *verb*
slops
slopping
slopped
slope *verb*
slopes
sloping
sloped
slope *noun*
slopes
sloppiness *noun*
sloppy *adjective*
sloppier
sloppiest
sloppily *adverb*
slops *plural noun*
slosh *verb*
sloshes
sloshing
sloshed
slot *noun*
slots
sloth *noun*
sloths
slouch *verb*
slouches
slouching
slouched
slovenly *adjective*
slow *adjective*
slower
slowest
slowly *adverb*
slow *verb*
slows
slowing
slowed
slowcoach *noun*
slowcoaches
slowness *noun*
sludge *noun*
slug *noun*
slugs
sluggish *adjective*
sluggishly
slum *noun*
slums
slumber *noun*
slumber *verb*
slumbers
slumbering
slumbered
slump *verb*
slumps
slumping
slumped
slump *noun*
slumps
slung *verb* SEE **sling**
slunk *verb* SEE **slink**
slur *noun*
slurs
slush *noun*
slushy *adjective*
slushier
slushiest
sly *adjective*
slyer
slyest
slyly *adverb*
slyness *noun*
smack *verb*
smacks
smacking
smacked
smack *noun*
smacks
small *adjective*
smaller
smallest
smallpox *noun*
smart *adjective*
smarter
smartest
smartly *adverb*
smart *verb*
smarts
smarting
smarted
smarten *verb*
smartens
smartening
smartened
smartness *noun*
smash *verb*
smashes
smashing
smashed
smash *noun*
smashes
smashing *adjective*
smear *verb*
smears
smearing
smeared
smear *noun*
smears
smell *verb*
smells
smelling
smelt
smelled
smell *noun*
smells
smelly *adjective*
smellier
smelliest
smelt *verb*
smelts
smelting
smelted
smile *noun*
smiles
smile *verb*
smiles
smiling
smiled
smirk *verb*
smirks
smirking
smirked
smith *noun*
smiths
smithereens *plural noun*
smock *noun*
smocks
smog *noun*
smoke *noun*
smoke *verb*
smokes
smoking
smoked

smokeless *adjective*
smoker *noun*
smokers
smoky *adjective*
smokier
smokiest
smooth *adjective*
smoother
smoothest
smoothly *adverb*
smooth *verb*
smooths
smoothing
smoothed
smoothness *noun*
smother *verb*
smothers
smothering
smothered
smoulder *verb*
smoulders
smouldering
smouldered
smudge *verb*
smudges
smudging
smudged
smudge *noun*
smudges
smug *adjective*
smugly *adverb*
smuggle *verb*
smuggles
smuggling
smuggled
smuggler *noun*
smugglers
smut *noun*
smuts
smutty *adjective*
smuttier
smuttiest
snack *noun*
snacks
snag *noun*
snags
snail *noun*
snails

snake *noun*
snakes
snaky *adjective*
snakier
snakiest
snap *verb*
snaps
snapping
snapped
snap *noun*
snaps
snappy *adjective*
snappier
snappiest
snappily *adverb*
snapshot *noun*
snapshots
snare *noun*
snares
snare *verb*
snares
snaring
snared
snarl *verb*
snarls
snarling
snarled
snarl *noun*
snarls
snatch *verb*
snatches
snatching
snatched
snatch *noun*
snatches
sneak *verb*
sneaks
sneaking
sneaked
sneak *noun*
sneaks
sneaky *adjective*
sneakier
sneakiest
sneakily *adverb*
sneer *verb*
sneers
sneering
sneered

sneeze *verb*
sneezes
sneezing
sneezed
sneeze *noun*
sneezes
sniff *verb*
sniffs
sniffing
sniffed
sniff *noun*
sniffs
snigger *verb*
sniggers
sniggering
sniggered
snigger *noun*
sniggers
snip *verb*
snips
snipping
snipped
snip *noun*
snips
snipe *verb*
snipes
sniping
sniped
sniper *noun*
snipers
snippet *noun*
snippets
snivel *verb*
snivels
snivelling
snivelled
snob *noun*
snobs
snobbery *noun*
snobbish *adjective*
snobbishly *adverb*
snooker *noun*
snoop *verb*
snoops
snooping
snooped
snooper *noun*
snoopers

snore *verb*
snores
snoring
snored
snorkel *noun*
snorkels
snort *verb*
snorts
snorting
snorted
snort *noun*
snorts
snout *noun*
snouts
snow *noun*
snow *verb*
snows
snowing
snowed
snowball *noun*
snowballs
snowdrop *noun*
snowdrops
snowflake *noun*
snowflakes
snowman *noun*
snowmen
snowplough *noun*
snowploughs
snowshoe *noun*
snowshoes
snowstorm *noun*
snowstorms
snowy *adjective*
snowier
snowiest
snub *verb*
snubs
snubbing
snubbed
snuff *noun* & *verb*
snug *adjective*
snugger
snuggest
snugly *adverb*

snuggle *verb*
snuggles
snuggling
snuggled
soak *verb*
soaks
soaking
soaked
so-and-so *noun*
so-and-sos
soap *noun*
soaps
soapy *adjective*
soapier
soapiest
soar★ *verb*
soars
soaring
soared
sob *verb*
sobs
sobbing
sobbed
sob *noun*
sobs
sober *adjective*
soberly *adverb*
sobriety *noun*
so-called *adjective*
soccer *noun*
sociability *noun*
sociable *adjective*
sociably *adverb*
social *adjective*
socially *adverb*
socialism *noun*
socialist *noun*
socialists
society *noun*
societies
sociological *adjective*
sociologist *noun*
sociologists
sociology *noun*

sock *noun*
socks
sock *verb*
socks
socking
socked
socket *noun*
sockets
soda *noun*
sodas
sodium *noun*
sofa *noun*
sofas
soft *adjective*
softer
softest
softly *adverb*
soften *verb*
softens
softening
softened
softness *noun*
software *noun*
soggy *adjective*
soggier
soggiest
soggily *adverb*
soil *noun*
soil *verb*
soils
soiling
soiled
solar *adjective*
sold *verb* SEE **sell**
solder *noun*
solder *verb*
solders
soldering
soldered
soldier *noun*
soldiers
sole☆ *noun*
soles
sole *adjective*
solely *adverb*

★ To **soar** is to rise or fly high. **! sore.**
☆ A **sole** is a fish or a part of a shoe. **! soul.**

a b c d e f g h i j k l m n o p q r s t u v w x y z

solemn *adjective*
solemnly *adverb*
solemnity *noun*
solicitor *noun*
solicitors
solid *adjective*
solidly *adverb*
solid *noun*
solids
solidarity *noun*
solidify *verb*
solidifies
solidifying
solidified
solidity *noun*
soliloquy *noun*
soliloquies
solitary *adjective*
solitude *noun*
solo *noun*
solos
soloist *noun*
soloists
solstice *noun*
solstices
solubility *noun*
soluble *adjective*
solution *noun*
solutions
solve *verb*
solves
solving
solved
solvent *adjective* & *noun*
solvents
sombre *adjective*
sombrely *adverb*
sombrero *noun*
sombreros
some★ *adjective* & *pronoun*
somebody *pronoun*
somehow *adverb*
someone *pronoun*
somersault *noun*
somersaults
something *noun*
sometime *adverb*
sometimes *adverb*
somewhat *adverb*
somewhere *adverb*
son☆ *noun*
sons
sonar *noun*
sonars
sonata *noun*
sonatas
song *noun*
songs
songbird *noun*
songbirds
sonic *adjective*
sonically *adverb*
sonnet *noun*
sonnets
soon *adverb*
sooner
soonest
soot *noun*
soothe *verb*
soothes
soothing
soothed
sooty *adjective*
sootier
sootiest
sophisticated *adjective*
sophistication *noun*
sopping *verb*
soppy *adjective*
soppier
soppiest
soppily *adverb*
soprano *noun*
sopranos
sorcerer *noun*
sorcerers
sorceress *noun*
sorceresses
sorcery *noun*
sore✪ *adjective*
sorer
sorest
sorely *adverb*
sore *noun*
sores
soreness *noun*
sorrow *noun*
sorrows
sorrowful *adjective*
sorrowfully *adverb*
sorry *adjective*
sorrier
sorriest
sort *noun*
sorts
sort *verb*
sorts
sorting
sorted
sought *verb* SEE **seek**
soul✦ *noun*
souls
sound *noun*
sounds
sound *verb*
sounds
sounding
sounded
sound *adjective*
sounder
soundest
soundly *adverb*
soundness *noun*
soundtrack *noun*
soundtracks
soup *noun*
soups

★ You use **some** in e.g. *Have some cake.* **! sum.**
☆ A **son** is a male child. **! sun.**
✪ You use **sore** in e.g. *I've got a sore tooth.* **! soar.**
✦ A **soul** is a person's spirit. **! sole.**

sour *adjective*
sourer
sourest
sourly *adverb*
source* *noun*
sources
sourness *noun*
south *adjective & adverb*
south☆ *noun*
south-east *noun, adjective, & adverb*
southerly *adjective & noun*
southerlies
southern *adjective*
southerner *noun*
southerners
southward *adjective & adverb*
southwards *adverb*
south-west *noun & adjective*
souvenir *noun*
souvenirs
sovereign *noun*
sovereigns
sow✪ *verb*
sows
sowing
sowed
sown
sow *noun*
sows
sower *noun*
sowers
soya bean *noun*
soya beans
space *noun*
spaces
space *verb*
spaces
spacing
spaced

spacecraft *noun*
spacecraft
spaceman *noun*
spacemen
spaceship *noun*
spaceships
spacewoman *noun*
spacewomen
spacious *adjective*
spaciousness
spade *noun*
spades
spaghetti *noun*
spam *noun*
span *verb*
spans
spanning
spanned
span *noun*
spans
spaniel *noun*
spaniels
spank *verb*
spanks
spanking
spanked
spanner *noun*
spanners
spar *noun*
spars
spar *verb*
spars
sparring
sparred
spare *verb*
spares
sparing
spared
spare *adjective & noun*
spares
sparing *adjective*
sparingly *adverb*
spark *noun*
sparks

spark *verb*
sparks
sparking
sparked
sparkle *verb*
sparkles
sparkling
sparkled
sparkler *noun*
sparklers
sparrow *noun*
sparrows
sparse *adjective*
sparser
sparsest
sparsely *adverb*
spastic *noun*
spastics
spat *verb* SEE **spit**
spate *noun*
spates
spatter *verb*
spatters
spattering
spattered
spawn *noun*
spawn *verb*
spawns
spawning
spawned
speak *verb*
speaks
speaking
spoke
spoken
speaker *noun*
speakers
spear *noun*
spears
spear *verb*
spears
spearing
speared
special *adjective*
specially *adverb*

* The **source** is where something comes from. **! sauce**.
☆ You use a capital S in **the South**, when you mean a particular region.
✪ To **sow** is to put seed in the ground. **! sew**.

special *noun*
specials
specialist *noun*
specialists
speciality *noun*
specialities
specialization *noun*
specialize *verb*
specializes
specializing
specialized
species *noun*
species
specific *adjective*
specifically *adverb*
specification *noun*
specifications
specify *verb*
specifies
specifying
specified
specimen *noun*
specimens
speck *noun*
specks
speckled *adjective*
spectacle *noun*
spectacles
spectacular *adjective*
spectacularly *adverb*
spectator *noun*
spectators
spectre *noun*
spectres
spectrum *noun*
spectra
speculate *verb*
speculates
speculating
speculated
speech *noun*
speeches
speechless *adjective*

speed *noun*
speeds
speed* *verb*
speeds
speeding
sped
speeded
speedboat *noun*
speedboats
speedometer *noun*
speedometers
speedway *noun*
speedways
speedy *adjective*
speedier
speediest
speedily *adverb*
spell *verb*
spells
spelling
spelled *or* spelt
spell *noun*
spells
spellchecker *noun*
spellcheckers
spelling *noun*
spellings
spend *verb*
spends
spending
spent
sphere *noun*
spheres
spherical *adjective*
spherically *adverb*
spice *noun*
spices
spicy *adjective*
spicier
spiciest
spider *noun*
spiders
spied *verb* SEE **spy**

spike *noun*
spikes
spiky *adjective*
spikier
spikiest
spill☆ *verb*
spills
spilling
spilt
spilled
spill *noun*
spills
spin *verb*
spins
spinning
spun
spin *noun*
spins
spinach *noun*
spindle *noun*
spindles
spin drier *noun*
spin driers
spine *noun*
spines
spinal *adjective*
spin-off *noun*
spin-offs
spinster *noun*
spinsters
spiny *adjective*
spiniest
spiniest
spiral *noun*
spirals
spire *noun*
spires
spirit *noun*
spirits
spirit *verb*
spirits
spiriting
spirited

* You use **sped** in e.g. *Cars sped past* and **speeded** in e.g. *They speeded up the process.*
☆ You use **spilled** in e.g. *I spilled the milk.* You use **spilt** in e.g. *I can see spilt milk.* You use **spilled** or **spilt** in e.g. *I have spilled/spilt the milk.*

spiritual *adjective*
spiritually *adverb*
spiritual *noun*
spirituals
spiritualism *noun*
spiritualist *noun*
spiritualists
spit *verb*
spits
spitting
spat
spit *noun*
spits
spite *noun*
spiteful *adjective*
spitefully *adverb*
spittle *noun*
splash *verb*
splashes
splashing
splashed
splash *noun*
splashes
splashdown *noun*
splashdowns
splendid *adjective*
splendidly *adverb*
splendour *noun*
splint *noun*
splints
splinter *noun*
splinters
splinter *verb*
splinters
splintering
splintered
split *verb*
splits
splitting
split
split *noun*
splits

splutter *verb*
splutters
spluttering
spluttered
spoil* *verb*
spoils
spoiling
spoilt
spoiled
spoils *plural noun*
spoilsport *noun*
spoilsports
spoke *noun*
spokes
spoke *verb* SEE **speak**
spoken *verb* SEE **speak**
spokesman *noun*
spokesmen
spokesperson *noun*
spokespersons
spokeswoman *noun*
spokeswomen
sponge *noun*
sponges
sponge *verb*
sponges
sponging
sponged
sponger *noun*
spongers
sponginess *noun*
spongy *adjective*
spongier
spongiest
sponsor *noun*
sponsors
sponsor *verb*
sponsors
sponsoring
sponsored
sponsorship *noun*
sponsorships
spontaneity *noun*
spontaneous *adjective*
spontaneously *adverb*

spooky *adjective*
spookier
spookiest
spookily *adverb*
spool *noun*
spools
spoon *noun*
spoons
spoon *verb*
spoons
spooning
spooned
spoonful *noun*
spoonfuls
sport *noun*
sports
sporting *adjective*
sportsman *noun*
sportsmen
sportsmanship *noun*
sportswoman *noun*
sportswomen
spot *noun*
spots
spot *verb*
spots
spotting
spotted
spotless *adjective*
spotlessly *adverb*
spotlight *noun*
spotlights
spotter *noun*
spotters
spotty *adjective*
spottier
spottiest
spout *noun*
spouts
spout *verb*
spouts
spouting
spouted

* You use **spoiled** in e.g. *They spoiled the party*. You use **spoilt** in e.g. *a spoilt child*. You use **spoiled** or **spoilt** in e.g. *They have spoiled/spoilt the party*.

a b c d e f g h i j k l m n o p q r s t u v w x y z

sprain *verb*
sprains
spraining
sprained
sprain *noun*
sprains
sprang *verb* SEE **spring**
sprawl *verb*
sprawls
sprawling
sprawled
spray *verb*
sprays
spraying
sprayed
spray *noun*
sprays
spread *verb*
spreads
spreading
spread
spread *noun*
spreads
spreadsheet *noun*
spreadsheets
spree *noun*
sprees
sprightliness *noun*
sprightly *adjective*
sprightlier
sprightliest
spring *verb*
springs
springing
sprang
sprung
spring *noun*
springs
springboard *noun*
springboards
spring-clean *verb*
spring-cleans
spring-cleaning
spring-cleaned
springtime *noun*
springy *adjective*
springier
springiest

sprinkle *verb*
sprinkles
sprinkling
sprinkled
sprinkler *noun*
sprinklers
sprint *verb*
sprints
sprinting
sprinted
sprinter *noun*
sprinters
sprout *verb*
sprouts
sprouting
sprouted
sprout *noun*
sprouts
spruce *noun*
spruces
spruce *adjective*
sprucer
sprucest
sprung *verb* SEE **spring**
spud *noun*
spuds
spun *verb* SEE **spin**
spur *noun*
spurs
spur *verb*
spurs
spurring
spurred
spurt *verb*
spurts
spurting
spurted
spurt *noun*
spurts
spy *noun*
spies
spy *verb*
spies
spying
spied

squabble *verb*
squabbles
squabbling
squabbled
squabble *noun*
squabbles
squad *noun*
squads
squadron *noun*
squadrons
squalid *adjective*
squall *noun*
squalls
squally *adjective*
squallier
squalliest
squalor *noun*
squander *verb*
squanders
squandering
squandered
square *adjective*
squarely *adverb*
square *noun*
squares
square *verb*
squares
squaring
squared
squareness *noun*
squash *verb*
squashes
squashing
squashed
squash *noun*
squashes
squat *verb*
squats
squatting
squatted
squat *adjective*
squatter
squattest
squatter *noun*
squatters
squaw *noun*
squaws

squawk *verb*
squawks
squawking
squawked

squawk *noun*
squawks

squeak *verb*
squeaks
squeaking
squeaked

squeak *noun*
squeaks

squeaky *adjective*
squeakier
squeakiest
squeakily *adverb*

squeal *verb*
squeals
squealing
squealed

squeal *noun*
squeals

squeeze *verb*
squeezes
squeezing
squeezed

squeeze *noun*
squeezes

squeezer *noun*
squeezers

squelch *verb*
squelches
squelching
squelched

squelch *noun*
squelches

squid *noun*
squid
squids

squint *verb*
squints
squinting
squinted

squint *noun*
squints

squire *noun*
squires

squirm *verb*
squirms
squirming
squirmed

squirrel *noun*
squirrels

squirt *verb*
squirts
squirting
squirted

stab *verb*
stabs
stabbing
stabbed

stab *noun*
stabs

stability *noun*

stabilize *verb*
stabilizes
stabilizing
stabilized

stabilizer *noun*
stabilizers

stable *adjective*
stabler
stablest
stably *adverb*

stable *noun*
stables

stack *verb*
stacks
stacking
stacked

stack *noun*
stacks

stadium *noun*
stadiums
stadia

staff *noun*
staffs

stag *noun*
stags

stage *noun*
stages

stage *verb*
stages
staging
staged

stagecoach *noun*
stagecoaches

stagger *verb*
staggers
staggering
staggered

stagnant *adjective*

stain *noun*
stains

stain *verb*
stains
staining
stained

stainless *adjective*

stair★ *noun*
stairs

staircase *noun*
staircases

stake☆ *noun*
stakes

stake *verb*
stakes
staking
staked

stalactite *noun*
stalactites

stalagmite *noun*
stalagmites

stale *adjective*
staler
stalest

stalk *noun*
stalks

stalk *verb*
stalks
stalking
stalked

stall *noun*
stalls

★ A **stair** is one of a set of steps. **! stare.**
☆ A **stake** is a pointed stick or post. **! steak.**

a b c d e f g h i j k l m n o p q r s t u v w x y z

stall *verb*
stalls
stalling
stalled
stallion *noun*
stallions
stalls *plural noun*
stamen *noun*
stamens
stamina *noun*
stammer *verb*
stammers
stammering
stammered
stammer *noun*
stammers
stamp *noun*
stamps
stamp *verb*
stamps
stamping
stamped
stampede *noun*
stampedes
stand *verb*
stands
standing
stood
stand *noun*
stands
standard *adjective* & *noun*
standards
standardize★ *verb*
standardizes
standardizing
standardized
standby *noun*
standbys
standstill *noun*
stank *verb* SEE **stink**
stanza *noun*
stanzas
staple *noun*
staples
staple *adjective*
stapler *noun*
staplers
star *noun*
stars
star *verb*
stars
starring
starred
starboard *adjective*
starch *noun*
starches
starchy *adjective*
starchier
starchiest
stare☆ *verb*
stares
staring
stared
starfish *noun*
starfish
starfishes
starling *noun*
starlings
starry *adjective*
starrier
starriest
start *verb*
starts
starting
started
start *noun*
starts
starter *noun*
starters
startle *verb*
startles
startling
startled
starvation *noun*
starve *verb*
starves
starving
starved
state *noun*
states
state *verb*
states
stating
stated
stateliness *noun*
stately *adjective*
statelier
stateliest
statement *noun*
statements
statesman *noun*
statesmen
statesmanship *noun*
stateswoman *noun*
stateswomen
static *adjective*
statically *adverb*
station *noun*
stations
station *verb*
stations
stationing
stationed
stationary✪ *adjective*
stationery✣ *noun*
stationmaster *noun*
stationmasters
statistic *noun*
statistics
statistical *adjective*
statistically *adverb*
statistician *noun*
statisticians
statistics *noun*
statue *noun*
statues

★ This word can also be spelled **standardise**.
☆ To **stare** is to look at something without moving your eyes. **! stair**.
✪ **Stationary** means 'not moving'. **! stationery**.
✣ **Stationery** means 'paper and envelopes'. **! stationary**.

status *noun*
statuses

staunch *adjective*
stauncher
staunchest
staunchly *adverb*

stave *noun*
staves

stave *verb*
staves
staving
staved
stove

stay *verb*
stays
staying
stayed

stay *noun*
stays

stead *noun*

steadiness *noun*

steady *adjective*
steadier
steadiest
steadily *adverb*

steady *verb*
steadies
steadying
steadied

steak★ *noun*
steaks

steal☆ *verb*
steals
stealing
stole
stolen

stealth *noun*

stealthy *adjective*
stealthier
stealthiest
stealthily *adverb*

steam *noun*

steam *verb*
steams
steaming
steamed

steamer *noun*
steamers

steamroller *noun*
steamrollers

steamship *noun*
steamships

steamy *adjective*
steamier
steamiest

steed *noun*
steeds

steel *noun*

steel✪ *verb*
steels
steeling
steeled

steely *adjective*
steelier
steeliest

steep *adjective*
steeper
steepest
steeply *adverb*

steepness *noun*

steeple *noun*
steeples

steeplechase *noun*
steeplechases

steeplejack *noun*
steeplejacks

steer *verb*
steers
steering
steered

steer *noun*
steers

stem *noun*
stems

stem *verb*
stems
stemming
stemmed

stench *noun*
stenches

stencil *noun*
stencils

step✣ *noun*
steps

step *verb*
steps
stepping
stepped

stepchild *noun*
stepchildren

stepfather *noun*
stepfathers

stepladder *noun*
stepladders

stepmother *noun*
stepmothers

steppe● *noun*
steppes

stereo *adjective* & *noun*
stereos

stereophonic *adjective*

stereotype *noun*
stereotypes

sterile *adjective*

sterility *noun*

sterilization *noun*

sterilize *verb*
sterilizes
sterilizing
sterilized

sterling *noun* & *adjective*

stern *noun*
sterns

★ A **steak** is a thick slice of meat. **! stake**.
☆ To **steal** is to take something that is not yours. **! steel**.
✪ To **steel** yourself is to find courage to do something hard. **! steal**.
✣ A **step** is a movement of the feet or part of a stair. **! steppe**.
● A **steppe** is a grassy plain. **! step**.

stern *adjective*
sterner
sternest
sternly *adverb*
sternness *noun*
stethoscope *noun*
stethoscopes
stew *verb*
stews
stewing
stewed
stew *noun*
stews
steward *noun*
stewards
stewardess *noun*
stewardesses
stick *verb*
sticks
sticking
stuck
stick *noun*
sticks
sticker *noun*
stickers
stickiness *noun*
stickleback *noun*
sticklebacks
sticky *adjective*
stickier
stickiest
stickily *adverb*
stiff *adjective*
stiffer
stiffest
stiffly *adverb*
stiffen *verb*
stiffens
stiffening
stiffened
stiffness *noun*
stifle *verb*
stifles
stifling
stifled
stigma *noun*
stigmas
stile *noun*
stiles
still *adjective*
stiller
stillest
still *adverb*
still *verb*
stills
stilling
stilled
stillness *noun*
stilts *noun*
stimulant *noun*
stimulants
stimulate *verb*
stimulates
stimulating
stimulated
stimulation *noun*
stimulus *noun*
stimuli
sting *noun*
stings
sting *verb*
stings
stinging
stung
stingy *adjective*
stingier
stingiest
stingily *adverb*
stink *noun*
stinks
stink *verb*
stinks
stinking
stank
stunk
stir *verb*
stirs
stirring
stirred
stir *noun*
stirs
stirrup *noun*
stirrups
stitch *noun*
stitches
stoat *noun*
stoats
stock *noun*
stocks
stock *verb*
stocks
stocking
stocked
stockade *noun*
stockades
stockbroker *noun*
stockbrokers
stocking *noun*
stockings
stockist *noun*
stockpile *noun*
stockpiles
stocks *plural noun*
stocky *adjective*
stockier
stockiest
stockily *adverb*
stodgy *adjective*
stodgier
stodgiest
stodgily *adverb*
stoke *verb*
stokes
stoking
stoked
stole *noun*
stoles
stole *verb* SEE **steal**
stolen *verb* SEE **steal**
stomach *noun*
stomachs
stomach *verb*
stomachs
stomaching
stomached
stone *noun*
stones
stone
stone *verb*
stones
stoning
stoned

stony *adjective*
stonier
stoniest
stood *verb* SEE **stand**
stool *noun*
stools
stoop *verb*
stoops
stooping
stooped
stop *verb*
stops
stopping
stopped
stop *noun*
stops
stoppage *noun*
stoppages
stopper *noun*
stoppers
stopwatch *noun*
stopwatches
storage *noun*
store *verb*
stores
storing
stored
store *noun*
stores
storey★ *noun*
storeys
stork *noun*
storks
storm *noun*
storms
storm *verb*
storms
storming
stormed
stormy *adjective*
stormier
stormiest

story☆ *noun*
stories
stout *adjective*
stouter
stoutest
stoutly *adverb*
stove *noun*
stoves
stove *verb* SEE **stave**
stow *verb*
stows
stowing
stowed
stowaway *noun*
stowaways
straddle *verb*
straddles
straddling
straddled
straggle *verb*
straggles
straggling
straggled
straggler *noun*
stragglers
straggly *adjective*
stragglier
straggliest
straight✪ *adjective*
straighter
straightest
straighten *verb*
straightens
straightening
straightened
straightforward *adjective*
straightforwardly *adverb*
strain *verb*
strains
straining
strained

strain *noun*
strains
strainer *noun*
strainers
strait✣ *noun*
straits
straits✱ *plural noun*
strand *noun*
strands
stranded *adjective*
strange *adjective*
stranger
strangest
strangely *adverb*
strangeness *noun*
stranger *noun*
strangers
strangle *verb*
strangles
strangling
strangled
strangler *noun*
stranglers
strangulation *noun*
strap *noun*
straps
strap *verb*
straps
strapping
strapped
strategic *adjective*
strategically *adverb*
strategist *noun*
strategists
strategy *noun*
strategies
stratum *noun*
strata
straw *noun*
straws
strawberry *noun*
strawberries

★ A **storey** is a floor of a building. **! story**.
☆ You use **story** in e.g. *read me a story*. **! storey**.
✪ **Straight** means 'not curving or bending'. **! strait**.
✣ A **strait** is a narrow stretch of water. **! straight**.
✱ You use **straits** in the phrase *in dire straits*.

a b c d e f g h i j k l m n o p q r s t u v w x y z

stray *verb*
strays
straying
strayed

stray *adjective*

streak *noun*
streaks

streak *verb*
streaks
streaking
streaked

streaky *adjective*
streakier
streakiest

stream *noun*
streams

stream *verb*
streams
streaming
streamed

streamer *noun*
streamers

streamline *verb*
streamlines
streamlining
streamlined

street *noun*
streets

strength *noun*
strengths

strengthen *verb*
strengthens
strengthening
strengthened

strenuous *adjective*
strenuously *adverb*

stress *noun*
stresses

stress *verb*
stresses
stressing
stressed

stressful *adjective*

stretch *verb*
stretches
stretching
stretched

stretch *noun*
stretches

stretcher *noun*
stretchers

strew *verb*
strews
strewing
strewed
strewn

stricken *adjective*

strict *adjective*
stricter
strictest
strictly *adverb*

strictness *noun*

stride *verb*
strides
striding
strode
stridden

stride *noun*
strides

strife *noun*

strike *verb*
strikes
striking
struck

strike *noun*
strikes

striker *noun*
strikers

striking *adjective*
strikingly *adverb*

string *noun*
strings

string *verb*
strings
stringing
strung

stringy *adjective*
stringier
stringiest

strip *verb*
strips
stripping
stripped

strip *noun*
strips

stripe *noun*
stripes

striped *adjective*

stripy *adjective*
stripier
stripiest

strive *verb*
strives
striving
strove
striven

strobe *noun*
strobes

strode *verb* SEE **stride**

stroke *noun*
strokes

stroke *verb*
strokes
stroking
stroked

stroll *verb*
strolls
strolling
strolled

stroll *noun*
strolls

strong *adjective*
stronger
strongest
strongly *adverb*

stronghold *noun*
strongholds

strove *verb* SEE **strive**

struck *verb* SEE **strike**

structural *adjective*
structurally *adverb*

structure *noun*
structures

struggle *verb*
struggles
struggling
struggled

struggle *noun*
struggles

strum *verb*
strums
strumming
strummed

strung *verb* SEE **string**

strut *verb*
struts
strutting
strutted

strut *noun*
struts

stub *verb*
stubs
stubbing
stubbed

stub *noun*
stubs

stubble

stubborn *adjective*
stubbornly *adverb*

stubbornness *noun*

stuck *verb* SEE **stick**

stuck-up *adjective*

stud *noun*
studs

student *noun*
students

studio *noun*
studios

studious *adjective*
studiously *adverb*

study *verb*
studies
studying
studied

study *noun*
studies

stuff *noun*

stuff *verb*
stuffs
stuffing
stuffed

stuffiness *noun*

stuffing *noun*
stuffings

stuffy *adjective*
stuffier
stuffiest

stumble *verb*
stumbles
stumbling
stumbled

stump *noun*
stumps

stump *verb*
stumps
stumping
stumped

stun *verb*
stuns
stunning
stunned

stung *verb* SEE **sting**

stunk *verb* SEE **stink**

stunt *noun*
stunts

stupendous *adjective*
stupendously *adverb*

stupid *adjective*
stupider
stupidest
stupidly *adverb*

stupidity *noun*

sturdiness *noun*

sturdy *adjective*
sturdier
sturdiest
sturdily *adverb*

stutter *verb*
stutters
stuttering
stuttered

stutter *noun*
stutters

sty* *noun*
sties

style *noun*
styles

style *verb*
styles
styling
styled

stylish *adjective*
stylishly *adverb*

stylus *noun*
styluses

subcontinent *noun*
subcontinents

subdivide *verb*
subdivides
subdividing
subdivided

subdivision *noun*
subdivisions

subdue *verb*
subdues
subduing
subdued

subject *adjective* & *noun*
subjects

subject *verb*
subjects
subjecting
subjected

subjective *adjective*
subjectively *adverb*

submarine *noun*
submarines

submerge *verb*
submerges
submerging
submerged

submersion *noun*

submission *noun*
submissions

submissive *adjective*
submissively *adverb*

submit *verb*
submits
submitting
submitted

subordinate *adjective* & *noun*
subordinates

* A **sty** is a place for pigs or a swelling on the eye. In the second meaning you can also use *stye*, plural *styes*.

a b c d e f g h i j k l m n o p q r s t u v w x y z

subordinate *verb*
subordinates
subordinating
subordinated

subordination *noun*

subscribe *verb*
subscribes
subscribing
subscribed

subscriber *noun*
subscribers

subscription *noun*
subscriptions

subsequent *adjective*
subsequently *adverb*

subside *verb*
subsides
subsiding
subsided

subsidence *noun*

subsidize *verb*
subsidizes
subsidizing
subsidized

subsidy *noun*
subsidies

substance *noun*
substances

substantial *adjective*
substantially *adverb*

substitute *verb*
substitutes
substituting
substituted

substitute *noun*
substitutes

substitution *noun*
substitutions

subtle *adjective*
subtler
subtlest
subtly *adverb*

subtlety *noun*
subtleties

subtract *verb*
subtracts
subtracting
subtracted

subtraction *noun*
subtractions

suburb *noun*
suburbs

suburban *adjective*

suburbia *noun*

subway *noun*
subways

succeed *verb*
succeeds
succeeding
succeeded

success *noun*
successes

successful *adjective*
successfully *adverb*

succession *noun*
successions

successive *adjective*
successively *adverb*

successor *noun*
successors

such *adjective*

suck *verb*
sucks
sucking
sucked

suck *noun*
sucks

suction *noun*

sudden *adjective*
suddenly *adverb*

suddenness *noun*

suds *plural noun*

sue *verb*
sues
suing
sued

suede *noun*

suet *noun*

suffer *verb*
suffers
suffering
suffered

sufficiency *noun*

sufficient *adjective*
sufficiently *adverb*

suffix *noun*
suffixes

suffocate *verb*
suffocates
suffocating
suffocated

suffocation *noun*

sugar *noun*

sugary *adjective*

suggest *verb*
suggests
suggesting
suggested

suggestion *noun*
suggestions

suicidal *adjective*
suicidally *adverb*

suicide *noun*
suicides

suit★ *noun*
suits

suit *verb*
suits
suiting
suited

suitability *noun*

suitable *adjective*
suitably *adverb*

suitcase *noun*
suitcases

suite☆ *noun*
suites

suitor *noun*
suitors

★ A **suit** is a set of matching clothes. **! suite.**
☆ A **suite** is a set of furniture or a group of rooms. **! suit.**

sulk *verb*
sulks
sulking
sulked
sulkiness *noun*
sulky *adjective*
sulkier
sulkiest
sulkily *adverb*
sullen *adjective*
sullenly *adverb*
sullenness *noun*
sulphur *noun*
sulphuric acid *noun*
sultan *noun*
sultans
sultana *noun*
sultanas
sum* *noun*
sums
sum *verb*
sums
summing
summed
summarize *verb*
summarizes
summarizing
summarized
summary *noun*
summaries
summer *noun*
summers
summertime *noun*
summit *noun*
summits
summon *verb*
summons
summoning
summoned
summons *noun*
summonses
sun☆ *noun*
suns
sun *verb*
suns
sunning
sunned
sunbathe *verb*
sunbathes
sunbathing
sunbathed
sunburn *noun*
sunburned *or* **sunburnt** *adjective*
sundae⊙ *noun*
sundaes
Sunday✢ *noun*
Sundays
sundial *noun*
sundials
sunflower *noun*
sunflowers
sung *verb* SEE **sing**
sunglasses *noun*
sunk *verb* SEE **sink**
sunlight *noun*
sunlit *adjective*
sunny *adjective*
sunnier
sunniest
sunrise *noun*
sunrises
sunset *noun*
sunsets
sunshade *noun*
sunshades
sunshine *noun*
sunspot *noun*
sunspots
sunstroke *noun*
suntan *noun*
suntans
suntanned *adjective*
super *adjective*

super- *prefix*
super- makes words meaning 'very good' or 'extra', e.g. **supermarket**, **supermodel**. They are normally spelled joined up.

superb *adjective*
superbly *adverb*
superficial *adjective*
superficially *adverb*
superfluous *adjective*
superintend *verb*
superintends
superintending
superintended
superintendent *noun*
superintendents
superior *adjective* & *noun*
superiors
superiority *noun*
superlative *adjective*
superlatively *adverb*
superlative *noun*
superlatives
Superman *noun*
supermarket *noun*
supermarkets
supernatural *adjective*
supernaturally *adverb*
supernova *noun*
supernova *verb*
superpower *noun*
supersonic *adjective*
supersonically *adverb*
superstition *noun*
superstitions
superstitious *adjective*
superstitiously *adverb*

★ A **sum** is an amount or total. **! some**.
☆ A **sun** is a large star. **! son**.
⊙ A **sundae** is a cocktail of fruit and ice cream. **! Sunday**.
✢ **Sunday** is a day of the week. **! sundae**.

a b c d e f g h i j k l m n o p q r s t u v w x y z

supervise *verb*
supervises
supervising
supervised
supervision *noun*
supervisor *noun*
supper *noun*
suppers
supple *adjective*
suppler
supplest
supplely *adverb*
supplement *noun*
supplements
supplementary *noun*
suppleness *noun*
supplicant *noun*
supply *verb*
supplies
supplying
supplied
supplier *noun*
suppliers
supply *noun*
supplies
support *verb*
supports
supporting
supported
support *noun*
supports
supporter *noun*
supporters
supportive *adjective*
suppose *verb*
supposes
supposing
supposed
supposedly *adverb*
supposition *noun*
suppositions
suppress *verb*
suppresses
suppressing
suppressed
suppression *noun*
supremacy *noun*
supreme *adjective*
supremely *adverb*
sure *adjective*
surer
surest
surely *adverb*
surf *noun*
surf *verb*
surfs
surfing
surfed
surface *noun*
surfaces
surface *verb*
surfaces
surfacing
surfaced
surfboard *noun*
surfboards
surfer *noun*
surfers
surge *verb*
surges
surging
surged
surge *noun*
surges
surgeon *noun*
surgeons
surgery *noun*
surgeries
surgical *adjective*
surgically *adverb*
surname *noun*
surnames
surpass *verb*
surpasses
surpassing
surpassed
surplus *noun*
surpluses
surprise *verb*
surprises
surprising
surprised
surprise *noun*
surprises
surprising *adjective*
surprisingly *adverb*
surrender *verb*
surrenders
surrendering
surrendered
surrender *noun*
surrenders
surround *verb*
surrounds
surrounding
surrounded
surroundings *plural noun*
surveillance *noun*
survey *noun*
surveys
survey *verb*
surveys
surveying
surveyed
surveyor *noun*
surveyors
survival *noun*
survive *verb*
survives
surviving
survived
survivor *noun*
survivors
susceptible *adjective*
suspect *verb*
suspects
suspecting
suspected
suspect *noun*
suspects
suspend *verb*
suspends
suspending
suspended
suspense *noun*
suspension *noun*
suspensions

suspicion *noun*
suspicions

suspicious *adjective*
suspiciously *adverb*

sustain *verb*
sustains
sustaining
sustained

sustainable *adjective*

swagger *verb*
swaggers
swaggering
swaggered

swallow *verb*
swallows
swallowing
swallowed

swallow *noun*
swallows

swam *verb* SEE **swim**

swamp *verb*
swamps
swamping
swamped

swamp *noun*
swamps

swampy *adjective*
swampier
swampiest

swan *noun*
swans

swank *verb*
swanks
swanking
swanked

swap *verb*
swaps
swapping
swapped

swap *noun*
swaps

swarm *noun*
swarms

swarm *verb*
swarms
swarming
swarmed

swastika *noun*
swastikas

swat* *verb*
swats
swatting
swatted

swatter *noun*
swatters

sway *verb*
sways
swaying
swayed

swear *verb*
swears
swearing
swore
sworn

sweat *verb*
sweats
sweating
sweated

sweat *noun*

sweater *noun*
sweaters

sweatshirt *noun*
sweatshirts

sweaty *adjective*
sweatier
sweatiest
sweatily *adverb*

swede *noun*
swedes

sweep *verb*
sweeps
sweeping
swept

sweep *noun*
sweeps

sweeper *noun*
sweepers

sweet *adjective*
sweeter
sweetest
sweetly *adverb*

sweet *noun*
sweets

sweetcorn *noun*

sweeten *verb*
sweetens
sweetening
sweetened

sweetener *noun*
sweeteners

sweetheart *noun*
sweethearts

sweetness *noun*

swell *verb*
swells
swelling
swelled
swollen

swell *noun*
swells

swelling *noun*
swellings

swelter *verb*
swelters
sweltering
sweltered

swept *verb* SEE **sweep**

swerve *verb*
swerves
swerving
swerved

swerve *noun*
swerves

swift *adjective*
swifter
swiftest
swiftly *adverb*

swift *noun*
swifts

swiftness *noun*

* To **swat** an insect is to hit it. **! swot**.

a b c d e f g h i j k l m n o p q r s t u v w x y z

swill *verb*
swills
swilling
swilled

swill *noun*

swim *verb*
swims
swimming
swam
swum

swim *noun*
swims

swimmer *noun*
swimmers

swimsuit *noun*
swimsuits

swindle *verb*
swindles
swindling
swindled

swindler *noun*
swindlers

swindle *noun*
swindles

swine *noun*
swine
swines

swing *verb*
swings
swinging
swung

swing *noun*
swings

swipe *verb*
swipes
swiping
swiped

swipe *noun*
swipes

swirl *verb*
swirls
swirling
swirled

swirl *noun*
swirls

swish *verb*
swishes
swishing
swished

swish *noun*
swishes

Swiss roll *noun*
Swiss rolls

switch *verb*
switches
switching
switched

switch *noun*
switches

switchboard *noun*
switchboards

swivel *verb*
swivels
swivelling
swivelled

swollen *adjective* SEE **swell**

swoon *verb*
swoons
swooning
swooned

swoop *verb*
swoops
swooping
swooped

swoop *noun*
swoops

swop *verb*
swops
swopping
swopped

sword *noun*
swords

swore *verb* SEE **swear**

sworn *verb* SEE **swear**

swot* *verb*
swots
swotting
swotted

swot *noun*
swots

swum *verb* SEE **swim**

swung *verb* SEE **swing**

sycamore *noun*
sycamores

syllabic *adjective*

syllable *noun*
syllables

syllabus *noun*
syllabuses

symbol *noun*
symbols

symbolic *adjective*
symbolically *adverb*

symbolism *noun*

symbolize *verb*
symbolizes
symbolizing
symbolized

symmetrical *adjective*
symmetrically *adverb*

symmetry *noun*

sympathetic *adjective*
sympathetically *adverb*

sympathize *verb*
sympathizes
sympathizing
sympathized

sympathy *noun*
sympathies

symphonic *adjective*

symphony *noun*
symphonies

symptom *noun*
symptoms

symptomatic *adjective*
symptomatically *adverb*

synagogue *noun*
synagogues

* To **swot** is to study hard. ! **swat**.

Try also words beginning with ci-, cy-, ps-, or sc-

synchronization *noun*

synchronize *verb*
synchronizes
synchronizing
synchronized

syncopated *adjective*

syndrome *noun*
syndromes

synonym *noun*
synonyms

synonymous *adjective*
synonymously *adverb*

synthesis *noun*
syntheses

synthesize *verb*
synthesizes
synthesizing
synthesized

synthesizer *noun*
synthesizers

synthetic *adjective*
synthetically *adverb*

syringe *noun*
syringes

syrup *noun*
syrups

syrupy *adjective*

system *noun*
systems

systematic *adjective*
systematically *adverb*

a b c d e f g h i j k l m n o p q r s t u v w x y z

Tt

-t
See the note at **-ed**.

tab *noun*
tabs
tabby *noun*
tabbies
table *noun*
tables
tablecloth *noun*
tablecloths
tablespoon *noun*
tablespoons
tablespoonful *noun*
tablespoonfuls
tablet *noun*
tablets
tabloid *adjective* & *noun*
tabloids
tack *noun*
tacks
tack *verb*
tacks
tacking
tacked
tackle *verb*
tackles
tackling
tackled
tackle *noun*
tackles
tacky *adjective*
tackier
tackiest
tackily *adverb*
tact *noun*
tactful *adjective*
tactfully *adverb*
tactical *adjective*
tactically *adverb*
tactics *plural noun*
tactless *adjective*
tactlessly *adverb*
tadpole *noun*
tadpoles
tag *noun*
tags
tag *verb*
tags
tagging
tagged
tagliatelle *noun*
tail* *noun*
tails
tail *verb*
tails
tailing
tailed
tailback *noun*
tailbacks
tailless *adjective*
tailor *noun*
tailors
take *verb*
takes
taking
took
taken
takeaway *noun*
takeaways
takings *plural noun*
talc *noun*
talcum powder *noun*
tale☆ *noun*
tales
talent *noun*
talents
talented *adjective*
talk *verb*
talks
talking
talked
talk *noun*
talks
talkative *adjective*
talkatively *adverb*
talker *noun*
talkers
tall *adjective*
taller
tallest
tally *verb*
tallies
tallying
tallied
Talmud *noun*
talon *noun*
talons
tambourine *noun*
tambourines
tame *adjective*
tamer
tamest
tamely *adverb*
tame *verb*
tames
taming
tamed
tameness *noun*
tamer *noun*
tamers
tamper *verb*
tampers
tampering
tampered

★ A **tail** is a part at the back of an animal. **! tale.**
☆ A **tale** is a story. **! tail.**

tan *noun*
tans
tan *verb*
tans
tanning
tanned
tandem *noun*
tandems
tang *noun*
tangs
tangent *noun*
tangents
tangerine *noun*
tangerines
tangle *verb*
tangles
tangling
tangled
tangle *noun*
tangles
tank *noun*
tanks
tanka *noun*
tankas
tankard *noun*
tankards
tanker *noun*
tankers
tantalize *verb*
tantalizes
tantalizing
tantalized
tantrum *noun*
tantrums
tap *noun*
taps
tap *verb*
taps
tapping
tapped
tap dance *noun*
tap dances
tap dancer *noun*
tap dancers
tap dancing *noun*
tape *noun*
tapes
tape *verb*
tapes
taping
taped
tape measure *noun*
tape measures
taper *verb*
tapers
tapering
tapered
taper *noun*
tapers
tape recorder *noun*
tape recorders
tapestry *noun*
tapestries
tapeworm *noun*
tapeworms
tapioca *noun*
tar *noun*
tar *verb*
tars
tarring
tarred
tarantula *noun*
tarantulas
target *noun*
targets
target *verb*
targets
targeting
targeted
tariff *noun*
tariffs
tarmac *noun*
tarmacadam *noun*
tarnish *verb*
tarnishes
tarnishing
tarnished
tarpaulin *noun*
tarpaulins
tarry *adjective*
tarrier
tarriest
tart *noun*
tarts
tart *adjective*
tarter
tartest
tartly *adverb*
tartan *noun*
tartans
task *noun*
tasks
tassel *noun*
tassels
taste *verb*
tastes
tasting
tasted
taste *noun*
tastes
tasteful *adjective*
tastefully *adverb*
tasteless *adjective*
tastelessly *adverb*
tasty *adjective*
tastier
tastiest
tastily *adverb*
tattered *adjective*
tatters *plural noun*
tattoo *noun*
tattoos
tattoo *verb*
tattoos
tattooing
tattooed
tatty *adjective*
tattier
tattiest
tattily *adverb*
taught *verb* SEE **teach**
taunt *verb*
taunts
taunting
taunted
taunt *noun*
taunts
taut *adjective*
tauter
tautest
tautly *adverb*
tautness *noun*

a b c d e f g h i j k l m n o p q r s t u v w x y z

tavern *noun*
taverns

tawny *adjective*
tawnier
tawniest

tax *noun*
taxes

tax *verb*
taxes
taxing
taxed

taxable *adjective*

taxation *noun*

taxi *noun*
taxis

taxi *verb*
taxis
taxiing
taxied

taxpayer *noun*
taxpayers

tea★ *noun*
teas

tea bag *noun*
tea bags

teacake *noun*
teacakes

teach *verb*
teaches
teaching
taught

teacher *noun*
teachers

teaching *noun*
teachings

tea cloth *or* **tea towel** *noun*
tea cloths
tea towels

teacup *noun*
teacups

teak *noun*

team☆ *noun*
teams

teapot *noun*
teapots

tear *verb*
tears
tearing
tore
torn

tear✪ *noun*
tears

tearful *adjective*
tearfully *adverb*

tear gas

tease *verb*
teases
teasing
teased

teaspoon *noun*
teaspoons

teaspoonful *noun*
teaspoonfuls

teat *noun*
teats

technical *adjective*
technically *adverb*

technicality *noun*
technicalities

technician *noun*
technicians

technique *noun*
techniques

technological *adjective*
technologically *adverb*

technology *noun*
technologies

teddy *noun*
teddies

teddy bear *noun*
teddy bears

tedious *adjective*
tediously *adverb*

tediousness *noun*

tedium *noun*

tee✣ *noun*
tees

teem✱ *verb*
teems
teeming
teemed

teenage *adjective*

teenager *noun*
teenagers

teens *plural noun*

teeth *plural noun* SEE **tooth**

teetotal *adjective*

teetotaller *noun*
teetotallers

telecom *noun*

telecommunications *plural noun*

telegram *noun*
telegrams

telegraph *noun*
telegraphs

telegraphic *adjective*

telegraphy *noun*

telepathic *adjective*
telepathically *adverb*

telepathy *noun*

telephone *noun*
telephones

telephone *verb*
telephones
telephoning
telephoned

telephonist *noun*
telephonists

telephoto *noun*

★ **Tea** is a hot drink. **! tee.**
☆ You use **team** in e.g. *a football team.* **! teem.**
✪ A **tear** is a drop of water from an eye and rhymes with 'here', or a split in something and rhymes with 'hair'.
✣ A **tee** is part of a golf course. **! tea.**
• You use **teem** in e.g. *a place teeming with people*. **! team.**

teleport *verb*
telescope *noun*
telescopes
telescopic *adjective*
teletext *noun*
televise *verb*
televises
televising
televised
television *noun*
televisions
tell *verb*
tells
telling
told
telltale *adjective* & *noun*
telltales
telly *noun*
tellies
temper *noun*
tempers
temperament *noun*
temperaments
temperate *adjective*
temperature *noun*
temperatures
tempest *noun*
tempests
tempestuous *adjective*
template *noun*
templates
temple *noun*
temples
tempo *noun*
tempos
temporary *adjective*
temporarily *adverb*
tempt *verb*
tempts
tempting
tempted
temptation *noun*
temptations
tempter *noun*
tempters
temptress *noun*
temptresses

ten *noun*
tens
tenancy *noun*
tenancies
tenant *noun*
tenants
tend *verb*
tends
tending
tended
tendency *noun*
tendencies
tender *adjective*
tenderer
tenderest
tenderly *adverb*
tender *noun*
tenders
tender *verb*
tenders
tendering
tendered
tenderness *noun*
tendon *noun*
tendons
tendril *noun*
tendrils
tennis *noun*
tenor *noun*
tenors
tenpin bowling *noun*
tense *adjective*
tenser
tensest
tensely *adverb*
tense *noun*
tenses
tension *noun*
tensions
tent *noun*
tents
tentacle *noun*
tentacles
tenth *adjective* & *noun*
tenthly *adverb*
tepid *adjective*

term *noun*
terms
term *verb*
terms
terming
termed
terminal *noun*
terminals
terminate *verb*
terminates
terminating
terminated
termination *noun*
terminations
terminology *noun*
terminus *noun*
termini
terrace *noun*
terraces
terrain *noun*
terrains
terrapin *noun*
terrapins
terrestrial *adjective*
terrible *adjective*
terribly *adverb*
terrier *noun*
terriers
terrific *adjective*
terrifically *adverb*
terrify *verb*
terrifies
terrifying
terrified
territorial *adjective*
territorially *adverb*
territory *noun*
territories
terror *noun*
terrors
terrorism *noun*
terrorist *adjective* & *noun*
terrorists
terrorize *verb*
terrorizes
terrorizing
terrorized

tessellation *noun*
tessellations

test *noun*
tests

test *verb*
tests
testing
tested

testament *noun*
testaments

testicle *noun*
testicles

testify *verb*
testifies
testifying
testified

testimonial *noun*
testimonials

testimony *noun*
testimonies

testy *adjective*
testier
testiest

tether *verb*
tethers
tethering
tethered

tether *noun*
tethers

tetrahedron *noun*
tetrahedrons

text *noun*
texts

textbook *noun*
textbooks

textile *noun*
textiles

texture *noun*
textures

than *conjunction* & *preposition*

thank *verb*
thanks
thanking
thanked

thankful *adjective*
thankfully *adverb*

thankless *adjective*
thanklessly *adverb*

thanks *plural noun*

that *adverb, pronoun,* & *conjunction*

thatch *noun*

thatch *verb*
thatches
thatching
thatched

thatcher *noun*
thatchers

thaw *verb*
thaws
thawing
thawed

theatre *noun*
theatres

theatrical *adjective*
theatrically *adverb*

thee

theft *noun*
thefts

their★ *adjective*

theirs☆ *posessive pronoun*

them *pronoun*

theme *noun*
themes

theme park *noun*
theme parks

themselves *pronoun*

then *adverb*

theologian *noun*
theologians

theological *adjective*
theologically *adverb*

theology *noun*

theorem *noun*
theorems

theoretical *adjective*
theoretically *adverb*

theory *noun*
theories

therapist *noun*
therapists

therapy *noun*
therapies

there✪ *adverb*

thereabouts *adverb*

therefore *adverb*

thermal *adjective*
thermally *adverb*

thermometer *noun*
thermometers

Thermos *noun*
Thermoses

thermostat *noun*
thermostats

thermostatic *adjective*
thermostatically *adverb*

thesaurus *noun*
thesauri
thesauruses

these

they *pronoun*

they'd *verb*

they'll *verb*

they're✣ *verb*

they've *verb*

thick *adjective*
thicker
thickest
thickly *adverb*

thicken *verb*
thickens
thickening
thickened

★ You use **their** in e.g. *this is their house.* **! there, they're.**
☆ You use **theirs** in e.g. *the house is theirs*. Note that there is no apostrophe in this word.
✪ You use **there** in e.g. *Look over there.* **! their, they're.**
✣ **They're** is short for *they are.* **! their, there.**

thicket *noun*
thickets
thickness *noun*
thicknesses
thief *noun*
thieves
theives *plural noun*
thigh *noun*
thighs
thimble *noun*
thimbles
thin *adjective*
thinner
thinnest
thinly *adverb*
thin *verb*
thins
thinning
thinned
thine *adjective* & *posessive pronoun*
thing *noun*
things
think *verb*
thinks
thinking
thought
thinker *noun*
thinkers
thinness *noun*
third *noun*
thirdly *adverb*
Third World *noun*
thirst *noun*
thirsty *adjective*
thirstier
thirstiest
thirstily *adverb*
thirteen *noun* & *adjective*
thirteenth *adjective* & *noun*
thirtieth *adjective* & *noun*
thirty *noun*
thirties

this *adjective* & *pronoun*
thistle *noun*
thistles
thorn *noun*
thorns
thorny *adjective*
thornier
thorniest
thorough *adjective*
thoroughly *adverb*
thoroughness *noun*
those
thou *pronoun*
though *adverb*
thought *noun*
thoughts
thought *verb* SEE **think**
thoughtful *adjective*
thoughtfully *adverb*
thoughtfulness *noun*
thoughtless *adjective*
thoughtlessly *adverb*
thoughtlessness *noun*
thousand *noun*
thousands
thousandth *adjective* & *noun*
thrash★ *verb*
thrashes
thrashing
thrashed
thread *noun*
threads
thread *verb*
threads
threading
threaded
threadbare *adjective*
threat *noun*
threats
threaten *verb*
threatens
threatening
threatened

three *noun*
threes
three dimensional *adjective*
three dimensionally *adverb*
thresh☆ *verb*
threshes
threshing
threshed
threshold *noun*
thresholds
threw *verb* SEE **throw**
thrift *noun*
thrifty *adjective*
thriftier
thriftiest
thrill *noun*
thrills
thrill *verb*
thrills
thrilling
thrilled
thriller *noun*
thrillers
thrive *verb*
thrives
thriving
thrived *or* throve
thriven *or* thrived
throat *noun*
throats
throb *verb*
throbs
throbbing
throbbed
throb *noun*
throbs
throne *noun*
thrones
throng *noun*
throngs

★ To **thrash** someone is to beat them. **! thresh.**
☆ To **thresh** corn is to beat it to separate the grain. **! thrash.**

throttle *verb*
throttles
throttling
throttled

throttle *noun*
throttles

through *adjective & adverb & preposition*

throughout *adverb & preposition*

throve *verb* SEE **thrive**

throw *verb*
throws
throwing
threw
thrown

throw *noun*
throws

thrush *noun*
thrushes

thrust *verb*
thrusts
thrusting
thrust

thud *noun*
thuds

thud *verb*
thuds
thudding
thudded

thug *noun*
thugs

thumb *noun*
thumbs

thump *verb*
thumps
thumping
thumped

thump *noun*
thumps

thunder *noun*

thunder *verb*
thunders
thundering
thundered

thunderous *adjective*
thunderously *adverb*

thunderstorm *noun*
thunderstorms

Thursday *noun*
Thursdays

thus *adverb*

thy *adjective*

tick *verb*
ticks
ticking
ticked

tick *noun*
ticks

ticket *noun*
tickets

tickle *verb*
tickles
tickling
tickled

ticklish *adjective*

tidal *adjective*

tiddler *noun*
tiddlers

tiddlywink *noun*
tiddlywinks

tide *noun*
tides

tide *verb*
tides
tiding
tided

tidiness *noun*

tidy *adjective*
tidier
tidiest
tidily *adverb*

tie *verb*
ties
tying
tied

tie *noun*
ties

tie break *noun*
tie breaks

tiger *noun*
tigers

tight *adjective*
tighter
tightest
tightly *adverb*

tighten *verb*
tightens
tightening
tightened

tightness *noun*

tightrope *noun*
tightropes

tights *plural noun*

tigress *noun*
tigresses

tile *noun*
tiles

tiled *adjective*

till *preposition & conjunction*

till *noun*
tills

till *verb*
tills
tilling
tilled

tiller *noun*
tillers

tilt *verb*
tilts
tilting
tilted

tilt *noun*
tilts

timber *noun*
timbers

time *noun*
times

time *verb*
times
timing
timed

timer *noun*
timers

times *plural noun*

timetable *noun*
timetables

timid *adjective*
timidly *adverb*

timidity *noun*

timing *noun*
timpani *plural noun*
tin *noun*
tins
tin *verb*
tins
tinning
tinned
tingle *verb*
tingles
tingling
tingled
tingle *noun*
tingles
tinker *verb*
tinkers
tinkering
tinkered
tinker *noun*
tinkers
tinkle *verb*
tinkles
tinkling
tinkled
tinkle *noun*
tinkles
tinny *adjective*
tinnier
tinniest
tinsel *noun*
tint *noun*
tints
tint *verb*
tints
tinting
tinted
tiny *adjective*
tinier
tiniest
tip *verb*
tips
tipping
tipped
tip *noun*
tips
tiptoe *verb*
tiptoes
tiptoeing
tiptoed
tiptoe *noun*
tire★ *verb*
tires
tiring
tired
tired *adjective*
tireless *adjective*
tirelessly *adverb*
tiresome *adjective*
tiresomely *adverb*
tissue *noun*
tissues
tit *noun*
tits
titbit *noun*
titbits
title *noun*
titles
titter *verb*
titters
tittering
tittered
to☆ *preposition*
toad *noun*
toads
toadstool *noun*
toadstools
toast *verb*
toasts
toasting
toasted
toast *noun*
toasts
toaster *noun*
toasters
tobacco *noun*
tobaccos
tobacconist *noun*
tobacconists
toboggan *noun*
toboggans
tobogganing *noun*
today *adverb*
toddler *noun*
toddlers
toe✪ *noun*
toes
toffee *noun*
toffees
toga *noun*
togas
together *adverb*
toggle *noun*
toil *verb*
toils
toiling
toiled
toilet *noun*
toilets
token *noun*
tokens
told *verb* SEE **tell**
tolerable *adjective*
tolerably *adverb*
tolerance *noun*
tolerant *adjective*
tolerantly *adverb*
tolerate *verb*
tolerates
tolerating
tolerated
toll *noun*
tolls
toll *verb*
tolls
tolling
tolled
tomahawk *noun*
tomahawks

★ To **tire** is to become tired. **! tyre.**
☆ You use **to** in e.g. *go to bed* or *I want to stay.* **! too, two.**
✪ A **toe** is a part of a foot. **! tow.**

a b c d e f g h i j k l m n o p q r s t u v w x y z

tomato *noun*
tomatoes
tomb *noun*
tombs
tombola *noun*
tombolas
tomboy *noun*
tomboys
tombstone *noun*
tombstones
tomcat *noun*
tomcats
tomorrow *noun & adverb*
tom-tom *noun*
tom-toms
ton★ *noun*
tons
tonal *adjective*
tonally *adverb*
tone *noun*
tones
tone *verb*
tones
toning
toned
tone-deaf *adjective*
tongs *plural noun*
tongue *noun*
tongues
tonic *noun*
tonics
tonight *noun & adverb*
tonne☆ *noun*
tonnes
tonsillitis *noun*
tonsils *plural noun*
too✪ *adverb*
took *verb* SEE **take**
tool *noun*
tools
tooth *noun*
teeth
toothache *noun*
toothbrush *noun*
toothbrushes
toothed *adjective*
toothpaste *noun*
toothpastes
top *noun*
tops
top *verb*
tops
topping
topped
topic *noun*
topics
topical *adjective*
topically *adverb*
topicality *noun*
topless *adjective*
topmost *adjective*
topping *noun*
toppings
topple *verb*
topples
toppling
toppled
topsy-turvy *adjective*
torch *noun*
torches
tore *verb* SEE **tear**
toreador *noun*
toreadors
torment *verb*
torments
tormenting
tormented
torment *noun*
torments
tormentor *noun*
tormentors
torn *verb* SEE **tear**
tornado *noun*
tornadoes
torpedo *noun*
torpedoes
torpedo *verb*
torpedoes
torpedoing
torpedoed
torrent *noun*
torrents
torrential *adjective*
torrentially *adverb*
torso *noun*
torsos
tortoise *noun*
tortoises
torture *verb*
tortures
torturing
tortured
torture *noun*
tortures
torturer *noun*
torturers
Tory *noun*
Tories
toss *verb*
tosses
tossing
tossed
toss *noun*
tosses
total *noun*
totals
total *adjective*
totally *adverb*
total *verb*
totals
totalling
totalled
totalitarian *adjective*
totem pole *noun*
totem poles
totter *verb*
totters
tottering
tottered

★ A **ton** is a non-metric unit of weight. **! tonne.**
☆ A **tonne** is a metric unit of weight. **! ton.**
✪ You use **too** in e.g. *it's too late* or *I want to come too.* **! to, two.**

touch *verb*
touches
touching
touched
touch *noun*
touches
touchable *adjective*
touchy *adjective*
touchier
touchiest
tough *adjective*
tougher
toughest
toughly *adverb*
toughen *verb*
toughens
toughening
toughened
toughness *noun*
tour *noun*
tours
tourism *noun*
tourist *noun*
tourists
tournament *noun*
tournaments
tow* *verb*
tows
towing
towed
tow *noun*
toward *or* **towards**
preposition
towel *noun*
towels
towelling *noun*
tower *noun*
towers
tower *verb*
towers
towering
towered
town *noun*
towns
towpath *noun*
towpaths

toxic *adjective*
toy *noun*
toys
toy *verb*
toys
toying
toyed
toyshop *noun*
toyshops
trace *noun*
traces
trace *verb*
traces
tracing
traced
traceable *adjective*
track *noun*
tracks
track *verb*
tracks
tracking
tracked
tracker *noun*
trackers
tracksuit *noun*
tracksuits
tract *noun*
tracts
traction *noun*
tractor *noun*
tractors
trade *noun*
trades
trade *verb*
trades
trading
traded
trademark *noun*
trademarks
trader *noun*
traders
tradesman *noun*
tradesmen
trade union *noun*
trade unions

tradition *noun*
traditions
traditional *adjective*
traditionally *adverb*
traffic *noun*
traffic *verb*
traffics
trafficking
trafficked
tragedy *noun*
tragedies
tragic *adjective*
tragically *adverb*
trail *noun*
trails
trail *verb*
trails
trailing
trailed
trailer *noun*
trailers
train *noun*
trains
train *verb*
trains
training
trained
trainer *noun*
trainers
trait *noun*
traits
traitor *noun*
traitors
tram *noun*
trams
tramp *noun*
tramps
tramp *verb*
tramps
tramping
tramped
trample *verb*
tramples
trampling
trampled

a b c d e f g h i j k l m n o p q r s **t** u v w x y z

* To **tow** something is to pull it along. **! toe.**

trampoline *noun*
trampolines

trance *noun*
trances

tranquil *adjective*
tranquilly *adverb*

tranquillity* *noun*

tranquillizer *noun*
tranquillizers

transact *verb*
transacts
transacting
transacted

transaction *noun*
transactions

transatlantic *adjective*

transcription *noun*
transcriptions

transfer *verb*
transfers
transferring
transferred

transfer *noun*
transfers

transferable *adjective*

transference *noun*

transform *verb*
transforms
transforming
transformed

transformation *noun*
transformations

transformer *noun*
transformers

transfusion *noun*
transfusions

transistor *noun*
transistors

transition *noun*
transitions

transitional *adjective*

transitive *adjective*

translate *verb*
translates
translating
translated

translation *noun*
translations

translator *noun*
translators

translucent *adjective*

transmission *noun*
transmissions

transmit *verb*
transmits
transmitting
transmitted

transmitter *noun*
transmitters

transparency *noun*
transparencies

transparent *adjective*
transparently *adverb*

transpire *verb*
transpires
transpiring
transpired

transplant *verb*
transplants
transplanting
transplanted

transplant *noun*
transplants

transplantation *noun*
transplantations

transport *verb*
transports
transporting
transported

transportation *noun*

transport *noun*

transporter *noun*
transporters

trap *verb*
traps
trapping
trapped

trap *noun*
traps

trapdoor *noun*
trapdoors

trapeze *noun*
trapezes

trapezium *noun*
trapeziums

trapezoid *noun*
trapezoids

trapper *noun*
trappers

trash *noun*

trashy *adjective*
trashier
trashiest

trauma *noun*
traumas

traumatic *adjective*

travel *verb*
travels
travelling
travelled

travel *noun*

traveller *noun*
travellers

traveller's cheque *noun*
traveller´s cheques

trawler *noun*
trawlers

tray *noun*
trays

treacherous *adjective*
treacherously *adverb*

treachery *noun*

treacle *noun*

tread *verb*
treads
treading
trod
trodden

tread *noun*
treads

treason *noun*

* Note that there are two 'l's in this word.

treasure *noun*
treasures

treasure *verb*
treasures
treasuring
treasured

treasurer *noun*
treasurers

treasury *noun*
treasuries

treat *verb*
treats
treating
treated

treat *noun*
treats

treatment *noun*
treatments

treaty *noun*
treaties

treble *adjective & noun*
trebles

treble *verb*
trebles
trebling
trebled

tree *noun*
trees

trek *verb*
treks
trekking
trekked

trek *noun*
treks

trellis *noun*
trellises

tremble *verb*
trembles
trembling
trembled

tremble *noun*
trembles

tremendous *adjective*
tremendously *adverb*

tremor *noun*
tremors

trench *noun*
trenches

trend *noun*
trends

trendiness *noun*

trendy *adjective*
trendier
trendiest
trendily *adverb*

trespass *verb*
trespasses
trespassing
trespassed

trespasser *noun*
trespassers

trestle *noun*
trestles

trial *noun*
trials

triangle *noun*
triangles

triangular *adjective*

tribal *adjective*
tribally *adverb*

tribe *noun*
tribes

tribesman *noun*
tribesmen

tribunal *noun*
tribunals

tributary *noun*
tributaries

tribute *noun*
tributes

trick *noun*
tricks

trick *verb*
tricks
tricking
tricked

trickery *noun*

trickster *noun*
tricksters

trickle *verb*
trickles
trickling
trickled

trickle *noun*
trickles

tricky *adjective*
trickier
trickiest
trickily *adverb*

tricycle *noun*
tricycles

tried *verb* SEE **try**

trifle *noun*
trifles

trifle *verb*
trifles
trifling
trifled

trifling *adjective*

trigger *noun*
triggers

trigger *verb*
triggers
triggering
triggered

trillion *noun*
trillions

trilogy *noun*
trilogies

trim *adjective*
trimmer
trimmest

trim *verb*
trims
trimming
trimmed

trim *noun*
trims

trio *noun*
trios

trip *verb*
trips
tripping
tripped

trip *noun*
trips

tripe *noun*

triple *adjective*
triply *adverb*

triple *noun*
triples

a b c d e f g h i j k l m n o p q r s t u v w x y z

triple *verb*
triples
tripling
tripled

triplet *noun*
triplets

tripod *noun*
tripods

triumph *noun*
triumphs

triumphant *adjective*
triumphantly *adverb*

trivial *adjective*
trivially *adverb*

triviality *noun*
trivialities

trod *verb* SEE **tread**

trodden *verb* SEE **tread**

troll *noun*
trolls

trolley *noun*
trolleys

trombone *noun*
trombones

troop *noun*
troops

troop *verb*
troops
trooping
trooped

troops *plural noun*

trophy *noun*
trophies

tropic *noun*
tropics

tropical *adjective*

trot *verb*
trots
trotting
trotted

trot *noun*
trots

trouble *noun*
troubles

trouble *verb*
troubles
troubling
troubled

troublesome *noun*

trough *noun*
troughs

trousers *plural noun*

trout *noun*
trout

trowel *noun*
trowels

truancy *noun*
truancies

truant *noun*
truants

truce *noun*
truces

truck *noun*
trucks

trudge *verb*
trudges
trudging
trudged

true *adjective*
truer
truest
truly *adverb*

trump *noun*
trumps

trump *verb*
trumps
trumping
trumped

trumpet *noun*
trumpets

trumpet *verb*
trumpets
trumpeting
trumpeted

trumpeter *noun*
trumpeters

truncheon *noun*
truncheons

trundle *verb*
trundles
trundling
trundled

trunk *noun*
trunks

trunks *plural noun*

trust *verb*
trusts
trusting
trusted

trust *noun*

trustful *adjective*
trustfully *adverb*

trustworthy *adjective*

trusty *adjective*
trustier
trustiest

truth *noun*
truths

truthful *adjective*
truthfully *adverb*

truthfulness *noun*

try *verb*
tries
trying
tried

try *noun*
tries

T-shirt *noun*
T-shirts

tsunami *verb*
tsunamis

tub *noun*
tubs

tuba *noun*
tubas

tube *noun*
tubes

tuber *noun*
tubers

tubing *noun*

tubular *adjective*

tuck *verb*
tucks
tucking
tucked

tuck *noun*
tucks

Tuesday *noun*
Tuesdays

tuft *noun*
tufts

tug *noun*
tugs

tug *verb*
tugs
tugging
tugged

tulip *noun*
tulips

tumble *verb*
tumbles
tumbling
tumbled

tumble *noun*
tumbles

tumble drier *noun*
tumble driers

tumbler *noun*
tumblers

tummy *noun*
tummies

tumour *noun*
tumours

tumult *noun*

tumultuous *adjective*
tumultuously *adverb*

tuna *noun*
tuna
tunas

tundra *noun*

tune *noun*
tunes

tune *verb*
tunes
tuning
tuned

tuneful *adjective*
tunefully *adverb*

tuneless *adjective*
tunelessly *adverb*

tunic *noun*
tunics

tunnel *noun*
tunnels

tunnel *verb*
tunnels
tunnelling
tunnelled

turban *noun*
turbans

turbine *noun*
turbines

turbulence *noun*

turbulent *adjective*
turbulently *adverb*

turf *noun*
turfs *or* turves

turkey *noun*
turkeys

Turkish bath *noun*
Turkish baths

turmoil *noun*

turn *verb*
turns
turning
turned

turn *noun*
turns

turncoat *noun*
turncoats

turnip *noun*
turnips

turnover *noun*
turnovers

turnstile *noun*
turnstiles

turntable *noun*
turntables

turpentine *noun*

turquoise *noun*

turret *noun*
turrets

turtle *noun*
turtles

tusk *noun*
tusks

tussle *verb*
tussles
tussling
tussled

tussle *noun*
tussles

tutor *noun*
tutors

tweak *verb*
tweaks
tweaking
tweaked

tweak *noun*
tweaks

tweed *noun*

tweezers *plural noun*

twelve *noun*
twelves

twelfth *adjective & noun*

twentieth *adjective & noun*

twenty *noun*
twenties

twice *adverb*

twiddle *verb*
twiddles
twiddling
twiddled

twiddle *noun*
twiddles

twig *noun*
twigs

twig *verb*
twigs
twigging
twigged

twilight *noun*

twin *noun*
twins

twin *verb*
twins
twinning
twinned

twine *noun*

twinkle *verb*
twinkles
twinkling
twinkled

twinkle *noun*
twinkles

twirl *verb*
twirls
twirling
twirled

twirl *noun*
twirls

twist *verb*
twists
twisting
twisted

twist *noun*
twists

twister *noun*
twisters

twitch *verb*
twitches
twitching
twitched

twitch *noun*
twitches

twitter *verb*
twitters
twittering
twittered

two★ *adjective* & *noun*
twos

tying SEE **tie**

type *noun*
types

type *verb*
types
typing
typed

typewriter *noun*
typewriters

typewritten *adjective*

typhoon *noun*
typhoons

typical *adjective*
typically *adverb*

typist *noun*
typists

tyranny *noun*
tyrannies

tyrannical *adjective*
tyrannically *adverb*

tyrant *noun*
tyrants

tyre☆ *noun*
tyres

★ You use **two** in e.g. *two people* or *there are two of them.* **! to**, **too**.
☆ A **tyre** is a rubber cover for a wheel. **! tire**.

Uu

udder *noun*
udders
ugliness *noun*
ugly *adjective*
uglier
ugliest
ulcer *noun*
ulcers
ultimate *adjective*
ultimately *adverb*
ultrasound *noun*
ultraviolet *adjective*
umbilical cord *noun*
umbilical cords
umbrella *noun*
umbrellas
umpire *noun*
umpires

> **un-** *prefix*
> *un-* makes words meaning 'not', e.g. **unable**, **unhappiness**. Some of these words have special meanings, e.g. **unprofessional**. See the note at **non-**.

unable *adjective*
unacceptable *adjective*
unacceptably *adverb*
unaided *adjective*
unanimity *noun*
unanimous *adjective*
unanimously *adverb*
unavoidable *adjective*
unavoidably *adverb*
unaware *adjective*
unawares *adverb*
unbalanced *adjective*
unbearable *adjective*
unbearably *adverb*
unbelievable *adjective*
unbelievably *adverb*
unblock *verb*
unblocks
unblocking
unblocked
unborn *adjective*
uncalled for *adjective*
uncanny *adjective*
uncannier
uncanniest
uncertain *adjective*
uncertainly *adverb*
uncertainty *noun*
uncle *noun*
uncles
uncomfortable *adjective*
uncomfortably *adverb*
uncommon *adjective*
uncommonly *adverb*
unconscious *adjective*
unconsciously *adverb*
unconsciousness *noun*
uncontrollable *adjective*
uncontrollably *adverb*
uncountable *adjective*
uncouth *adjective*
uncover *verb*
uncovers
uncovering
uncovered
undecided *adjective*
undeniable *adjective*
undeniably *adverb*
under *adverb*
underarm *adjective*
underclothes *plural noun*
underdeveloped *adjective*
underdone *adjective*
underestimate *verb*
underestimates
underestimating
underestimated
underfoot *adjective*
undergo *verb*
undergoes
undergoing
underwent
undergone
undergraduate *noun*
undergraduates
underground *adjective & noun*
undergrounds
undergrowth *noun*
underhand *adjective*
underlie *verb*
underlies
underlying
underlay
underlain
underline *verb*
underlines
underlining
underlined
undermine *verb*
undermines
undermining
undermined
underneath *preposition*
underpants *plural noun*
underpass *noun*
underpasses
underprivileged *adjective*
understand *verb*
understands
understanding
understood

a b c d e f g h i j k l m n o p q r s t u v w x y z

understandable *adjective*
understandably *adverb*
understanding *adjective*
undertake *verb*
undertakes
undertaking
undertook
undertaken
undertaker *noun*
undertakers
undertaking *noun*
undertakings
underwater *adjective & adverb*
underwear *noun*
underworld *noun*
undesirable *adjective*
undesirably *adverb*
undeveloped *adjective*
undo *verb*
undoes
undoing
undid
undone
undoubted *adjective*
undoubtedly *adverb*
undress *verb*
undresses
undressing
undressed
unearth *verb*
unearths
unearthing
unearthed
unearthly *adjective*
unease *noun*
uneasiness *noun*
uneasy *adjective*
uneasier
uneasiest
uneasily *adverb*
uneatable *adjective*
unemployed *adjective*
unemployment *noun*
uneven *adjective*
unevenly *adverb*
unevenness *noun*
unexpected *adjective*
unexpectedly *adverb*
unfair *adjective*
unfairly *adverb*
unfairness *noun*
unfaithful *adjective*
unfaithfully *adverb*
unfamiliar *adjective*
unfamiliarity *noun*
unfasten *verb*
unfastens
unfastening
unfastened
unfavourable *adjective*
unfavourably *adverb*
unfinished *adjective*
unfit *adjective*
unfold *verb*
unfolds
unfolding
unfolded
unforgettable *adjective*
unforgettably *adverb*
unforgivable *adjective*
unforgivably *adverb*
unfortunate *adjective*
unfortunately *adverb*
unfounded *adjective*
unfreeze *verb*
unfreezes
unfreezing
unfroze
unfrozen
unfriendliness *noun*
unfriendly *adjective*
ungrateful *adjective*
ungratefully *adverb*
unhappiness *noun*
unhappy *adjective*
unhappier
unhappiest
unhappily *adverb*
unhealthy *adjective*
unhealthier
unhealthiest
unhealthily *adverb*
unheard of *adjective*
unicorn *noun*
unicorns
unification *noun*
uniform *noun*
uniforms
uniform *adjective*
uniformly *adverb*
uniformed *adjective*
uniformity *noun*
unify *verb*
unifies
unifying
unified
unilateral *adjective*
unilaterally *adverb*
unimportance *noun*
unimportant *adjective*
uninhabited *adjective*
unintentional *adjective*
unintentionally *adverb*
uninterested *adjective*
uninteresting *adjective*
union *noun*
unions
unique *adjective*
uniquely *adverb*
uniqueness *noun*
unisex *adjective*
unison *noun*
unit *noun*
units
unite *verb*
unites
uniting
united
unity *noun*
unities
universal *adjective*
universally *adverb*
universe *noun*
universes
university *noun*
universities
unjust *adjective*
unjustly *adverb*

unkind *adjective*
unkinder
unkindest
unkindly *adverb*

unkindness *noun*

unknown *adjective*

unleaded *adjective*

unleash *verb*
unleashes
unleasing
unleashed

unless *conjunction*

unlike *preposition* & *adjective*

unlikely *adjective*
unlikelier
unlikeliest

unload *verb*
unloads
unloading
unloaded

unlock *verb*
unlocks
unlocking
unlocked

unlucky *adjective*
unluckier
unluckiest
unluckily *adverb*

unmistakable *adjective*
unmistakably *adverb*

unnatural *adjective*
unnaturally *adverb*

unnecessary *adjective*
unnecessarily *adverb*

unoccupied *adjective*

unofficial *adjective*

unpack *verb*
unpacks
unpacking
unpacked

unpick *verb*

unpleasant *adjective*
unpleasantly *adverb*

unpleasantness *noun*

unplug *verb*
unplugs
unplugging
unplugged

unpopular *adjective*

unpopularity *noun*

unprecedented *verb*

unravel *verb*
unravels
unravelling
unravelled

unreal *adjective*

unreasonable *adjective*
unreasonably *adverb*

unrest *noun*

unroll *verb*
unrolls
unrolling
unrolled

unruliness *noun*

unruly *adjective*
unrulier
unruliest

unscrew *verb*
unscrews
unscrewing
unscrewed

unseemly *adjective*

unseen *adjective*

unselfish *adjective*
unselfishly *adverb*

unselfishness *noun*

unsightly *adjective*

unskilled *adjective*

unsound *adjective*
unsoundly *adverb*

unsteadiness *noun*

unsteady *adjective*
unsteadier
unsteadiest
unsteadily *adverb*

unsuccessful *adjective*
unsuccessfully *adverb*

unsuitable *adjective*
unsuitably *adverb*

unsuspecting *adjective*

unthinkable *adjective*
unthinkably *adverb*

untidiness *noun*

untidy *adjective*
untidier
untidiest
untidily *adverb*

untie *verb*
unties
untying
untied

until *preposition* & *conjunction*

untimely *adjective*

unto *preposition*

untold *adjective*

untoward *adjective*

untrained *adjective*

untrue *adjective*

untruthful *adjective*
untruthfully *adverb*

unused *adjective*

unusual *adjective*
unusually *adverb*

unveil *verb*
unveils
unveiling
unveiled

unwanted *adjective*

unwell *adjective*

unwilling *adjective*
unwillingly *adverb*

unwillingness *noun*

unwind *verb*
unwinds
unwinding
unwound

unwittingly *adverb*

unwrap *verb*
unwraps
unwrapping
unwrapped

unzip *verb*
unzips
unzipping
unzipped

upbeat *adjective*

a b c d e f g h i j k l m n o p q r s t u v w x y z

update *verb*
updates
updating
updated
upgrade *verb*
upgrades
upgrading
upgraded
upheaval *noun*
upheavals
uphill *adverb & adjective*
uphold *verb*
upholds
upholding
upheld
upholstery *noun*
upkeep *noun*
uplands *plural noun*
upon *preposition*
upper *adjective*
upright *adjective*
upright *noun*
uprights
uprising *noun*
uprisings
uproar *noun*
uproars
upset *verb*
upsets
upsetting
upset
upset *noun*
upsets
upshot *noun*
upside down *adverb & adjective*
upstairs *adverb & adjective*
upstart *noun*
upstarts
upstream *adjective*
uptake *noun*
uptight *adjective*
upward *adjective & adverb*
upwards *adverb*
uranium *noun*
urban *adjective*
urbanization *noun*
urbanize *verb*
urbanizes
urbanizing
urbanized
urchin *noun*
urchins
Urdu *noun*
urge *verb*
urges
urging
urged
urge *noun*
urges
urgency *noun*
urgent *adjective*
urgently *adverb*
urinary *adjective*
urinate *verb*
urinates
urinating
urinated
urination *noun*
urine *noun*
urn *noun*
urns

> **-us**
> Most nouns ending in *-us* come from Latin words, e.g. **bonus** and **terminus**. They normally have plurals ending in *-uses*, e.g. **bonuses** and **terminuses**. Some more technical words have plurals ending in *-i*, e.g. **nucleus – nuclei**.

usable *adjective*
usage *noun*
usages
use *verb*
uses
using
used
use *noun*
uses
useful *adjective*
usefully *adverb*
usefulness *noun*
useless *adjective*
uselessly *adverb*
uselessness *noun*
user *noun*
users
user-friendly *adjective*
user-friendlier
user-friendliest
usher *noun*
ushers
usher *verb*
ushers
ushering
ushered
usherette *noun*
usherettes
usual *adjective*
usually *adverb*
usurp *verb*
usurps
usurping
usurped
usurper *noun*
usurpers
utensil *noun*
utensils
uterus *noun*
uteri
utilization *noun*
utilize *verb*
utilizes
utilizing
utilized
utmost *adjective*
utter *adjective*
utter *verb*
utters
uttering
uttered
utterance *noun*
utterances
utterly *adverb*
U-turn *noun*
U-turns

Vv

vacancy *noun*
vacancies
vacant *adjective*
vacantly *adverb*
vacate *verb*
vacates
vacating
vacated
vacation *noun*
vacations
vaccinate *verb*
vaccinates
vaccinating
vaccinated
vaccination *noun*
vaccinations
vaccine *noun*
vaccines
vacuum *noun*
vacuums
vague *adjective*
vaguer
vaguest
vaguely *adverb*
vagueness *noun*
vain★ *adjective*
vainer
vainest
vainly
vale☆ *noun*
vales
valentine *noun*
valentines
valiant *adjective*
valiantly *adverb*
valid *adjective*
validly *adverb*
validity *noun*
valley *noun*
valleys
valour *noun*
valuable *adjective*
valuably *adverb*
valuables *plural noun*
valuation *noun*
valuations
value *noun*
values
value *verb*
values
valuing
valued
valueless *adjective*
valuer *noun*
valuers
valve *noun*
valves
vampire *noun*
vampires
van *noun*
vans
vandal *noun*
vandals
vandalism *noun*
vane✪ *noun*
vanes
vanilla *noun*
vanish *verb*
vanishes
vanishing
vanished
vanity *noun*
vanquish *verb*
vanquishes
vanquishing
vanquished
vaporize *verb*
vaporizes
vaporizing
vaporized
vapour *noun*
vapours
variable *adjective*
variably *adverb*
variable *noun*
variables
variant *noun*
variants
variation *noun*
variations
varied *adjective*
variety *noun*
varieties
various *adjective*
variously *adverb*
varnish *noun*
varnishes
varnish *verb*
varnishes
varnishing
varnished
vary *verb*
varies
varying
varied
vase *noun*
vases
vast *adjective*
vastly *adverb*
vastness *noun*
vat *noun*
vats

★ **Vain** means 'conceited' or 'proud'. **! vane, vein.**
☆ A **vale** is a valley. **! veil.**
✪ A **vane** is a pointer that shows which way the wind is blowing. **! vain, vein.**

vault *verb*
vaults
vaulting
vaulted
vault *noun*
vaults
veal *noun*
vector *noun*
vectors
Veda *noun*
veer *verb*
veers
veering
veered
vegan *noun*
vegans
vegetable *noun*
vegetables
vegetarian *noun*
vegetarians
vegetate *verb*
vegetates
vegetating
vegetated
vegetation *noun*
vehicle *noun*
vehicles
veil★ *noun*
veils
veil *verb*
veils
veiling
veiled
vein☆ *noun*
veins
velocity *noun*
velocities
velvet *noun*
velvety *adjective*
vendetta *noun*
vendettas
vendor *noun*
vendors
venerable *adjective*
venetian blind *noun*
venetian blinds
vengeance *noun*
venison *noun*
Venn diagram *noun*
Venn diagrams
venom *noun*
venomous *adjective*
venomously *adverb*
venue *noun*
venues
vent *noun*
vents
ventilate *verb*
ventilates
ventilating
ventilated
ventilation *noun*
ventilator *noun*
ventilators
ventriloquism *noun*
ventriloquist *noun*
ventriloquists
venture *verb*
ventures
venturing
ventured
venture *noun*
ventures
veranda *noun*
verandas
verb *noun*
verbs
verbal *adjective*
verbally *adverb*
verdict *noun*
verdicts
verge *verb*
verges
verging
verged
verge *noun*
verges
verification
verify *verb*
verifies
verifying
verified
vermin *noun*
verruca *noun*
verrucas
versatile *adjective*
versatility *noun*
verse *noun*
verses
version *noun*
versions
versus *preposition*
vertebra *noun*
vertebrae
vertebrate *noun*
vertebrates
vertex *noun*
vertices
vertical *adjective*
vertically *adverb*
very *adverb & adjective*
Vesak *noun*
vessel *noun*
vessels
vest *noun*
vests
vested *adjective*
vested
vestment *noun*
vestments
vestry *noun*
vestries
vet *noun*
vets
veteran *noun*
veterans
veterinary *adjective*
veto *verb*
vetoes
vetoing
vetoed

★ A **veil** is a covering for the face. **! vale.**
☆ A **vein** carries blood to the heart. **! vain, vane.**

veto *noun*
vetoes
vex *verb*
vexes
vexing
vexed
vexation *noun*
via *preposition*
viable *adjective*
viaduct *noun*
viaducts
vibrant *adjective*
vibrate *verb*
vibrates
vibrating
vibrated
vibration *noun*
vibrations
vicar *noun*
vicars
vicarage *noun*
vicarages
vice *noun*
vices
vice-president *noun*
vice-presidents
vice versa *adverb*
vicinity *noun*
vicinities
vicious *adjective*
viciously *adverb*
viciousness *noun*
victim *noun*
victims
victimize *verb*
victimizes
victimizing
victimized
victor *noun*
victors
Victorian *adjective* & *noun*
Victorians
victorious *adjective*
victoriously *adverb*
victory *noun*
victories

video *noun*
videos
video *verb*
videoes
videoing
videoed
videotape *noun*
videotapes
view *noun*
views
view *verb*
views
viewing
viewed
viewer *noun*
viewers
vigilance *noun*
vigilant *adjective*
vigilantly *adverb*
vigorous *adjective*
vigorously *adverb*
vigour *noun*
Viking *noun*
Vikings
vile *adjective*
viler
vilest
vilely *adverb*
villa *noun*
villas
village *noun*
villages
villager *noun*
villagers
villain *noun*
villains
villainous *adjective*
villainy
vine *noun*
vines
vinegar *noun*
vineyard *noun*
vineyards
vintage *noun*
vintages
vinyl *noun*

viola *noun*
violas
violate *verb*
violates
violating
violated
violation *noun*
violations
violator *noun*
violators
violence *noun*
violent *adjective*
violently *adverb*
violet *noun*
violets
violin *noun*
violins
violinist *noun*
violinists
VIP *noun*
VIPs
viper *noun*
vipers
viral *adjective*
virtual *adjective*
virtually *adverb*
virtue *noun*
virtues
virtuous *adjective*
virtuously *adverb*
virus *noun*
viruses
visa *noun*
visas
visibility *noun*
visible *adjective*
visibly *adverb*
vision *noun*
visions
visit *verb*
visits
visiting
visited
visit *noun*
visits
visitor *noun*
visitors

visor *noun*
visors
visual *adjective*
visually *adverb*
visualize *verb*
visualizes
visualizing
visualized
vital *adjective*
vitally *adverb*
vitality *noun*
vitamin *noun*
vitamins
vivid *adjective*
vividly *adverb*
vividness *noun*
vivisection *noun*
vivisections
vixen *noun*
vixens
vocabulary *noun*
vocabularies
vocal *adjective*
vocally *adverb*
vocalist *noun*
vocalists
vocals *plural noun*
vocation *noun*
vocations
vocational *adjective*
vocationally *adverb*
vodka *noun*
vodkas
voice *noun*
voices
voice *verb*
voices
voicing
voiced
voicemail *noun*
voicemails
void *noun*
voids
volcanic *adjective*
volcano *noun*
volcanoes
vole *noun*
voles
volley *noun*
volleys
volleyball *noun*
volt *noun*
volts
voltage *noun*
voltages
volume *noun*
volumes
voluntary *adjective*
voluntarily *adverb*
volunteer *verb*
volunteers
volunteering
volunteered
volunteer *noun*
volunteers
vomit *verb*
vomits
vomiting
vomited
vote *verb*
votes
voting
voted
vote *noun*
votes
voter *noun*
voters
vouch *verb*
vouches
vouching
vouched
voucher *noun*
vouchers
vow *noun*
vows
vow *verb*
vows
vowing
vowed
vowel *noun*
vowels
voyage *noun*
voyages
voyager *noun*
voyagers
vulgar *adjective*
vulgarly *adverb*
vulnerable *adjective*
vulnerably *adverb*
vulture *noun*
vultures

Try also words beginning with **wh-**

Ww

wad *noun*
wads
waddle *verb*
waddles
waddling
waddled
waddle *noun*
waddles
wade *verb*
wades
wading
waded
wafer *noun*
wafers
wag *verb*
wags
wagging
wagged
wag *noun*
wags
wage *noun*
wages
wage *verb*
wages
waging
waged
wager *noun*
wagers
wager *verb*
wagers
wagering
wagered
waggle *verb*
waggles
waggling
waggled
wagon *noun*
wagons
wagtail *noun*
wagtails
wail *verb*
wails
wailing
wailed
wail★ *noun*
wails
waist☆ *noun*
waists
waistband *noun*
waistcoat *noun*
waistcoats
wait✪ *verb*
waits
waiting
waited
wait *noun*
waits
waiter *noun*
waiters
waitress *noun*
waitresses
waive✣ *verb*
waives
waiving
waived
wake *verb*
wakes
waking
woke
woken
wake *noun*
wakes
waken *verb*
wakens
wakening
wakened
wakeful *adjective*
walk *verb*
walks
walking
walked
walk *noun*
walks
walkabout *noun*
walkabouts
walker *noun*
walkers
walkie-talkie *noun*
walkie-talkies
Walkman *noun*
Walkmans
wall *noun*
walls
wall *verb*
walls
walling
walled
wallaby *noun*
wallabies
wallet *noun*
wallets
wallflower *noun*
wallflowers
wallop *verb*
wallops
walloping
walloped
wallow *verb*
wallows
wallowing
wallowed
wallpaper *noun*
wallpapers

★ A **wail** is a loud sad cry. **! whale.**
☆ A person's **waist** is the narrow part around their middle. **! waste.**
✪ To **wait** is to delay, pause, or rest. **! weight.**
✣ To **waive** a right is to say you do not need it. **! wave.**

Try also words beginning with **wh-**

walnut *noun*
walnuts

walrus *noun*
walruses

waltz *noun*
waltzes

waltz *verb*
waltzes
waltzing
waltzed

wand *noun*
wands

wander *verb*
wanders
wandering
wandered

wanderer *noun*
wanderers

wane *verb*
wanes
waning
waned

wangle *verb*
wangles
wangling
wangled

want *verb*
wants
wanting
wanted

want *noun*
wants

war *noun*
wars

warble *verb*
warbles
warbling
warbled

warble *noun*
warbles

warbler *noun*
warblers

ward *noun*
wards

ward *verb*
wards
warding
warded

warden *noun*
wardens

warder *noun*
warders

wardrobe *noun*
wardrobes

ware★ *noun*
wares

warehouse *noun*
warehouses

warfare *noun*

warhead *noun*
warheads

wariness *noun*

warlike *adjective*

warm *adjective*
warmer
warmest
warmly *adverb*

warm *verb*
warms
warming
warmed

warmth *noun*

warn *verb*
warns
warning
warned

warning *noun*
warnings

warp *verb*
warps
warping
warped

warp *noun*
warps

warrant *noun*
warrants

warrant *verb*
warrants
warranting
warranted

warren *noun*
warrens

warring *adjective*

warrior *noun*
warriors

warship *noun*
warships

wart *noun*
warts

wary *adjective*
warier
wariest
warily *adverb*

was *verb*

wash *verb*
washes
washing
washed

wash *noun*
washes

washable *adjective*

washbasin *noun*
washbasins

washer *noun*
washers

washing *noun*

washing-up *noun*

wash out *noun*
wash outs

wasn't *verb*

wasp *noun*
wasps

wastage *noun*

waste☆ *verb*
wastes
wasting
wasted

waste *adjective* & *noun*
wastes

★ **Wares** are manufactured goods. **! wear, where.**
☆ To **waste** something is to use more of it than is needed. **! waist.**

Try also words beginning with **wh-**

wasteful *adjective*
wastefully *adverb*
watch *verb*
watches
watching
watched
watch *noun*
watches
watchdog *noun*
watchdogs
watcher *noun*
watchers
watchful *adjective*
watchfully *adverb*
watchfulness *noun*
watchman *noun*
watchmen
water *noun*
waters
water *verb*
waters
watering
watered
watercolour *noun*
watercolours
watercress *noun*
waterfall *noun*
waterfalls
waterlogged *adjective*
watermark *noun*
watermarks
waterproof *adjective*
waterskiing *noun*
watertight *adjective*
waterway *noun*
waterways
waterworks *noun*
waterworks
watery *adjective*

watt★ *noun*
watts
wave☆ *verb*
waves
waving
waved
wave *noun*
waves
waveband *noun*
wavebands
wavelength *noun*
wavelengths
waver *verb*
wavers
wavering
wavered
wavy *adjective*
wavier
waviest
wax *noun*
waxes
wax *verb*
waxes
waxing
waxed
waxwork *noun*
waxworks
waxy *adjective*
waxier
waxiest
way✪ *noun*
ways
we *pronoun*
weak✧ *adjective*
weaker
weakest
weakly *adverb*
weakness *noun*
weaknesses

weaken *verb*
weakens
weakening
weakened
weakling *noun*
weaklings
wealth *noun*
wealthy *adjective*
wealthier
wealthiest
weapon *noun*
weapons
wear● *verb*
wears
wearing
wore
worn
wear *noun*
wearer *noun*
wearers
weariness *noun*
weary *adjective*
wearier
weariest
wearily *adverb*
weasel *noun*
weasels
weather *noun*
weather *verb*
weathers
weathering
weathered
weathercock *noun*
weathercocks
weave✻ *verb*
weaves
weaving
weaved
wove
woven

★ A **watt** is a unit of electricity. **! what.**
☆ To **wave** is to move your arm in greeting. **! waive.**
✪ You use **way** in e.g. *can you tell me the way?* **! weigh, whey.**
✧ **Weak** means 'not strong'. **! week.**
● To **wear** clothes is to be dressed in them. **! ware, where.**
✻ The past tense is **weaved** in e.g. *she weaved her way through the crowd* and **wove** in e.g. *she wove a shawl.*

a b c d e f g h i j k l m n o p q r s t u v w x y z

weaver *noun*
weavers
web *noun*
webs
webbed *adjective*
webcam *noun*
webcams
website *noun*
websites
wed *verb*
weds
wedding
wedded
wed
we'd *verb*
wedding *noun*
weddings
wedge *noun*
wedges
wedge *verb*
wedges
wedging
wedged
Wednesday *noun*
Wednesdays
weed *noun*
weeds
weed *verb*
weeds
weeding
weeded
weedy *adjective*
weedier
weediest
week* *noun*
weeks
weekday *noun*
weekdays
weekend *noun*
weekends
weekly *adjective & adverb*
weep *verb*
weeps
weeping
wept
weft *noun*
weigh☆ *verb*
weighs
weighing
weighed
weight✪ *noun*
weights
weightless *adjective*
weightlifting *noun*
weighty *adjective*
weightier
weightiest
weir *noun*
weirs
weird *adjective*
weirder
weirdest
weirdly *adverb*
weirdness *noun*
welcome *noun*
welcomes
welcome *verb*
welcomes
welcoming
welcomed
weld *verb*
welds
welding
welded
welder *noun*
welders
welfare *noun*
well *noun*
wells
well *adjective & adverb*
better
best
we'll *verb*
well-being *noun*
wellington boots
plural noun
well-known *adjective*
went *verb* SEE **go**
wept *verb* SEE **weep**
were *verb* SEE **are**
we're *verb*
werewolf *noun*
werewolves
west *adjective & adverb*
west✣ *noun*
westerly *adjective & noun*
westerlies
western *adjective*
western *noun*
westerns
westward *adjective & adverb*
westwards *adverb*
wet *adjective*
wetter
wettest
wet *verb*
wets
wetting
wetted
wetness *noun*
we've *verb*
whack *verb*
whacks
whacking
whacked
whack *noun*
whacks
whale● *noun*
whales
whaler *noun*
whalers
whaling *noun*

---

* A **week** is a period of seven days. **! weak.**
☆ You use **weigh** in e.g. *how much do you weigh?* **! way, whey.**
✪ **Weight** is how heavy something is. **! wait.**
✣ You use a capital W in **the West**, when you mean a particular region.
● A **whale** is a large sea mammal. **! wail.**

wharf *noun*
wharves *or* wharfs
what★ *adjective*
whatever *pronoun* & *adjective*
wheat *noun*
wheel *noun*
wheels
wheel *verb*
wheels
wheeling
wheeled
wheelbarrow *noun*
wheelbarrows
wheelchair *noun*
wheelchairs
wheeze *verb*
wheezes
wheezing
wheezed
whelk *noun*
whelks
when *adverb* & *conjunction*
whenever *conjunction*
where☆ *adverb. conjunction,* & *pronoun*
whereabouts *plural noun* & *adverb*
whereas *conjunction*
whereupon *conjunction*
wherever *adverb*
whether *conjunction*
whey✪ *noun*
which✣ *adjective* & *pronoun*
whichever *pronoun* & *adjective*
whiff *noun*
whiffs
while *adjective* & *noun*

while *verb*
whiles
whiling
whiled
whilst *conjunction*
whimper *verb*
whimpers
whimpering
whimpered
whimper *noun*
whimpers
whine *verb*
whines
whining
whined
whine● *noun*
whines
whinny *verb*
whinnies
whinnying
whinnied
whip *noun*
whips
whip *verb*
whips
whipping
whipped
whirl *verb*
whirls
whirling
whirled
whirl *noun*
whirls
whirlpool *noun*
whirlpools
whirlwind *noun*
whirlwinds
whirr *verb*
whirrs
whirring
whirred
whirr *noun*
whirrs

whisk *verb*
whisks
whisking
whisked
whisk *noun*
whisks
whisker *noun*
whiskers
whisky *noun*
whiskies
whisper *verb*
whispers
whispering
whispered
whisper *noun*
whispers
whist *noun*
whistle *verb*
whistles
whistling
whistled
whistle *noun*
whistles
whistler *noun*
whistlers
white *adjective*
whiter
whitest
whiteboard *noun*
whiteboards
whiteness *noun*
whitish *adjective*
white *noun*
whites
whiten *verb*
whitens
whitening
whitened
whitewash *noun*

a b c d e f g h i j k l m n o p q r s t u v **w** x y z

★ You use **what** in e.g. *what are they doing?* or *I don't know what you mean.* **! watt.**
☆ You use **where** in e.g. *where are you?* **! ware, wear.**
✪ **Whey** is a watery liquid from milk. **! way, weigh.**
✣ You use **which** in e.g. *which one is that?* **! witch.**
● A **whine** is a high piercing sound. **! wine.**

Try also words beginning with **wh-**

whitewash *verb*
whitewashes
whitewashing
whitewashed
whiz *verb*
whizzes
whizzing
whizzed
who *pronoun*
whoever *pronoun*
whole★ *adjective*
wholly *adverb*
whole *noun*
wholes
wholefood *noun*
wholefoods
wholemeal *adjective*
wholesale *adjective*
wholesome *adjective*
wholly *adverb*
whom *pronoun*
whoop *noun*
whoops
whoopee *interjection*
whooping cough *noun*
who's☆ *verb*
whose✪ *adjective*
why *adverb*
wick *noun*
wicks
wicked *adjective*
wickeder
wickedest
wickedly *adverb*
wickedness *noun*
wicker *noun*
wickerwork *noun*
wicket *noun*
wickets
wicketkeeper *noun*
wicketkeepers

wide *adjective & adverb*
wider
widest
widely *adverb*
widen *verb*
widens
widening
widened
widespread *adjective*
widow *noun*
widows
widower *noun*
widowers
width *noun*
widths
wield *verb*
wields
wielding
wielded
wife *noun*
wives
wig *noun*
wigs
wiggle *verb*
wiggles
wiggling
wiggled
wiggle *noun*
wiggles
wigwam *noun*
wigwams
wild *adjective*
wilder
wildest
wildly *adverb*
wilderness *noun*
wildernesses
wildness *noun*
wildlife *noun*
wilful *adjective*
wilfully *adverb*
wilfulness *noun*
wiliness *noun*

will *verb*
would
will *noun*
wills
willing *adjective*
willingly *adverb*
willingness *noun*
willow *noun*
willows
wilt *verb*
wilts
wilting
wilted
wily *adjective*
wilier
wiliest
wimp *noun*
wimps
win *verb*
wins
winning
won
win *noun*
wins
wince *verb*
winces
wincing
winced
winch *noun*
winches
winch *verb*
winches
winching
winched
wind *noun*
winds
wind *verb*
winds
winding
wound
windfall *noun*
windfalls
windiness *noun*

★ You use **whole** in e.g. *I saw the whole film.* **! hole.**
☆ You use **who's** in *who's* (who is) *that?* and *I don't know who's* (who has) *done it.* **! whose.**
✪ You use **whose** in *whose is this?* and *I don't know whose it is.* **! who's.**

windmill *noun*
windmills
window *noun*
windows
windpipe *noun*
windpipes
windscreen *noun*
windscreens
windsurfer *noun*
windsurfing *noun*
windward *adjective*
windy *adjective*
windier
windiest
windily *adverb*
wine★ *noun*
wines
wing *noun*
wings
wing *verb*
wings
winging
winged
winged *adjective*
winger *noun*
wingers
wingless *adjective*
wingspan *noun*
wingspans
wink *verb*
winks
winking
winked
wink *noun*
winks
winkle *noun*
winkles
winkle *verb*
winkles
winkling
winkled
winner *noun*
winners
winnings *plural noun*
winter *noun*
winters
wintertime *noun*
wintry *adjective*
wintrier
wintriest
wipe *verb*
wipes
wiping
wiped
wipe *noun*
wipes
wiper *noun*
wipers
wire *noun*
wires
wire *verb*
wires
wiring
wired
wireless *noun*
wirelesses
wireless *adjective*
wiring *noun*
wiry *adjective*
wirier
wiriest
wisdom *noun*
wise *adjective*
wiser
wisest
wisely *adverb*
wish *verb*
wishes
wishing
wished
wish *noun*
wishes
wishbone *noun*
wishbones
wishful *adjective*
wisp *noun*
wisps
wispy *adjective*
wispier
wispiest
wistful *adjective*
wistfully *adverb*
wistfulness *noun*
wit *noun*
wits
witch☆ *noun*
witches
witchcraft *noun*
with *preposition*
withdraw *verb*
withdraws
withdrawing
withdrew
withdrawn
withdrawal *noun*
withdrawals
wither *verb*
withers
withering
withered
withhold *verb*
withholds
withholding
withheld
within *preposition & adverb*
without *preposition*
withstand *verb*
withstands
withstanding
withstood
witness *noun*
witnesses
witness *verb*
witnesses
witnessing
witnessed
wittiness
witty *adjective*
wittier
wittiest
wittily *adverb*

★ **Wine** is a drink. **! whine.**
☆ A **witch** is someone who uses witchcraft. **! which.**

Try also words beginning with **wh-**

a b c d e f g h i j k l m n o p q r s t u v w x y z

wizard *noun*
wizards
wizardry *noun*
wobble *verb*
wobbles
wobbling
wobbled
wobble *noun*
wobbles
wobbly *adjective*
wobblier
wobbliest
woe *noun*
woes
woeful *adjective*
woefully *adverb*
wok *noun*
woks
woke *verb* SEE **wake**
woken *verb* SEE **wake**
wolf *noun*
wolves
woman *noun*
women
womb *noun*
wombs
won *verb*★ SEE **win**
wonder *noun*
wonders
wonder *verb*
wonders
wondering
wondered
wonderful *adjective*
wonderfully *adverb*
won't *verb*
wood☆ *noun*
woods
wooded *adjective*
wooden *adjective*
woodland *noun*
woodlands
woodlouse *noun*
woodlice

woodpecker *noun*
woodpeckers
woodwind *noun*
woodwork *noun*
woodworm *noun*
woodworm *or*
woodworms
woody *adjective*
woodier
woodiest
woof *noun*
wool *noun*
woollen *adjective*
woollens *plural noun*
woolliness *noun*
woolly *adjective*
woollier
woolliest
word *noun*
words
word *verb*
words
wording
worded
wording *noun*
wordy *adjective*
wordier
wordiest
wore *verb* SEE **wear**
work *noun*
works
work *verb*
works
working
worked
workable *adjective*
worker *noun*
workers
workforce *noun*
workforces
workings *plural noun*
workman *noun*
workmen
workmanship *noun*

workout *noun*
workouts
works *plural noun*
worksheet *noun*
worksheets
workshop *noun*
workshops
world *noun*
worlds
worldliness *noun*
worldly *adjective*
worldlier
worldliest
worldwide *adjective*
worm *noun*
worms
worm *verb*
worms
worming
wormed
worn *verb* SEE **wear**
worry *verb*
worries
worrying
worried
worrier *noun*
worriers
worry *noun*
worries
worse *adjective* & *adverb*
worsen *verb*
worsens
worsening
worsened
worship *verb*
worships
worshipping
worshipped
worship *noun*
worshipper *noun*
worshippers
worst *adjective* & *adverb*
worth *adjective* & *noun*
worthiness *noun*

★ You use **won** in e.g. *I won a prize.* **! one**.
☆ **Wood** is material from trees or a lot of trees growing together. **! would**.

worthless *adjective*
worthlessly *adverb*
worthlessness *noun*
worthwhile *adjective*
worthy *adjective*
worthier
worthiest
worthily *adverb*
would★ *auxiliary verb* SEE **will**
wouldn't *verb*
wound *noun*
wounds
wound *verb*
wounds
wounding
wounded
wound *verb* SEE **wind**
wove *verb* SEE **weave**
woven *adjective* SEE **weave**
wrap☆ *verb*
wraps
wrapping
wrapped
wrap *noun*
wraps
wrapper *noun*
wrappers
wrapping *noun*
wrappings
wrath *noun*
wrathful *adjective*
wrathfully *adverb*
wreath *noun*
wreaths
wreathe *verb*
wreathes
wreathing
wreathed
wreck *verb*
wrecks
wrecking
wrecked
wreck *noun*
wrecks
wreckage *noun*
wreckages
wrecker *noun*
wreckers
wren *noun*
wrens
wrench *verb*
wrenches
wrenching
wrenched
wrench *noun*
wrenches
wrestle *verb*
wrestles
wrestling
wrestled
wrestler *noun*
wrestlers
wretch *noun*
wretches
wretched *adjective*
wretchedly *adverb*
wriggle *verb*
wriggles
wriggling
wriggled
wriggle *noun*
wriggles
wriggly *adjective*
wrigglier
wriggliest
wring✪ *verb*
wrings
wringing
wrung
wrinkle *noun*
wrinkles
wrinkle *verb*
wrinkles
wrinkling
wrinkled
wrist *noun*
wrists
wristwatch *noun*
wristwatches
write✢ *verb*
writes
writing
wrote
written
writer *noun*
writers
writhe *verb*
writhes
writhing
writhed
writing *noun*
writings
written *adjective* SEE **write**
wrong *adjective & adverb*
wrongly *adverb*
wrong *noun*
wrongs
wrong *verb*
wrongs
wronging
wronged
wrote *verb* SEE **write**
wrought *noun*
wrung *verb* SEE **wring**
wry✸ *adjective*
wryer
wryest

★ You use **would** in e.g. *would you like to come to tea?* **! wood**.
☆ To **wrap** something is to cover it in paper etc. **! rap**.
✪ To **wring** something is to squeeze it hard. **! ring**.
✢ You use **write** in e.g. *to write a letter*. **! right, rite**.
✸ You use **wry** in e.g. *a wry smile*. **! rye**.

Xx

xenophobia *noun*

Xmas *noun*
Xmases

X-ray *noun*
X-rays

X-ray *verb*
X-rays
X-raying
X-rayed

xylophone *noun*
xylophones

Yy

> **-y and -ey**
> Nouns ending in *-y* following a consonant, e.g. **story**, make plurals ending in *-ies*, e.g. **stories**, and verbs, e.g. **try**, make forms in *-ies* and *-ied*, e.g. **tries, tried**. Nouns ending in *-ey*, e.g. **journey**, make plurals ending in *-eys*, e.g. **journeys**.

yacht *noun*
yachts

yachtsman *noun*
yachtsmen

yachtswoman *noun*
yachtswomen

yam *noun*
yams

yank *verb*
yanks
yanking
yanked

yap *verb*
yaps
yapping
yapped

yap *noun*
yaps

yard *noun*
yards

yard *noun*
yards

yarn *noun*
yarns

yawn *verb*
yawns
yawning
yawned

yawn *noun*
yawns

year *noun*
years

yearly *adjective & adverb*

yearn *verb*
yearns
yearning
yearned

yeast *noun*

yell *noun*
yells

yell *verb*
yells
yelling
yelled

yellow *adjective & noun*
yellower
yellowest

yelp *verb*
yelps
yelping
yelped

yelp *noun*
yelps

yen* *noun*
yens *or* yen

yeoman *noun*
yeomen

* The plural is **yens** when you mean 'a longing' and **yen** for Japanese money.

yesterday *adjective & noun*
yesterdays
yet *adverb & conjunction*
yeti *noun*
yetis
yew* *noun*
yews
yield *verb*
yields
yielding
yielded
yield *noun*
yields
yippee
yodel *verb*
yodels
yodelling
yodelled
yodeller *noun*
yodellers

yoga *noun*
yoghurt *noun*
yoghurts
yoke☆ *noun*
yokes
yoke *verb*
yokes
yoking
yoked
yolk✪ *noun*
yolks
Yom Kippur *noun*
yonder *adjective & adverb*
you✣ *pronoun*
you'd *verb*
you'll *verb*
young *adjective*
younger
youngest

youngster *noun*
youngsters
your *adjective*
you're *verb*
yours *posessive pronoun*
yourself *pronoun*
yourselves
youth *noun*
youths
youthful *adjective*
youthfully *adverb*
you've *verb*
yo-yo *noun*
yo-yos
yuppie *noun*
yuppies

* A **yew** is a tree. **! ewe, you.**
☆ A **yoke** is a piece of wood put across animals pulling a cart. **! yolk.**
✪ A **yolk** is the yellow part of an egg. **! yoke.**
✣ You use **you** in e.g. *I love you.* **! ewe, yew.**

For words beginning with a **z-** sound, try also **x-**

Zz

zany *adjective*
zanier
zaniest
zanily *adverb*

zap *verb*
zaps
zapping
zapped

zeal *noun*

zealous *adjective*
zealously *adverb*

zebra *noun*
zebras

zenith *noun*
zeniths

zero *noun*
zeros

zest *noun*

zigzag *noun*
zigzags

zigzag *verb*
zigzags
zigzagging
zigzagged

zinc *noun*

zip *noun*
zips

zip *verb*
zips
zipping
zipped

zodiac *noun*

zombie *noun*
zombies

zone *noun*
zones

zoo *noun*
zoos

zoological *adjective*

zoologist *noun*
zoologists

zoology *noun*

zoom *verb*
zooms
zooming
zoomed

Zulu *noun*
Zulus

Chief languages of the world

Chief languages of the world (*spoken by over 6m people*)

language	where it is spoken
Afrikaans	southern Africa
Albanian	Albania
Amharic	Ethiopia
Arabic	northern Africa and the Middle East
Armenian	Armenia and nearby areas
Assamese	India and Bangladesh
Awadhi	India, Nepal
Azerbaijani	Azerbaijan, Russia, Iraq
Belorussian	Belarus, Poland
Bengali	Bangladesh, India
Bhojpuri	India, Nepal
Bihari	India, Nepal, and nearby areas
Braj Bhasha	India
Bulgarian	Bulgaria and nearby areas
Burmese	Myanmar
Catalan	north-east Spain, France
Cebuano	Philippines
Chattisgarhi	India
Chinese	China
Czech	Czech Republic
Danish	Denmark
Dutch	The Netherlands, Belgium, Suriname
English	UK, USA, Canada, Ireland, Australia, New Zealand, South Africa, (and worldwide as a second language)
Farsi (Persian)	Iran and nearby areas
Finnish	Finland
French	France, Canada, Belgium, Switzerland, Monaco, (and widespread as a second language)
German	Germany, Austria, Switzerland, eastern Europe, (and widespread as a second language)
Greek	Greece, Cyprus, Turkey
Gujarati	India, Pakistan
Hausa	Nigeria, Niger, and nearby areas
Hebrew	Israel, Europe, USA
Hindi	India, parts of Africa
Hungarian	Hungary, Romania
Icelandic	Iceland
Igbo	Nigeria
Indonesian	Indonesia
Italian	Italy, Switzerland, San Marino
Japanese	Japan, USA, Brazil
Javanese	Indonesia
Kannada (Kanarese)	India
Kazakh	Kazakhstan, Russia, China
Khmer (Cambodian)	south-east Asia

language	where it is spoken
Korean	North and South Korea, Japan
Kurdish	Iraq, Iran, Turkey
Lanna	Thailand, Laos
Lingala	central Africa
Magahi	India
Maithili	India, Nepal
Malagasy	Madagascar
Malay	Indonesia, Malaysia, Singapore, and nearby areas
Malayalam	India
Marathi	India
Marwari	India, Pakistan
Nepali	Nepal, India, Bhutan
Norwegian	Norway
Occitan	France
Oriya	India, Bangladesh
Oromo	Ethiopia, Kenya
Panjabi	Pakistan, India
Pashto	Afghanistan, Pakistan, Arabia
Persian (see Farsi)	
Polish	Poland and nearby areas
Portuguese	Portugal, Brazil
Quechua	Peru, Bolivia, Ecuador
Romanian	Romania, Moldova
Russian	Russia and nearby areas
Rwandan	central Africa
Serbian	Balkans
Sinhalese	Sri Lanka
Siraiki	Pakistan, India
Slovak	Slovak Republic and nearby areas
Spanish	Spain, North, Central, and South America
Sunda	Indonesia
Swahili	central Africa
Swedish	Sweden, Finland
Tagalog	Philippines
Tamil	India, Sri Lanka, Vietnam
Telugu	India, south-east Asia
Thai	Thailand
Turkish	Turkey
Ukrainian	Ukraine and nearby areas
Urdu	India, Pakistan
Uzbek	Uzbekistan and nearby areas
Vietnamese	Vietnam, Cambodia, Laos
Yiddish	Israel, USA, Russia
Yoruba	Nigeria, Benin
Zulu	South Africa

Oxford Children's Dictionaries

Think Dictionaries. Think Oxford. www.oup.com

Age 4+

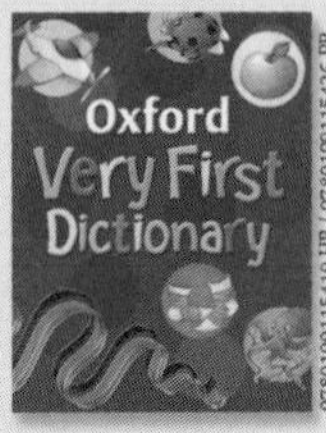

9780199115419 HB / 9780199115426 PB

Age 5+

9780199115198 HB / 9780199115204 PB

9780199115433 HB / 9780199115457 PB

Age 7+

9780199115211 HB / 9780199115228 PB

9780199113194 HB / 9780199113200 PB

9780199115129 HB

9780199115136 HB

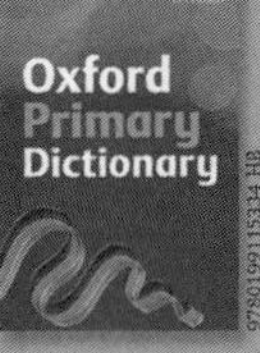

9780199115334 HB

9780199115167 HB

9780199114931 HB / 9780199113088 PB

9780199115242 PB

9780199115341 HB

9780199115358 HB

9780199115365 HB / 9780199115372 PB

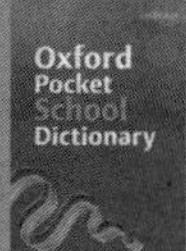

9780199115389 PB

9780199115396 PB

9780199115174 PB

9780199115181 PB

9780199113736 PB

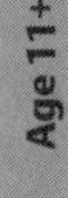

9780199116416 HB
9780199116423 PB

9780199115280 PB

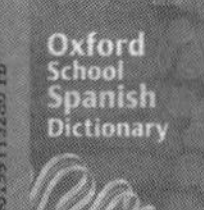

9780199115297 PB

9780199115303 PB

9780199115273 PB

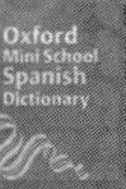

9780199115259 PB

9780199115266 PB

9780199115327 HB
9780199115310 PB

9780199116522 PB

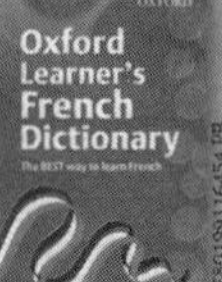

9780199116454 PB

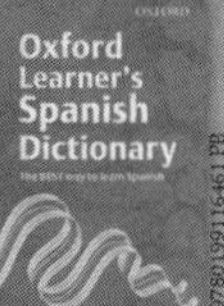

9780199116461 PB